DOUGLAS OWEN

DECLARATION OF WAR

A SURVEY OF THE POSITION OF

BELLIGERENTS AND NEUTRALS

WITH RELATIVE CONSIDERATIONS OF

SHIPPING AND MARINE INSURANCE DURING WAR

Elibron Classics
www.elibron.com

Elibron Classics series.

ISBN 0-543-96610-0 (paperback)
ISBN 0-543-96609-7 (hardcover)

This Elibron Classics Replica Edition is an unabridged facsimile of the edition published in 1889 by Stevens ans Sons, Ltd., London.

DECLARATION OF WAR:

A SURVEY OF THE POSITION OF

BELLIGERENTS AND NEUTRALS

WITH RELATIVE CONSIDERATIONS OF

SHIPPING AND MARINE INSURANCE

DURING WAR.

BY

DOUGLAS OWEN,

OF THE INNER TEMPLE, BARRISTER-AT-LAW.

SECRETARY OF THE ALLIANCE MARINE ASSURANCE COMPANY, LIMITED, AND OF
THE ASSOCIATION OF AVERAGE ADJUSTERS OF GREAT BRITAIN.

AUTHOR OF "MARINE INSURANCE NOTES AND CLAUSES."

LONDON:

STEVENS AND SONS, LIMITED,

Law Publishers and Booksellers,

119 & 120, CHANCERY LANE.

1889.

LONDON:

PRINTED BY C. F. ROWORTH, GREAT NEW STREET, FETTER LANE, E.C.

TO

THE RIGHT HONORABLE

LORD ROTHSCHILD,

PRESIDENT OF

THE ALLIANCE MARINE ASSURANCE

COMPANY, LIMITED,

THIS WORK

IS

BY HIS LORDSHIP'S PERMISSION

RESPECTFULLY DEDICATED

BY

THE AUTHOR.

PREFACE.

For three-quarters of a century British property at sea has remained practically free from the risk of hostile capture. This immunity has produced in our sea-girt land an oblivion of those mercantile contingencies which require to be specially provided against during a period of maritime warfare. Even had the conditions of ocean traffic remained as the Peace of 1815 found them, the above result might well have been anticipated. But, as it is, the substitution of the steel or iron steamship for the wind-driven sailing vessel, and the altered conditions of ocean traffic and communication generally, have imported into mercantile contracts features essentially new and important, and with these constantly developing conditions it has been necessary to keep pace. This necessity has not unnaturally caused to be put still further into the shade contingencies which a long-continued immunity from hostile acts at sea has caused to be regarded as remote.

That this is so becomes especially apparent whenever a rumour of impending war calls forth a common desire for better information as to the rights and obligations both of belligerents and neutrals, and for more accurate knowledge touching collateral mercantile considerations generally. But inquiries thus induced are sometimes difficult to satisfy, or, at any rate, to answer with the promptitude and sufficiency desired by men of affairs. Treatises there are on International Law, it is true, and there are also works readily accessible, both on Shipping and on Marine Insurance, more numerous still; but with respect to the first-named treatises, they are for the most part so interlarded with the views and opinions of learned theorists, both ancient and modern, and amplified with various international considerations of a purely political character, as to be much more valuable to the student of International Law than for purposes of ready mercantile reference.

Of relative essays of a more practical kind there are few indeed, and of these the writers are more to be congratulated for their research than for the appreciation which they have shown of the importance of dissecting and classifying its results.

The works on Shipping and Marine Insurance, on the other hand, dealing as they do with these important subjects as a whole, naturally do not class by themselves questions in connexion with the subject of warlike exigencies; but subdivide and discuss them, in common with others not specially relating to war, under various heads. Besides which, such treatises, however valuable in other respects, mostly possess the already indicated common tendency to give more consideration to the risks and liabilities generally attendant on maritime transactions, than to those which have become comparatively uninteresting during several generations of freedom from hostile capture.

The practical inquirer is ordinarily quite indifferent to the views, however otherwise interesting, of the learned Grotius, the erudite Puffendorf and Bynkershoek, and the various other publicists of bygone days. He wants rather to be succinctly informed as to his position under international law as it stands; and as a rule, indeed, he does not greatly care whether this law be good or bad. But to inform himself fully respecting it he is compelled to read and collate reviews of the three several subjects—law of nations, shipping, and marine insurance; and he has at present no opportunity to turn to any one work in which these three important considerations are treated collectively.

Any such reference can, perhaps, be dispensed with altogether so long as no warlike cloud shows itself on the political horizon. But the attitude of mutual watchfulness which is so marked a characteristic of some international relations at the present time, can scarcely be regarded as a satisfactory assurance of permanent peace. And as it is not solely the condition but almost as much the rumour of war which emphasises the need of a work of the above comprehensive kind, this work I have now endeavoured to provide.

In observing that no such treatise is in existence, I should, perhaps, rather have said that I have failed to discover any such. Consequently, in the endeavour to submit a system of classification and arrangement calculated to meet the requirements already referred to, I have been thrown on my own resources. To deficiencies in these, then, must be attributed any imperfection of which the reader may become aware, and for which I trust I may receive his kind indulgence.

DOUGLAS OWEN.

LONDON,

July, 1889.

I desire to record my indebtedness to the following works which, amongst the many referred to, have been found especially valuable, viz.:—

Wheaton's International Law.
Kent's International Law.
Maritime Warfare (Hazlitt & Roche).
Leading Cases on International Law (Pitt Cobbett).
Law of Nations: War (Twiss).
Story's "Prize Courts" (Pratt).
Park's Marine Insurance.
Arnould's Marine Insurance.
Carver's Carriage by Sea.

D. O.

CONTENTS.

TABLE OF CASES.

A

B

M

N

"DECLARATION OF WAR"

AND WARFARE GENERALLY.

EXPLANATORY.

THAT the scheme of arrangement followed in these pages is unassailable on the score of its strict accuracy is by no means supposed. It is, indeed, difficult to imagine any system having the same object which would not be open to such an objection. But the various rights and obligations which constitute what is called the Law of Nations seem especially to require, in order that they may be readily appreciated, careful dissection and classification. In this view a method of arrangement has been here attempted which, if not beyond the reach of criticism as to its technical accuracy, may, it is hoped, yet be found to possess the merit of simplicity. What this system is will sufficiently appear on reference to the table of contents supplied above; but seeing that a perusal of these pages will not necessarily be prefaced by such a reference, a few words of explanation at the outset may be useful to the reader.

First, then, there is submitted—

I. **A Retrospect** showing the harsh foundation on which the Law of Nations is supported, and briefly reviewing the circumstances which have placed this law on the footing which it now occupies amongst civilized states.

Enemy property being ordinarily liable to, and neutral property being ordinarily exempt from, confiscation, the next subject for consideration is the principles adopted by prize courts in deciding whether captured property is to be deemed to belong to an enemy or to a neutral: that is, to a friend,—for a neutral is to be regarded as the friend of both belligerents, impartially. Therefore, under

II. **Domicile and Ownership** are set forth the principles governing the decision of this all-important question.

As the position alike of belligerents and neutrals has been largely affected by the so-called Declaration appended to the Treaty of Paris of 1856, it is necessary to hold the Declaration well in view when discussing the Law of Nations as it stands. The Declaration cannot, of course, alter this law: but, as an international agreement to substitute the rules defined by the treaty for the principles of the Law of Nations, the latter, so long as the treaty remains in force, must be regarded as subordinated to its rules. The next chapter for consideration then is

III. **The Declaration of Paris.**

By the above three preliminary chapters the way is cleared for a review of the rights and obligations which it is the object of this work to place succinctly before the reader.

On the outbreak of war the community of nations becomes divided under two heads, viz.: (1) Those who fight;
(2) Those who look on.

By the law of Nature the only rule of the prize-ring, whether nations or individuals be the combatants, is the rule of the strongest. Civilization has, however, toned down the brutality of this rule, and there must nowadays be no hitting below the belt, in the case either of the individual or of the nation. There are now, in fact, rules of the ring, and the combatant or belligerent setting these rules at naught risks the hatred and contempt, if not the actual interposition, of the lookers on,—individuals or nations, as the case may be. The rules consist partly of Rights, partly of Obligations. As the former put the latter completely into the shade, the Rights may reasonably be considered first. And these, for greater convenience, may be divided into three distinct heads, viz.: first,

IV. **Belligerent Rights against the Enemy**—which, as well as the various other rights and obligations, are scheduled in detail in the table of contents; second,

V. **Belligerent Rights against Neutrals,** who are bound both to respect the rights of belligerents and to honourably fulfil their own obligation to preserve a strict neutrality; and, third,

VI. **Belligerent Municipal Rights**; such as the placing of restrictions on the trade and transactions of the national subjects, appropriating their property for warlike purposes, and so forth.

Having thus dealt with the belligerent rights, the next subject for consideration is

VII. **Belligerent Obligations**; namely, respect of neutral territory; the bringing of captured property to prompt adjudication by a prize court of the captors, &c. The obligations, as compared with the rights, are few enough. But to them must be added the general duty not to unduly interfere with neutral trade,—a subject which it has been found better to treat from its corresponding aspect, Neutral Rights; to which we shall come presently.

The position of those who fight having been discussed, there remains to consider that of the lookers-on. It may, perhaps, be suggested—and with some truth—that in scheduling the belligerent rights against neutrals we have already practically enumerated the obligations of neutrals to belligerents:

and similarly, that "belligerent obligations" is only another way of expressing "neutral rights." The circumstance has not been overlooked; but there yet remain certain neutral rights and obligations which—especially so far as they are of an abstract nature—it has been considered preferable to treat directly from the neutral aspect. These special rights and obligations of neutrals should in strictness be subjected to the same system of analysis as that applied in the case of those of belligerents: but this has proved impracticable. The rights and the obligations so dovetail and sometimes overlap that they have to be dealt with together. The next chapter, therefore, is entitled

VIII. **Neutral Rights and Obligations.**— These, so far as they have not already been scheduled from the corresponding belligerent aspect, although they do not lend themselves to useful analysis, are at any rate collectively capable of a rough classification. Some are rather of a mercantile character, others political; and this distinction has been made use of in considering the subject as a whole.

With this chapter ends our study of the Law of Nations from its maritime point of view. There are, however, certain mercantile considerations arising out of a condition of warfare which, at any rate to the mercantile reader, are of much importance; and without some reference to these, the objects of this work would scarcely be fulfilled. These considerations are more especially interesting and important in relation to Marine Insurance, and they are accordingly submitted under their several heads, as follows, viz.:—

IX. **War Warranties.** — The word warranty in marine insurance may, for convenience, be regarded as having two different meanings, the one, in which the assured guarantees, as a fact, a certain condition on which the underwriter undertakes the insurance, as, "Warranted neutral"; the other, in which it may be said that the underwriter excludes a certain risk from the risks otherwise covered under the policy, as, "Warranted free from capture." This chapter treats of the warranties specially met with during or in view of hostilities. Similarly in the case of the subjects following: items not specially connected with the question of hostilities not being referred to.

X. **Misrepresentation and Concealment** of facts material to a risk submitted for insurance.— Illustrates the obligations of insurers, in time of hostilities, to inform the underwriter truthfully and fully touching the nature and circumstances of risks offered for insurance; and the consequences of failure in this respect.

XI. **Void Insurances.**—Indicates those insurances which are ordinarily incapable of being effected in time of hostilities, and those which are rendered void by the outbreak of hostilities.

XII. **Insurable Interest of Captors.**—Discusses the position of captors as regards their right to insure their interest in property seized at sea and sent in by them for adjudication.

XIII. **Effect of War on Contract.**—Shows in what manner the outbreak of war affects contracts existing between the national subjects and alien enemies; and especially the effect of war on the Contract of Affreightment.

XIV. **Piracy.**—Included mainly in order to indicate the characteristics which mark the distinction between the lawful belligerent and the unlawful combatant, or pirate.

To the reviews of the various rights and obligations dealt with in this work there has been appended, wherever necessary, a special summary of the relative Law of Marine Insurance. These summaries speak for themselves; but it may be remarked respecting them that the reader interested more especially in the marine insurance aspect of the subject will find it to his advantage to first examine in each case the review of the Law of Nations to which the summary relates. Inquirers respecting the Law of Nations are, on the other hand, likely to find under the head Insurance useful illustrations of the practical application of the principles embodied in the review.

N.B.—The references to cases in the American Law Reports are printed in italics.

I.

RETROSPECT.

The rights and obligations subsisting between nations are, by some, comprehended under the denomination Law of Nations, whilst others prefer to designate them by the title International Law. Titles, like names, being for the most part rather labels than definitions, this difference of denomination may be of no great moment. But as the propriety of accepting the two terms as synonymous, and therefore interchangeable, seems open to question, it may be well to indicate the meaning which, rightly or wrongly, is attached to them in these pages.

The term Law of Nations, then, is, as we hold, correctly used to describe that condition of mutual rights and obligations subsisting between nations, based on what is, by some writers, called the Law of Nature,—that law to which we should revert if the softening influences of civilization were to be done away. Whereas, by International Law we understand that condition of mutual relations which results from special convention; such convention being commonly, though by no means necessarily, in mitigation of the sterner rights of the Law of Nations. As, for example: By the Law of Nations enemy goods are liable to confiscation none the less that they may be on board a neutral vessel. But by treaties now subsisting between the powers, or most of them, this right has been disavowed; so that International Law here expressly prohibits that which the Law of Nations as clearly permits.

Municipal Law, it is scarcely necessary to observe, is, as distinguished from International Law, the domestic law of a state, binding all persons within the national jurisdiction to do, or to refrain from doing, such acts and things as may by the governing body be decided to be necessary for, or contrary to, the public interests respectively.

The object of this work is rather to set forth the state of the Law of Nations, as it now subsists, than to inquire into and discuss those changes which have, in bygone days, conduced to the present condition. The history of international rights, from the earliest times of which we have records, may therefore be very briefly summed up. The warlike rights of nation against nation were originally, and till within a measurable distance of modern times, limited not by any sense of right and wrong, but apparently only by the power of nations to conceive and execute deeds of violence one against the other. The Old Testament abounds in instances of such unrestrained cruelty. Thus, we read how the army of the Chaldeans under Nebuchadnezzar having besieged and captured Jerusalem, and caught the unhappy King Zedekiah, after some process described as "giving judgment" upon him, slew his sons before his eyes, and then, having put out his eyes, bore him in fetters to Babylon. The walls of the Jewish stronghold were levelled, and such of the nation as were worth anything were also carried captive to the same destination. In the days of ancient Rome, contemporary history makes it abundantly plain that very similar views prevailed as to the rights of the vanquisher over the vanquished. The Romans, indeed, considered it permissible to enslave or kill any of the enemy race on whom they could lay their hands, in Roman territory, on the breaking out of war. An enemy was regarded as a criminal and an outlaw, to be hunted down and slain wherever found; whilst his wife and children were sold into slavery. And even at the close of the 13th century our own King Edward I., on capturing Berwick from the Scotch, put the citizens to the sword by thousands, without distinction of age or sex; so that, as we read, for two days the city ran with blood like a river.

From time to time some nation or another would seek, by municipal enactments, to restrain its subjects from perpetrating such deeds, but until Christian influences had begun to be generally felt, the precedents handed down from the ancients were commonly accepted and followed with but little modification. The crusades, binding together as they did the Christian nations, were no doubt a factor of some importance; but it was not until the 16th century that a more enlightened sense of justice and humanity came into general acceptance amongst Christian powers. Maritime commerce was then rapidly extending, with the inevitable result of bringing nations into closer relationship; whilst the power of appeal to the Head of the Church at Rome, and the knowledge that any outrage of the principles there propagated would entail the risk of punishment, materially supported the advance of civilization and the dictates of humanity.

Until the early part of the 17th century there was no such thing as a recognised code of the rights subsisting between the nations, but this was in a great measure supplied by the writings of the learned Grotius, 1583—1645, regarded by many as the father of the Law of Nations. Following in his steps came Puffendorf, Bynkershoek, Vattel, Valin, Emerigon, and others, who, though not always in accord on disputed points, served to beat into a firm and well-defined road the path first traced by Grotius. The adoption in subsequent wars of the principles contended for by such writers crystallized into accepted law what had before been but matter of belief. So that at the present day the writings of Wheaton, Kent, and other publicists may be regarded as an exposition of the Law of Nations as now accepted by the powers and acted upon in the various national tribunals.

Whether a formal declaration of war communicated to the enemy should precede the outbreak of offensive operations is somewhat of an open question. As a matter of fact, the various powers appear to consider themselves under the obligation to make such a declaration only at such time as it may suit them. Thus, in 1877 the Russian declaration of war against Turkey was preceded by some hours by the entry of the Russian forces into Turkey. A nation may convey its warlike intentions to the state with which it is at variance by the recall of its minister, or by a public declaration of war within its own territory, or by announcement of an ultimatum followed by hostile acts; or, indeed, by any such unambiguous mode of intimation as may grow out of the circumstances at the time. War having once been commenced, a formal declaration to the enemy can, it would seem, be formulated and communicated at leisure if it so please the aggressor. But it is of course open to nations to provide for such a case by a clause in international treaties.

Previous to the actual declaration of war or commencement of active hostilities a provisional seizure is occasionally made of enemy ships and goods within the national jurisdiction. Such seizures are of the nature of embargo or reprisal, and may be relinquished on adjustment of the difficulty which resulted in the hostile act. This subject will be considered under the head Embargo and Reprisals (*b*). The disputed right of confiscation of enemy debts and property within the national territory will also be considered in its place (*c*).

(*b*) *Vide* p. 36, *infra*.

(*c*) *Vide* p. 49, *infra*.

When war is entered upon, every individual of the nations engaged is considered to be involved in the hostilities, since every man is considered to be a party to the acts of his own government. According to the letter of the law of nations this condition of affairs warrants the arrest of any subject of the enemy found within the national territory. But this right, if right it be, is now obsolete, though if one nation at war were to revive and execute it, the other would probably claim the same right by retortion if not by the law of nations. The effect of this taint of hostilities, as regards individuals, is to stop all intercourse between citizens of the nations at war. The individual members of the nations are embarked in one common bottom and must share one common fate. Therefore, all trading with the common enemy becomes at once illicit, and is usually so proclaimed on the outbreak of hostilities (*d*).

But the extension of this spirit of hostility to individuals does not, by the usage of nations, entitle individuals to engage in independent hostile acts against the enemy or subjects of the enemy. Only those persons who have been expressly empowered or commissioned by their government to engage in active hostility are entitled to exercise any such aggressive acts.

The circumstance that two nations decide to settle their differences by resort to war is not to be allowed to interfere with legitimate trade on the part of neutrals. It is now a fundamental principle of the public law of Europe that neutral nations shall, in time of war, be allowed to carry on their accustomed trade, subject only to such restrictions on the part of belligerents as may be necessary for the safety and protection of the latter. The nature of such restrictions will be set forth in its place (*e*).

(*d*) *Vide sub* "Trading with the Enemy," p. 258, *infra*.

(*e*) *Vide* p. 345, *infra*.

By the law of nations it is permissible to seize and confiscate enemy property found on board a neutral vessel; but this right, as will presently appear, has been disavowed by the Declaration of Paris. Ships of the enemy may of course be seized and confiscated, and any enemy property found on board of them will be involved in the same fate, though neutral goods, except contraband of war, must be restored. These subjects will receive fuller consideration later on, but meantime it may be observed that a fruitful source of difficulty and irritation between belligerents and neutrals is the decision of the crucial point as to the ownership of goods found on enemy vessels. That is, whether the property in such goods is to be regarded as vested in neutral subjects, and the goods therefore exempt from confiscation; or in subjects of the hostile nation, and the goods consequently the subject of legal condemnation to the captors. The answer to this important question frequently turns on the domicile of the owner. Before proceeding further it will be well to give some special consideration to this subject.

II.

DOMICILE AND OWNERSHIP.

Domicile and nationality are not of necessity the same thing. Thus a British subject may have a commercial domicile or domiciles in foreign countries, or the subject of a foreign state may have a domicile in Great Britain. In deciding as to the nationality of captured goods, the courts of prize are not ordinarily concerned to inquire of what nation the owner of the property is a member: what they do set themselves to ascertain is, whether the property is to be deemed to be owned by an enemy subject or—which is the same thing—by a person who has cast in his lot with the enemy. Of what particular nationality the owner may himself be is another matter altogether, and not ordinarily material to the point at issue. No matter of what nationality a person may be, if he establishes himself in business in a neutral or hostile state, he becomes, so far as the transactions of such business are concerned, to all intents and purposes a neutral or an enemy, as the case may be. And in such capacity he must accept all its inconveniences, just as he shares its advantages. Therefore all persons trading in the enemy's country are considered *pro hac vice* to be enemy subjects so far as concerns the interests of their alien domicile. Aliens are deemed to be under no obligation to remain in the enemy country, and the fact that they do so remain is to be taken as an admission of their willingness to cast in their lot with the foe. The theory acted upon is that an alien subject resident in a country against which war is declared by his government must at once return to the national territory. To hesitate is to be lost; and even if, on at once returning with his goods, the latter should be captured by his government, the Courts, before restoring them, will require the clearest proof of his intention to abandon the hostile domicile (*a*). A distinction is drawn between a temporary and a permanent residence, though the mere fact that a person has only just recently entered the country with which hostilities have broken out will not absolve him if it be clear that he came there with intent to remain. Nor will the circumstance of a longer residence necessarily convict him if he should succeed in rebutting the presumption that such prolonged stay was evidence of his intention to remain. What has in all cases to be looked at is the *animus manendi* or the *animus revertendi*, the onus of disproof or of proof lying on the claimant (*b*). "A mere intention to remove has never been held sufficient, without some overt act" (*c*).

Whether, on the outbreak of war, a subject domiciled in the enemy country can withdraw his property from such country, free from risk of confiscation on the part of his own government, without first obtaining a licence or safe-conduct from his government, is disputed. But to take such a precaution would, in any case, be a prudent act on the citizen's part (*d*). An instance of double domicile is supplied by the case of *The Portland* (*e*), where the property of a German subject was seized on the ground that he had a domicile on French territory, Great Britain being then at war with

(*a*) *Vide* Passports and Safe-conducts, p. 277, *infra*.
(*b*) *Vide* The Diana, 5 Rob. 60.
(*c*) The President, 5 Rob. 277.
(*d*) *Vide* p. 266, *infra*.
(*e*) 3 Rob. 41.

France. It turned out that the transaction was connected with a neutral domicile in Germany, and not with the enemy domicile, and the cargo was accordingly declared neutral.

The Jonge Klassina (*f*) was a case where, during war between Great Britain and Holland, a British citizen named Ravie obtained a special licence (*g*) to import from Holland goods belonging to him, presumably as a Birmingham merchant. The citizen was, as it turned out, not only the importer to England, but also the exporter from Holland, and it was held that the licence was given to protect Ravie in his capacity of a British importer, and did not extend to cover his exportation from Holland in the capacity of a Dutch merchant. That he held no fixed counting-house in the enemy's country was held to be a consideration of secondary importance. The goods were condemned.

If an alien subject be domiciled in a country with which war is declared, the fact that he shipped goods thence before the declaration of war does not exempt them from capture by his government as being enemy goods. This was decided by the American Court (which, however, was not unanimous) in *The Venus* (*h*).

If a British subject be domiciled in a neutral country, he is entitled to carry on his lawful trade unmolested, even with nations with which his government is at war (*i*).

If, however, he should trade in articles contraband of war, or of a contraband nature, such traffic would be deemed contrary to his allegiance (*k*). And if he should engage in the

(*f*) 5 Rob. 297; and p. 283, *infra*.

(*g*) *Vide* p. 277, *infra*, for the subject of Special Licences.

(*h*) 8 *Cranch*, 253. (*Vide* Wheaton's comments on this case; Int. Law, 2 Eng. ed. pp. 388—395.)

(*i*) The Danaous, cited in 4 Rob. 255; Bell *v*. Reid, 1 M. & S. 726.

(*k*) The Neptunus, p. 270, *infra*.

privileged trade of the enemy, the act would imbue the undertaking with a hostile character, whatever his domicile (*l*).

If a neutral and an enemy subject engage in a joint undertaking, and a shipment of the joint property be captured, the share of the neutral will be released, while that of the enemy is confiscated (*m*).

But if, as in *The Primus* (*n*), a neutral be part-owner of an enemy's ship, his share will be confiscated. The neutral owner, said the Court in this case, enjoys the privileges attached to the enemy's flag and must take its risks.

All produce of soil in the enemy's territory is impressed with a hostile character, whatever the nationality or domicile of the owner, provided that at the time of capture this produce be owned by the proprietor of the soil (*o*).

In *The Boedes Lust* (*p*), till December, 1803, the inhabitants of Demerara had remained British subjects, but the colony was then surrendered to the Dutch in virtue of the Treaty of Amiens. In January and February, 1804, certain property, the produce of the island during the British occupation, was shipped by the above vessel, which sailed in March, and was captured in May under an embargo laid on all Dutch property at sea, a month before the declaration of war against Holland. Before adjudication the settlement had again been acquired by the British. The circumstances were, on the one hand, submitted to the Court as justifying condemnation, and on the other as requiring restoration, of the property. Sir William Scott (afterwards Lord Stowell), in a lucid and interesting judgment, which does not admit of a brief summary, decided that the property at the time of its seizure was vested in Dutch owners; that the declaration of war

---

(*l*) The Ann, Dodson, 222; The Anna Catharina, 4 Rob. 107.

(*m*) The Franklin, 6 Rob. 120.

(*n*) 24 L. T. 15. *Cf. The Napoleon, Blatch. Pr. Ca.* 357.

(*o*) The Phœnix, 5 Rob. 20; *The Mary Clinton, Blatch. Pr. Ca.* 556.

(*p*) 5 Rob. 233.

had a retroactive effect, applying to all property previously detained; that the fact that the owners of the property had since become friends of this country would not relieve them; and, finally, that the property was liable to confiscation.

As regards factories or colonial establishments in Asia or Africa, there is attributed to them the national character of the European mother state to which they belong (*q*).

Insurances on enemy property being void by statute, the property of subjects domiciled with the enemy is, so far as concerns property attaching to the domicile, also within the statute (*r*). To an inquiry, in 1854, on the part of British merchants domiciled in Riga, as to what respect would be paid by British cruisers to *bonâ fide* British property, the produce of Russia, if shipped on board neutral vessels, a reply was sent from the Foreign Office that such property, even if purchased before the outbreak of war, would not be respected unless specially licensed or exempted by instructions to the officers of the British navy (*s*). Shortly afterwards, however, it was by proclamation announced that her Majesty had decided to waive the right to seize enemy's property laden on neutral vessels (*t*). The Treaty of Paris (*u*), in 1856, having embodied the principle "free ships, free goods," all property, except contraband of war, covered by the neutral flag must, so long as the treaty holds good, be deemed, as between the signatories of the treaty, free from capture.

The privilege of trading, in time of war, through the enemy's ports is allowed to inland states, such as Switzerland, in consideration of the hardship to which they would be exposed were this denied them. But such a trade, as being necessarily exposed to great suspicion, must, according to

(*q*) 5th ed. Arnould's Insce. 146.

(*r*) *Vide sub* Void Insurances, p. 405, *infra*.

(*s*) 44 State Papers, 1853-4, pp. 106, 108.

(*t*) 1 Bulletins, 1854, p. 356.

(*u*) P. 27, *infra*.

Sir W. Scott, in *The Magnus*, be justified by proofs of more than ordinary strictness (*x*).

In like manner as domicile is the test of the ownership of goods, so the national character of a ship is deemed to depend on the domicile of the owner (*y*). Thus, in *Tabbs* v. *Bendlebrack* (*z*), a vessel built and registered in America, and owned by an American subject, was deemed British property, the owner being domiciled in Great Britain. But a vessel sailing under the flag or pass of the enemy is regarded as enemy property, irrespective of the real ownership (*a*). Except that if a country have no national maritime flag, and a vessel belonging to subjects of such country be, in consequence, sailed under an alien flag, the flag is not to be deemed conclusive as to the vessel's nationality. This was decided in *The Palme*, a Swiss vessel, captured by a French cruiser in 1871, whilst sailing under the German flag (*b*). And if a vessel be engaged in the privileged trade of the enemy, or be habitually engaged in the trade of the enemy's country, or sail under his licence and passport, she will be regarded as enemy property: as will be illustrated presently (*c*). This principle of the law of nations is not to be evaded by a colourable transfer. Thus, in *The Jemmy*, which had been purchased of the enemy, but left in the trade and under the management of the former owner, the Court, regarding the transfer as colourable, declined to admit further proofs (*d*). *The Odin* (*e*) is another

(*x*) 1 Rob. 31. See also The Active, Ho. Lords, 10 March, 1798.

(*y*) The Elizabeth, 5 Rob. 2; The Vigilantia, 1 Rob. 1, 19, 26; The Vrow Anna Catharina, 5 Rob. 161; The Success, 1 Dodson, 131; The Magnus, 1 Rob. 31.

(*z*) 4 Esp. 108; 3 Bos. & Pul. 207, note, *S. C.*

(*a*) *Vide* pp. 233 *et seq.*, *infra.*

(*b*) Wheat. Int. Law, 2 Eng. ed. 401.

(*c*) *Vide* p. 233, *infra.*

(*d*) 4 Rob. 31; The Christine, 2 Spinks' Ec. & Ad. Rep. 24.

(*e*) 1 Rob. 248. *Vide* The Ocean Bride, p. 335, *infra*, for a special exception to the rule.

instance of condemnation consequent on a transfer not recognized by the Court. This was a vessel belonging to British subjects at Calcutta, who had been in the habit of trading with Batavia. On the outbreak of war with Holland, an ostensible transfer was made to a Norwegian domiciled at a Danish establishment near Calcutta, by whom the trade with Batavia was continued. When seized, the vessel was on a voyage from Batavia to Copenhagen, having on board an English ship-master (the former master of the vessel), but who, it was asserted, was not acting as master. The Court, finding that the allegation of transfer had not been sufficiently supported, condemned the property, of which the value was assessed at 150,000*l.* In *The Omnibus* (*f*), also, Sir William Scott declared that "the Court had often had occasion to observe that where a ship, asserted to have been transferred, is continued under the former agency and in the former habits of trade, not all the swearing in the world will convince it that it is a genuine transaction."

It being established as a general principle that domicile is the test of ownership, the question remains, in whom is the property in goods captured on the high seas to be deemed to be vested:—in the shipper; the consignee at destination, or the purchaser; or other apparent proprietor, domiciled perhaps in the country neither of the ship's port of loading nor destination? The common rule is, that goods entrusted to a ship-master by a consignor for delivery to a consignee are regarded as the property of the latter (*g*). But notwithstanding this general rule, if at the commencement of the transit the goods are enemy-owned, the circumstance that they are destined to a neutral consignee will not be considered material (*h*). In short, neutral goods with a hostile destination, or hostile goods with a neutral destination, shipped

(*f*) 6 Rob. 71.

(*g*) Packet de Bilboa, 2 Rob. 133; *The Sally Magee, Blatch. Pr. Ca.* 385.

(*h*) The Sally; The Atlas; The Anna Catharina, *infra*.

under contract made during or, it may be supposed, in anticipation of war, are by the law of nations *primâ facie* liable to hostile capture (*i*). This position must, however, owing to the Declaration of Paris (*k*), be regarded as now essentially modified; for, by the Declaration, all permissive goods under a neutral flag are to be free from condemnation.

During the Crimean war a question arose as to the ownership of cargo on *The Abo* (*l*), which had been brought in as a prize. The cargo, claimed as neutral property, had been shipped *flagrante bello*, and the bills of lading did not show on whose account the shipment had been made. In other respects, also, the shipping documents were incomplete. Dr. Lushington, in ordering further proof as to ownership, observed that Lord Stowell had, in *The Cousine Marianne* (*m*), laid it down as a settled principle of the Court that, in order to constitute an effectual transfer of the property, there must be either an order for the goods or an acceptance of them by the consignee prior to the capture. That, whatever the common law might be, the Court of Admiralty acted independently, and must be satisfied that the title to the property was substantiated by the Court's own rules and practice (*n*).

The real ownership of goods has in each case to be established by the documentary evidence and depositions at the port or place of adjudication in the captor's territory. Whatever may be the practice or law in times of peace, no transfer is recognized by the captor which has taken place during the transit of the goods, if war was at that time either actually existent or imminent, and if the goods have borne a hostile character at the commencement of the

---

(*i*) 5th ed. Arnould's Insce. 613.
(*k*) P. 27, *infra*.
(*l*) 24 L. T. 5.
(*m*) Edw. 347.
(*n*) *Cf. The Hannah M. Johnson, Blatch. Pr. Ca.* 37.

voyage (*o*). For it is obvious that in the absence of such a rule no limit could be placed upon colourable transfers effected with the express object of defeating the rights of captors (*p*). Efforts to evade this restriction are frequent in time of war, but it in all cases lies upon the claimants of the goods to prove the ownership; so that the question becomes purely one of evidence.

Sales to neutrals must be absolute and unconditional in their nature, and any equity of redemption or other reservation in favour of the seller will be held fatal to the *bona fides* of the transaction (*q*).

Any reservation of risk on the part of the neutral consignor of goods until their delivery to a belligerent consignee is similarly held to be void; for otherwise all shipments of the kind would doubtless have such a stipulation attached to them. The result would be to defeat the right of capture until, delivery having been effected, it was too late to exercise it (*r*).

The title of the captors, on failure of the claimants to establish neutral ownership, is absolute; and no claim can be set up against it on the part of any persons asserting equitable rights over the property (*s*). A bill of lading transmitted to a party to cover his advances on cargo shipped, does not pass the title to the cargo (*t*). And property consigned by an enemy to his creditor to be applied in payment of a debt, is regarded by captors as enemy property (*u*). A

(*o*) The Soglasie, 2 Spinks, Ecc. & Adm. 101; The Danckebaar Africaan, 1 Rob. 107; The Herstelder, 1 Rob. 114; The Jan Frederick, 5 Rob. 128.

(*p*) The Vrow Margaretha, 1 Rob. 337; The Negotie en Zeevaart, 1 Rob. 111.

(*q*) The Anoydt Gedacht, 2 Rob. 137; The Sechs Geschwistern, 4 Rob. 100; The Sally, 5 Rob. 300.

(*r*) The Atlas, 3 Rob. 299; The Anna Catharina, 4 Rob. 107, 113, note. But see note in 5 Arnould's Insce. 613, as to the view of the U. S. Courts.

(*s*) The Josephine, 4 Rob. 25; The Tobago, 5 Rob. 218; The Mariana, 6 Rob. 24; *The Francis*, 1 *Gall.* 445; The Sisters, 5 Rob. 155; *The Mersey*, *Blatch. Pr. Ca.* 187.

(*t*) *The Lynchburg*, *Blatch. Pr. Ca.* 49; *The Winifred*, *ib.* 33.

(*u*) *The Hannah M. Johnson*, *ib.* 97; *The Mary Clinton*, *ib.* 556.

lien upon a captured vessel for repairs effected prior to the hostilities will similarly be disregarded (*x*). If a vessel be transferred at the time of hostilities, satisfactory evidence will be required as to *boná fide* payment of the purchase-money, and as to the character of the transaction generally (*y*); but any sale by a belligerent to a neutral will be regarded with great suspicion, and, to save from condemnation property so transferred, the good faith of the transfer will have to be clearly established. Several cases of this kind occurred during the Crimean war. Thus, in *The Johan Christophe* (*z*), the vessel, seized as enemy property, was claimed by a Russian subject, setting himself forth as a Dane. He had, in fact, become a burgher of Altona, and taken the oath of allegiance to the King of Denmark, but with the express object, as it would seem, of qualifying himself to buy the vessel in the latter capacity. The Court decided that no such adoption of neutral nationality would invest him with the character claimed by him. In all such cases the Court will closely examine the claim to neutral nationality, and will not accept the claim if it should appear that an enemy subject has, under the guise of neutrality, gone into neutral territory in order to purchase an enemy ship. And in *The Ernst Merck* (*a*), seized at Hull whilst sailing under the Mecklenburg colours, the Court condemned the vessel, which had been sold by a Russian owner very shortly before the outbreak of war. The real ownership of the vessel was not established: there were deficiencies in the evidence; and the Court, in reference to this circumstance, declared that it "was not required to declare affirmatively that the enemy's interest remained; it was sufficient to bar restitution if the neutral claim was not unequivocally sustained by the evidence."

(*x*) *The Nassau, Blatch. Pr. Ca.* 665.

(*y*) The Soglasie, 2 Spinks, Ecc. & Ad. 101.

(*z*) 24 L. T. 52.

(*a*) *Ibid.* 303.

In *The Industrie* (*b*), where the vessel was seized whilst sailing under the Russian flag, and carrying Russian papers, it was held that these conditions imprinted a hostile character on the whole ship. Three-fourths of the latter were Russian owned, and one-fourth was claimed by the master, who alleged himself to be a native of Denmark; but the Court declined, in the above circumstances, to regard the property as other than that of an enemy.

In 1870, during the Franco-Prussian war, *The Sophia Rickmers* (*c*), having been captured by the French in the China Seas, the owner, P. A. Rickmers, as a British subject, petitioned the British Government to interfere to obtain the release of his vessel. This latter, he declared, he had bought at Singapore shortly before her capture, she being then registered at the port of Geestemunde, and he claimed that, as neutral property, her seizure was unjustifiable. The following is an extract from the reply to this petition:—

"It is for the Prize Court of the captors to determine whether *The Sophia Rickmers* is a good prize of war; and Lord Granville is of opinion that the French Prize Courts, if they observe their long-established practice, will not recognise the sale of an enemy's vessel made in a neutral port after the commencement of the war: the necessity of such sale being caused by the exigencies of the war, and the object of such sale being to defeat the exercise of the belligerent right as regards the capture of enemy's property on the high seas."

In the United States Courts it has also been clearly laid down that the sale of vessels in an enemy port to neutrals during or in contemplation of hostilities, by persons domiciled and trading there, does not pass the title, the property still remaining subject to capture as prize (*d*).

(*b*) 1 Ecc. & Ad. Rep. (Spinks) 444.

(*c*) State Papers, 61 (1870-1), 1092. See also The Minerva, 6 Rob. 396.

(*d*) *The Sarah Starr*, *Blatch. Pr. Ca.* 69; *The Cheshire*, *ib.* 151; *The Mersey*, *ib.* 187; *The Stephen Hart*, *ib.* 388. See also The Georgia, and relative note, p. 402, *infra*.

(The subject of transfer *in transitu*, in presence of hostilities, is exhaustively discussed in Story's Practice of Prize Courts, p. 63 *et seq*. Wheaton's International Law, 2 Eng. ed. p. 427, may also be referred to in this connexion.)

Having thus endeavoured to clear the ground with a view to the due consideration of the question of rights and obligations as between belligerents and neutrals, a brief space may fitly be devoted to the consideration of a highly important modern treaty, by which such rights and obligations are largely affected, viz., the Treaty, or, as it is more commonly termed, the Declaration, of Paris.

III.

THE DECLARATION OF PARIS.

On 30th March, 1856, on conclusion of the war with Russia, there was signed the so-called Treaty of Paris. Subsequently, viz. on 16th April, there was appended to it a Declaration on the part of the signatories that—

1. Privateering is and remains abolished.
2. The neutral flag covers enemy's goods, with the exception of contraband of war.
3. Neutral goods, except contraband of war, are not liable to capture under the enemy's flag.
4. Blockades, in order to be binding, must be effective, that is to say, maintained by a force sufficient in reality to prevent access to the coasts of the enemy.

The Declaration not to be binding except between the Powers acceding to it (*e*).

The important bearing of this international treaty on the interests of this country can hardly be understated. That it was distinctly to the advantage of other maritime states that such an engagement should be entered into by a country having command of the seas, must be admitted. With respect to clauses 3 and 4, they are comparatively unimportant: practically they do nothing more than codify principles of maritime warfare which were not in dispute. With respect to clause 1, it certainly tells against this country;

(*e*) Annual Reg. 1856, p. 322; 46 State Papers, 1855-6, pp. 8, 26.

especially since, owing to the general introduction of municipal regulations by which the chief powers prohibit the fitting out, by their subjects, of vessels to be used in the service of belligerents, this country has little to fear from privateers other than those originally belonging to an enemy state. Besides which, privateering could nowadays in no case be profitably undertaken by other than steam vessels, and it would needs be a difficult problem for such vessels, so far as the other European states are concerned, either to keep themselves adequately supplied with coal or to carry their prizes safely into the national ports. For the resources of this country are such that, even if it were found impracticable to establish an effective blockade of the enemy's chief ports, our cruisers would presumably be sufficiently numerous and alert to render it an exceedingly hazardous task for his privateers to bring in their prizes in safety.

The main object of privateering being plunder, there is little to fear from privateers if the prospects of this be reduced to a minimum: to risk life and liberty in the sole desire to destroy the enemy's commerce without hope of plunder is not the aim of privateers. *The Alabama*, which, in the American civil war, wrought such destruction upon the Federal commerce, was not, be it remembered, a privateer, but a Confederate warship.

That this country, in signing away its right to make use of privateers, must be considered to have lost the use of a very powerful weapon of offence, is sufficiently obvious. But, notwithstanding, the system of privateering, with the thirst for gain and the evil passions which it engenders, is so out of harmony with the principles of modern progress and civilization, that, from this view, the loss is attended by conditions which go far to mitigate it. And in abandoning the right to commission private vessels of war, this country has by no means necessarily deprived itself of the power to throw into the scale against the enemy such of the vessels of the national merchant marine as could with advantage be turned to this use. There is nothing to prevent the equipment and commissioning of these vessels as national cruisers. During the Franco-Prussian war, a decree was issued by Prince Bismarck authorizing the formation of such a, so-called, Volunteer Navy (*f*); and a similar fleet is at the present moment sailing under the Russian flag.

A mail steamer, with its high speed and great capacity for carrying coal, would, with a few long-range quick-firing guns and a torpedo launch, be readily converted into a highly effective public vessel. And the prohibition against privateering would not, it may be supposed, prevent mail or other steamers from carrying such defences under letters of marque for their own protection.

The most serious item in the treaty is clause 2, which exempts from capture enemy goods under the neutral flag. In abandoning this right, Great Britain has, it is asserted, not only given away the power to harass the enemy by cutting off his supplies, but what is far more important, has suspended over the national shipowning interest a sword which, on this country's becoming engaged in hostilities, may descend upon it with consequences the most disastrous. To the loss of the right to seize the enemy's goods is presumably to be attached but a secondary importance, for the facilities of inland carriage are in the present day such that a continental power at war with this country would have little difficulty in trading through neighbouring neutral ports, the property being so documented as to place it beyond the reach of condemnation by a Prize Court of the captors. What is to be especially feared is lest, on the outbreak of war directly involving Great Britain, shipment under the British flag should be universally

(*f*) *Vide* p. 100, *infra*.

avoided. British vessels being liable to capture by the enemy, it may reasonably be supposed that merchants, whether British or foreign, would not, during hostilities, ship by a British vessel so long as a neutral bottom was available; for although the neutral cargo could not be condemned, it would, under the British flag, be exposed to the risks of war; and in the event of the capture and condemnation of the vessel, it might be indefinitely detained in some foreign port. Other objections are raised to the Declaration of Paris by writers who have made it their special study, but the foregoing brief reference to the subject is considered sufficient for the purposes of this work (*g*). The circumstances in which the Declaration was signed by the British representatives seem to be involved in some obscurity, and certainly it might well have been expected that the signing and ratification of a treaty of such exceptional importance would have been attended with a greater degree of formality than was actually observed. The engagement itself is, moreover, of the crudest description. It establishes principles, but makes no sort of attempt to define their application to cases. Thus, for example, supposing that this country, bound by the Declaration not to seize the enemy's goods in neutral vessels, were to be engaged in war with the United States—a country not bound by the Declaration—what, as has been very pertinently enquired, would, under the Declaration, be the position? For while, according to the Treaty, we should be precluded from taking American property out of vessels owned by neutral states, signatories of the treaty, American cruisers would be under no corresponding disadvantage, but would, under the law of nations, have an undoubted right to carry into port, for examination, any neutral vessels reasonably

(*g*) For an exhaustive criticism of the Declaration, see copy of an Address delivered by T. G. Bowles to the London Chamber of Commerce, 17th July, 1888.

supposed to be engaged in conveying the property of British subjects.

Again, while prohibiting the capture of neutral goods on enemy vessels, the Declaration makes no provision for the case where the belligerent carrying-ship is destroyed by the enemy, and the neutral goods are thus involved in the destruction of the vessel (*h*). And if the Declaration is to be accepted—as, indeed, it reads—as an abstract and unqualified enunciation of the principle that neutral goods (except contraband of war: and "*Expressio unius est exclusio alterius*") are always to be free from capture under the enemy's flag, it follows that neutrals may henceforth with impunity ship by *armed* vessels of the enemy or under enemy convoy, though goods so shipped have hitherto been held by our Courts to be subject to confiscation (*i*).

Lord Mansfield's remark (*k*) on the subject of marine policy clauses—that it was amazing that some advice was not taken in framing them, or that more consideration was not bestowed upon them by the framers—might with advantage have been borne in mind by those concerned in framing, at any rate, clause 2 of a document of such vital importance to the national interests of this country.

If the Declaration is to be regarded as finally and irrevocably adopted by this country, it is much to be desired that its clauses should be carefully considered and so supplemented as to provide for the various important contingencies which are likely, sooner or later, to arise in connexion with them. If, on the other hand, the Declaration as it now stands should be deemed detrimental to the national wellbeing of this country, the sooner that steps are taken to withdraw from it the better. Any parties to the treaty

(*h*) *Vide* The Ludwig and Vorwärts, pp. 333, 357, *infra*.

(*i*) *Vide* p. 213, *infra*.

(*k*) In Simond *v*. Boydell, Doug. 255.

have, presumably, a perfect right to withdraw from it on giving due notice to the other contractors; but such notice cannot be honourably given at a time when hostilities seem imminent.

The Declaration has now been acceded to by all civilized states, except the United States, Spain, and Mexico. The United States declined to accept the proposition as to the abolition of privateering, unless it were further agreed that *all* private property except contraband of war should be exempt from capture: that is, practically, that merchant ships and their cargoes should not in case of hostilities be the subject of belligerent capture. The United States having no regularly constituted navy, it was contended by the American Government that their adhesion to the above proposition would, in the event of their engaging in hostilities with a country having a powerful navy, place the United States at a great disadvantage. Having themselves a large merchant fleet, it was argued, they would be especially exposed to depredations on the part of an enemy possessing a large and powerful fleet of public war vessels; and in such case their only means of placing themselves at all on an equality with the favoured belligerent would be by commissioning privateers. And they contended, further, that the extension of clause 1 in the sense of their requirement was a legitimate development of the true spirit of the Declaration. This may or may not be so, but it is obvious that there is no necessary connexion between privateering and the right of capture by national vessels. The strength of some nations lies in the possession of or the power to raise large standing armies, whilst other nations, having a comparatively small population, may nevertheless possess a powerful navy, by means of which they may be in a measure placed on an equality with nations of the former class. The abandonment by such a maritime nation of its right to capture enemy property on the high seas would be to cast away the advantage of a legitimate and most powerful weapon. It is true that privateering, like some other anachronisms, is sanctioned by the law of nations, but the system has ever been a blot on civilization, encouraging in the individual a spirit of cruelty and greed, and tending to subordinate, on the part of those concerned in it, the sense of patriotism to the love of pelf. In the hands especially of a maritime power such as Great Britain, which has voluntarily consented to forego the right to use it, privateering would become a highly effective offensive weapon.

The United States Government could hardly have seriously supposed that Great Britain, having renounced the right of privateering for herself, would consent to forego the, to her, all-important right of capture by public vessels as a set-off against America's abandonment of the same right of privateering. Indeed, it would seem that the United States Government are not very closely tied to the principle asserted by them, for on the revolt of the Southern States in 1861 the Northern Government expressed to the European Powers its desire to abandon the stipulation hitherto contended for, and to accept the terms of the Declaration. This intimation was willingly received by the Powers, who were about to give effect to it, when it occurred to Her Majesty's Government that serious complications might result in respect of the Southern States. For both the United States Government and the European Powers having thus agreed in effect to class privateering with piracy, the Powers might be placed in an awkward predicament if they then refused to take this view of the naval operations likely to be undertaken by the Southern against the Northern States. Earl Russell, therefore, on behalf of Her Majesty's Government, explained to the American Minister that in agreeing to the proposed treaty Her Majesty did not intend thereby to undertake any engagement bearing on the internal differences then prevailing in the United States; and in this course the French Government also concurred. That this change of views on the part of the American Government had been rightly appreciated seems evident, for the result was that the American Minister was directed to break off the negotiations, if the reservation was insisted upon; and the negotiations were broken off accordingly.

The Second clause of the Declaration embodies the abbreviated proposition, "Free ships, free goods." A belligerent has, under the law of nations, an unquestionable right to seize and confiscate enemy goods found on board a neutral vessel. But this right is now waived by the nations signatories to the Treaty of Paris. The United States and the other non-signatories presumably possess the right to seize goods so found where they have not contracted themselves out of it by express treaty. Contraband of war is in all cases liable to confiscation.

The Third clause asserts the proposition that permissive neutral goods are exempt from capture, though shipped under an enemy flag. This principle has been explicitly incorporated into the jurisprudence of the United States. It is indeed so obvious that war gives no right to capture the goods of a friend that it, at first sight, seems needless to have embodied the principle in the Declaration of 1856. It has, however, been by some considered that the proposition, "Enemy ships, enemy goods," is the logical converse of "Free ships, free goods," and it may have been for this reason thought convenient to publicly express the contrary view of the signatories to the treaty.

It may here be observed that since the acceptance of the Declaration of Paris a disposition has been shown to go even further in the direction of providing immunity to merchant shipping to whomever belonging. Thus, in 1866, it was agreed between Austria on the one hand, and her adversaries Prussia and Italy on the other, that enemy merchandise and enemy merchant ships should both be exempt from capture on the high seas. And in the war between France and Prussia in 1870, the latter power issued a declaration that all French merchant vessels should be exempt from capture. This decree was, however, subsequently annulled in consequence of France having refused to waive her right of capture of Prussian merchant vessels.

The principles embodied in clauses 2 and 3 of the treaty, as well as the final declaration relative to Blockade, will be more fully discussed in their proper place under the general head Belligerent Rights. These Rights may for convenience be divided into three classes—viz.: (1) Rights against the Enemy; (2) Rights against Neutrals; and (3) Municipal Rights. The rights falling under these several heads have now to be set forth and considered according to this classification.

IV.

BELLIGERENT RIGHTS AGAINST THE ENEMY

ACCORDING TO THE LAW OF NATIONS.

EMBARGO AND REPRISALS.

THE right of embargo may be exercised either as a stop or arrest of the departure of ships or goods from within the national jurisdiction, or as a restraint laid upon ships and goods prohibitive of their entering the national ports or certain of them. Or it may be in the nature of an order to the national public vessels to seize and bring into port vessels belonging to or sailing under an alien flag, such vessels and their cargoes to be carefully saved from harm pending further notification (*a*).

Thus, in 1840, in consequence of a monopoly of the sulphur trade granted by Sicily to France, contrary, as was

(*a*) *Vide* 5th ed. Arnould's Insce. 698.

alleged by Her Majesty's Government, to treaty between this country and Sicily, orders were sent to the Mediterranean fleet to seize and detain all Sicilian and Neapolitan vessels, pending compliance with the demands of Her Majesty's Government. A number of Neapolitan vessels were seized in consequence, an embargo being also placed at Malta on all vessels flying the Sicilian flag. On the intervention of the French Government the obnoxious contract was dissolved by Sicily, and the vessels under arrest were released. During this time the British Minister remained at Naples, the British Government having instructed him that the reprisals which Her Majesty's Government had been compelled to institute were not to be regarded as constituting war. In 1857, in *The Cagliari* case (*b*), the Neapolitan Government were induced to accede to the British demands mainly under the threat to place an embargo on Neapolitan vessels.

Embargo may be ordered by public authority or by the royal proclamation. It may be either municipal, applying to subjects; or aggressive, applying to the property of aliens. The property of aliens arrested under such a proclamation may be restored on the establishment of a satisfactory understanding between the arresting and the alien power, or, failing such an understanding, it may be declared confiscated. A declaration of embargo affords to an aggrieved nation a convenient weapon of reprisal in the event of a refusal of justice by another power; for the property seized may be either confiscated in compensation, or held as a hostage pending restitution, for a wrong committed.

Other forms of reprisal are pacific blockade (*c*); the issuing of letters of marque to privateers (*d*); and retortion generally—

(*b*) *Vide* pp. 295, 435, *infra*.

(*c*) Respecting which, *vide* p. 121, *infra*.

(*d*) *Vide sub* Blockade and Privateering respectively, *infra*.

an instance of the last named being the rigorous confinement of prisoners of war as a set-off against similar harshness initiated by the enemy: or the imposition of a poll or other tax on alien subjects within the national jurisdiction in retaliation for the like measures adopted by the alien power. In the year 1748, Prussia, by way of reprisal against Great Britain for alleged illegal captures by the latter, confiscated certain funds lent by British subjects in respect of a Prussian loan. The ultimate result of this proceeding was that, in consideration of Prussia undertaking to pay off the loan, Great Britain agreed to pay Prussia £20,000 in discharge of all claims. On the declaration of war against Russia in 1854 a proclamation was issued by Her Majesty, ordering that "general reprisals be granted against the ships, vessels, and goods" of the Emperor of all the Russias and of his subjects or the inhabitants of Russian territory; but such an announcement is rather of the nature of a declaration of general hostilities than of the intention to resort to reprisals in the above sense.

With respect to the right of pacific blockade, it should perhaps not yet be included amongst the rights recognised by the law of nations, although at times claimed as such. Instances of this form of reprisal are given below, *sub* Blockade (*d*).

Although not strictly within the limits of the present subject, it may be convenient here to observe that it is permissible by the law of nations for a Power to seize neutral property for State purposes, with the intention to ultimately either restore or appropriate it. In either case the neutral owners have to be compensated. This class of seizure is rather to be called an "arrest" than described by the hostile term "capture." This point will be more fully dealt with when considering the subject of Belligerent Rights

(*d*) P. 121.

against Neutrals, under the head Pre-emption (*e*). A government is, of course, entitled to execute similar rights municipally against its own subjects, as will be set forth when dealing with the Municipal Rights of Belligerents.

A familiar instance of arrest is that of the Genoese cornship, generally quoted by the marine insurance text-writers. The ship was seized by Venetian cruisers and taken into Corfu for the relief of that place, then in a state of famine, the corn being sold for the benefit of the islanders, and the owners being paid for it.

Insurance (*f*).

The leading distinction between arrest and capture lies in the circumstance that, while in the former case the property is seized with the intention to ultimately restore it or pay its value, a capture is effected with the intention to condemn and confiscate (*g*). On the Continent, the enforced abandonment of a voyage owing to embargo at the port of destination gives rise to a claim on underwriters. But this is not so under British law (*h*). It has, on the contrary, been clearly laid down that the abandonment of a voyage consequent on embargo, hostile occupation, blockade, or interdiction of trade at the port of destination, gives rise to no such claim. The proximate cause of damages thus resulting is deemed to be the *fear* of capture—a peril not contemplated under the policy. Of course, if the vessel were to proceed and be captured the loss would then be one of capture, for which, in the absence of an exceptive clause, underwriters would be liable, provided the master in so proceeding did not break the conditions of the insurance or the laws of this country. Whether a loss thus deliberately incurred could be

---

(*e*) *Vide sub* Pre-emption, p. 244, *infra*.

(*f*) The observations following under this head deal, to some extent, with embargo, restraint, and detainment generally, whether exercised against an enemy, a neutral, or a national subject.

(*g*) Rodocanachi *v.* Elliott, 8 L. R. C. P. 649.

(*h*) 5th ed. Arnould's Insce. 726.

attributed to barratry of the master would depend upon the circumstances of the case.

If, on approaching his destination, the master finds it blockaded, the alternatives present themselves of either waiting as near by as he safely can until the port is re-opened, or of sailing away for some other port, definitely abandoning the voyage (*i*), or of returning to his port of loading. In the first case the policy will apparently remain in force (*j*); but in the alternative cases the voyage insured will be deemed to be abandoned, and there will be an arrival under the policy (*k*). The moment the master puts his ship about with the intention to abandon the voyage, the underwriters' risk is concluded. That is, unless any special clause relating to deviation or change of voyage should provide otherwise,—as, for example, in *The Monarch*, mentioned on p. 125, *infra*, where the voyage insured was declared to be "to any ports or places in the river Plata, with liberty, in the event of a blockade or being ordered off the river Plata, to proceed to any other port and there wait or discharge." The shipowner is not justified in abandoning the voyage, unless he has reserved the option to do so under the terms of his contract of affreightment. But if he merely proceeds to another port and there awaits the raising of the embargo or blockade, this will appa-

(*i*) The following are special clauses framed to protect the assured in the event of their property being discharged short of its destination :—

> "In case of blockade, to include the risk of landing the goods at any other port or ports, whilst there, and thence to port of destination by same or other conveyance; premium to be arranged." Owen's Marine Insce. Notes and Clauses, 2nd ed. p. 49.
>
> "In the event of the vessel being prevented, either by blockade or other cause connected with hostilities, from proceeding to her port of destination, and consequently discharging the property hereby insured at any other port or place, we hereby agree to pay all charges for landing, warehousing, and forwarding, as well as freight from the port or place, and all charges until the goods shall be safely delivered into the hands of the consignees." *Ib.*

(*j*) Blanckenhagen *v.* London Assurance Co., 1 Camp. 454; *Graham* v. *Commercial Insurance Co.*, 11 *Johnson's Rep.* 352, cited 1 Phillips' Insce., No. 1023. *Vide* also pp. 421-2, *infra.*

(*k*) Parkin *v.* Tunno, 11 East, 22; Lubbock *v.* Rowcroft, 5 Esp. 49; Hadkinson *v.* Robinson, 3 B. & P. 388.

rently not be deemed a breach of his carriage contract (*l*). Wages and cost of provisions of the crew incurred during embargo, or consequent on blockade, are not recoverable either as general average or from underwriters on ship or freight. Such charges are, at any rate under British law, held to be within the scope of the shipowner's obligations under the contract of affreightment, and, in the absence of any stipulation to the contrary, he must bear them accordingly (*m*). Arrest, detention, and embargo do not effect an annulment or discharge of the contract of affreightment, but act merely as a temporary suspense of its operation.

If a foreign power place an embargo on neutral vessels within its territory, the assured is entitled to abandon to his underwriters, and claim as for a total loss by "arrest, restraint, and detainment of princes" (*n*). If, however, the detention be on the face of it merely a temporary obstruction of the voyage, the case is otherwise (*o*). The assured cannot recover as for a total loss by embargo without abandonment, and if he allow the time to pass without abandoning, the loss may have to be considered merely as an average claim, as in other cases of abandonment deferred. An instance of a "detainment" was furnished by the Franco-Prussian war, certain silk in course of despatch from the East to this country having been detained in Paris owing to the Prussian investment of that city. It was decided that this was a loss for which the underwriters were liable (*p*).

If a neutral ship be seized by belligerents and carried into port with the intent to procure the condemnation of the cargo and not further to detain the vessel, such an arrest is not in the nature of embargo, but must, within the meaning of the policy, be regarded as a detainment or capture (*q*).

In *Fowler* v. *Eng. and Scot. M. I. Co.* (*r*), the policy contained the following clause:—"To pay a total loss thirty days after receipt of official news of capture or embargo, without waiting

(*l*) Blanckenhagen's case, *supra*.
(*m*) Robertson *v.* Ewer, 1 T. R. 129.
(*n*) Rotch *v.* Edie, 6 T. R. 413.
(*o*) 5th ed. Arnould's Insce. 998.
(*p*) Rodocanachi *v.* Elliott, L. R. 8 C. P. 649.
(*q*) *Vide* p. 71, *infra*.
(*r*) 34 L. J. C. P. 253.

for condemnation." The vessel having been detained under an embargo, as contemplated under the clause, it was held that when the thirty days after official news of the embargo had expired, the assured was entitled to recover for a total loss, although, before action—but subsequently to such thirty days—the embargo had been taken off and the vessel released (*r*).

The contract to indemnify the assured in respect of arrests, restraints, and detainments by princes, being in general terms—that is, not limited to the acts of alien powers—underwriters are liable also for arrests on the part of the nation of which the assured is a member, whether such nation be British or foreign. But this is subject to the reservation that any insurance against British capture, and, consequently, of British hostile embargo, is illegal and void, whether such insurance be effected before or after the outbreak of hostilities (*s*). Insurance against capture or embargo on the part of an ally of or co-belligerent with Great Britain would stand on the same footing.

With respect to loss by what may be termed British municipal embargo,—that is, the arrest and detainment of British property by the national government, the assured, who is a British subject, is entitled to recover under the policy (*t*). The position of an alien in this country, who has sustained a loss by the action of his own government, has been the subject of no little discussion; and although the law in this respect must now be taken to be clearly defined, it may be convenient to here briefly review the legal decisions bearing on the point. First in order came the important case of *Touteng* v. *Hubbard* (*u*), in which a London merchant had chartered a Swedish vessel to proceed (restraint of

---

(*r*) The following are further examples of this clause:—

"In case of capture it is hereby agreed that the loss shall be payable within thirty days after reliable information of the same shall be received in London, without waiting for adjudication in a prize Court." Owen's Marine Insce. Notes, 2nd ed. p. 21.

"Against all risks whatsoever, British as well as foreign capture, seizure, and detention included. Detention for a period of six months to be deemed equivalent to a condemnation." *Ib.* 22. (*Vide* p. 405, *sub* Void Insurances, relative to this clause.)

(*s*) *Vide sub* Void Insurances, *infra*, p. 405.

(*t*) Page *v.* Thompson, 8th ed. Park's Insce. 175; Green *v.* Young, 2 Ld. Raym. 840; 2 Salk. 444. And see 5th ed. Arnould's Insce. 725, n.

(*u*) 3 B. & P. 291.

princes and rulers excepted) to St. Michael's for a cargo of fruit. Shortly after sailing from London, the vessel put into Ramsgate, where, in consequence of an embargo then placed on all Swedish vessels, she was detained for six months. On release of the vessel, the charterer gave notice to the shipowner that the contract was at an end, the fruit season being over. The shipowner on this sued for damages. The Court held that a distinction was to be drawn between an embargo laid on for general purposes and an embargo, as in this case, in the nature of partial hostilities; that this embargo had been laid on by the British Government in order to resist the injustice of the Swedish Court; and that it would be a violation of all principle if it were competent for a Swedish subject, by a contract of affreightment, to defeat all the efforts of the British Government, and throw the burden on a British subject; that, from a political point of view, the plaintiff's loss might be considered as arising from his own fault, since it was the consequence of an act of aggression on the part of his (the Swedish) Government; and that where a party had been disabled from performing his contract by his own default, he could not allege the circumstances by which he had been prevented as an excuse for his omission. The reasoning here is intelligible enough; but in *Conway* v. *Gray* (*v*), which followed in 1809, Lord Ellenborough seems to have given it too wide an application. In this case an insurance had been effected in England on an American vessel bound from New York to Liverpool. The American Government having placed an embargo on all vessels in the United States ports, the assured abandoned, and claimed a total loss. The Court, however, decided in favour of the underwriters, on the ground that the assent of every man is implied to the acts of his own government, and makes such an embargo as the present his own voluntary act. "In all questions arising between the subjects of different states," said his lordship, "each is a party to the public authoritative acts of his own government," as, was added, seemed to be established by *Touteng* v. *Hubbard*. But the circumstances were not the same in these cases. In *Touteng's* case the embargo was in the nature of hostilities. In *Conway's* case it was for

(*v*) 10 East, 536.

general purposes unconnected with hostilities. *Conway's* decision was followed in 1812 by *Mennett* v. *Bonham* (*w*), *Flindt* v. *Crockett* (*x*), and *Flindt* v. *Scott* (*y*). In *Simeon* v. *Bazett* (*z*), however, a distinction was drawn between the two sets of circumstances, and the decision in *Conway's* case was practically overruled. An insurance had been effected in London on ship and goods from London under special licence, to any ports in the Baltic, with liberty to carry false papers, the goods to be covered till warehoused. The intended voyage was to a port in Prussia, with which country England was at peace. Prussia was, however, under control of Napoleon's continental system, in force of which all British cargoes to the Baltic had been interdicted. These facts were common knowledge, and it was also well known that an extensive commerce was, notwithstanding, carried on between Great Britain and the Baltic ports by means of simulated papers. The Prussian Government having confiscated the property insured, the underwriters, averring that the owners of the goods were Prussian subjects, repudiated liability and based their defence on *Touteng* v. *Hubbard* and *Conway* v. *Gray*. But Lord Ellenborough gave judgment for the plaintiff, though it can hardly be said that his reasons for so doing were very conclusive. Without disavowing the decision in *Conway* v. *Gray* he laid stress on the circumstance that whereas, in the cases relied on, the embargo was never an object of the insurance nor contemplated by the underwriter, in the present case the cause of loss arose from the course of the commerce itself. It was carried on, he said, by simulated papers: the parties had leave to carry these papers, and it was clear that the perils of the trade were contemplated under the policy.

The underwriters appealed against this decision—*Bazett* v. *Meyer* (*survivor of Simeon* (*a*))—but the judgment was affirmed. In 1821 the question again arose in *Campbell* v. *Innes* (*b*), and

(*w*) 15 East, 477.

(*x*) *Ibid.* 522.

(*y*) *Ibid.* 525. Overruled by Flindt *v.* Scott, 5 Taunt. 674 (1814), on appeal.

(*z*) 2 M. & S. 94. Confirmed on appeal, Bazett *v.* Meyer, 5 Taunt. 824 (1814).

(*a*) 5 Taunt. 824, An. 1814.

(*b*) 4 B. & Ald. 423.

was decided in favour of the underwriters on a different issue, viz.: concealment of nationality (*c*). In 1861 it again came before the Courts in *Aubert* v. *Gray* (*d*). An insurance had been effected on carpets by *The Jovellanos*, from London to Alicante, the assured being Spaniards. The vessel, having put into Corunna, was there restrained and seized by the Spanish Government. The cargo was turned out upon the quay during the prevalence of tempestuous weather in order to make room for Spanish troops, to be conveyed to Malaga *en route* for Morocco, with which country Spain was on hostile relations. The cargo having sustained damages, and sue-and-labour charges having been incurred in its behalf, plaintiffs sued for indemnification. The underwriters disclaimed liability, basing their defence on the judgment in *Conway* v. *Gray*. The Court, in rejecting this defence, observed that if *Conway* v. *Gray* really decided that in such a case as the present the assured must be taken to be consenting parties to the acts of their own government, the judgment in that case must be overruled. "This judgment" (*i.e.* in *Aubert* v. *Gray*), observed the Court, "recognises a marked distinction between an embargo in a time when there is peace between the countries of the insurer and the assured, laid on for a purpose wholly unconnected with hostility, either existing or expected; and an embargo connected with such hostility. Therefore this judgment does not interfere with any of the decisions on points connected with war." To this was added a declaration that it was also to be understood that the Court did not say that if the act of seizure was a lawful act under the municipal law of Spain, as against a Spanish subject such seizure would be within the insurance. By which, as it appears, the Court indicated that a distinction was equally to be drawn between a seizure consequent on a breach of ordinary municipal enactments and a seizure consequent on a government proclamation, issued, as in the present case, under pressure of some special emergency. This decision must presumably be regarded as a final expression of the law on the subject.

The assured being entitled to abandon to his underwriters on receipt of news that his property insured is restrained by the

---

(*c*) *Vide* p. 403, *infra*.

(*d*) 3 B. & S. 163, 169; 32 L. J. Q. B. 50.

embargo of a foreign power, the underwriter or the several underwriters have to provide for realisation of the property in the event of the embargo being taken off. The various underwriters on the ship and cargo having paid as for a total loss, and the property in those several interests having accordingly become vested in the said underwriters respectively, it becomes necessary for them to appoint trustees to act on their joint behalf. It may be arranged with the shipowner that he shall undertake this responsibility, or the property may be formally vested in certain persons as trustees on behalf of all concerned. Inasmuch as abandonment of the ship carries with it the title to unpaid freight, shipowners, as in other cases of abandonment of a vessel which may yet earn her freight, have to take care that the underwriters on the freight also accept abandonment. Otherwise it may result that after acceptance of abandonment by underwriters on ship, but before such acceptance by those on freight, the ship may be released, the shipowners thus losing their rights against the underwriters on freight. The result being that the freight becomes due to the ship underwriters, and the owners of the vessel have no rights under the policy on freight; there being no loss of this interest by a peril insured against (*d*). In Sir James Park's work on marine insurance a case is reported in which the shipowners, in consideration of payment of the sum insured by the underwriters on freight, expressly assigned to them any freight which might be earned. The ship arrived, and the freight was claimed by the underwriters on ship. Held, that the shipowners were, notwithstanding, bound by their voluntary undertaking with the underwriters on freight (*e*).

To sail in contravention of an embargo is an unlawful act, and if the vessel be insured within the dominions of the power laying on the embargo, the insurance will be voided by the offence (*f*).

If on the entry of a vessel into a port she find herself under an embargo, she cannot be said to have been "moored in safety" for twenty-four hours within the meaning of the policy. On the

(*d*) McCarthy *v.* Abel, 5 East, 388; Scottish Mar. Ins. Co. *v.* Turner, 1 Macq. H. L. Cas. 334.

(*e*) Thompson *v.* Rowcroft, 4 East, 34.

(*f*) *Vide* Delmada *v.* Motteux, pp. 289, 308, *infra*.

contrary, from the moment of her arrival, instead of being "moored in safety" she is practically detained as a prize by the enemy (*g*). In a somewhat similar case judgment went for the underwriters on the ground that the vessel was carrying simulated papers without leave (*h*). The offence of carrying simulated papers will be discussed in its place (*i*).

The brief reference to the subject of insurance *sub* Blockade may also be referred to in this connexion, p. 123, *infra*.

In the late war against Russia an example was set which, if it should meet with general adoption in the future, will do much to mitigate the losses and inconveniences consequent on embargo on declaration of war. War was declared by Great Britain on 28th March, 1854, and on the following day a Royal Proclamation was issued, ordering a general embargo or stop to be made of all Russian vessels then or which might thereafter arrive in her Majesty's dominions, together with all persons and effects thereon. But by a second proclamation of the same date it was declared that all Russian merchant vessels then in the dominions should be allowed until 10th May, a period of six weeks, for loading their cargoes and departing, such vessels to be free from arrest at sea unless carrying any officer in the naval or military service of the enemy, any article contraband of war, or any despatch of or to the Russian Government (*k*).

By another proclamation it was declared that any Russian merchant vessel which prior to the date of the said order had sailed for any port in her Majesty's dominions, should be permitted to enter and discharge at such port and thereafter depart unmolested and be permitted to proceed to any port not blockaded.

On 7th April it was further ordered that Russian merchant vessels at that date at any port within her Majesty's dominions or possessions should be allowed thirty days in which to load and depart, and should not be molested or detained if met with at sea, or on an examination of the ship's papers establishing the

(*g*) Minett *v.* Anderson, Peake, 211.

(*h*) Horneyer *v.* Lushington, 15 East, 46.

(*i*) *Vide* p. 219, *infra*.

(*k*) 1 Bulletins, 1854, 359-60. *Vide* also p. 92, *infra*.

fact that the sailing took place within such period. And on 15th April it was declared that this order extended to all Russian merchant vessels which prior to 15th May had sailed from any Russian port of the Baltic Sea or White Sea for any port in the British dominions.

Vessels having on board officers in the enemy's public service, contraband of war, or hostile despatches were excluded from these concessions.

Concessions on the above lines were in like manner proclaimed by the governments of France and Russia. The above proclamations, it will be observed, make no reference to the case of vessels on voyages to other than British ports.

The subject of restraint, seizure, and detention of property of the national subjects, which may be usefully referred to in this connexion, will be considered separately, in its place (*l*). The reference to "Letters of Marque and Reprisal" (p. 91, *infra*) is also of interest in relation to this subject.

Analogous to the right to seize, on the outbreak of hostilities, vessels of the enemy within the national jurisdiction, is the less obvious right to seize and confiscate property of and debts due to the enemy within the dominions. This subject will now be briefly considered.

(*l*) *Vide* p. 254, *infra*.

Confiscation of Enemy Debts and Enemy Property within the National Territory.

Whether such assets of the enemy as above can be lawfully confiscated as a right of war is matter of controversy on the part of writers on the law of nations. The letter of the law would certainly appear to recognise the right, and that the ancients had no scruples on the point is manifest. On the outbreak of hostilities between Great Britain and France in 1793, France sequestrated the debts to and property of British subjects, which proceeding was retorted upon by Great Britain as regards property of French subjects. But in 1814 the sequestrations were removed on both sides, and the claims of individual sufferers at the hands of the French were liquidated. By modern international usage, however, the right, if right it be, is presumably deemed to be extinct, and in many cases the contingency is probably specially provided for by treaty. In the absence of such a treaty all civilized powers would, it may be confidently assumed, now refrain from claiming any such rights, unless, indeed, the property were of such national importance that its seizure would result in diminishing the capacity of the enemy for carrying on the war. But in the event of the maintenance of the right on the part of one belligerent, the other might assert it by way of retaliation. One of the stipulations of Magna Charta provides that at the commencement of a war the enemy's merchants shall be kept and treated as English merchants are treated by the enemy. Subsequent enactments in this and other countries provide that enemy subjects shall, on outbreak of war, be allowed to depart from the country of their domicile in safety, taking with them or selling their goods on departure. In 1854 it was declared by the government of this country that the persons and property of Russian subjects domiciled in Great Britain would be respected to the full extent promised by the government of Russia to British subjects domiciled in that country. To confiscate the property of an alien who has entered the country with the sanction and under the implied protection of the government of the country would certainly, according to the enlightened opinion of the present day, be considered a discreditable breach of the national good faith. This principle does not apply to the seizure of enemy ships and cargoes temporarily within the jurisdiction, for it is obvious that there is a wide difference between seizing the property of an alien domiciled in the country, contributing to the national taxes, and sharing the lot common to individuals of the nation; and seizing ships and cargoes in port belonging to enemy subjects domiciled in the hostile territory. During the war between Great Britain and the United States in 1814, certain timber found within the jurisdiction of the latter power was confiscated on the ground that being British property it was lawful prize of war. On appeal this order was reversed, the Supreme Court declaring that though the right of seizure was undoubtedly possessed by the sovereign power, the right did not of itself operate as a confiscation of enemy property, but that the intention to exercise it must first be declared by the State. No such intention having in this case been expressed, the right of seizure had not attached (*m*).

During the American civil war, cotton, the property of individuals in the Southern States, was seized and confiscated by the Federal troops, on the ground that it was the mainstay of the Confederates, and ministered directly to their power to

---

(*m*) *Brown* v. *United States*, 8 *Cranch*, 110.

carry on hostilities (*n*). The Confederate States, on their side, passed an act confiscating property, of whatever nature, except public stocks and securities, held by an alien enemy. Lord Russell strongly protested against this measure, declaring "that whatever may have been the abstract law of nations on this point in former times, the instances of its application in the manner contemplated, in modern and more civilized times, are so rare, and have been so generally condemned, that it may almost be said to have become obsolete" (*o*).

On the outbreak of hostilities, debts due from a belligerent State to alien enemies are in strict law subject to confiscation, but modern usage does not sanction the exercise of this right. The case is, probably, now commonly expressly provided for by international conventions (*p*).

As regards private debts, the rule appears to be that the right of enemy subjects to moneys owed to them by individuals of this country is not annulled on outbreak of war, but is held in suspense until the conclusion of hostilities. During war an alien enemy has no *locus standi* in our Courts, and therefore cannot sue for payment. With the renewal of peace his right revives, so far as it relates to debts contracted before hostilities, but any contract made during hostilities would be void (*q*). In *Wolff* v. *Oxholm* (*r*) Lord Ellenborough declined to recognise as legal the confiscation by the Danish Government of debts due from Danish to British subjects. On an action being brought against a Danish subject in the British Courts, the Court held that the payment by such subject to

(*n*) Wheat. Int. Law, 2 Eng. ed. 412.

(*o*) Edinburgh Review, July 1884, 273.

(*p*) In the case of government bonds, it is sometimes expressly declared upon them that payment of interest shall be made, and redemption of principal take place, as well in time of war as during peace, and whether the holders be subjects of a friendly or hostile state.

(*q*) Alcinous *v.* Nigreu, 4 E. & B. 217. *Vide* Effect of War on Contract, p. 412, *infra*.

(*r*) 6 M. & S. 92.

his government did not furnish a defence to the demand of the creditor in this country, and judgment was given against him accordingly.

The rights of embargo, reprisals, and confiscation may be roughly described as rights more especially internal—that is, which can be exercised by a belligerent against the enemy within the national territory. Other and more important or, at any rate, better known rights are those to be exercised outside the jurisdiction. Foremost amongst these stands the right to seize and confiscate enemy shipping on the high seas. This we will now consider.

Capture of Enemy Vessels and Enemy Cargo therein.

Capture may for present purposes be defined as the forcible seizure of the ships and goods of an enemy, or of enemy subjects, with intent to appropriate the same to the captors' use, and it may be effected either (1) by the public vessels or national forces; or (2) by individuals commissioned by letters of marque to engage in hostilities against the enemy on the high seas and within the enemy jurisdiction. The subjects of Letters of Marque and Privateers will be specially considered presently (*s*), and the subject of Neutral Territory (as opposed to "enemy jurisdiction") will be referred to in its place under the general head Belligerent Obligations (*t*).

On the outbreak of hostilities the right of capture at once becomes active, but having regard to the example in moderation set by the belligerent powers in recent wars, it is not unreasonable to suppose that the right to capture any enemy vessels within the dominions on the outbreak of hostilities will henceforth be postponed. Thus, in the war with Russia in 1854, six weeks was allowed for Russian merchant vessels within British territory to load and proceed; whilst such vessels which had sailed for British ports prior to the outbreak were permitted to enter, discharge, and proceed unmolested to any port not blockaded (*u*). And on the occurrence of the

(*s*) *Vide* p. 91, *infra*.
(*t*) *Vide* p. 311, *infra*.
(*u*) 1 Bulletins, 1854. *Vide* also p. 47, *supra*.

Franco-German war in 1870, thirty days were allowed for German merchant vessels in French ports to load or unload and depart, whilst those vessels which had sailed prior to the war with cargoes on French account were also to be free from capture (*v*). To French vessels in German ports a period of six weeks was allowed in which the vessels might load or unload and depart (*x*).

To constitute a capture it is not necessary that the captured vessel should be actually boarded and seized by the enemy, or even that a prize master should be sent on board. The striking of the colours of the assailed vessel is deemed a token of surrender and capture (*y*); or the vessel may be driven on shore or into port (*z*). In *The Edward and Mary* (*a*) Sir W. Scott mentioned as an instance of this a famous case in which a small British vessel, having only three men on board, and with no weapons except two swivel-guns, drove into Ostend, then the port of an ally, a French row-boat full of heavily armed men. The British seamen dared not attempt to board the row-boat, but forced the enemy into port, by following them all the way at a suitable distance, covering the boat meantime with the swivels. And in another case, that of *The Resolution* (*b*), which was seized by a British vessel and claimed as a capture, it was held that the vessel had already been captured by another British vessel, although the first captors, instead of putting a prize crew on board, had accepted the master's voluntary promise that he would proceed to a

(*v*) 60 State Papers, 879; and *vide* p. 269, *infra*.

(*x*) 60 State Papers, 899.

(*y*) The Rebekah, 1 Rob. 233.

(*z*) Cf. Powell *v.* Hyde, p. 79, *infra*, where an abandoned ship, deliberately sunk by the enemy, was held to have been "captured."

(*a*) 3 Rob. 306.

(*b*) 6 Rob. 13.

British port, which promise, however, was not kept. The vessel was a neutral, and had been seized on the ground that she had enemy goods on board.

A capture is none the less a capture if illegally made, or if it prove on adjudication that the property is not subject to condemnation (*c*). A reasonable suspicion on the part of the captors will justify seizure, and a ship may be liable to capture though not to condemnation. But every capture, whether by a public vessel or by a privateer, is at the peril of the captors, who, on failure to show reasonable and sufficient justification, are liable to a suit for restitution, and may in addition be mulcted in costs and damages (*d*).

All captured vessels must be brought without unnecessary delay and with due care to a port within the jurisdiction of the nation of which the captor is a member, or to the port of an ally, for adjudication (*e*). The Prize Act (*vide* Appendix) allows captors considerable latitude as to the port to which to take their prize, but they must not select any port they please. It must be a convenient port, and one of the first considerations in this connexion should be the convenience of the claimants in proceeding to adjudication (*f*).

If a captor finds himself unable to bring his prize into port —because, for example, he cannot spare men to man her; or because his own national ports are too closely watched by the enemy; or for any other sufficient reason—in default of other means of disposing of the vessel he may destroy her. But before resorting to such an extreme exercise of the rights of war he should satisfy himself that the vessel, if brought in

(*c*) Hobbs *v*. Henning, p. 196, *infra*.

(*d*) Story on Prize Courts, p. 35. *Vide* also p. 324, *infra*.

(*e*) *Vide* p. 316, *infra*, "Adjudication and Condemnation."

(*f*) The Wilhelmsberg, 5 Rob. 143; *The Lively and Cargo*, 1 *Gall*. 318; The Washington, 6 Rob. 275.

for adjudication, would be condemned, and in case of doubt upon this point she should be released. If destruction be resorted to, the vessel's papers should be preserved, for it will be open to innocent sufferers to demand adjudication and compensation, though ship and cargo be destroyed (*g*). During the American civil war many Federal vessels were burnt by the Confederate cruisers, and in so doing the Confederates followed, as was subsequently admitted by the Federal law officers, the example of the United States during the war with this country in 1812—1814 (*h*). And during the recent war between Russia and Turkey, a similar course was, it is alleged, adopted by Russian cruisers against merchant vessels of the latter power (*i*). But failing such evidence as in captors' opinion would secure the confiscation of the property, the capture should be released (*j*). If a prize be destroyed on insufficient grounds, compensation may be ordered to the claimants (*k*). But great indulgence is allowed to errors in cases where captors act in good faith and without gross misconduct (*l*).

Formerly, fishermen engaged in their occupation were deemed non-combatants and their property exempt from capture, but Sir W. Scott, in *The Young Jacob* (*m*), observing that the rule was one of comity and not of law, condemned the vessel as being constantly and exclusively employed in the enemy's trade. But by an Order in Council dated May,

(*g*) But *vide* p. 357, *infra*, relative to neutral property on belligerent vessels destroyed in the Franco-Prussian War.

(*h*) *Vide Jecker* v. *Montgomery*, p. 299, *infra*. Also Wheat. Int. Law, 2 Eng. ed. 432.

(*i*) *Ibid.*

(*j*) The Felicity, 2 Dod. 381.

(*k*) The Felicity, *supra;* The Actæon, 2 Dod. 381.

(*l*) *The Lively and Cargo*, *supra ; The Anne*, 3 *Wheat.* 435; *The George*, 1 *Mason*, 24; The John, 2 Dod. 339.

(*m*) 1 Rob. 20.

1806, all fishing vessels engaged for the purpose of catching fish and conveying them fresh to market, with their crews, cargoes, and stores, were declared to be free from molestation (*n*).

"Whenever the captors are justified in the capture they are considered as having a *bonâ fide* possession, and are not responsible for any subsequent losses or injuries arising to the property from mere accident or casualty, as from stress of weather, recapture by the enemy, shipwreck, &c. (*o*). They are, however, in all cases bound for fair and safe custody; and if the property be lost from the want of proper care, they are responsible to the amount of the damage; for subsequent misconduct may forfeit the fair title of a *bonâ fide* possessor, and make him a trespasser from the beginning" (*p*).

An unduly postponed claim for damages in respect of illegal capture is not specifically barred by the Statute of Limitations, but after a great lapse of time the Court will by equity extend to prize causes the principle of that Statute (*q*). When damages are allowed, in the case of loss of the property, the measure of damages is usually the actual loss sustained. And if after assessment of damages, payment be delayed, interest will be allowed on the whole sum awarded, from date of the assessment (*r*). The person immediately liable for damages in the case of illegal seizure by a public vessel is he who effects the capture, and not his superior in command, such as the admiral or commodore; though the actual captor may have rights over against his superiors within the scope of whose authority he is acting. It is the

(*n*) 5 Rob. Appendix.

(*o*) The Betsey, 1 Rob. 93; The Catharine and Anna, 4 Rob. 39; The Caroline, 4 Rob. 256; *Del Col* v. *Arnold*, 3 *Dall.* 333.

(*p*) Story on Prize Courts, p. 37.

(*q*) The Mentor, 1 Rob. 179; The Huldah, 3 Rob. 235.

(*r*) Story's Prize Courts, p. 41.

actual wrong-doer who must be brought before the Court (*s*). In the case of a capture by privateers the matter stands on a somewhat different footing, as will be set forth under the head Privateering and Letters of Marque (*t*).

All persons found on board a captured vessel have, as provided by Art. VI. of the Instructions for Commanders of Her Majesty's Ships of War as to the Disposal of Captured Vessels, to be treated as prisoners of war, and they must accordingly be handed over to the authorities charged with the duty of receiving such prisoners. And by Art. III. of the same instructions, when a vessel is captured, bulk must not in ordinary circumstances be broken until judgment has been given in the Court of Admiralty. In case of the capture of a neutral vessel the crew must not in the absence of special reason to the contrary be handcuffed or put in irons (*u*). Damages will be awarded by a Prize Court against captors acting contrary to this general rule. If the master of a captured vessel have cause to complain of the treatment received at the hands of the captors, the proper course is for him to set forth his complaint in the form of a public instrument of protest, sworn before a notary public in the customary form. Any damages sustained by the ship or cargo in consequence of the mismanagement, neglect, or malfeasance of the captors should in like manner be protested against by the master.

If a belligerent vessel having prisoners on board puts into a neutral port, the prisoners are lawfully under the belligerent's jurisdiction so long as they remain on board ship, and the neutral power has no right of interference; but if once they set foot on land they become free (*x*).

(*s*) The Mentor, 1 Rob. 179; The Diligentia, 1 Dod. 404; The Ostsee, p. 325, *infra*.

(*t*) *Vide* pp. 94 and 332, *infra*.

(*u*) The St. Juan Baptista, 5 Rob. 33; The Die Fire Damer, 5 Rob. 357.

(*x*) *Vide* reply of H. M. Government to a complaint by the French Govern-

If the ship be condemned, the master's private effects are apparently subject to the same fate (*y*).

Where on adjudication the property is condemned, the costs of discharging, warehousing, &c., have to be defrayed by the captors. Where it is restored, payment of the charges will be awarded as the Court, having regard to the circumstances, may in its discretion deem proper (*z*).

Costs may be awarded to captors, notwithstanding a decree of restitution, if it appear that sufficient grounds existed for the seizure (*a*).

The precise point or moment at which captured property is deemed to be vested absolutely in the captor has never been universally decided, and different rules exist respecting it. According to the United States laws, when a ship has once been condemned in a competent Court of the captors she becomes thenceforth vested absolutely in the captors; whereas, according to the laws of this country, if the vessel be re-captured from enemy subjects even after condemnation, she is deemed to be re-vested in the original owners, who accordingly become entitled to enter again into possession on paying salvage to the re-captors (*b*).

The circumstance that the sailing of a vessel took place before the outbreak of hostilities entails, as may be perceived on a consideration of the observations *sub* Embargo (*c*), no security against capture, unless this immunity be voluntarily

---

ment as to a Prussian vessel in the Firth of Forth: State Papers, 61 (1870-1), 1093. Also The Sitka, 1854. "Opinions of the Attorneys-General of the United States:" Tom. 7, p. 123. See also Twiss's Internat. Law (War), p. 454, for a reference to the views (in 1855) of the United States Government, which harmonize with those of H. M. Government.

(*y*) *The Ouachita*, *Blatch. Pr. Ca.* 306.

(*z*) The Industrie, 5 Rob. 88.

(*a*) Berens *v*. Rucker, 1 Black. 313; *vide sub* Adjudication and Condemnation, p. 316, *infra*.

(*b*) *Vide sub* The Right of Recapture, p. 126, *infra*.

(*c*) *Vide* p. 36, *supra*.

declared by the nation at war with the power by which such vessel is deemed to be owned. In the war with Russia, in 1854-5, privilege was, by an Order in Council, granted to enemy ships which had sailed for a British port prior to 29th March, 1854. A Russian vessel (*d*), which had left Antwerp for Havannah in November, 1853, proceeded from Havannah to Matanzas in February, 1854, left Matanzas for Cork on 2nd April, and was seized and carried into Cork as an enemy ship not protected by this Order. Restitution was decreed, the Court holding that the voyage must be deemed to have commenced with the sailing from Havannah in ballast in the month of February, and that the subsequent putting into Matanzas did not alter this fact.

No capture may be effected or attempted in neutral waters, though a capture so made cannot be called in question except by the sovereign whose neutrality has been invaded. It is one of the first duties of belligerents to respect neutral waters (*e*).

The right to capture enemy goods in neutral vessels calls for separate consideration in its place (*f*).

The subject of **Joint Capture** need scarcely be closely considered in these pages. The question may become on occasion highly interesting to rival claimants of captured property, but it is of little concern to the owner of property lawfully seized by others to know on what basis the spoil is to be divided between such captors. Great Britain having, by the Declaration of Paris, renounced the right to commission privateers, British shipowners have no longer the interest in the subject of joint capture which they possessed so long as it was open to them to send their vessels to sea under commission of war. Suffice it, therefore, to say, generally, that in

(*d*) The Argo, 24 L. T. 16.

(*e*) *Vide sub* Belligerent Obligations, p. 311, *infra*.

(*f*) *Vide* p. 88, *infra*.

the case of claim for joint capture the British Courts are mainly guided by the following principles:—If the claim to constructive capture be grounded on the fact that the claimant ship was in sight, it must be established that she was seen both by the captured vessel (whose yielding may be presumed to have been induced by the approach of the claimants) and by the immediate captors. In the absence of some antecedent agreement, a vessel in harbour cannot claim as joint captor merely on the ground that one of her boats was in sight of the parties to the engagement or pending engagement. If the claimant be a privateer, the mere being in sight is not sufficient; some overt act must also be shown in support of the claim: for a privateer is under no obligation to fight in all cases, so that the *animus capiendi* is not necessarily to be assumed in his favour. In ordinary cases revenue cutters cannot claim, their primary duty being to protect the revenue, and not to enter upon active hostilities. Warships forming part of a fleet associated in a common enterprise of capture may be entitled to share though not actually in sight, but the decision must in each case rest upon the particular facts (*g*). If two vessels engage in joint chase of an enemy ship, and one of them effects the capture out of sight of the other, the capture is, nevertheless, deemed to be joint. Decisions bearing upon these and other relative points will be found reported and discussed in Hazlitt and Roche's valuable "Manual of the Law of Maritime Warfare"; and numerous cases before the Courts appear in Robinson's "Admiralty Reports." Sect. 35 of the Naval Prize Act, 1864, provides that allies of Her Majesty shall be entitled to share in joint captures on such basis as may be from time to time agreed upon between Her Majesty and such ally. And by sect. 36 it is provided that claimants for

(*g*) *Vide The Anglia*, *Blatch. Pr. Ca.* 566.

joint capture shall give security for a due proportion of any costs or damages which may be awarded against the actual captors on account of improper capture or detention (*h*).

It is lawful by maritime law to chase under false colours, but to fire under false colours is illegal (*i*). By the French "Ordonnance de 17 Mars, 1696," it is strictly provided that French vessels firing under false colours shall lose all right to the prize captured if the vessel be declared an enemy, and shall be condemned in costs, damages, and interest if she be adjudged neutral (*k*).

If, without the sanction of the neutral power, a belligerent vessel be fitted out or her force be augmented in neutral territory, any captures made by such vessel during the succeeding cruise are illegal, and in the event of the prizes being brought within the neutral jurisdiction proceedings may be instituted for restitution (*l*). No such sanction should, however, be granted by neutrals, but if on any occasion conceded, it should be granted to both belligerents impartially (*m*). Prizes may be taken into neutral ports, but it rests with neutral powers to impose such limitations to this right as they may deem consonant with their obligations as neutrals.

A prize lying in a neutral port in possession of the captors is not properly the subject of valid condemnation in a Prize Court in the captors' territory. This principle was strongly enunciated by Sir W. Scott in *The Henric and Maria* (*n*); but inasmuch as it had not always been acted upon in the British Courts, his lordship declared himself unable to enforce

(*h*) *Vide sub* The Right of Recapture, p. 130, *infra*, as to prize money payable to captors.

(*i*) The Peacock, 4 Rob. 185.

(*k*) Story on Prize Courts, p. 38.

(*l*) *The Santissima Trinidad*, 7 *Wheaton*, 283. *Vide* also p. 380, *infra*.

(*m*) *Vide* as to this, *sub* Neutral Rights and Obligations, generally, pp. 345, 363, &c., *infra*.

(*n*) 4 Rob. 43; 6 *ib.* 139, n. *Vide* also The Purissima Conception, 6 Rob. 45.

it to the detriment of alien captors who asserted the contrary right (*o*).

If the master of a neutral ship resists an attempt to board her on the part of a belligerent, he exposes his vessel to confiscation (*p*). But if the vessel assailed be enemy property condemnation will naturally succeed capture; so that, in this respect, the master has, so far as his property is concerned, little to lose and everything to gain by resistance. An enemy subject (master or seaman), even if there be a fair prospect of rescuing the vessel, is ordinarily under no obligation to offer resistance, unless required to do so by the terms of the contract of service under which he has been engaged. An old statute (*q*), after setting forth the loss and discredit to which the country has been subjected by shipmasters yielding up their cargoes to pirates, sea-rovers, and Turks, lays it down that no master of an English vessel of 200 tons or upwards, and mounted with sixteen or more guns, shall yield to any such foe without fighting, and that no smaller or less-armed vessel shall without fighting yield to any such vessel as aforesaid unless the latter shall have at least double the number of guns carried by the English vessel. Any shipmaster found guilty under this statute to suffer the pains and penalties therein provided, and any one of his crew refusing to fight when ordered to do so, or uttering words to discourage the other mariners from defending their ship, to suffer imprisonment. This law was called forth by the tactics of the Turks and others, who induced shipmasters not to fight, by promising to release the ship and the master's property on condition that the rest of the property was yielded up. The provision exists as a gratifying testimony

(*o*) For observations in this connexion, and relative to the question of Compensation and Costs, *vide sub* pp. 316, 325, *infra*.

(*p*) *Vide sub* Resistance to Search, p. 212, *infra*. Also p. 216, *infra*.

(*q*) 22 & 23 Car. II. c. 11, s. 7.

to the estimation in which the fighting powers of the English seaman were in old times held by the legislature; but seeing that merchant vessels now go for the most part unarmed, while "pirates, sea-rovers, and Turks" are no longer an occasion of dread, the enactment must now be considered obsolete.

If the crew of a vessel seized for examination attempt to rescue her from the prize crew put in charge, the attempt, if ultimately defeated, involves confiscation (*r*).

Captures after Cessation of Hostilities.—The effect of a truce or treaty of peace is that, in the absence of express provision otherwise, hostilities between the contracting parties terminate on the signing of the treaty. It may, however, very easily happen that, owing to ignorance on the part of the captors that peace has been concluded, a capture or re-capture may be effected after cessation of hostilities. Thus the American ship *Mentor* (*s*) was, in 1783, destroyed by British warships after the cessation of hostilities, but before either of the parties had become aware of the fact. Unfortunately, owing to the manner in which the injured party prosecuted his claim for compensation, little more is to be learned from the decision in this case than that the proper person to be sued in respect of a wrongful capture is the actual captor. The claimants appear to have proceeded, in the first instance, against the captor; but the Admiralty Court, for reasons which do not appear, refused redress. No appeal seems to have been made by the claimants against this decision; but ten years later they instituted proceedings against the admiral under whose general orders the captor was acting at the time of the capture. Sir W. Scott decided (*t*) that no action lay against the admiral; that the

(*r*) *Vide*, as to this, Attempt at Rescue, p. 216, *infra*.

(*s*) Kent's Int. Law, 2nd ed. 388.

(*t*) 1 Rob. 179.

proper person to proceed against was the actual wrongdoer; and as at the trial already mentioned it had been held that the captor was not liable, the sufferer thus obtained no compensation. The learned judge intimated that if through ignorance an act of mischief had been done by the king's officers, the ignorance would not necessarily protect them from civil responsibility, though if in such case held liable the government should indemnify them. He was, therefore, inclined to think that the determination of the judge in the former case did not turn upon the fact of ignorance only, but upon all the circumstances of the case.

Queen's officers who act wrongfully are personally responsible to the party aggrieved, but so long as their action has been within the general scope of their authority they may reasonably look to their government for indemnification (*t*).

A few years later arose the case of *The Swineherd* (*u*), seized whilst on a voyage from Calcutta to England by the French privateer *Bellona*. By the Treaty of Amiens it had been *inter alia* provided that hostilities between Great Britain and France should cease in the Indian Seas five months after a date fixed by the treaty. *The Swineherd* sailed after news of the peace had reached Calcutta, but before the period of five months had elapsed. The master of *The Bellona* had been made aware, though unofficially, that peace had been concluded, but, notwithstanding, he seized *The Swineherd*, which vessel was finally condemned in the French Courts. The grounds of this decision were that the master of *The Bellona* was not bound to accept notice of cessation of hostilities unless such notice were attested by the French authorities; and, further, that until the aforesaid period of five months had elapsed hostilities remained in force in the Indian Seas.

Again, in 1814 (*x*), a question arose in a British Vice-

(*t*) *Vide* The Ostsee, p. 328, *infra*.

(*u*) Kent's Int. Law, 2nd ed. p. 389, n.

(*x*) *Ibid.* 390. *Vide* also The Sophia, 6 Rob. 138.

Admiralty Court on the validity of a recapture, by a British warship, of a British vessel which had been previously seized by an American privateer. The original capture was in itself valid, but the prize had not been carried into port and condemned, and the recapture was effected after the cessation of hostilities, but whilst the parties were still in ignorance of the fact. It was held that the British vessel could not, after the peace, lawfully use force to divest the original captor of a possession which was lawful. The restoration of peace put an end, from the time limited, to all force, and the general principle then applied that things acquired in war remain, as to title and possession, precisely as they stood when the peace took place. "Peace gives a final and perfect title to captures without condemnation, and, as it forbids all force, it destroys all hopes of recovery as much as if the vessel was carried *infra præsidia* and condemned."

Neutral Goods on Enemy Ships: the question of Freight.—If an enemy ship be captured with neutral cargo on board, the captors are entitled, if they so elect, to carry the cargo to its intended destination, and to earn the freight there payable. But captors cannot claim freight unless they carry the property to its port of destination, or at any rate to the country in which the latter is situated (*y*). There have, however, been cases in which freight has been allowed to captors where the goods, instead of being taken to destination, have been carried to the claimants in their own country (*z*). In *The Weldsborgaren* (*a*), the vessel, bound from Philadelphia to Lisbon, had been brought into a British port under an embargo on Swedish vessels, and it became necessary to discharge the cargo, which was forwarded in another vessel. On the release of the vessel a claim was made against the cargo for freight, but the Court rejected this application, observing that the cargo had itself been a sufferer on account of the ship.

But when the goods have been sold short of their destination, even though the sale be to the advantage of the owners, the captors cannot lay claim to freight (*b*). And where freight is allowed to the captors, if they have done any damage to the cargo, the amount may be deducted by way of set-off or compensation (*c*).

No exception, as regards captured cargo, is made by the Court to the rule respecting payment of *pro-ratâ* freight. Thus, delivery by a neutral carrier to the captor, at a port selected by the latter, is deemed a delivery under the original contract, and the full freight due at destination must be paid by the captor. On the other hand, as appears above, a captor, in order to earn freight from a neutral consignee, must carry the cargo to its destination, and he has no right to part-payment for delivery at a port

---

(*y*) The Diana, 5 Rob. 67; The Vrow Henrietta, *ib.* 75. But cf. The Wilhelmina Eleonora, 3 Rob. 234.

(*z*) The Fortuna, 4 Rob. 278; The Diana, *supra;* The Vrow Anna Catharina, 6 Rob. 269.

(*a*) 4 Rob. 17. *Vide* also The Isabella Jacobina, 4 Rob. 77.

(*b*) The Vrow Anna Catharina, *supra.*

(*c*) The Fortuna, *supra.*

short of such destination. (The converse view,—Belligerent Obligations: payment of Freight to Neutral Carriers (p. 339, *infra*) is of some interest in connexion with the foregoing remarks.)

Insurance,—*Capture generally.*

The common form of the English policy of marine insurance expressly protects the assured against the risk of capture. "Touching the adventures and perils which we, the assurers, are contented to bear, and do take upon us in this voyage, they are,"—says the Lloyd's policy—"of the seas, men of war, fire, enemies, pirates, rovers, thieves, jettisons, letters of mart and counter-mart, surprisals, takings at sea, restraints and detainments of all kings, princes, and people, of what nation, condition or quality soever" (*d*). In cases where the underwriters intend to exclude hostile risks, they do so by inserting a special clause commonly known as the "F. C. & S." or "free of capture" clause (*e*). The risk of hostile capture is thus covered in the body of all the marine policy forms in common use in England; and if the underwriter in any case decides to exclude the risk, he does so, as just stated, by inserting a clause expressly to override the words including it. A large proportion of British tonnage is, however, insured in the so-called Mutual Insurance Clubs or associations of shipowners. Whether war risks are covered by the conditions of the insurance in such clubs must in each case be ascertained by reference to the club terms.

It is now settled law in this country that as between the underwriters and the assured, the vessel insured, if captured, is *primâ facie* to be deemed a loss within the policy, notwithstanding that she be never condemned or even taken into port (*f*). It is the fact of the capture which constitutes the loss; and the circumstance that the vessel may possibly be subsequently released or recaptured, and that by the law of Great

(*d*) The following clause is sometimes inserted in policies on vessels chartered by the government for employment in connexion with hostilities: "To include war risks except those taken by H. M. Government." Owen's Mar. Insce. Notes and Clauses, 2nd ed. p. 100.

(*e*) *Vide* as to this clause, *sub* War Warranties, p. 386, *infra*.

(*f*) Goss *v.* Withers, 2 Burr. 694; and p. 73, *infra*.

Britain the property is deemed to remain vested in the owners until the vessel has been condemned by a Court of prize, does not affect the position. It can never be positively affirmed that a captured vessel remaining afloat can by no possibility come again into the owners' possession, and ships may be justifiably captured, though the captors fail to obtain condemnation by the tribunals of prize. And whether the capture be legal or illegal (*g*), or effected under a mistake (*h*), the underwriters are equally liable. Capture is *primâ facie* a case of constructive total loss (*i*), and gives the right to abandon to the underwriters on receipt of the announcement of the capture. If the underwriters accept the tender, the question of liability becomes thereby definitely fixed. If on the other hand the abandonment be declined, it remains for the assured either to bring their action forthwith, or to abide the issue of events and claim ultimately as for an average loss. As a general principle, if a loss be in fact total, there is nothing to abandon, and the assured can claim for payment of the sum insured without previous abandonment. In the case of constructive total loss, however, the position is different, and notice of abandonment is a necessary preliminary to the right to recover as for a total loss. If, before action brought, news be received of the safety of the ship, by release, rescue, recapture, or otherwise; or if the assured so proceed as to indicate their intention to claim as for an average loss and to waive the right to claim as for a total loss; then the claim will be not for total loss, but for the actual damages and costs caused by the capture. As in other cases giving rise to tender of abandonment, the assured must make up their mind as to the course to be taken so soon as the facts communicated to them enable them to come to a decision. They must not stand by from day to day before deciding to abandon, as by so doing they may be deemed to have elected to claim as

(*g*) Goss *v.* Withers, 2 Burr. 683, 694-5, and p. 73, *infra*.

(*h*) Lozano *v.* Janson, 2 E. & E. 100; 28 L. J. (Q. B.) 337.

(*i*) Of course, if, in the case of cargo, only a portion of it be on board on capture of the vessel, and only such portion be captured, the loss will not be total; and in this case, if the insurance be free of particular average, a question may arise as to the liability of underwriters. As to this, see McArthur's Contract of Insce., 1st ed. 254-5.

for an average loss. The reason for this is that, if immediate notice of abandonment be given to underwriters, they are thus put in a position to take prompt steps to protect their interests, whereas by the indecision of the assured the opportunity to take such protective measures at the outset may have been lost to them. But though the assured may thus lose their right to abandon, the right will revive if circumstances should subsequently occur to renew the option of decision.

In *Stringer* v. *English Mar. Insce. Co.* (*k*), the assured, instead of abandoning on news of the capture, as they might have done, intervened in the suit for condemnation, with the result that judgment was given in their favour. Against this decision, however, an appeal was lodged by the captors, and pending the final judgment the goods insured were ordered by the Court to be sold, in default of bail or deposit in American currency up to their full value. The condition of the American currency was at that time very unsatisfactory, and the assured declined to provide the security. The underwriters similarly declining to interfere, proceedings were instituted against them for payment of a total loss under the policy. The Court decided for the plaintiffs. The latter had, it was true, tendered at the outset no notice of abandonment, but the subsequent material alteration in the circumstances revived, it was held, their right to abandon.

As has already been mentioned *sub* Embargo and Reprisals (*l*), abandonment of the ship carries with it the right to the freight in course of being earned by her. Shipowners, therefore, have to take care, when abandoning their ship to underwriters, to secure themselves for payment of total loss by underwriters on freight. For if underwriters on ship accept abandonment, and the ship be, for example, released before action brought against those on freight, the shipowner will be in the position of having alienated his freight in favour of the hull underwriters, without having any right to claim for a total loss under the policy on freight. Apparently it may, during hostilities, be on occasion a politic course for underwriters on ship to accept abandonment, as by so doing they may acquire the title to a considerable

(*k*) L. R. 4 Q. B. 676; 5 Q. B. 599.

(*l*) P. 36, *supra*.

amount of unearned freight,—the more so as the bare risk of capture or detention may have forced the rate of freight to a point much in excess of rates current in times of peace.

If after acceptance of abandonment, but before payment of loss, the ship be again in safety, underwriters have, notwithstanding, to consummate their acceptance by paying the sum insured under the policy (*m*). They are under no legal obligation to accept abandonment, but if they elect to do so they must needs abide by their decision. On abandonment being accepted, or on a total loss being paid, the assured's title to the property becomes transferred to the underwriters, with whom it rests until divested by condemnation. If the vessel be ultimately released, then the various underwriters concerned will have to decide as to the course to be adopted with the property. For this purpose, as has been already mentioned *sub* Embargo and Reprisals (*n*), it may be necessary for all concerned to vest the property in trustees to be by them sold and apportioned over the various interests involved.

The assured cannot abandon to underwriters on the ground that, though restitution may in fact have been decreed, they are meantime out of possession of the property (*o*).

If a neutral vessel be seized by a belligerent, and taken into port in order to be examined as to the nature or ownership of her cargo, such a seizure, although not intended as a capture, is a detainment for which underwriters are expressly liable under the policy. And as between underwriter and assured, a loss so arising is to be dealt with as if the seizure had been with a view to condemnation of the vessel in a prize court of the captors (*p*). Belligerents have a right to visit and search all neutral private vessels, and, in case of need, to carry them into port for further examination (*q*).

If in case of capture the claim under the policy be treated as

---

(*m*) Smith *v.* Robertson, 2 Dow's P. C. 474. *Vide* also Hudson *v.* Harrison, 3 Brod. & B. 153.

(*n*) *Vide* p. 46, *supra*.

(*o*) Arnould's Insce., 5th ed. p. 1016.

(*p*) Barker *v.* Blakes, 9 East, 283.

(*q*) *Vide* as to this, *sub* Belligerent Rights against Neutrals, "Visit and Search," p. 144.

in the nature of an average loss—as, for instance, if the vessel be released or escape before action brought against underwriters—expenses or costs resulting to the property insured, in consequence of the capture, are claimable under the policy (*r*). For example, the vessel may be recaptured, in which case salvage will be payable to the recaptors (*s*). Or special charges may be incurred by ship and cargo in the port of detention; or expenses may be incurred in contesting the captors' suit for condemnation, or in appealing against a judgment in their favour. Or, as in *Berens* v. *Rucker* (*t*), where a neutral assured pays to belligerent captors a sum of money as a compromise *bonâ fide* made in order to prevent condemnation in a prize Court,—whether as a fact the property be legally subject to condemnation or not.

If during the process of adjudication the cargo be exposed to material deterioration the Court may order it to be sold in default of bail being provided.

If, as has already been observed, the underwriters elect to accept abandonment, their liability under the policy becomes *ipso facto* fixed; and the assured are also precluded from going back on their tender. On acceptance of abandonment the whole interest becomes vested in the underwriters as from the time of the occurrence giving rise to it, and all consequent costs and charges are accordingly for their account. If, on the other hand, underwriters decline the tender, and the assured decide to proceed for payment of total loss, it will lie on the latter to prove the existence of the facts on which their claim is based. Mere rumour or report will not serve their purpose; and if it should turn out that the state of circumstances on which they relied in support of their claim had ceased to exist at the time of bringing the action, the fact that the report relied upon was true at the time they heard of it will not benefit them. In other words, although a (constructive) total loss may have occurred, if, nevertheless, it shall have ceased to exist before action brought, it cannot be enforced against underwriters. In such a case the real damnification under the contract of insurance is such loss or damages as may have been incurred in conse-

(*r*) *Vide* as to this, *sub* Costs and Damages, p. 336, *infra*.

(*s*) *Vide sub* Recapture, p. 126, *infra*.

(*t*) 1 W. Bl. 313. *Vide* also 2 Burr. 683.

quence of the capture, and for this only are the underwriters liable (*u*).

If underwriters decline to accept abandonment, and in place of doing so make a compromise with the assured, they cannot afterwards lay claim to any sum awarded to the assured in respect of the circumstances which led to the tender of abandonment. Thus, where a British vessel was condemned by the Brazilian Government for an alleged breach of blockade, and the underwriters came to a compromise with the assured, they were subsequently held to have no claim on a sum paid by the said government as compensation to the assured (*x*).

It does not necessarily follow that if there be a recapture there can be no claim for total loss. If, for example, the voyage be practically lost, or the property be so deteriorated in value, or the charges for salvage and for bringing the property to its destination be so heavy, that the assured may reasonably decline to resume possession, a total loss will be due under the policy. This was decided in *Goss* v. *Withers* (*y*). This was an insurance on the vessel *David and Rebecca* with fish from Newfoundland to Portugal, Spain, or England; and there was a second insurance on the fish. The vessel was captured by the French and manned by a prize crew. After eight days she was recaptured by a British privateer and brought into Milford Haven, when the assured tendered abandonment. It appeared that before the capture by the French the vessel had been rendered practically unseaworthy by violent weather, and that a part of her cargo had been jettisoned. And whilst she was at Milford Haven, after the offer of abandonment and before she could be refitted, the rest of the cargo was spoiled. And, besides all this, there was due to the recaptors as salvage, under the law then prevailing, fifty per cent. of the value salved. The real destination was, it would appear, Spain or Portugal. Lord Mansfield found that in these circumstances the voyage was as absolutely defeated as if the ship had been wrecked and a third or a fourth of the goods

(*u*) Patterson *v.* Ritchie, 4 M. & S. 393; Bainbridge *v.* Neilson, 10 East, 329; Parsons *v.* Scott, 2 Taunt. 363; Falkner *v.* Ritchie, 2 M. & S. 290. *Vide* also Arnould, 5th ed. 982-6.

(*x*) Brooks *v.* McDonnell, 1 Y. & C. 502. See also Tunno *v.* Edwards, 12 East, 488; and Blaawpot *v.* Da Costa, 1 Eden, 130.

(*y*) 2 Burr. 683.

saved. The cargo must from its nature have been sold where it was brought in, and as to the ship, the loss could not be estimated, and the salvage due in respect of it could not be better fixed than by a sale. In such a case there was no colour to say that the assured might not disentangle himself from unprofitable trouble and further expense, and leave the insurers to save what they could. Judgment accordingly. In this case Lord Mansfield laid considerable stress on the fact that the *voyage* was lost, and for a long period subsequently the same doctrine was recognised by the Courts. It has, however, since been definitely decided that the loss of the voyage has nothing to do with the loss of the ship (*z*).

The application of the principle laid down in *Goss* v. *Withers* will of course depend in every case upon the state of facts existing at the time of action brought, and the tendency at the present day will, it is apprehended, not be in favour of a wider application of the principle. In *Hamilton* v. *Mendes* (*a*) the ship *Selby*, bound from Virginia to London with tobacco in hogsheads, was captured by the French and taken towards France in charge of a prize crew. On the voyage she was recaptured and brought into Plymouth. The assured abandoned to the underwriters on the ship, who declined acceptance, and the ship was then brought to London under an order of the owners of the cargo and of the recaptors. The Court, dealing with plaintiffs' pleas, found (1) that the shipowners had never been divested of their property, the ship not having been condemned, though (2) it was true that after the capture there was a total loss under the policy, but only until the recapture; (3) that the voyage was not totally lost, ship and cargo being safe, and the obstruction being but temporary; the recaptors having no right to demand a sale; and (4) that, the thing insured being in safety, the assured had no right to abandon: their claim was for the damnification sustained at the time the action was brought, and not for a total loss. Judgment for defendants.

The case of *McIver* v. *Henderson* (*b*) was decided for the

---

(*z*) Parsons *v.* Scott, 2 Taunt. 363; Falkner *v.* Ritchie, 2 M. & S. 290. See also Arnould's Insce., 5th ed. p. 992, n.

(*a*) 2 Burr. 1209.

(*b*) 4 M. & S. 576.

assured somewhat on the lines of *Goss* v. *Withers*, *supra.* A ship bound from Liverpool to the African coast, after being captured and plundered by the French, was by them given up to the master of a Portuguese prize, who took her into Fayal and claimed her as a gift from the captors. The local Court decided against this claim, and the possessors appealed. Pending this appeal, the English owners, by allowing what remained of the cargo to be sold and the proceeds to be deposited, obtained the release of the ship, and brought her to Liverpool. On her arrival, the owners proceeded for a total loss on the ground that, owing to the small value of the vessel in her dismantled condition, together with the expenses of bringing her from Fayal and the liabilities overhanging at that place, they were exposed to the prospect of having to pay more than the ship was worth. The Court decided that the peculiar circumstances of the case justified the demand for payment as for a total loss, and gave judgment accordingly.

In *Brown* v. *Smith* (*c*) the facts were somewhat analogous, and the decision was also given for the assured. In this case the crew ran away with the ship, which was, however, subsequently brought by a British man-of-war into Barbados, where the authorities sold the cargo and stores to pay salvage, and left nothing but the hull and rigging.

The judgments in *Holdsworth* v. *Wise* (7 B. & Cr. 794); *Chapman* v. *Benson* (5 C. B. 330); *Thorneley* v. *Hebson* (2 B. & Ald. 513), referred to in Arnould's Insce., pp. 994—996, relate to cases of privation of property arising from causes other than capture, but in which the same principles apply between underwriters and assured. The cases of *Dean* v. *Hornby* (3 E. & B. 180) and *Lozano* v. *Janson* (2 E. & E. 100; 28 L. J. (Q. B.) 337; Arnould's Insce., 5th ed. 996, 997), also show decisions based on the principles already set forth. The decisions mentioned *sub* Embargo (pp. 36—48, *supra*) may also be referred to in this connexion.

If a vessel be sold in a prize court of the captors, purchased by the master, and brought back to the country of her owners, can the last named assert a claim for total loss under the policy? Judgments in the United States appear to go upon the lines that

(*c*) 1 Dow's P. C. 349.

the master in re-purchasing is acting as the owners' agent, and the decisions in this country seem to favour the same view.

In *McMasters* v. *Shoolbred* (*d*) a ship, having been condemned by a tribunal incompetent to adjudicate, was purchased by the master and conveyed home before action brought by the owners. The latter refused to adopt the purchase, and claimed for a total loss. Lord Kenyon held that the loss was to be treated as an average loss, especially as no notice of abandonment had been given. A similar decision was given in *Wilson* v. *Forster* (*e*), where the ship was illegally seized at her port of discharge, and condemned and sold. The master bought the vessel, repaired her under bottomry, and brought her home; but the owners, refusing to satisfy the bond and allowing the vessel to be sold, claimed for a total loss without notice of abandonment. Held, that the seizure and condemnation having been illegal, the owners had never been divested of the property, and that the claim was to be settled on the basis of an average loss.

But the master of a vessel captured by the national enemy, before entering upon any scheme of re-purchase, must well consider whether such an operation on his part may not involve him or his owners in the consequences attending a breach of the laws prohibiting ransom (*f*) or trading with the enemy (*g*).

In *Kulen Kemp* v. *Vigne* (*h*), a vessel was captured and subsequently released, but not until her cargo, which was of a perishable nature, had been sold. Instead of proceeding on her voyage she deviated to another port and was lost by perils of the seas. The assured claimed for a loss as by capture, but the Court decided against this averment, declaring that after the capture the policy might still have been complied with by the vessel's proceeding to her original destination.

If a loss be apparently due to the joint operation of capture and of perils of the sea, the circumstances must, in case of need, be analysed, and the loss ascribed to the cause to which it has rightly to be attributed, or applied to both causes in such pro-

(*d*) 1 Esp. 238.
(*e*) 6 Taunt. 25; 1 Marsh. Rep. 425.
(*f*) *Vide* p. 296, *infra*.
(*g*) *Ibid.* 258.
(*h*) 1 T. R. 304.

portion as the facts as ascertained may indicate. In *Green* v. *Elmslie* (*i*), a vessel insured "against total loss only" was driven ashore, sustaining no hurt, but being captured by the enemy. This was held to be a loss by capture and not by perils of the sea, Lord Kenyon remarking that if the vessel had been driven on any other coast but that of an enemy she would have been in perfect safety. And in *Hahn* v. *Cobbett* (*k*), where goods insured free of capture were placed in imminent risk of total loss owing to the vessel having been driven on a sandbank, and were saved from such loss only by being salved by the enemy, by whom they were confiscated, the Court held that the loss was due to perils of the sea. Again, in *Livie* v. *Janson* (*l*), where a ship warranted free from American condemnation was driven on the American shore, and there seized and condemned, it was held that the total loss by capture discharged the underwriters from any claim in respect of the antecedent stranding, any damage caused thereby not having prejudiced the assured. But the recent decision in *Ionides* v. *Universal Insurance Co.* (*m*) very plainly sets forth the law governing cases of loss arising jointly from capture and from perils of the seas. This was an insurance on some 6,000 bags of coffee shipped during the American Civil War from Rio de Janeiro to New York, and the policy was warranted "free from all consequences of hostilities." The Confederates having extinguished the Cape Hatteras Light, the vessel went ashore, and ultimately broke up. Before this latter event, however, about 120 bags of coffee were saved by local fishermen, and other 1,000 bags could have been also saved but for a dispute which occurred between the Confederate soldiers and the fishermen. The Court held that the 120 bags salved and confiscated were lost owing to the hostilities, and that the 1,000 bags which ought to have been salved must also be deemed to have been lost owing to the same cause. That as to the remainder, which could not have been salved, its loss had to be attributed to perils of the sea. Erle, C. J., illustrated his

(*i*) Peake, 212.
(*k*) 2 Bing. 205.
(*l*) 12 East, 648.
(*m*) 14 C. B. N. S. 259; 32 L. J. (C. P.) 170.

judgment in words to the following effect (*n*):—Suppose a ship-master, chased by a cruiser, to avoid capture runs ashore, or runs into a bay where there is neither harbour nor anchorage, and being unable to beat out is driven ashore, the loss or damage by such grounding is a consequence of hostilities, and within the exception: not so if, in the second case supposed, she does come out of the bay and pursue her voyage, but is afterwards lost in a storm which she would have escaped had she not been pursued and changed her course. Suppose, again, the ship is going to a port where there are two channels, in one of which a torpedo has been laid by the enemy. If the master, not knowing this, goes into the channel where the torpedo is, and is blown up, this is within the exception: not so if, knowing of the torpedo, he takes the other channel to avoid it, and by unskilful navigation runs aground there.

The "consequences" intended were, it was held, such as constantly follow the operation of the same cause; and it could not be maintained on behalf of the underwriters that a vessel could not pass the Cape in the ordinary course of a coasting voyage in the absence of the light.

In effect, as regards the 5,000 bags lost by perils of the seas, their loss was to be ascribed to the stranding on the reef as the proximate cause; the extinction of the light, the consequence of the hostilities, being the remote cause. For this loss could not be predicated as the constant effect of the light being out, and the going ashore could, therefore, not be regarded as such a "consequence of hostilities" as was contemplated under the clause in the policy. Judgment accordingly for the assured in respect of the (about) 5,000 bags lost by perils of the seas; for the underwriters in respect of the 1,120 bags lost by hostile capture.

If a ship be lost by being barratrously delivered into the hand of the enemy, the loss can be claimed for as being due either to capture or to barratry (*o*). But if, as in the case of *Stamma* v. *Brown* (*p*), a vessel be destroyed by the enemy owing to the captain having put into a port where he was exposed to this contingency, barratry cannot be alleged against him if in so doing he was acting with the privity of his owners.

(*n*) Lowndes's Law of Marine Insce., p. 113. But see the judgment at length.
(*o*) Arcangelo *v.* Thompson, 2 Camp. 620. But cf. Cory *v.* Burr, *infra*.
(*p*) 2 Str. 1173.

In *Powell* v. *Hyde* (1854) (*q*), a ship had been insured "warranted free from capture and seizure, and the consequences of any attempt thereof." Her crew, on a demonstration by a Russian battery, dropped anchor and fled from the vessel, which was thereupon fired upon and sunk. The Court held that this was a capture within the meaning of the warranty. The vessel was as much "seized" as if the Russians had sunk her by means of a boat's crew from the shore. They could have brought her to the shore, but they preferred to send her to the bottom. The warranty, said the Court, extends "to any capture or seizure whereby the ship is destroyed or lost or damnified . . . . any capture or seizure whereby the ship is lost to the assured."

In *Cory* v. *Burr* (*r*) a vessel similarly insured was seized by the Spanish authorities for smuggling, and for the consequent expenses the owners claimed under the policy, notwithstanding the warranty, on the plea of barratry. It was, however, decided that the warranty against capture extended to capture however caused, and that it therefore practically overrode the agreement to indemnify in respect of barratry so far as concerned barratry resulting in capture.

Though a seizure be only of a temporary nature, it must none the less be regarded as a seizure within the meaning of the warranty "free from capture and seizure." Thus, in *Johnston* v. *Hogg* (*s*), where a vessel aground in a river was boarded by natives and abandoned, leaving her in such a condition that she was not worth repairing, it was held that the underwriters were discharged by the words of the above warranty (*t*).

The marine policy expressly mentions "enemies," "takings at sea," and "arrests, restraints, and detainments" as risks covered by the underwriters; and other perils *ejusdem generis* are comprehensively referred to in the general agreement to bear "all other perils, losses, and misfortunes" happening to the subject-matter of the insurance. This agreement becomes operative when property issued is lost or damaged as the immediate consequence of hostilities provided against by the insurance. Thus, in *Cullen* v. *Butler* (*u*), it was decided that the

---

(*q*) 25 L. J. Q. B. 65. *Vide* also p. 54, *supra*.

(*r*) L. R. 9 Q. B. D. 463; 8 App. Cas. 404.

(*s*) 10 Q. B. D. 432.

(*t*) *Vide sub* Piracy, p. 438, *infra*.

(*u*) 5 M. & S. 461.

sinking of the British vessel *Industry* by another British vessel *The Midas*, the latter thinking that the other was an enemy and about to attack her, was claimable under the above general words. The plaintiffs had pleaded "perils of the seas" in their first count; and the general words in the second; but the Court, being strongly of opinion that the loss was recoverable under the second count, considered it less material to discuss the first. The inclination of the Court, however, seemed to be against the first plea. On this count it should be noticed that Lord Herschell, in a recent case (*x*), observed that the opinion of the Court in *Cullen* v. *Butler* that the loss was not a loss by perils of the sea stood, he believed, alone, and had not been sanctioned by subsequent cases. In his opinion, every loss by incursion of the sea, due to a vessel coming accidentally (using this word in its popular sense) into contact with a foreign body which penetrates it and causes a leak, is a loss by perils of the sea.

Again, in *Butler* v. *Wildman* (*y*), the loss of a bag of dollars thrown overboard at the moment of capture by an enemy was held to be recoverable under the head of jettison. If, said Abbott, C. J., the loss was not by jettison in its technical sense, it was something *ejusdem generis*, and therefore within the general words "all other losses and misfortunes." The jettison was of an extraordinary species, but was not in principle distinguishable from the case where the master sets fire to his ship in order to prevent her falling into the hands of the enemy, for which, according to Emerigon and Pothier, the underwriters are liable. Bayley, J., expressed the opinion that the facts would have supported the claim whether set forth as a loss by jettison, by enemies, or by the "other losses and misfortunes" mentioned in the policy.

In *Hagedorn* v. *Whitmore* (*z*), damage caused to cargo by the vessel shipping seas when in tow of a British man-of-war which had wrongfully arrested her, was held to come within the meaning of the "perils of the seas" specially mentioned in the policy; though, as Arnould points out (*a*), such a loss may also be attributed to seizure.

(*x*) Wilson *v.* Owners of Cargo *per* Xantho, 12 App. Cas. 503.

(*y*) 2 B. & Ald. 398.

(*z*) 1 Stark. 157.

(*a*) Arnould's Insce., 5th ed. 1131.

If a shipmaster finds his port of destination blocked, he can presumably, as was suggested by Lord Ellenborough in *Blanckenhagen* v. *London Assurance Corporation* (*b*), make the nearest practicable port, there to remain until his destination is again open, the underwriters' risk continuing. But if through *fear of capture* he definitely abandons the voyage, such abandonment of the adventure terminates the underwriters' liability, "fear of capture" not being a risk contemplated under the policy (*c*).

In 1815, many of the Baltic ports being under French influence, and the risk of confiscation of British shipping on arrival at such ports being consequently considerable, underwriters frequently provided against this contingency by some such special clause as the following:—"Free of capture and seizure in the ship's port of discharge;" "Free from confiscation by the government in the ship's port or ports of discharge;" "Free from capture in the ship's port of destination" (*d*). If to avoid such capture or confiscation the ship should put to sea and proceed to a port out of the course of the voyage insured, the underwriters will not, for the reason stated below, be liable for a subsequent loss. Without such a clause they are liable. Thus in *O'Reilly* v. *Gonne* (*e*), where freight was insured *inter alia* against capture in the port of loading, and the ship put to sea in order to avoid capture when only half loaded and not prepared to sail, and subsequently put into a port out of the course of her voyage in order to repair damage consequent on her hasty and unprepared departure, it was held that the deviation was justifiable, and therefore that the underwriters were liable for the loss. But in an insurance by the same vessel, warranted free from capture and seizure and the consequences thereof in the port of loading, the underwriters were held not to be liable (*f*). The latter case is but briefly reported, but the Court appears to have found that the cause of leaving La Guayra—the loading port—was to avoid capture; and that, as the underwriters were not liable for the risk of capture, they were not to be held responsible for a loss consequent on her

(*b*) 1 Camp. 453.

(*c*) *Vide sub* Embargo, p. 39, *supra*.

(*d*) *Vide* cases in Park's Marine Insce.

(*e*) 4 Camp. 249.

(*f*) O'Reilly *v.* Royal Exch. Assce. Co., 4 Camp. 246.

leaving, unfitted for sea, in order to avoid that risk. In the United States several cases have been decided on this principle, the main point of inquiry being apparently in each case whether the danger was so real and immediate as to justify the deviation (*g*).

The state of political affairs just mentioned rendering it not unfrequently a matter of uncertainty at which port the vessel would finally discharge, it became in several cases a question under the policy whether a port in which the vessel insured was seized was the "port of discharge" intended by the parties. Such a consideration has necessarily in each case to be settled in accordance with the facts as ascertained. If the circumstances point to the conclusion that but for the capture the voyage would have been terminated at the port of capture, that port must be deemed to have been intended as the port of discharge (*h*). And a vessel may for the purposes of the warranty be deemed to be at her port of discharge though she be in fact in an open roadstead where ships usually unload (*i*), or lie on and off in a river forming the estuary of a port, waiting for intelligence (*k*). But she must be there with intent to discharge there,—a question of fact to be answered by the jury (*l*). If the vessel be captured when at anchor outside the roadstead where ships usually discharge, she is deemed not to be in port of discharge (*m*). If the warranty be against capture in "port of discharge," then the underwriters may in some cases be exempt, though the vessel be captured in an open roadstead; but a warranty against capture "in port" receives a more literal interpretation, so that a capture in the roads or in an estuary will not under such a warranty discharge the underwriters (*n*).

A warranty against "confiscation of the government in the port

(*g*) Arnould's Insce., 5th ed. p. 501.

(*h*) Levin *v.* Newnham, 4 Taunt. 722.

(*i*) Dalgleish *v.* Brooke, 15 East, 295. See Arnould's Insce., 5th ed. pp. 806-8, generally on this subject.

(*k*) Jarman *v.* Coape, 13 East, 394; *S. C.* 2 Camp. 613.

(*l*) Reyner *v.* Pearson, 4 Taunt. 662.

(*m*) Mellish *v.* Staniforth, 3 Taunt. 499; Levy *v.* Vaughan, 4 Taunt. 387; Keyser *v.* Scott, *ibid.* 660.

(*n*) Jarman *v.* Coape, *supra*; Brown *v.* Tierney, 1 Taunt. 517; Baring *v.* Vaux, 2 Camp. 541.

of discharge" received in *Levi* v. *Allnutt* (*o*) an interpretation based strictly on the words of the clause. The ship was seized in a Prussian port simultaneously by a French privateer and by Prussian soldiers, the Prussians being at that time in a state of subjection to France. The Prussian Government referred the conflicting claims for possession to a French tribunal, who awarded in favour of the privateer. On this award, it was held in the British Court that the confiscation was not on the part of the "government in the port of discharge," and the underwriters were consequently held liable.

As indicated above (*p*), a mere detention of the vessel by embargo or arrest does not work a dissolution of the contract of affreightment; nor is this necessarily otherwise in cases where the vessel is actually captured or subjected to hostile seizure (*q*). If, on the capture and taking into port, the services of the master and crew be given with the object of procuring the release of the ship and cargo, their wages and provisions, and all other relative expenses, must be deemed a general average charge (*r*). If such charges be incurred solely on behalf of the ship or of the cargo, they will presumably be in the nature of a special charge to be borne by the interest in behalf of which they were incurred.

Ransom from the enemy being now, by statute, illegal, moneys paid with this object are not recoverable. The statute does not apply to moneys paid *bonâ fide* as a voluntary composition to pirates, money so paid being recoverable in general average (*s*). Insurance against British capture is also illegal (*t*).

If a merchant vessel carry defensive weapons as part of her equipment, and sustain damage in resisting hostile attack, such damages are not recoverable in general average, as they are presumably within the shipowner's liability under his contract of affreightment. Expenses attending the curing of wounds

---

(*o*) 15 East, 267.

(*p*) *Sub* Embargo, p. 40, *supra*.

(*q*) *Vide* Effect of War on Contract, p. 412, *infra*.

(*r*) The Hiram, 3 Rob. 180; Liddard *v.* Lopes, 10 East, 526. And *vide sub* Adjudication, p. 337, *infra*.

(*s*) Hicks *v.* Palington, 4 T. R. 783.

(*t*) *Vide sub* Void Insurances, p. 405, *infra*.

sustained by the crew in fighting are similarly not recoverable (*u*). Any expenses falling within the shipowner's contract to carry, however otherwise exceptional, must, as has been abundantly established by the Courts, be borne by the shipowner. In the above case (*Taylor* v. *Curtis*) the ship carried guns as part of her outfit; but if the contract had not been made under such a warranty, the damages in question, having been voluntarily incurred for the general benefit in a moment of emergency, would, it may be presumed, have been a charge in general average.

If a vessel crowd on all sail in order to escape from an enemy and so sustain damage, the damage is not recoverable in general average, inasmuch as it immediately results from an ordinary sea risk (*x*). But if, for the same reason, a master cut or slip his cable, whereby it and the anchor are lost, the loss must be made good in general average (*y*).

Loss caused by Torpedoes.—The liability of underwriters for loss caused by these modern engines of destruction depends upon too many circumstances to be briefly and comprehensively summarized. The first question which suggests itself is, under which, if any, of the heads enumerated in the marine policy, would such a loss be recoverable? If a vessel be blown up by a torpedo (from without) the loss could apparently be ascribed to "explosion"; and in *West India Telegraph Co.* v. *Home and Colonial Insurance Co.* (*z*), it was decided that damage caused by the explosion of ship's boiler (from within) was *ejusdem generis* with damage caused by "fire," a risk specially mentioned in the policy.

In *Wilson* v. *Xantho* (*a*), where the House of Lords was called upon to decide whether a collision ascribed to negligence was a

(*u*) Taylor *v.* Curtis, 2 Marsh. 309.
(*x*) Covington *v.* Roberts, 2 N. R. 378.
(*y*) Arnould, 5th ed. p. 831.
(*z*) 6 L. R. Q. B. D. 51.
(*a*) 12 App. Ca. 513.

"peril of the seas" within the meaning of the bill of lading, Lord Bramwell delivered himself thus: "Was it a peril of the sea that the defendants' ship foundered? The facts are, that the sea-water flowed into her through a hole, and flowed in such quantities that she sank. It seems to me that the bare statement shows she went to the bottom through a peril of the sea. If the hole had been small, there being a piece of bad wood, a plank starting, or a similar cause, it would be called a leak, and no one would doubt that she foundered from a peril of the sea. Does it make any difference that the hole was large, and occasioned by collision? I cannot think it does. It is admitted that if the question had arisen on an insurance against loss by perils of the sea, this would have been within the policy a loss by perils of the sea." And Lord Herschell, commenting in the same case on the decision in *Cullen* v. *Butler* already referred to (*b*), expressed his opinion that every loss by incursion of the sea, due to a vessel coming accidentally (using the word in its popular sense) into contact with a foreign body which penetrates it and causes a leak, is a loss by perils of the sea. And Lord Halsbury, in *Hamilton* v. *Pandorf* (*c*), similarly held that damage caused to cargo by water admitted into a ship through a hole gnawed in a pipe by rats, is a peril of the seas. "I cannot," said he, "think that it was less such a peril or accident (*i. e.*, of the seas) because the hole through which the sea came was made by vermin from within the vessel, and not by a sword fish from without: the sea-water did get in." Lord Macnaghten described the damage as being due to "an accidental or unforeseen incursion of the sea that could not have been guarded against by the exercise of reasonable care," and therefore to be regarded as within the exceptions of the bill of lading. If, therefore, a vessel be blown up by a torpedo, the loss, it would seem, may be claimed either as caused by perils *ejusdem generis* with fire, or as directly attributable to the operation of perils of the sea. And if a ship be sunk by the impact of a "fish" torpedo starting her plates, without explosion—not an impossible event during practice with torpedoes, at any time—such a loss would apparently be similarly recoverable. Whether the loss of a

(*b*) *Vide* p. 79, *supra*.

(*c*) 12 App. Ca. 518.

vessel sunk by shot from a shore battery should be regarded as a loss by perils of the sea, or not—and in face of the above decisions there can scarcely be a doubt that it would be so regarded (b)—that a loss caused by a blow from an unloaded "fish" torpedo would be a loss due to perils of the seas, seems evident. And even if not a loss actually by perils of the sea, certainly it would be *ejusdem generis* with such a loss: for there is not a great difference between a loss caused by the impact of an uncharged torpedo and a loss caused by the blow of a sword fish or a whale. Both are *primâ facie* "due to an accidental or unforeseen incursion of the sea that cannot reasonably be guarded against."

If a vessel warranted free merely from "capture, seizure, and detention" be sunk by a torpedo, the warranty would not ordinarily exclude the loss (b). But if the presence of the torpedo be attributable to hostilities, and the words "and all consequences of hostilities" be added to the warranty, then, no doubt, the loss would be so excluded (c). But if the contact with the torpedo be brought about by the barratrous act of the master, then—unless, indeed, barred by the decision in *Cory* v. *Burr* (d)—the loss might be claimed under the head of barratry.

If an enemy's ship be sunk by a torpedo, the loss of the enemy property would not be recoverable, all insurances on enemy property being void (e). And if a British vessel be sunk whilst trading with the enemy without a licence, recovery of the loss would similarly be barred by the illegality of the insurance (f).

If a vessel, warranted neutral, be blown up in consequence of an act entered upon in breach of the neutral warranty, the loss (unless attributable to barratry) would be barred by the breach of warranty (g). If a vessel be blown up whilst attempting to run a blockade, the loss, unless the underwriters knew that

(b) Cf. *Powell* v. *Hyde*, p. 79, *supra*.

(c) *Vide* remark of Erle, C. J., in *Ionides* v. *Universal Insurance Co.*, p. 77, *supra*.

(d) *Vide* p. 79, *supra*.

(e) *Vide* p. 262, *infra*. *Vide* also p. 357, relative to neutral goods on enemy vessels.

(f) *Vide* p. 258, *infra*.

(g) *Vide* p. 386, *infra*.

breach of blockade was intended, would also be barred, the concealment of this material fact (*h*) rendering the insurance void.

If a British ship be blown up by the enemy, the loss will be recoverable, provided it be not excluded by the clause freeing the underwriters from all consequences of hostilities, or by some act by which the policy is rendered void.

If a British or neutral vessel be blown up by other than an enemy nation—either accidentally or of deliberate design: as, for instance, in execution of a design to block a channel—the loss will be recoverable, even though caused by the government of the country of which the owner of the vessel is a subject (*i*). But in such a case the owner would presumably have a claim against the authorities.

The foregoing are some of the chief points which suggest themselves for consideration in this connexion. But inasmuch as losses caused by torpedoes have not yet been adjudicated in our Courts, the above remarks are necessarily submitted with diffidence.

Having thus considered the subject of belligerent capture of enemy shipping, we may proceed to review the right of seizure of enemy goods shipped on neutral vessels, a right recognised by the law of nations, though nowadays, owing to the Declaration of Paris, fallen considerably into abeyance.

(*h*) *Vide* p. 398, *infra*.

(*i*) *Vide* pp. 252, 256, *infra*, and Cullen *v*. Butler, *supra*, p. 79.

CAPTURE OF ENEMY GOODS IN NEUTRAL VESSELS.

Neutrals have an indisputable right to trade with belligerent nations in lawful merchandise, and an equally clear right to carry goods the property of belligerents (*k*). This latter right exists, however, subject to the co-existent right—which has at times been disputed—of a belligerent power to seize all property of the enemy found out of neutral jurisdiction, and therefore to seize and confiscate such property if found on board a neutral vessel on the high seas or within the jurisdiction of the country of the captors. This belligerent right carries with it the antecedent right to stop and examine neutral merchant vessels in order to ascertain the nature and ownership of their cargo (*l*).

That a belligerent is by the common law of nations entitled to seize his enemy's property when being lawfully carried by a neutral has been on several occasions vigorously controverted by particular nations to whose interests the claim was detrimental. Notably in 1780 Russia asserted her intention to dispute the claim of Great Britain to exercise the right, if necessary, by force of arms; and Sweden, Denmark, Prussia, Germany, Holland, France, Spain, Portugal, and Naples, with the United States, gave their adhesion to the principle contended for by Russia. The contention of this Armed Neutrality, however, Great Britain steadily repudiated, with the result that the so-called Baltic Code was in 1793 finally abandoned as being contrary to the law of nations, and to be adopted only when

(*k*) *Vide* as to this, *sub* Rights and Obligations of Neutrals, pp. 345 *et seq.*, *infra*.

(*l*) *Vide sub* Visit and Search, p. 144, *infra*.

its principles are incorporated in international treaties. But notwithstanding this conclusion, the Baltic powers early in 1801, led by Russia, sought to revive and insist upon the adoption of the principles contended for in 1780. The new confederacy was, however, promptly defeated by the naval supremacy of this country; so that in June of the same year Russia abandoned the contention, and by express convention with Great Britain agreed that enemy property is not by the law of nations protected by the neutral flag. It may be observed that the argument on which the contention of the Baltic powers was based was that a belligerent has admittedly no right to seize property of the enemy when in neutral territory, and that a neutral vessel must for this purpose be deemed part of the territory to which she belongs. But this proposition clearly cannot be maintained in its entirety, for when a vessel comes into an alien port she comes under the alien jurisdiction; and, further, the same argument would equally deprive belligerents of the right to seize contraband goods found under the neutral flag, a right than which none is more clearly recognised by the common law of nations. In 1543, indeed, France went to the length of publicly expressing her determination to confiscate neutral vessels found to be laden with goods belonging to the enemies of France.

Such being the position according to the law of nations, it remains to be considered how this right is regarded by modern international law. The principle of "free ship, free goods" has frequently been adopted by international treaty; so far back as 1667, for example, it was expressly agreed to by a convention between England and Spain. In 1795, the United States adopted it in a treaty of commerce with the latter power, and in 1825 the principle was also embodied in similar treaties with Columbia and Bolivia. The American Government simultaneously declared that the rule of public law that the property of an enemy is liable to capture in the vessel of a friend has no foundation in natural right, and that the usage to the contrary rested entirely on force. This general view was, however, at the same time stated to be subject to the limitation that a belligerent nation admitting the milder principle might justly refuse to extend its benefit to neutrals to whom it was denied by the enemy of such belligerent. In 1854, on the outbreak of war between Great Britain and Russia, it was publicly announced by the British Government that Great Britain waived the right of seizing enemy property on a neutral vessel unless it were contraband of war. This principle was subsequently adopted by the signatories to the Treaty of Paris (*m*); and the United States, Mexico, and Spain, though declining to sign the treaty, have nevertheless expressed their intention to be bound by it, except so far as it deals with the subject of privateering. It may presumably, therefore, be now considered that the right to capture enemy goods in neutral vessels has given way to the modern usage summed up in the common phrase "free ships, free goods"; but should the Declaration of Paris be at any future time disavowed by any of the signatories, the old right will to such extent be again revived. That is, unless expressly relinquished by special treaty independent of the Declaration.

Although by the law of nations a belligerent is entitled to seize the goods of the enemy whilst being carried by a neutral vessel, there is attached to this right the obligation to pay to the neutral carrier the freight due to the latter on his delivering the goods at their destination. This is the general rule, but there are exceptions to it; as, for example, if the goods be contraband of war or the conduct of the carrier be fraudulent. This subject will be dealt with separately under the head Belligerent Obligations: Payment of Freight to Neutral Carriers (*n*). We will now pass on to the consideration of the right to grant letters of marque to privateers.

(*m*) *Vide* p. 27, *supra*.

(*n*) *Vide* p. 339, *infra*.

PRIVATEERING AND LETTERS OF MARQUE AND REPRISAL.

Privateers, as distinguished from national public vessels (*o*), are armed vessels fitted out by private persons and sailed by a commander to whom a belligerent power has granted a commission to seize the ships and goods of the enemy. There is properly a clear distinction between a privateer and a vessel sailing under a letter of marque; but nowadays the general term privateer is used indiscriminately to comprehend vessels of both these classes. Thus, for example, in the British Declaration, published on the outbreak of war with Russia in 1854, it was announced that her Majesty had not the present intention "to issue letters of marque for the commissioning of privateers." Privateers are essentially vessels intended to undertake hostile operations; but letters of marque—or, to give them their full title, letters of marque and reprisal—may by the law of nations be granted to the commander of a private vessel in time of peace, empowering the bearer to make reprisals against the ships and goods of the subjects of a power which has refused to make reparation for an injury done by its subjects as individuals. Thus, in 1599, Spain having captured a British vessel carrying tobacco to the Dutch, then at war with Spain, on the ground that tobacco was "victuals," the English owner, in order that he might make good his loss, obtained from the king of England letters of reprisal against the subjects of the king of Spain (*p*).

(*o*) "Public vessels." *Vide infra* (p. 205) for consideration of definition.
(*p*) *Vide* p. 176, *infra*.

The right to grant reprisals in such cases was accepted as in accord with the law of nations, and was not inconsistent with peaceful relations between the powers. When redress was refused, but not till then, it was the privilege of the person aggrieved to obtain compensation by his own hand—provided, that is, that his sovereign considered him entitled to so proceed, and licensed him accordingly. In the sixteenth century it was not infrequently stipulated in treaties of commerce that reprisals should be granted only against the principal delinquents and their goods, and then only in the event of manifest delay or denial of justice. And at a later time a definite period was fixed—three, four, or six months, as the case might be—in which justice should be sought before reprisals might be granted. Letters of marque and reprisal may no doubt now be looked upon as features of an extinct barbarism, but they were in their inception a distinct advance on the road to civilization; for at one time there was no restriction on the right of private warfare and sea-roving—a condition of affairs which was eventually amended by the salutary provision that no vessel should engage in acts of war or reprisal without being furnished with a letter of marque on the part of the sovereign to whom her owner was subject. As to the precise original meaning of the term "letter of marque," there seems to be some uncertainty. Of French origin, it has by some writers been identified with the German "mark," or Latin "marcha," in the sense of a boundary; and "letter of marque" has accordingly been interpreted to mean a letter of licence to cross the frontier and attach hostile goods beyond it. Others consider it to mean a licence from an independent prince to "set a mark upon" or seize as a pledge the goods of others. The "right of marque" is found recognised in the twelfth century as a royal prerogative, granting to certain subjects rights against certain other subjects of the same sovereign against whom a complaint has been made—*i. e.*, to seize their persons or goods. From references given by Professor Skeats, the words marque and reprisals appear to have borne in old statutes much the same meaning as the old French "marquer," apparently meaning "to pillage"—literally, "to catch within one's borders." The form "letter of mart" is a corruption, and need not therefore be discussed.

A privateer is to be regarded as essentially a ship of war; but a vessel sailing under a letter of marque may be, in many cases, simply an armed merchantman. The master of such a vessel may be ordered either to proceed to his destination without engaging in any hostilities which can be avoided; or to attack only such ships of the enemy as come in his path; or to cruise in search of prizes. It would seem that it was at one time no uncommon thing for an owner to procure a letter of marque for a vessel about to sail, solely as an inducement to seamen to ship by her, and not with any intention to take hostile action unless forced to do so. An owner petitioning for a letter of marque had to make a formal application (*q*), giving detailed particulars as to build, rig, voyage, crew, arms, &c.; and, before issue of the letter, security had to be given under a bail bond on the part of the owner and two sureties. The security was declared to be in respect of any damage or injury done to any British subjects or subjects of foreign states in amity with Great Britain, and to cover also customs dues in respect of ships and goods taken and adjudged as prize. And the letter, a lengthy document, provided, amongst other things, that the master should keep a journal of his proceedings, and take particular note as to the station, motion, and strength of the enemy, and transmit an account of same, with any other useful information extracted from prisoners or otherwise gained, to the Admiralty. Having

(*q*) See Story on Prize Courts for forms of Petition, Surety, &c.

regard to the serious difficulties which might be created by improper conduct on the part of privateers, maritime nations have commonly made it their business to place such vessels under all needful restrictions and to keep their proceedings under close supervision. By the British Prize Act, provision was made for the cancelling of the commission granted to a privateer master in the event of breach of instructions or of other misconduct.

The master as well as the owner of a privateer or vessel sailing under letter of marque is responsible for all costs or damages which may be awarded against either in a prize court, for unjustifiable capture or for other misconduct, the amount of such liability not being limited to the amount of the bond, nor, according to some writers, to the value of the privateer outfit; but these points would doubtless be the subject of express municipal provision. And a person may be held liable as part owner, though not registered as such. Every part owner is liable, not merely for his own proportion of any damages, but for the whole amount (*r*).

Seeing that all captures are made at the risk of the captors, in the event of a seizure being adjudged unlawful and without reasonable excuse, the owners of a privateer and their sureties may be called upon to pay damages and costs, and generally to pay compensation for any misconduct giving rise to reclamation in a tribunal of prize. As already indicated, this liability extends to the value of the property unlawfully injured or destroyed, and is not limited to the amount of the bond. As in the case of captures made by public vessels, all vessels taken as prize must be brought in for adjudication, a sentence of condemnation being necessary to transfer the property in the prize to the captors. Every privateer must have her commission of war on board, for if seized and found to be without this indispensable evidence of recognised right to

(*r*) The Khorasan, 5 Rob. 291.

engage in hostilities her crew are liable to be harshly dealt with, and in some cases—as, for instance, on seizure of a neutral vessel—to be treated as pirates; and a prize court might refuse to condemn neutral property so seized if the captor had on board no commission at the time of the capture. And the actual commission must be produced: no mere transcript, however attested, will serve in its stead. But if the document be lost or destroyed between the capture and the adjudication, the Court may accept oral evidence that it was on board at the time of capture (*s*). And as the commission is granted to the master personally, it is necessary that he shall be on board when the capture is effected; otherwise the prize, if condemned, will be adjudged a droit of Admiralty (*t*). To this an exception appears to have been in one instance made where, the commander being dead, the capture was effected by his lieutenant (*u*).

No commander of a privateer may accept concurrent commissions from two belligerents, even if they be co-belligerents, though he may hold two commissions from the same belligerent,—as, for instance, if the power to which he is subject gives him a commission to act against a single enemy and another power unite with the latter; in which case a further commission would be required by the privateer. It is obvious that if a privateer were to sail under commissions from two distinct powers, the common municipal regulation would be defeated which requires that all prizes shall be brought for adjudication into a port of the state under whose flag the captor sails (*x*). These further powers would not be required merely to enable the privateer to assail the foe, for by the law of nations (apart from conventions and municipal regulations)

(*s*) *The Estrella*, 6 *Wheaton*, 304.

(*t*) The Charlotte, 5 Rob. 280.

(*u*) Law of Nations by Twiss, 2nd ed. vol. 2, p. 393.

(*x*) Twiss's Law of Nations, p. 390.

it is apparently lawful for the master of a private ship, though uncommissioned, to attack a vessel belonging to subjects of his country's enemy, without such conduct being deemed piratical. This right, however, would not extend to enable him to board or assail a neutral ship carrying contraband or otherwise acting unlawfully; and the engagement in any such enterprise would expose the uncommissioned assailant to be dealt with as a pirate. Moreover, in the case of capture from the enemy, the uncommissioned British captor would find himself deprived of the fruits of his action by a municipal law declaring all such captures to be droits of Admiralty, though as a matter of modern practice the Crown has in cases of meritorious capture, on their petition, commonly ceded such prizes to the captors.

By the British Naval Instructions of 1826 it was declared that any vessel taken whilst acting as a ship of war or privateer without being duly commissioned in that behalf should be regarded as a pirate, and her crew should be treated accordingly. But such acts are by the law of nations not acts of piracy, however otherwise irregular and dangerous, and no declaration on the part of any one country can alter this position (*x*). As between contracting powers such a regulation may be good enough; but as Twiss observes, "No power can make an offence to be piracy within the purview of the law of nations by declaring it to be so" (*y*).

By international convention it is commonly expressly provided that, in the event of hostilities arising, neither party to the treaty shall engage aliens to serve against the other; and the municipal laws of the various nations will doubtless in most cases be found to impose obligations on their subjects to prevent them enlisting under an alien flag (*z*). But by the

(*x*) The subject of Piracy is referred to below, p. 433.

(*y*) Law of Nations, 2nd ed. vol. 2, p. 418.

(*z*) *Vide sub* Neutral Rights and Obligations, Political, p. 363, *infra*.

common law of nations there is nothing to prevent a belligerent from raising levies in neutral territory, nor from granting letters of marque or commissions of war to alien subjects. Two nations may agree as between themselves that if any subjects of either shall be found by the other acting under a commission of war granted against the latter by a third nation, such subjects may be condemned as pirates in the Courts of the captors; but the operation of this compact must, it is apprehended, be confined strictly to the contracting parties. Thus, if two states, A and B, mutually agree on the basis, for example, that A may treat as pirates the subjects of B commissioned against A by a third power, C; and C shall in fact grant a commission to a subject of B, who is seized by A; A will be entitled to proceed against such subject of B as a pirate within the convention, but C may on the other hand claim in protection of B's subject, holding the commission, that the claimant C had by the law of nations an indisputable right to grant the commission; that this being so, any private arrangement entered into between A and B is beside the question; and that the subject of B is by the law of nations to be dealt with not under any such private arrangement, but as a lawful combatant. That such a complication might, as Twiss suggests, arise, is certainly within the bounds of possibility; but having regard to the general and growing disposition of non-combatant powers to prevent by severe municipal regulations any such acceptance of commissions from belligerents, the contingency is probably now remote. Under the head Neutral Rights and Obligations (a) the subject of such municipal regulations will receive more detailed consideration, and the right of privateers to enter neutral ports will be at the same time reviewed.

Privateers sailing under British commission are required

(a) *Vide* p. 363, *infra*.

to "wear a red Jack, with the Union Jack described in the canton at the upper corner thereof near the staff," in addition to the colours usually borne by merchant ships (*a*). In *The Minerva* (*b*) a warrant of arrest was, on a declaration by officers of a public vessel, granted against a privateer master for sailing under false colours. Amongst other nations there would appear to be no settled practice as to the flag to be carried by privateers. Public war ships possess over privateers the same right of visitation as over non-commissioned private vessels, for it is only by visiting the vessel and examining her papers that her occupation can be ascertained to be lawful (*c*).

Although by the Declaration of Paris privateering "is and remains abolished," it must be remembered that this convention is operative only as between the nations parties to it, and that certain nations—the United States, Spain, and Mexico—have hitherto held aloof. In the event of hostilities between one of the latter powers and a signatory to the declaration, the one would have the right to commission privateers, while the other would at first sight seem to have no such right. But privateering being permissible by the common law of nations, no treaties between individual states can extinguish the existing right of recusant powers to commission privateers; and, this being so, it stands to reason that the signatories, whilst agreeing upon the course to be adopted as between themselves, have not intended to sign away, and have not signed away their several rights to commission privateers by way of retortion against a belligerent not a party to the compact who asserts his right under the law of nations. So that France and Prussia, for example, being

(*a*) In a note in the "Times" of 25th May, 1889, it is stated that a Bill introduced by the First Lord of the Admiralty declares (*inter alia*) that the red ensign usually worn by merchant ships, without any modification whatever, shall be the proper national colours for all ships in her Majesty's mercantile navy.

(*b*) 3 Rob. 34.

(*c*) *Vide sub* Visit and Search, p. 144, *infra*.

signatories to the treaty, neither could, in the event of war, commission privateers against the other. But Spain is not a signatory, and if she were to engage in hostilities and commission privateers against say France or Prussia, no doubt these powers could lawfully retaliate by issuing similar commissions. For privateering being, by the law of nations, a recognised weapon for the use of belligerents, the various signatories to the declaration would have no right to combine against Spain in order to compel her to abandon such a weapon. "Mr. Lawrence, in his last edition of Wheaton's Elements, has very justly remarked," says Travers Twiss (*d*), "that this declaration is only binding upon the parties to it, and does not constitute privateering an offence against the law of nations. The declaration, he says, is only a pledge, on the part of the states adhering to it, not to issue commissions for that purpose, and does not of itself create any new offence against the law of nations; while the admission of the congress, made at the suggestion of the Russian plenipotentiary, that it would not be obligatory on the signers of the declaration to maintain the principle of the abolition of privateering against those which did not accede to it, received a practical construction in the course adopted by England and France, and other countries, in their declarations with respect to the pending contest in America" (*e*). But as Twiss proceeds, very justly, to point out, while in such a case a non-signatory would be entitled to instruct his privateers to visit and search, and, on reason found, to capture neutral vessels, the instructions given by a signatory to privateers commissioned by him would not extend to authorize the molestation of neutral vessels, the property of other signatories to the declaration (*f*). So that, while the belligerent non-signatory

(*d*) Law of Nations, 2nd ed. vol. 2, p. 423.

(*e*) *Vide* p. 33, *supra*.

(*f*) *I. e.*, that the mere carriage of belligerent goods would not, of itself, justify the capture of such vessels.

would, without breach of any obligation towards neutrals, be able to seize enemy property carried by neutral signatories, the belligerent signatory would be restrained by his compact with such neutrals.

Whether those nations who have hitherto stood out from the treaty will ultimately, like others who delayed to sign, give in their adhesion to it; or whether warlike or other exigencies may cause the retirement of any of the present signatories, the future will show. And in this connexion it may be apposite to remember that a similar treaty between Prussia and the United States, in 1785, was not renewed on expiring, and that Sweden failed to observe a parallel compact made with the States General in 1679. For damages sustained by the commerce of the States General in consequence of this breach of treaty, however, Sweden at the conclusion of the war was held liable to pay compensation.

One result of the Franco-Prussian War of 1870 has been to show that a new sort of armed fleet may be made use of, the vessels of which may approach more nearly to privateers or to national warships, according as the laws and regulations for their supervision and control are carefully or loosely framed. Thus, in July 1870, a Prussian decree was issued, approving the formation of a, so-called, Voluntary Naval Force, on certain prescribed conditions, and providing, *inter alia*, for the indemnification of the owners of ships destroyed in the service of the country, and fixing the reward payable to such vessels for the capture or destruction of ships of the enemy (*f*). To this decree the French Government objected as being a breach of the Declaration of Paris against privateering. Earl Granville, however, expressed his opinion that substantial distinctions existed between the proposed naval force and the system of privateering intended in the Declaration of Paris; and that the vessels in question were,

---

(*f*) State Papers, 61 (1870-1), 692.

apparently, to all intents and purposes, in the service of the Prussian Government, and under the ordinary description of the navy of that State. These vessels were, it would appear, intended to be used against war ships, and not against merchant vessels; for the Prussian Government had on the outbreak of hostilities declared their intention of not seizing merchant ships of the enemy, except such as would be subject to capture if they were neutral vessels (*g*). But the declaration announced in 1870 was annulled by an ordinance in 1871, France having declined to abandon her right of capture of German merchant vessels.

Insurance.

As regards marine insurance in connexion with this subject, if it be intended that a vessel shall carry letters of marque, this intention should be set forth in the policy under some such wording as the following:—"With leave to cruise," "With leave to carry letters of marque," &c., such permissions being strictly construed by the Courts (*h*). The liberty to carry letters of marque is not a permission to cruise, and a deviation with this object will vitiate the policy (*i*).

In *Lawrence* v. *Sydebotham* (*h*), where the ship was insured to trade, "with or without letters of marque, with leave to chase, capture, and man prizes," it was held that this liberty could not be extended beyond the strict intention, and did not, therefore, entitle the assured to shorten sail and lie-to, in order to convoy the prize into port. But, as Arnould (5th ed. 493) observes, the mere act of convoying under such a liberty is not *per se* a deviation unless it involves delay or departure from the direct course of the voyage, and this has been so held in the United States (*k*).

(*g*) State Papers, 60 (1869-70), 923.
(*h*) Lawrence *v.* Sydebotham, 6 East, 45, 51; Syers *v.* Bridge, Dougl. 527.
(*i*) Parr *v.* Anderson, 6 East, 202, 205.
(*k*) *Ward* v. *Wood*, 13 *Mass. R.* 539; 1 Phillips' Insce., No. 1030

And in *Jarratt* v. *Ward* (*l*) it was held that a permission "to cruise for, chase, capture, man, and see into port any enemy's ships" did not authorize the assured to remain in port whilst the prize was being repaired there. Again, in *Hibbert* v. *Halliday* (*m*) it was decided that a permission "to chase, capture, and man prizes, &c." did not cover a lying-to for nine days for the purpose of effecting a capture, but that this was a "cruising;" and that a permission to cruise on this side of Cape Horn could not be construed to cover a cruising on the other side of that cape. From which case it appears that any substantial variation of the risk insured will operate as a deviation, and void the insurance whenever such deviation can be shown to have arisen from culpable intention or negligence.

It was at one time decided that if a trading vessel carried letters of marque without the knowledge or consent of the underwriters, the circumstance voided the policy on the ground that such letters offered a temptation to deviate. But Lord Ellenborough, in *Jarratt* v. *Walker* (*n*), observed that a "mere irritation of this sort shall not operate as a deviation," a dictum in harmony with the judgment of Lawrence, J., in *Raine* v. *Bell* (*o*). How far the sailing under letters of marque with the knowledge and consent of underwriters, but without express liberty in the policy so to do, will justify deviation, seems to have been, according to Arnould (*p*), the subject of doubt; and he indicates that departure from the usual course should not be regarded as a deviation if fairly attributable to motives of self-defence; but that to diverge in the hope of meeting with prizes is a deviation (*q*); and that if a ship of the enemy comes in the way it is no deviation to depart from the direct course whilst engaging her, or even, apparently, to continue the pursuit after she has been lost sight of. *Jolly* v. *Walker* (*r*) seems to establish that a vessel having letters of marque, but no express liberty to carry

(*l*) 1 Camp. 264.
(*m*) 2 Taunt. 428.
(*n*) 1 Camp. 263, 266.
(*o*) 9 East, 195, 201.
(*p*) 5th ed. p. 489.
(*q*) Cock *v.* Townson, 8th ed. Park's Insce. 630.
(*r*) Jolly *v.* Walker, 8th ed. Park's Insce. 630.

them, may give chase to an enemy ship without committing a deviation; but Lord Ellenborough, in the subsequent case of *Parr* v. *Anderson* (*s*), was disposed to think that such a deviation is permissible only if in self-defence—as, for instance, for the purpose of showing the enemy a bold front—but is not permissible if purely with the object of effecting a capture. For a summary of the United States law in this connexion, *vide* Arnould (5th ed. p. 491) on the case of *Haven* v. *Holland* (*t*), in which it was held that it was no deviation for a merchant ship, carrying letters of marque without express authority to do so, to man a prize justifiably captured by her.

(*s*) 6 East, 202.
(*t*) 2 *Mason's Rep.* 230.

BLOCKADE.

Blockade of the enemy's ports is a warlike expedient of much antiquity, carrying with it in ancient times the right to put to death persons found guilty of its contravention. In the thirteenth century and for some time subsequently we find European belligerent nations prohibiting on the outbreak of war all shipments of victuals or merchandise to the enemy's territory generally,—the disregard of any such proclamation involving seizure and confiscation of ships and cargoes implicated. Towards the end of the seventeenth century this arbitrary exercise of belligerent rights, in deference to the more moderate views then prevailing, underwent material modification, and the right to confiscate goods shipped to the enemy was confined in its application to the case of shipments to ports publicly declared to be blockaded. The general right to seize victuals was, indeed, preserved, but subject to the obligation on the part of the captor to compensate the neutral owner (*u*).

The right of blockade, so far as it operates against neutrals, should properly be also considered under the general head "Belligerent Rights against Neutrals"; but seeing that the prime object of the right is to cripple and harass the enemy, whilst the recourse against neutrals is secondary and pendant, and only to be enforced when defied by them; and that the two rights are so bound up, the one with the other, that it is undesirable to treat them separately; it has been thought

(*u*) The subject of Pre-emption is specially considered below, p. 244.

better to discuss the right of blockade at large under the general head "Belligerent Rights against the Enemy."

The immediate motive of blockade is to force the enemy to surrender by cutting off the supplies on which he relies. A belligerent is plainly entitled to resort to such a measure, and it follows that he is entitled to confiscate the property of persons setting this right at defiance. Merely to order off approaching vessels would be idle, and the only means of effectually deterring neutral traders from attempting thus to succour the enemy is to attach to such attempts the risk of confiscation of both ship and cargo. It is true that the circumstance that nations A and B choose to engage in conflict between themselves is not to be allowed to deprive nation C of its right to carry on its lawful trade in the accustomed manner, and in this sense, therefore, it is not unlawful for a neutral to carry goods to a blockaded port (*x*). But this right to trade on the part of neutrals is subject to the countervailing right of belligerents to prohibit interference with the course of hostilities; so that if neutrals elect to attempt such interference they must do so at their own risk.

With respect to the ports which may be blockaded, if the belligerent power is able to effectively close every port of the enemy he is entitled to do so. Thus, in 1854 the Allies established a blockade of all the Russian ports in the Baltic and in the Gulfs of Finland and Bothnia. But a blockade, in order to be so considered, must be effective: no mere proclamation of blockade, or "paper blockade," as it has been termed, will suffice. This, although specially formulated by the Declaration of Paris, is no new principle. "A blockade," said Bynkershoek, in his ancient treatise, "is virtually relaxed if the coast be slothfully watched." "To

(*x*) The Helen, L. R. 1 A. & E. 1.

constitute a violation of blockade," said Sir W. Scott, in *The Betsey* (z), "three things must be proved—1st. The existence of an actual blockade; 2nd. The knowledge of the party supposed to have offended; and 3rd. Some act of violation either by going in or coming out with a cargo laden after the commencement of blockade." The learned judge rightly placed first the proof of the existence of the actual blockade; for a shipmaster can scarcely be charged with violating a blockade of the existence of which there is no proof.

The law of nations being as above, it is obvious that the 4th clause of the Declaration of Paris, that "blockades, in order to be binding, must be effective," is a declaration of no new thing; any more than is the 3rd clause, that neutral permissive goods are free from capture under the enemy's flag. It may, indeed, be observed, by the way, that it is not evident why these clauses should have been incorporated at all, any more than clauses embodying other principles of the law of nations not in dispute: unless the framers of the declaration were fearful that the novel clauses 1 and 2, if allowed to stand by themselves would be more likely to evoke excessive criticism. Clause 4 is as follows: "Blockades to be binding must be effective, that is to say, maintained by a force sufficient in reality to prevent access to the coast of the enemy." By "effective" or "effectual" it is not to be understood that the blockaded port must be so closely invested that it is absolutely impossible for a vessel to obtain ingress or egress; but merely that any attempt to enter or leave the port will necessarily be attended by the imminent danger of capture (*a*). Whether in any given case the blockade fulfils this condition must be determined on the evidence. A blockade is rendered effectual, in the words of Sir William

(z) 1 Rob. 92.

(*a*) Geipel *v*. Smith, L. R. 7 Q. B. 410.

Scott, "by stationing a number of ships and forming, as it were, an arch of circumvallation round the mouth of the prohibited port. Then, if the arch fails in any one part, the blockade fails altogether" (*b*).

If several ports be included in the declaration of blockade when only one of such ports is in fact blockaded, the whole declaration is nullified, and a neutral cannot be condemned for an attempt to break the blockade of that port which really is invested (*c*). During the civil war in America the Federal States declared a blockade of the whole Confederate coast line, and vessels captured for endeavouring to enter or leave Confederate ports were condemned, though their officers swore that they saw no blockading vessels (*d*). If an exception be made in favour of one nation the blockade is invalid; for partiality voids the declaration. This was decided in the Russian war of 1854, when it was held in *The Franciska* (*e*), a Danish vessel captured by a British cruiser, that inasmuch as the Allies had authorized the Russians to export goods from certain Russian ports declared to be blockaded, the blockade could not be maintained against other nations. It is, however, within the right of belligerents to declare a limited or modified blockade, provided that, as in other cases, the blockade be applied impartially.

In the Turko-Russian war, the Porte having, by means of cruisers in the Bosphorus, captured certain vessels which had managed to elude the blockading squadron in the Black Sea, it was claimed on behalf of such vessels that, having escaped capture in the Black Sea, they thus became free from further seizure. The Turkish prize court, however, condemned the

---

(*b*) The Arthur, 1 Dods. 425; The Stert, 4 Rob. 66.

(*c*) The Henrick and Maria, 1 Rob. 146; The Mercurius, *ibid.* p. 83; The Betsey, *ibid.* p. 93.

(*d*) Wheat. Int. Law, 2 Eng. ed. 596.

(*e*) Northcote *v.* Douglas, 10 Moore, P. C. C. 37.

vessels—mostly Greek—so captured, a decision supported by the foreign ambassadors at the Porte. The ambassadors represented that to allow such vessels to go uncondemned, would be to relieve Greece from the rigours of the blockade, of which the effect would be to invalidate the whole blockade (*e*). But the blockading power has, it would seem, the right to permit or to deny admission of neutral war vessels to blockaded ports, and the fact that such vessels are admitted will not invalidate the blockade.

In 1884, during the hostilities between France and China, the former power declared a blockade of certain Formosan ports, but the British Government protested against this notification on the ground that the French fleet available was insufficient to render the blockade effectual in accordance with the requirement of the Declaration of Paris (*ee*).

When in the American civil war the Federal States declared all the Southern ports blockaded, the Supreme Court decided that this did not apply to the western side of the Rio Grande, which was in neutral (Mexican) territory (*f*).

Proof of discontinuance of a blockade by notification lies on the captured vessel pleading this defence (*g*).

A blockade otherwise effective is not to be deemed ineffective owing to what may be called accidental circumstances. "The only exception to the general rule which requires the actual presence of an adequate force to constitute a lawful blockade arises out of the circumstance of the occasional temporary absence of the blockading squadron, produced by accident, as in the case of a storm, which does not suspend

(*e*) Wheat. Int. Law, 2 Eng. ed. 597.

(*ee*) Cf. reference in *Times*, 13 July, 1889, to declaration of inefficiency of blockade of Haytian ports by the Haytian Government.

(*f*) Wheat. Int. Law, 2 Eng. ed. 595; The Peterhoff, p. 186, *infra*.

(*g*) *The Circassian*, 2 *Wall.* 150.

the legal operation of the blockade": so says Wheaton (*h*). Thus the temporary absence of the blockading squadron, owing to adverse weather (*i*), or to chase of suspicious vessels (*j*), provided the chase be not unduly prolonged (*k*), has been held not to justify an attempt to break the investment; but in such cases the blockading vessels must return to their station so soon as circumstances may permit. If, however, the squadron should be despatched elsewhere, leaving an insufficient force on the spot (*l*), this would be held to invalidate the blockade. If the blockade be once raised, through whatever cause, neutrals must be served with a fresh notice if the investment be resumed (*m*).

The occasional success of attempts to break the blockade is not necessarily evidence of ineffectiveness of the investment, for such successful attempts may be owing to temporary absence of some of the squadron, or to other circumstances specially favouring the blockade runner, and not arguing any inefficiency in the blockade as such. The onus of showing that, at the time of capture, a *de facto* blockade was actually existing, lies upon the captors (*n*).

A maritime blockade must be construed literally, and not in such a general sense as to involve confiscation of goods being carried to the blockaded port by means of canals or other internal conveyances (*o*). Nor can it be applied to ships carrying goods to neighbouring ports with a view to their being forwarded to the blockaded port by inland routes; or to goods similarly forwarded from the blockaded port to a

(*h*) Int. Law, 2 Eng. ed. 596.
(*i*) The Columbia, 1 Rob. 156. *Vide* also p. 118, *infra*.
(*j*) The Eagle, 1 Acton, 65.
(*k*) La Melanie, 2 Dod. 130.
(*l*) The Nancy, 1 Acton, 58.
(*m*) The Hoffnung, 6 Rob. 112; The Tisketeir, *ibid.* 65.
(*n*) *The Circassian*, 2 *Wall.* 150.
(*o*) The Stert, 4 Rob. 65; The Ocean, 3 Rob. 297.

neighbouring open port, thence to be carried over sea (*p*). But if a British subject ship goods to the enemy through a neutral country, confiscation will attach (*q*).

Goods cannot be sent along the coast in lighters so as to evade a blockade. Thus, where a ship left a blockaded port in ballast for a neighbouring river, and there took on board goods which had been previously sent to the same place by lighter, the goods were declared confiscated (*r*).

The rigorous application of a blockade is usually postponed for a greater or less time in favour of any neutral vessels which, at the time the declaration is made, may be within the port declared to be blockaded. On declaration of blockade, such neutral vessels are entitled to depart free from interference on the part of the blockading squadron, and with any cargo which they may have on board at the time. If this cargo be neutral property, it is entitled to pass freely; and, as has been submitted above (Enemy Cargo on Neutral Vessels) (*s*), if it be the property of the enemy, where the principle of "free ships, free goods" is accepted, it will similarly be allowed to pass. But no cargo must be taken on board after declaration of the blockade, unless already lying in lighters for the shipment. Cargo found to have been shipped subsequently will, with the vessel, be liable to confiscation (*t*); and when any portion of the cargo has been so shipped, the departure of the vessel will be regarded as a fraudulent act (*u*). Ships in ballast may leave at any time,

---

(*p*) The Ocean, 3 Rob. 297. But compare as to this the United States decisions in *The Stephen Hart*, *Springbok*, and *Peterhoff*, p. 185, *infra*.

(*q*) The Jonge Pieter, 4 Rob. p. 83. *Vide sub* Trading with the Enemy, p. 258, *infra*.

(*r*) Wheat. Int. Law, 2 Eng. ed. 606.

(*s*) P. 88, *supra*.

(*t*) The Rolla, 6 Rob. 367; The Vrow Judith, 1 Rob. 151; The Comet, Edwards, 33; The Frederick Molke, 1 Rob. 86.

(*u*) The Calypso, 2 Rob. 298.

but the maximum limit of time within which cargo may be carried out is subject to the discretion of the blockading power, to be announced in the public declaration of blockade. Fifteen days would seem to be the minimum time allowed in practice, and on the blockade of Buenos Ayres by France in 1838 forty-two days were allowed (*w*).

On the blockade of Archangel by the Allies, the port authorities appear to have exhibited to the masters of all neutral vessels in the port a copy of the declaration of the blockade; and each master was required to sign a certificate that the notice had been exhibited to him, and that he had read and understood it.

If a neutral vessel shall have been compelled by stress of weather or similar necessity to enter a blockaded port, she may leave without violating the blockade; and she may also leave free from risk of confiscation if she shall have entered under special licence of the blockading power (*x*); or if she shall have reloaded neutral goods sent into the port before blockade, and *bonâ fide* withdrawn by the owner as being unsaleable (*y*); or if she shall have on board goods purchased by a neutral subsequent to declaration of the blockade, if the ground for carrying the goods out of port is the *bonâ fide* and well-founded belief in the immediate outbreak of war between the nation owning the blockaded port and that of which the neutral purchaser is a subject, involving risk of confiscation of the goods (*z*); or she may leave in ballast, notwithstanding that she has entered during the blockade, if she arrived off the port in ignorance of the blockade, and was allowed to enter (*a*); or, similarly, if she knew of the blockade, and was allowed to enter (*b*); or if she shall have been informed by

(*w*) *Vide* also p. 53, *supra*. Only three days were allowed by France in 1884 to vessels in Formosan ports. 2 Lon. Gaz. 1884, p. 4571.

(*x*) The Charlotta, Edw. 252; The Byfield, *ibid.* 188.

(*y*) The Juffrow Maria Schrœder, 4 Rob. 89, *in not.*

(*z*) The Drie Frienden, 1 Dod. 269.

(*a*) The Christina Margaretta, 6 Rob. 63.

(*b*) The Juffrow Maria Schrœder, 3 Rob. 149; The Vrow Barbara, *ibid.* [158, *in not.*

one of the belligerent cruisers that the blockade was raised, and entered the port unmolested (*c*); or, apparently, if she leaves solely for the purpose of carrying home distressed neutral seamen thrown out of work by the hostilities and detained in the various ports of the belligerent country (*d*). But although such excuses may secure neutral vessels from condemnation, they will not necessarily avert capture. For breach of blockade is *primâ facie* good ground for seizure, and it may be that only on resort to adjudication will the true circumstances appear in which the breach occurred.

No vessel can be condemned in respect of breach of blockade unless it can be shown in fact or constructively that the master was aware of the existence of the blockade. This is a condition precedent to condemnation most clearly laid down. It follows, therefore, that public notification of blockade must be given by the belligerent declaring it before or immediately on its enforcement. Mere proclamation of blockade does not, as already observed, itself constitute blockade, the proclamation or notice being simply *primâ facie* evidence of the fact; and a blockade, however effective, is not regarded as in force as against neutrals until the fact of it has been brought to their knowledge. All that is necessary is to prove knowledge on the part of the individuals attempting the breach (*e*). In the case of uncivilized powers, whilst they are not to be held bound by all the rules of the law of nations, no indulgence is to be shown them in respect of any breach of the well-known law of blockade (*f*). Notification to a foreign government is constructive notice to the individual members of the nation, for it is the duty of such government to inform its subjects, and a neutral master can never be heard to aver in his defence

(*c*) The Neptunus, 2 Rob. 110.

(*d*) The Rose in Bloom, 1 Dod. 58. For comments on the above exceptions *vide* Twiss, Law of Nations, 2nd ed. pp. 217, 218.

(*e*) The Mercurius, 1 Rob. 82.

(*f*) The Hurtige Hane, 3 Rob. 324.

that his government failed to inform him. If the defence be true, it may give rise to a claim as between him and the government, but into this the captors will decline to enter (*g*); and a shipmaster cannot rely upon the circumstance that no notification has been given to the country from which he is about to sail, if the blockade be a matter of common notoriety.

There are, however, two kinds, or, rather, two views to be taken, of blockade: blockade in the one case by notice, and in the other *de facto*.

If a neutral vessel shall have sailed for a blockaded port, after notice of the blockade has been given to the country from which she sailed, she will, *primâ facie*, be liable to condemnation. If, however, she shall have departed before any such notification, then the blockade will be, so far as she is concerned, *de facto*, and she is then, unless otherwise informed of it, entitled to notification on the part of the blockading squadron. But a vessel approaching a blockaded port with intent to violate the blockade is not entitled to be warned off (*h*).

If a ship be seized whilst hovering off a port under blockade by notice, the plea that she was going to the blockading squadron to ask for authority to continue her voyage will not be accepted (*i*).

In *The Union* (*j*), where a Danish vessel had been seized by a British cruiser for attempting to run the blockade during the Anglo-Russian war, it was held that inasmuch as it was practicable to inquire at a neighbouring neutral port as to the maintenance of the blockade, there was no excuse for making

(*g*) The Spes and Irene, 5 Rob. 79.

(*h*) *The Hallie Jackson, Blatch. Pr. Ca.* 42.

(*i*) *The Admiral*, 3 *Wall.* 603; *The Josephine, ibid.* 83; *The Cheshire, ibid.* 231.

(*j*) 2 Ec. & Ad. Rep. (Spinks), 161.

inquiries of the blockading squadron. "When it is intended to prove ignorance of a blockade which was a matter of general notoriety," said Dr. Lushington, "it must be proved by the clearest and most satisfactory evidence to the judgment of the Court."

In *The Jeanne Marie* (*k*), where a cargo had been bought before war occurred, and the purchasers were moreover ignorant at the time the vessel sailed of the fact that the loading port was under blockade, the cargo was restored. It was true that the shippers, who were purchasers' agents, were aware of the facts when they shipped the cargo; but it was held by the Court that the cargo-owner is not necessarily bound by the act of his agent, when the latter has become a belligerent, and the cargo-owner has no control over him. But where, as in *The Nornen* (*l*), the cargo has been purchased in the blockaded port by an agent of the cargo-owners specially sent for that purpose, condemnation will follow.

There is this main difference between a blockade by notification and a blockade *de facto*;—in the former case the act of sailing for the invested port is *primâ facie* considered an attempted breach *ab initio*, whereas, in the latter, the mere sailing in ignorance is no offence, and a vessel may even, on a doubtful or provisional destination, sail for a port blockaded *de facto*, on the prospect of the blockade having been raised by the time of her arrival (*m*). But in this event she must, on approaching her destination, apply for information, not at the mouth of the blockaded port, but at some other port lying in the way,—if possible, a port of the blockading power (*n*). Otherwise, a neutral vessel, on being

(*k*) 2 Ec. & Ad. Rep. (Spinks), 165.

(*l*) *Ibid.* 169.

(*m*) The Neptunus, 2 Rob. 110; The Columbia, 1 Rob. 130. Cf. The Monarch, p. 125, *infra*.

(*n*) The Betsey, 1 Rob. 334; The Shepherdess, 5 Rob. 262; *The Delta, Blatch. Pr. Ca.* 133; *The Empress, ibid.* 175; *The Cheshire, ibid.* 643.

seen by one of the blockading squadron, would seek information of her; but in the temporary absence of belligerent cruisers she would be tempted to run direct into the blockaded port (*o*). This is the general rule, but if, in any case, a master has in departing from it acted *bonâ fide* and reasonably, an exception may be made to it (*p*). In *The Betsey* (*q*) (1799) the rule was relaxed in favour of a master who had sailed from an American port, on the ground that at such a distant port he could not have had constant notice of the state of the blockade. But this was before the days of telegraphs and rapid postal communication.

A master, when informed that his port of destination is blockaded, must forthwith turn away. "It must be clear and obvious that the neighbourhood of the blockaded port cannot be considered as the fit *locus deliberandi* of his future plans," whatever may be his difficulty in determining where he should go (*r*).

In *The Franciska* (*Northcote* v. *Douglas*) (*s*) it was declared not to be the law that the neutral is always entitled to warning from the blockading squadron before seizure, in case of a *de facto* blockade of which there has been no official notification. If he has obtained knowledge anyhow of such blockade, he is liable to seizure. And when the acts of the belligerent are generally known, such knowledge may be presumed without distinct proof of personal knowledge. But the facts with the knowledge of which the individual is to be fixed must be such as to admit of no reasonable doubt; and the notice which is to be inferred from general notoriety must be such that if given in the form of a public notification or of a particular warning it would have been legal and effectual.

(*o*) The Spes and Irene, 5 Rob. 76.
(*p*) The Empress, *supra*.
(*q*) *Supra*.
(*r*) The Apollo, 5 Rob. 289.
(*s*) 26 L. T. 113.

As, for instance, the notice of a blockade must not be more extensive than the blockade itself, otherwise a neutral may safely disregard it.

In the case of vessels coming out of a blockaded port, no notice is necessary after a blockade shall have existed *de facto* for any length of time, for it is obvious that knowledge of the blockade must in such case exist on the part of vessels within the port (*t*).

In the Franco-Prussian war, French naval officers were instructed that ships approaching a blockaded port were not to be deemed to intend a violation of the blockade until its notification had been inscribed on their register or ship's papers by an officer of one of the blockading vessels (*u*).

If a neutral vessel whose master has no knowledge of the blockade, arrives off a blockaded port, she must be warned off by the blockading squadron; but until such warning has been given, and has been disregarded, no grounds exist for condemnation. If the captors have reason to believe that the averment of ignorance is fraudulent, they are entitled to capture the vessel, and send her before a court of prize for adjudication (*v*). If a vessel be thus warned off by a blockading cruiser, the commander of the cruiser is required to write a notice of the blockade upon one or more of the principal ship's-papers (*x*).

When a vessel has been captured and brought into port, her master, and such of the ship's company as may be considered necessary, are subjected to a most minute and searching examination on all points material to the purposes of adjudication. As will be concluded on perusal of the Standing

---

(*t*) The Vrow Judith, 1 Rob. 153.

(*u*) Wheat. Int. Law, 2 Eng. ed. 597.

(*v*) *Vide sub* Adjudication and Condemnation, p. 316, *infra*.

(*x*) Instructions to the Navy, Art. X.; Story on Prize Courts, p. 257.

Interrogatories (*y*), the chances of a vessel escaping condemnation by suppression, or false statements, on the part of the master are exceedingly remote. It may, indeed, well happen that though the immediate grounds for the capture prove to be erroneous, other circumstances may, under the examination, appear by which condemnation may be justified; as, for example, if the capture be made under the erroneous belief that the ship carried contraband, or had falsified her papers, and it should come out that she had been guilty of violating a blockade.

To sail for a blockaded port with knowledge of the blockade, and with intent to violate it, warrants condemnation (*z*); and the intent, failing sufficient evidence to the contrary, of which the onus of proof lies on the captured vessel, will be deduced from the sailing with knowledge. So that, in such case, the act of sailing will be held to constitute an attempted breach. And on proof of the sailing with intent, condemnation will be involved, notwithstanding that, at the moment of capture, the vessel may, owing to stress of weather, be out of the course for the blockaded port. But if the master shall be able to show to the satisfaction of the Court that he had voluntarily abandoned the voyage to such port (*a*), and had altered his original intention to attempt a violation of the blockade, the vessel will no longer be subject to confiscation. A mere intention to commit the breach, unsupported by an overt act, such as starting for the blockaded port, will not, of itself, involve condemnation (*b*). But if false papers be used (*c*), or the papers be destroyed, or the

---

(*y*) 1 Spinks' Ec. & Ad. Rep., p. xiii, App.

(*z*) The Columbia, 1 Rob. 155, An. 1799; cf. The Monarch, p. 125, *infra*.

(*a*) The Imina, 3 Rob. 169, and p. 184, *infra; The John Gilpin, Blatchfd.* 291.

(*b*) *Fitzsimmons* v. *Newport Insce. Co.*, 4 *Cranch*, 199; *The John Gilpin, Blatchfd.* 291; *Yeaton* v. *Fry*, 9 *Cranch*, 446.

(*c*) *The Louisa Agnes, Blatchfd. Pr. Ca.* 112; The Mentor, Edw. 207.

voyage be altered in order to avoid search, such circumstances will be deemed evidence of fraudulent intention (*d*). There are, however, certain cases in which the intentional bearing up for a blockaded port may be excused, as, for instance, if the cause be stress of weather, want of water or provisions, or some other imperative necessity (*e*); but in all such cases the burden of proof of unavoidable necessity and of good faith will be upon the vessel seized (*f*). Similarly, if the excuse for violating the blockade be that the master required to ascertain the land, the excuse will be subjected to severe criticism (*g*).

In *The Neutralitet* (*h*), the vessel, bound ostensibly from Bordeaux to Embden, went to Ostend, which was blockaded, under the pretence of procuring a pilot. The master anchored the vessel in such a position that at daylight he would have been under protection of the shore batteries. The Court, observing that a neutral vessel has no right to anchor in a spot where she may have an opportunity of slipping into the blockaded port without molestation, ordered the confiscation of ship and cargo.

Intoxication of the master will not be accepted as an excuse, as in such case it becomes the duty of his officers to dispossess him and to give a proper direction to the ship (*i*). If the master of the captured vessel have been previously master of a vessel which has been condemned, the Court will notice the

---

(*d*) *The Circassian*, 2 *Wall.* 135; *The Bargorry*, *ibid.* 474; *The Andromeda*, *ibid.* 482; *The Cornelius*, 3 *Wall.* 214.

(*e*) The Fortuna, 6 Rob. 27; *The Diana*, 7 *Wall.* 369; *The Major Barbour*, *Blatchfd.* 167; *The Forest King*, *ibid.* 2; The Panaghia Rhomba, 12 Moo. P. C. 168.

(*f*) The Hurtige Hane, 2 Rob. 127; The Arthur, Edw. 263; The Charlotta, *ibid.* 232.

(*g*) The Adonis, 5 Rob. 256.

(*h*) 6 Rob. 30. See also The Charlotte Christina, *ibid.* 101, and The Gute Erwartung, *ibid.* 182.

(*i*) The Shepherdess, *ibid.* 262.

fact (*j*). If a port be once blockaded the prohibition against entry applies both to private vessels and, ordinarily, to neutral war-ships; and no private vessel, whether in ballast or laden, can, subject to the above exceptions, be allowed to attempt to enter without a special licence from the government of the blockading power. And any such licence will be strictly interpreted; so that a mere general licence to trade with the enemy will be held not to give admission to enter blockaded ports (*k*).

Breach or attempted breach of blockade is *primâ facie* ground for confiscation of both ship and cargo, the presumption being that the breach was intended to benefit both of these interests (*l*). The presumption of complicity may, however, be rebutted in favour of the cargo if the documents found on board at the time of capture should exonerate it. There may indeed be cases in which the presumption is in favour of the innocence of the cargo-owners: as, for instance, if the blockade shall have been declared after sailing of the vessel (*m*). In such event, in order to affect the cargo-owners with complicity, it would be necessary to prove that the act of the master personally bound them. In *The Panaghia Rhomba* (*n*) it was laid down that when at the time of shipment the blockade is or might be known to cargo-owners, their privity to the intended violation must be assumed as an irresistible inference of law, and is not capable of rebutment by evidence. In *The Juffrow Maria Schrœder* (*o*), the ship was released and the cargo condemned, on the exceptional ground that,

---

(*j*) *The Diana*, 7 *Wall.* 360; *The Wm. H. Northrop*, *Blatchfd.* 235.
(*k*) The Byfield, Edw. 188.
(*l*) The Alexander, 4 Rob. 93; The Shepherdess, 5 Rob. 262.
(*m*) The Mercurius, 1 Rob. 80; The Adonis, 5 Rob. 262.
(*n*) 12 Moo. P. C. C. 168.
(*o*) 3 Rob. 147.

whereas the vessel had a licence to enter the blockaded port with a cargo, and consequently to come out again, presumably also with a cargo, no such licence existed in favour of the cargo taken on board in the blockaded port.

If the master of a ship deviate into a blockaded port contrary to his duty to his owners, the latter are nevertheless not allowed to plead this as against condemnation. The decision in the case in which this principle was laid down (*p*) deals especially with the owners' plea of barratry of the master. But in such cases the master is regarded as the servant of the shipowners, who are responsible for his illegal acts, a reasoning which does not necessarily hold good in the case of the cargo. Unless, therefore, the master be agent for the cargo-owner (or his servant, if the ship and cargo be both under the same ownership), or the cargo-owner be held privy to the intended breach, the cargo will not be subjected to the fate of the ship if she be condemned (*q*).

In *The Crenshaw* (*r*), the vessel, leaving a blockaded port for England, was captured by the United States Government and condemned, the cargo sharing the fate of the ship, except a portion belonging to British consignees who could have had no knowledge of the blockade, and could not consequently be presumed to have instructed or authorized the master to sail in violation of it.

So long as a blockade continues, the penalty for its breach, either by ingress or egress, remains in force, and may be exacted until completion of the return voyage (*s*). The end of the voyage is the only natural termination of the offence;

(*p*) The Adonis, 5 Rob. 256.

(*q*) The Alexander; The Imina, *supra*. See also The Vrouw Judith, 1 Rob. 150; The Rosalie and Betty, 2 Rob. 343, 351; The Elsebe, 5 Rob. 173.

(*r*) *Blatch. Pr. Ca.*, 1861-5, p. 30.

(*s*) Welvaart van Pillau, 2 Rob. 128; The Christiansberg, 6 Rob. 376; The General Hamilton, *ibid.* 61.

consequently a successful evasion of the blockading squadron does not purge the offence. And this position will not be affected by the circumstance that a vessel which has evaded the blockade has subsequently put into an intermediate port or has been driven into such port by stress of weather. If, however, the blockade should have been raised before capture for the breach, the offence will be deemed to have been purged, and the vessel *ipso facto* will cease to remain *in delicto* (*t*). "The blockade being gone," said Sir W. Scott, in *The Lisette*, "the necessity of applying the penalty to prevent future transgression cannot continue." The case of *The General Hamilton*, *supra*, affords an exception to the rule that termination of voyage purges offence. This vessel, being blockaded in the port of Rotterdam, was enabled to sail in virtue of an indulgence allowing neutral vessels to sail out if bound to a neutral port. The vessel sailed apparently for the neutral port of Smyrna, but, putting into Alicante ostensibly for repairs, she sold her cargo there and took on board a cargo for Copenhagen. On returning towards Copenhagen she was captured by a British cruiser, and, with her cargo, condemned, Sir W. Scott observing that the permission to go to a neutral port implied a contract that that destination would be *bonâ fide* pursued, and that the evasion of this obligation was an act of perfidy.

Pacific Blockade, a measure short of actual hostilities, is occasionally resorted to as a means of reprisal or of extorting redress or concession. Thus in 1827 England, France, and Russia blockaded the coasts of Greece with the view of coercing Turkey, and similar measures were threatened but not executed against the same State in 1880. In 1884 the

---

(*t*) The Lisette, 6 Rob. 387.

French declared a blockade between certain fixed points of the island of Formosa. This blockade, however, the British Government declined to recognise as pacific, and further protested against it that it was invalid because not effectual as required by the Declaration of Paris.

The affair known as the *Don Pacifico* case supplies an exceptional instance of blockade short of actual hostilities. Don Pacifico was a Jew at that time resident in Athens, but a British subject born at Gibraltar. Owing to some question of religious observance, the mob attacked and plundered Pacifico's house at Athens, and this gentleman claimed compensation—a grotesquely exaggerated sum, as it turned out—through the British Government. The Greek Government being slow to afford redress, the British Government adopted the very extreme measure of blockading the Greek ports, so as to prevent the egress of the national public vessels, and went to the further length of capturing and detaining any such vessels found upon the sea. Eventually the matter was settled by arbitration. (On this case, and on the subject of Pacific Blockade generally, see Pitt Cobbett's Leading Cases, pp. 100—102.)

Again, in 1861, owing to the plundering of a British vessel wrecked on the Brazilian coast—for which compensation was demanded by the British Government and refused—the British Government blockaded the port of Rio de Janeiro, and captured five Brazilian vessels. Ultimately these were restored, compensation being paid by the Brazilian Government under protest; but some years elapsed before international relations were resumed between the two countries (*u*).

Still more recently, viz., in 1886, on the refusal of Greece, Bulgaria, and Servia, to disarm in response to a collective note of the powers, orders were given to the commanders of

(*u*) Wheat. Int. Law, 2 Eng. ed. 352.

the united squadrons "to establish a blockade of the coasts of Greece against all ships under the Greek flag." The notification of the blockade stated that "every ship under a Greek flag, which may attempt to violate the blockade, will render itself liable to be detained." The instructions given to the British commander, in view of the determination of the blockade, ran as follows:—"Whenever the blockade is raised, you will receive instructions to release the vessels which you have detained. . . . . Her Majesty's Government do not admit any liability whatever to compensation to the owners of such vessels on the ground of damage suffered during such detention" (*x*).

(For an instructive treatise on the subject of Pacific Blockade generally, reference may be made to the Law Magazine for February, 1889.)

Insurance.

The subject of blockade is, for purposes of marine insurance, in many respects identical with that of Embargo, and under this head (pp. 36—48, *supra*) the question of liability under the marine policy in respect of blockade has in some measure already been considered.

As has been observed, there is nothing illegal in the attempt to violate or break, or, as it is currently termed, to run a blockade, but vessels engaging in this enterprise do so with the knowledge that if the attempt fail—or indeed, possibly, as has been shown, though for the moment it may succeed—confiscation of ship and cargo may ensue. The fact that such a risk is to be encountered must consequently be communicated to the underwriter when the insurance is effected; or it must be established that this material

(*x*) State Papers, 1886, Nos. 4731-2, 4765-6.

fact was within his knowledge notwithstanding that no such special communication was made to him. For otherwise the concealment will be held to have vitiated the insurance (*y*). But in the event of this country becoming a belligerent, any such insurance in favour of neutral vessels contemplating breach of British blockade would be void on the ground, first, of insurance against British capture, and, secondly, it may be supposed that vessels having as destination a blockaded port and seeking to evade the blockade must be regarded as engaged in the trade of the enemy, and therefore not capable of British insurance. So that knowledge on the part of the underwriter would in such a case be beside the question (*z*).

If a vessel be warranted neutral property, it is implied that she shall be so navigated as not to forfeit her character of neutrality; and any attempt to violate a blockade would consequently be held a breach of the neutral warranty, and the underwriter would be freed from all liability under the policy (*a*).

That blockade of the port of destination is not a peril within the policy has already been set forth *sub* Embargo (pp. 39—48, *supra*).

If a master, without the knowledge or consent and in disobedience to the orders of his owners, be guilty of intentional breach of blockade, and the vessel be seized in consequence, the loss may be attributed to barratry (*b*). But if the policy be warranted free from capture and seizure, this warranty, according to the decision in *Cory* v. *Burr* (*vide* p. 79, *supra*), would exclude capture consequent on barratry (*c*).

(*y*) Arnould, 5th ed. vol. 2, 700.

(*z*) *Vide sub* Void Insurances, p. 405, *infra*.

(*a*) Arnould's Insce., 5th ed. p. 609. *Vide*, also, *sub* War Warranties, p. 386, *infra*.

(*b*) Goldschmidt *v.* Whitmore, 3 Taunt. 508.

(*c*) The following are instances of clauses apparently intended to exclude risks consequent on breach of blockade, or carriage of contraband:—

"Warranted free from capture, seizure, or damage received consequent on being engaged in trades contraband of war, or consequent on any breach, or attempted breach, of blockade." Owen's Marine Insce. Notes and Clauses, 2nd ed. 20.

"Warranted free from capture, seizure, or consequence of any attempt thereat, arising from any breach, or attempted breach, of blockade, or from

Whether the master is to be presumed in law to have had notice of the blockade is a question for the Court; but as was decided in *The Monarch*, whether breach of blockade has been intentional or otherwise must be left to the jury to determine. In this case the vessel was seized when approaching the blockaded port, but the master disclaimed any intention of violation; as to which Lord Tenterden observed that the vessel might have sailed for Buenos Ayres—the blockaded port—without contravening the law of nations, provided it was a part of the original intention to inquire as to the continuance of the blockade at some port of the blockading country; and that inquiry might have been made at Monte Video or of any of the Brazilian ships met with in the River Plata; and that the sailing for Buenos Ayres did not of itself indicate any intention to violate the blockade(*d*).

With respect to capture in connexion with violation of blockade, reference may be made to the subject of capture generally, p. 68, *supra*.

---

being employed in any contraband or unlawful trade, or performing any unlawful act." *Ibid.*

(*d*) Naylor *v.* Taylor, 9 B. & C. 718, An. 1829. *Vide* also Medeiros *v.* Hill, An. 1832, p. 419, *infra;* and Harratt *v.* Wise, *ibid.* 712, An. 1829; and cf. The Columbia, p. 117, *supra.*

RECAPTURE

CONSIDERED IN CONJUNCTION WITH THE LAW OF POSTLIMINY AND THE PAYMENT OF SALVAGE TO RECAPTORS.

The term recapture is used to denote the retaking, by force of arms or by stratagem from without, of property seized by the enemy. If the recaptors be from within—as, for instance, if the crew of the captured vessel rise and overpower the prize-crew placed on board by the captors—then the recovery of the property is termed "rescue."

Postliminium.—"The *jus postliminii*," says Wheaton, in his "International Law" (*e*), "was a fiction of the Roman law, by which persons or things taken by the enemy were held to be restored to their former state when coming again under the power of the nation to which they formerly belonged." The effect of this law is, that property recaptured or rescued from the enemy and brought within the territory of the original ownership does not vest in the recaptor or rescuer, but is held still to belong to the original owners, to whom it must be restored, against payment of salvage by them. If the property be brought into neutral territory, the law of postliminy does not apply to it, but in the case of prisoners it does apply. Or rather, so long as prisoners remain on board the vessel of their captors, they are appa-

(*e*) 2 Eng. ed. 438.

rently held to be out of neutral jurisdiction, but if once they set foot on shore in neutral territory, then the captors lose all right over them.

By the ancient and strict law of nations, property, when captured by the enemy, was held to become his absolutely, to the complete divestment of the original owner. This rule, however, in course of time, underwent modification, different laws being passed in different countries fixing the point of time, after capture, at which the rights of the original owner became divested. Early writers held that when once the property seized had been carried by the captors *infra præsidia*, the title of the original owner was *ipso facto* divested. The law of France and Portugal, and presumably of various other countries is, that this result is effected by twenty-four hours of safe possession by the enemy. In the United States the property is changed only by condemnation in the prize courts of the captors. In Great Britain it is expressly provided by statute that the *jus postliminii* continues for ever—that is, to the end of the war—whether the property be condemned or not. If after lawful condemnation the prize be sold to a neutral, the right of recapture will be extinguished.

These different regulations may in case of hostilities be subject to revision as between allies. If, to put an example, Great Britain and France were jointly to engage in war, say, with Spain, and vessels belonging to each of these powers were to be captured by Spain: British property recaptured by France would after twenty-four hours' possession by the captors, according to French municipal law, be vested absolutely in the recaptors; whereas French property similarly recaptured by this country would, according to the letter of British municipal law, have to be restored to the French owners against payment of salvage. It would not be difficult to instance similar anomalies existing to the prejudice of British shipping in times of peace; but in times of war—possibly because the sense of injustice and inequality may then be especially alert—a common-sense view is taken, and we do not grant to our allies privileges which they refuse to us. The principle of reciprocity steps in, and we annex as a reasonable condition to the liberality of this country that our allies shall meet us on a common basis of restitution (*f*). The same principle obtains in the United States.

There is, however, an exception to the above general rule of postliminy. If a private vessel be captured and subsequently recaptured, but between these two events she be set forth as a public vessel by the first captors, she will be held to belong wholly to the recaptors. And the same rule will prevail if the property when first captured was engaged in an illegal trade (*g*). A vessel recaptured as above will be deemed a public vessel, notwithstanding that, although fitted out as a privateer by the enemy, she was when recaptured navigating as a merchant vessel (*h*). But the mere putting on board of an additional number of men will not of itself constitute the vessel a public vessel (*i*). And if it can be shown that the recaptured vessel has been employed in the public military service, although never regularly commissioned or sent out of port—as, for instance, if she be dismantled and fitted out as a prison ship—the original owners will be debarred from claiming under the general rule of postliminy (*k*). The circumstance that the recaptured vessel had guns on board will be a material element in deciding as to the recaptors' right to the property (*l*). And if the person

(*f*) The Santa Cruz, 1 Rob. 49; The San Francisco, Edw. 279.

(*g*) The Walsingham Packet, 2 Rob. 77.

(*h*) L'Actif, Edw. 186.

(*i*) The Horatio, 6 Rob. 320.

(*k*) The Ceylon, 1 Dods. 105.

(*l*) The Nostra Signora del Rosario, 3 Rob. 10; The Ceylon, *supra*.

directing the vessel to be employed in the public service be invested with a fair semblance of authority, the Court will presume due authorization (*m*).

The rule of postliminy does not apply where the cause of the original capture has been a breach solely of municipal regulations. "The seizure and condemnation in time of peace," said Sir W. Scott, in *The Jeune Voyageur* (*n*), "will have the effect of working an entire defeasance of the British title; and a ship must be condemned to the captor, as property of the enemy, taken in the ordinary course of prize." The vessel had been confiscated during peace, and sold to a French subject; and on the outbreak of war she fell into the possession of British captors.

If a British vessel be captured, lawfully condemned, and sold to a neutral, and the neutral purchaser become, owing to subsequent hostilities, an enemy subject, and the vessel then be captured by the British, she will be held, as in the case of *The Purissima Conception* (*o*), to have become the rightful property of an enemy, and so not the subject of restoration to the original British owner. For if a neutral purchase a vessel lawfully condemned, his title is secured, and that of the original owner is divested.

If a treaty of peace makes no provision relative to captured property, it remains in the possession of the holders, the right of postliminium ceasing to operate on the conclusion of peace. And the circumstance that such property has come into possession of the holder improperly—as, for example, by illegal condemnation—will not affect the position (*p*).

(*m*) The Georgiana, 1 Dods. 397.
(*n*) 5 Rob. 1.
(*o*) 6 Rob. 45.
(*p*) The Sophie, 6 Rob. 138.

Salvage.—If a British-owned vessel be recaptured from the enemy by subjects of this country, it has, subject to the above exceptions, to be restored, as we have already seen, to its original owners. But the original owners, although entitled to claim restitution of the property, are none the less under the obligation to compensate the recaptors for their meritorious services; money so earned or paid being comprehended under the general term "salvage." By the Naval Prize Act, 1864 (*q*), s. 40, it is provided that property recaptured by any of Her Majesty's ships of war shall be restored to the owner "on his paying as prize salvage one-eighth part of the value of the prize, to be decreed and ascertained by the Court, or such sum not exceeding one-eighth part of the estimated value of the prize, as may be agreed on between the owner and the recaptors, and approved by order of the Court: provided that where the recapture is made under circumstances of special difficulty or danger, the Prize Court may, if it thinks fit, award to the recaptors as prize salvage a larger part than one-eighth part, but not exceeding in any case one-fourth part of the value of the prize. Provided also, that where a ship, after being so taken, is set forth or used by any of Her Majesty's enemies as a ship of war, this provision for restitution shall not apply, and the ship shall be adjudicated on as in other cases of prize." This enactment, it will be noticed, makes no reference to the case where the vessel recaptured was, when originally captured, engaged in illegal trade.

In the *London Gazette* of 28th March, 1854, is published the British Prize Proclamation, which makes detailed provision for the apportionment of prize money amongst the various officers and members of the crew of the vessel effecting a capture. The 1864 Prize Act provides for the case of

(*q*) *Vide* Appendix.

joint capture, appraisement of property salved, proceedings by captors, &c., and deals with the various questions arising out of capture generally. Sect. 41 provides that recaptured vessels shall, with consent of the recaptors, be allowed to proceed on their voyage, and deals with the award and enforcement of salvage in case of non-return of the vessel to a port in the United Kingdom. The recaptors may, under the same section, permit the master to discharge and dispose of the cargo before adjudication. At one time, if a vessel was captured, recaptured, captured again, and again recaptured, the interest in the prize was held to be vested wholly in the recaptors. The 1864 Prize Act, however, contains no such exception in favour of second recaptors. In *The Charlotte Croom* (r), it was decided that where a ship has been captured, recaptured, captured again and condemned, but is finally released, the recaptors' right to salvage is still existent.

It was decided in *The Belle* (s) that, in the event of a hired transport being recaptured by a ship of war, no salvage is due. But in the Act of 1864 no such provision appears. A convoying vessel is entitled to salvage, though the recapture immediately succeed the capture (t).

If a vessel be captured and condemned and sold to a neutral purchaser, the legal sentence of condemnation is by the general practice of the law of nations regarded as one of the title-deeds of the vessel. But if the condemnation be made by an improper tribunal, and the vessel be recaptured, the Court will refuse to recognise the title of the neutral purchaser, and will decree restitution to the British owners on payment of the usual salvage (u). If a neutral vessel be

(r) 1 Dod. 192.
(s) Edw. 66.
(t) The Wight, 5 Rob. 315.
(u) The Flad Oyen, 1 Rob. 135; Nostra Signora de los Angelos, 3 Rob. 287. *Vide* also The Cosmopolite, 3 Rob. 333.

seized by the subjects of a country with which Great Britain is at war, and be recaptured by a British vessel, salvage will or will not be payable by the neutral, according to whether the vessel would or would not be subject to condemnation by a competent prize court of the captors. The principle on which this practice is based is that a neutral vessel ought to be respected by all nations, and, if unjustly seized by one belligerent, the other should not be an accomplice to and seek to profit by the injustice. But if the original capture would in all probability, whether rightly or wrongly, be followed by condemnation, then the recaptors are fairly entitled to be recompensed for their meritorious services in effecting the recapture (*v*). In decreeing salvage in *The War Onskan*, a neutral vessel recaptured from the French, Sir W. Scott said that he knew perfectly well that it was not the modern practice of the law of nations to grant salvage on recapture of neutral vessels, on the principle that, inasmuch as the neutral would presumably be restored on adjudication, no essential service was rendered to him by the recaptors. But that, inasmuch as in the present war it was notorious to all Europe that a constant struggle was being maintained between the governing powers of France and its maritime tribunals which should most outrage the rights of neutral property, the one by its decrees, the other by its decisions, the liberation of neutral property had been deemed, even in the Courts of the neutrals themselves, a most substantial benefit conferred upon them, in a delivery from danger against which no clearness and innocence of conduct could have afforded any protection. And that when such lawless and irregular practices ceased, the rule of paying salvage for the liberation of neutral property must cease likewise.

(*v*) The Carlotta, 5 Rob. 54; The Eleonora Catharina, 4 Rob. 156; The War Onskan, 2 Rob. 299; The Huntress, 6 Rob. 104; The Samson, *ibid.* 410; The Barbara, 3 Rob. 171; The Cygnet, 2 Dods. 299.

In *The Barbara* (*x*), where a neutral ship had been recaptured from the Spaniards, the Court declined to discuss the principle whether salvage was due, the recaptors having been guilty of the irregularity of making a private settlement with the asserted owners, and having thus forfeited the right to demand the aid of the Court.

A neutral vessel recaptured may, if necessary for her protection, be armed and equipped for purposes of defence, and if she be lost or damaged while resisting the enemy, no claim for compensation will lie against the recaptors (*y*).

The absence of intention to effect a recovery of captured property cannot be pleaded by the owners of the property as a reason for non-payment of salvage, if the recovery be the immediate and necessary result of the service rendered (*z*). But the mere stopping a vessel from going into an enemy's port does not give rise to a claim for salvage (*a*).

The 1864 Prize Act declares that prizes captured by ships other than warships shall, on condemnation, belong to Her Majesty. It may, however, be assumed that if special circumstances should in any such case appear to warrant it, a petition for salvage would be favourably considered (*b*).

In cases of salvage by merchant ships, the master and crew are, in strictness, to be regarded as the salvors, though the owners are entitled to equitable consideration in respect of damage or risk accruing to their property owing to the operation (*c*).

A capture made by a naval force in a river, 130 miles from its mouth, was held by the United States Courts to be a

---

(*x*) 3 Rob. 171.

(*y*) The Swift, 1 Act. 1.

(*z*) The Progress, Edw. 211.

(*a*) *The Ann Green*, 1 *Gall.* 293.

(*b*) The Helen, 3 Rob. 224; The Haase, 1 Rob. 286; The Amor Parentum, *ibid.* 303. *Vide* also p. 136, *infra*.

(*c*) The San Bernardo, 1 Rob. 178.

capture upon "inland waters," and, therefore, not to be regarded as a maritime capture (*d*). On the other hand, it was by the same Courts held that property seized in a warehouse by gunboats which had entered a river in the enemy's country was maritime prize (*e*).

Formerly, whereas the salvage due to public vessels was one-eighth, non-commissioned vessels received one-sixth, on the ground that the officers and crews of public vessels sacrificed no time of their own, and did not jeopardize, in the case of the vessel, their own private property.

If a vessel be purchased from the captors for the purpose of returning her to the owners, salvage is due from the latter,—or so it was decided in *The Henry* (*f*). But such a purchase from the enemy by a British subject would now presumably come within the prohibition against ransom (*g*), and would, consequently, be illegal. Freight, of course, has to contribute to salvage, as well as the ship and cargo (*h*). The valuation of property recaptured has for purposes of salvage to be assessed at the place of restitution, and not of recapture (*i*).

Re-captors may, in addition to salvage in the nature of prize-money, also become entitled to ordinary marine salvage. As, for instance, if after the recapture the vessel be in distress, from which she is succoured and preserved owing to their meritorious services (*j*). In *The Franklin* (*k*) the vessel had been captured on the suspicion—reasonable, but,

(*d*) *The Cotton Plant*, 10 *Wall.* 577.
(*e*) 1,253 *Bags Rice*, *Blatch. Pr. Ca.* 211.
(*f*) Edw. 192.
(*g*) *Vide* p. 296, *infra*.
(*h*) The Dorothy Foster, 6 Rob. 88.
(*i*) The Progress, Edw. 210, 222.
(*j*) The Louisa, 1 Dods. 317.
(*k*) 4 Rob. 147.

as it turned out, erroneous—that she was intending to deliver her cargo at an enemy's port. She was, however, declared by the master to have been, in fact, forced to proceed to the nearest port on account of her leaky condition; and on this the captors pleaded a claim for salvage. If the vessel had not been seized by them, they said, she would have been confiscated by the enemy. They also claimed as for a marine salvage, as they had carried the vessel (alleged to be leaky) into Jersey. The Court held that, the vessel being neither actually nor virtually within the grasp of the enemy, no military salvage was due. She had not arrived at the enemy's port: as well might salvage be claimed for giving the first intimation of a war. As to the marine salvage, it was one of no high merit. He could not, however, say that no service had been rendered, and he therefore awarded 500*l.*, —the appraised value of the property being 30,000*l.*

In *The Gage* (*l*), where a vessel captured by a French privateer had been abandoned by her and subsequently picked up at sea, with a fire burning in her cabin, the Court held the case not to fall under the restrictions of the Prize Act, and decreed a special salvage.

If after capture a vessel be rescued by her own crew, or by such of them as are left on board, they are entitled to salvage. The crew are not bound by their general duty as mariners to attempt a rescue; and if they by their voluntary act successfully undertake such a meritorious service, they are to be compensated (*m*). But if a captured vessel makes her escape owing to the captors having allowed her own officers and crew to continue in charge, this is not for salvage purposes to be deemed a rescue (*n*). (The subject of Rescue

(*l*) 6 Rob. 273.
(*m*) The Two Friends, 1 Rob. 271; The Dispatch, 3 Rob. 278.
(*n*) The Pennsylvania, 1 Act. 33.

is further dealt with on p. 216, *infra*, under the general head Belligerent Rights against Neutrals.)

In *The Abigail* (o), where a capture had been effected by a non-commissioned privateer, the proceeds were condemned as a droit of Admiralty. In *The Haase* (p), however—another case of seizure by non-commissioned captors—the whole proceeds, condemned as droit of Admiralty, were awarded to the captors in consequence of their meritorious services and the loss of voyage entailed upon them by their action. In *The Melomane* (q), where a capture had been effected by a boat hired by a king's ship for the purpose of impressing homeward-bound seamen, the prize was condemned as a droit of Admiralty, the boat having no commission or authority from the Admiralty (qq).

In *The Racehorse* (r), Sir W. Scott remarked:—"It is much to be regretted that charter parties do not contain provisions for the case of capture and recapture; it is an accident that frequently occurs" (s).

The instructions furnished to Lloyd's agents impress upon the agents the obligation to prevent the sale of recaptured vessels at foreign ports for the purpose of payment of salvage. The salvage is, wherever practicable, to be adjusted without such sale, in order that the vessel may proceed with her cargo to the port of destination. And in the event of any salvage proceeds finding their way into the agent's possession, the money is to be remitted to Lloyd's for distribution amongst the parties entitled to it.

(o) 4 Rob. 72.

(p) 1 Rob. 286.

(q) 5 Rob. 41.

(qq) *Vide* also cases cited p. 133, *supra*.

(r) *Vide* p. 426, *infra*.

(s) The subject of the payment of freight in such cases is discussed below, *sub* Effect of War on Contract, p. 412.

Insurance.

The word salvage, like the word insurer, is used in two distinct and opposite senses. On the one hand, it means a sum of money payable to persons who have saved the ship from loss; on the other, it means the property or proceeds of property which may remain after a loss has been incurred. As regards salvage in the former sense, it may be broadly stated that wherever the underwriters are liable for a loss, they are liable for charges incurred in averting the same. Therefore, if the property insured be captured, and the owners, in order to regain possession of it, have to pay salvage to recaptors, such a payment, unless the risk of capture be excluded by the policy, gives rise to a claim against underwriters. The salvage must, however (*t*), have been properly ascertained and paid by the assured.

As regards salvage in the sense of proceeds, an instance may be mentioned of a so-called salvage of a very exceptional kind which attached to goods in vessels destroyed by the Confederate cruiser *Alabama*. Part of the compensation paid by the British Government under the Geneva award (*u*) was ordered by the United States Government to be applied in payment of any deficiencies as between the actual and the insured values of property so destroyed. This difference was, in *Burnand* v. *Rodocanachi* (*x*), claimed from the assured by the underwriters, who had paid as for a total loss of certain goods in respect of which this compensation had been received. The Court, however, decided against this claim, on the ground that defendant had received the money under the Act of Congress and judgment of the American Court expressly to keep it for himself, and not to pay it over to the plaintiff (*y*).

(*t*) Arnould's Insce., 5th ed., 779.

(*u*) *Vide* p. 364, *infra*.

(*x*) L. R. 7 App. Cases, House of Lords, 333.

(*y*) The following clause is sometimes used in marine policies on vessels chartered by the government during hostilities:—

"To include war risk, but all money received from H. M. Government as compensation for value of ship if lost or captured to be treated as salvage": Owen's Marine Insce. Notes and Clauses, 2nd ed. p. 100.

THE BOMBARDMENT OF SEABOARD TOWNS.

According to first principles, the individual is, by the law of nations, so identified with the government to which he is subject, that acts of aggression or reprisal which may lawfully be exercised against his government, may equally be put in force against himself. He may be slain or imprisoned wherever found. But as the influences of civilization and religious sentiment have gathered force, the crudeness of this original principle has been greatly toned down in practice. So that at the present day it is, on the outbreak of hostilities, regarded as a matter of course that the non-combatant individual, so long as he stands aloof, will be allowed to go unharmed, and that his property will not be seized or destroyed, unless as a measure of necessity or safety on the part of the hostile forces. It is, indeed, nowadays, nothing uncommon for an invading force to tender payment for supplies gathered from residents in the hostile country traversed, and this practice, to whatever motives it may be attributed, seems destined to be in time regarded as a rule binding on civilized nations. Therefore, whatever may have been the rights or usages sanctioned or tolerated under less mature conditions of civilization, it must now, there can scarcely be a doubt, be taken as a recognised principle of modern warfare, that the lives and property of non-combatants are to be respected; and any nation wantonly, and without valid reason, burning or destroying defenceless cities, would undoubtedly become the object of the hatred and contempt of the world at large.

This is no doubt true. But, on the other hand, the well-established principle has to be kept in view, that the aim and object of a belligerent is to force his adversary to sue for peace, and that he is justified in taking such measures as may, by creating panic, dismay, and loss, incline the foe to come to terms. The application of this principle would scarcely justify a belligerent in wantonly bombarding an unfortified town; but it seems by no means evident that a hostile fleet, finding a wealthy and important seaboard town of the enemy at the moment without its defences, would not be held justified in demanding money or supplies from such a town, under penalty of bombardment in case of refusal (z).

During the great maritime war which prevailed at the beginning of the present century, this question does not seem to have arisen. Seaboard towns, such as now exist, for example, along our own south-eastern coast-line, were comparatively unknown, their growth since then being almost entirely due to facilities of communication afforded by the railways. Owing to the great range and power of modern projectiles, these seaboard towns are probably incapable of defence against bombardment, except by warships; and, should

---

(z) "A ship at 4,000 or 5,000 yards range is so insignificant an object that she need fear no sort of fire from the shore at her; whilst the town aimed at is a very large target indeed. But two jokes which are current amongst naval and military men give a point to the modern ideas of bombardment, which nothing else rivals. It is said that ships intending to bombard will shelter themselves under the curvature of the earth; and it has been stated that one of the ships in the late manœuvres laid her guns 'W.S.W. by compass, eight and a quarter miles,' for a large inland town." —*Edinburgh Review*, October, 1888, p. 473.

But if the above be jokes, a note in the *Times* of 26th December, 1888, under the head "Monster Russian Guns," would seem to invest them with a spice of reality. For the note attributes to the weapons referred to a range of over thirteen miles, and remarks that as a consequence of this range "the fire of the guns can only be directed by the map, the object fired at being out of sight."

the enemy succeed in bringing his naval forces near one of such towns, in the temporary absence of the defending fleet, the temptation to turn the opportunity to solid advantage might, perhaps, not be resisted. That such a contingency is not to be regarded as outside the range of the contingencies or conditions of modern naval warfare, may not unreasonably be inferred from the proceedings of some of the vessels of the British fleet during the naval war-game which took place between two opposing fleets in the summer of 1888. Professor Holland, in a letter which appeared in the *Times* of 29th August in that year, whilst protesting against what he describes as this "buccaneering precedent," remarks, that "It should be remembered that operations conducted with the apparent approval of the highest naval authorities, and letters in the *Times* from distinguished admirals, are, in truth, the stuff that public opinion, and, in particular, that department of public opinion known as 'international law,' is made of." Concluding, he observes that "We are as yet far from having disposed of the comparatively simple question as to the operations which may be properly undertaken by a naval squadron against an undefended seaboard." On the question of precedent, it may be here mentioned that in 1866 the city of Valparaiso, which was left absolutely undefended, was bombarded by the Spanish fleet, after a delay—conceded by the Spanish admiral, it is stated, on the representations of the commander of the British fleet then off the port—had been granted in order to give the inhabitants time to withdraw.

It is true that the delegates of all the States of Europe laid it down, *inter alia*, at the Brussels Conference of 1874, assembled at the invitation of the Emperor of Russia, that open or undefended towns cannot be attacked or bombarded; but such irresponsible expressions of opinion or sentiment cannot be looked upon as binding upon any one. Lord Derby, indeed, writing on the subject of this Conference, declared that "A careful consideration of the whole matter has convinced her Majesty's Government that it is their duty firmly to repudiate, on behalf of Great Britain and her allies in any future war, any project for altering the principles of international law upon which this country has hitherto acted; and, above all, to refuse to be a party to any agreement the effect of which would be to facilitate aggressive wars and to paralyse the patriotic efforts of an invaded people" (*a*).

The *Times*, treating on this subject (*b*), writes as follows: "The rules of international law are singularly precarious agreements, observable just so long as it may suit the strongest nations to observe them, and not a moment longer. It is but a very few years since Admiral Aube, a French officer of the highest distinction, and afterwards for a considerable time Minister of Marine, published in the *Revue des Deux Mondes* an article in which he laid it down that France, in any future war with a country like England, would make at once for the coast towns, and either bombard them without mercy or hold them to heavy ransom." And Admiral De Horsey, writing to the same journal (*c*), expresses himself thus: "A state of war, I venture to maintain, not only warrants, but makes it the duty of a belligerent to do everything in his power, consistent with humanity and the rights of neutrals, to induce his enemy to sue for peace. Few will deny the above brief definition of a belligerent's duty, and if that be granted, it is obvious that in pursuance of this object everything belonging to an enemy, whether afloat or on land, which can afford shelter, means of repair, aid or subsistence to his forces, is subject to capture or destruction; and that

(*a*) This expression of sentiment is interesting in conjunction with any consideration of the novelties formulated by the Declaration of Paris.

(*b*) 10th August, 1888.

(*c*) 25th August, 1888.

rich towns are liable to reasonable ransom, and, in default of compliance, to bombardment. This appears to be the common-sense view of war, in order to make it short, sharp, and decisive, and to render so terrible a scourge one of rare occurrence. . . . What towns should be subjected to ransom, and what ransom would be reasonable, are matters which must be left to the judgment and humanity of the commander at the time—of course, under general instructions from his government."

So that, as matters now stand, the whole question of bombardment of seaboard towns must be considered open; and, unless meantime dealt with by international treaty, or otherwise determined, it may not unreasonably be assumed that in the event of the occurrence of naval hostilities in the future, the example of the peaceful British naval manœuvres already referred to will, should occasion arise for following it, be regarded as a precedent to be observed in actual war.

Insurance,—*Fire.*

The ordinary form of fire policy excludes the risk of loss or injury caused by enemies or hostilities, by the following or similar words:—

"This policy does not cover . . . . any loss or damage occasioned by or in consequence of invasion, foreign enemy, hostilities, riot, civil commotion, or earthquakes."

The Right to Bombard Seaboard Towns is the last of the direct belligerent rights against the enemy scheduled on p. 36, *supra*. The rights next demanding consideration are those indirect rights which consist in prohibiting neutrals from carrying supplies to the enemy, and generally from acting in opposition to the principles of neutrality which are by the common law of nations to be observed by neutral powers. Let us now proceed to classify these indirect rights under the head "Belligerent Rights against Neutrals."

V.

BELLIGERENT RIGHTS AGAINST NEUTRALS.

VISIT AND SEARCH.

THE right of visitation and search is one of great antiquity, having apparently been commonly recognised so far back as the twelfth century. It is obvious that if the right of maritime capture be admitted, the precedent right of visit and search must also be admitted. For how otherwise can it be ascertained whether a merchant ship really belongs to the country whose flag she is flying; or that she is engaged on a legitimate voyage or in a legitimate trade; or that no part of her cargo is confiscable under the law of nations? It is, in fact, an incontestable right founded on necessity, and one which has survived all attempts to dispute or deny it. As was observed by Sir W. Scott in the well-known case of *The Swedish Convoy*, to be referred to presently, even those who contend for the inadmissible rule that "free ships make (by the law of nations) free goods," must admit the exercise of the right for the purpose of ascertaining whether the ships are free or not. The right may, of course, be dealt with by treaty, but any such special conventions will doubtless confine themselves to the mode in which the right is to be exercised, and will not operate as its renunciation or abandonment. For it is difficult to see how any nation which maintains the right to effect maritime capture can abandon the necessarily antecedent right of visit and examination. The right of visit and search is distinctly a war right, though there are apparently cases in which the right of visit may be exercised in time of peace,—as, for example, on suspicion of piracy, of breaking revenue laws, and of aiding rebels; and special treaty provisions have been made respecting it, with a view to enforcement of the international provisions against the slave trade. At one time the British Government drew a distinction between the right of visit, to which it laid claim in time of peace, and the right of search. The Government of the United States, however, declined to recognise such a distinction, arguing that the right of visit, logically considered, practically carried with it the right of search. This difference of view arose out of the British endeavours to suppress the trade in slaves on the African coast, but it was apparently ultimately overcome by the formulation of special provisions to meet the case. That these two rights are technically different, and that the right of visit does not of necessity involve the right to search, seems evident. But whether they should by the law of nations be regarded as altogether distinct, or as practically indistinguishable, appears to be unsettled. Twiss makes a distinction between the right of visit and the right of external inspection, which he terms the right of approach (*a*). No such right as the latter, however, appears ever to have been either asserted or denied under the law of nations, and seeing that the high seas are the property of no one, and that all have an equal right to their free use, there can scarcely be any question as to the right of one vessel to approach as closely to another as may be consistent with the safe and unimpeded navigation of both. At the same time, as he indicates, the right of approach rests upon a different footing in times of peace and in times of hostilities; and an approach which in the former case would pass unnoticed might in the latter be regarded by the vessel approached as evidence of a design to effect a capture, and, therefore, to justify the initiation of hostile defensive proceedings.

The right of search exists only as against private vessels and not against ships of war. The proposition that public warships are, as such, exempt from all jurisdiction beyond that of the sovereign power to which they belong, has been uniformly conceded. It is less obvious whether war vessels, though exempt from search, are equally exempt from the right of visit; but presumably, if a vessel's public character be manifest it would be unlawful to claim the right of visit

(*a*) Law of Nations in Time of War, pp. 179, 180.

against her. This exemption does not, however, exist in favour of privateers, for the right of a vessel to sail under this title can only be verified by visit and inspection of her commander's commission of war.

Notwithstanding that the right of visit and search is supported by the accepted usage of centuries, and is clearly in accord with the principles of the common law of nations, several attempts have been made in European history to resist it. Thus, in 1780, Russia, Sweden, Denmark, and some inferior States, entered into a league of armed neutrality—in reality against England, but professedly for the purpose of supporting the principle that "free ships make free goods," and that the neutral flag should exclude the right of search. The British Government at once declared their intention to resist, and persistently resisted, this attempt to introduce by force a new code of maritime law, inconsistent with England's maritime rights, and hostile to her interests. In 1799 this determination on the part of the British Government was manifested in a sufficiently marked manner. War was at that time prevailing between this country and France, and a convoy of Swedish vessels was encountered by a British squadron. This squadron having proposed to exercise the right of search over the vessels under convoy, the convoying Swedish war ship interposed, and refused to allow the search. Whereupon, without further ado, the squadron captured the whole fleet under convoy, and brought the vessels in for adjudication. The case of *The Maria* (*b*), one of the fleet, was heard before Sir W. Scott, who affirmed the right of visit and search in regard to merchant ships as being an incontestable right of a belligerent, and he decreed condemnation for contravention of the right (*c*).

(*b*) 1 Rob. 340.

(*c*) For a review of the consequences of Resistance to Visit and Search, *vide* p. 212, *infra*.

That Great Britain was determined at all costs to resist any such obnoxious pretension as the foregoing, was sufficiently obvious, her action in the case of the Swedish convoy being evidence, as Wheaton aptly expresses it, of an intention to throw down the glove to all the world. But, notwithstanding, in the wars ensuing on the French Revolution, a second armed neutrality was formed between Russia, Denmark, Sweden and Prussia, under the title of "The Baltic Confederacy," in which the former pretensions were revived. The confederacy agreed that a declaration by officers in charge of a convoy that the vessels under convoy had no contraband on board, should exclude the right of visit and search. The league was, however, met by such prompt and vigorous opposition on the part of Great Britain that it was rendered abortive, and the right of search became on all hands admitted to the fullest extent. As a result, a convention was, in 1801, settled between this country and Russia, to which the other northern powers subsequently acceded, providing (*d*) (1) that the right of search should only be exercised by war-ships, and should not extend to privateers; (2) That the owners of merchantmen should, before being allowed to sail under convoy, produce to the commander of the convoy passports and certificates; (3) That the convoy and merchant ships should keep out of cannon-shot, if possible, and that for the purpose of making a search a boat should be sent by the belligerent to the convoy; (4) That no search should be made if the papers were in form and there was no good motive for suspicion; in the contrary case, the commander of the convoy was to detain the merchantman for sufficient time to allow of search, which was to be made in the presence of officers selected by the commanders of both war-ships; (5) If there appeared sufficient reason for making further search, notification of the intention

(*d*) *Vide* Cobbett's Leading Cases, p. 249.

to do so was to be made to the commander of the convoy, the latter having the right to appoint an officer and to remain on board and assist at the examination; the merchant ship in such case to be taken as soon as possible to the nearest and most convenient port of the belligerent, and the search to be made with all possible despatch; (6) If a merchantman under convoy should be detained without sufficient cause, the commander of the visiting ship not only to be bound to make compensation, but to suffer further punishment for every act of violence committed; on the other hand, a convoying ship not to be allowed to resist by force the detention of a merchantman.

By the municipal regulations of some of the European powers it is provided that merchant vessels under convoy shall be exempt from search on a satisfactory declaration being made by the convoying officer; but Great Britain has always refused to admit, so far as she is concerned, any such restriction of the belligerent right of visitation and search. The United States Government, in this case and in that of most other principles of the law of nations, has laid down rules similar to those maintained by this country; but on one somewhat important detail in this connexion, the two countries are at issue. For whereas Great Britain claims the right to search for her seamen or other subjects on the high seas, into whatever service they may have entered, the government of the United States declines to admit any such right. This difference was one principal cause of the war between Great Britain and the United States in 1812.

The mode in which the right of visit and search is to be exercised may be, and probably commonly is, regulated by international treaty. In the absence of stipulation to the contrary, it would appear that private ships of war have an equal right with public vessels to visit and search neutral vessels, their commission of war being a sufficient warrant in this respect. It has sometimes been stipulated that no war-ship shall come within cannon-shot, or half cannon-shot, as the case may be, whilst exercising the right of visit. On or before arriving at such a distance, the intention to visit should be intimated by the firing of a blank charge, and on this intimation the neutral vessel should at once signify her acquiescence by lowering her sails or otherwise bringing herself to. That an affirming gun should be fired seems a reasonable requirement; but Mr. Justice Story, in the case of *The Mariana Flora* (e), did not admit the existence of any universal rule or obligation to this effect. Such a provision might exist by regulation or usage in the case of particular states, but the circumstance did not bind other nations. The authorities cited by Twiss, in his Law of Nations (f), go to confirm the soundness of Mr. Justice Story's view; and it would seem that, however usual and reasonable the affirming gun may be, any other mode of communication equally intelligible on board the neutral vessel would answer the purpose. There must, however, be no room for mistake as to the intention to exercise the right of visit, as otherwise the visiting vessel may be found liable for damage resulting to the neutral vessel consequent on a resistance or endeavour to escape, founded on ignorance. But until both the intention and the right to visit shall have been unequivocally conveyed to the neutral vessel, the latter is under no obligation to shorten sail or lie to (g). The visiting vessel must also hoist her military flag in evidence of her true character, and of her consequent right to visit; and when these two conditions shall have been fulfilled, it is presumably incumbent on the neutral to at once shorten sail or lie to.

(e) 11 *Wheaton*, p. 50.

(f) "War," pp. 182-3.

(g) The San Juan Baptista, 5 Rob. 34.

If, notwithstanding, she should continue on her course without heeding the intimation, the visiting vessel would be warranted in regarding such conduct as evidence of an attempt to evade the right of visit, and the neutral vessel would have no right to complain if, on attempting flight, she should be fired into by the belligerent war-ship. And the neutral must not decline to permit visit by a privateer until the commander of the latter shall have exhibited his commission of war. To proceed otherwise will be to subject the vessel to capture on the ground of illegal resistance to the right of visit. When the neutral has stopped on her course, the war-ship is entitled to send a boat's crew on board for examination of the ship's papers, and, if found necessary, for instituting a search. The visit and search must be conducted in such a manner as to cause no unnecessary alarm to the neutral, and for this reason the boat sent off should be manned by a small crew, in order to avoid any needless demonstration of force. For it must be remembered that the neutral vessel is presumably engaged in a lawful and pacific trade, in conformity with the law of nations, and that her officers and crew are accordingly entitled to be treated with the courtesy due to peaceable subjects of a friendly nation until, by their conduct or actions, they shall have forfeited this right. And the visit and search must be conducted generally with due care and regard to the safety and rights of the vessel (*h*); and, of course, to the stipulations of any treaties covering the case. Should a belligerent vessel, in exercising the right, proceed in an aggressive manner, the circumstance may be regarded by the neutral nation as an unfriendly act demanding satisfactory explanation and reparation.

It is the duty of merchant vessels to show their real colours on meeting with a ship of war, in order that their nationality

(*h*) *The Anna Maria*, 2 *Wheaton*, 327.

may be verified. And in time of war especially the neutral master is required to have knowledge as to his cargo. A prudent master, having regard to the possible consequences of insufficient knowledge on this point, will take care to be provided with such documentary evidence as will relieve him from the possible inconvenience of search or detainment—events which may be rendered necessary by unsatisfactory replies on his part (*i*). He must also produce all the ship's papers, and his instructions (*k*). If his voyage or destination be alternative, the fact should appear on the papers, for otherwise belligerent cruisers may be misled (*l*). General clearances are regarded critically, and, if available to an enemy's port, should be attended by affidavit as to the inoffensive nature of the cargo (*m*). It is essential that the ship's papers should be regular and in order (*n*). A deficiency of the usual and proper documents, or inconsistency amongst the documents themselves, though not necessarily entailing condemnation, may involve the carrying of the vessel into port for adjudication, and render the neutral liable for the captors' costs. The carrying of false papers, and the suppression or destruction of papers, is ordinarily a heinous offence, which may involve confiscation of the property (*o*).

It has on occasion been provided by treaty that the neutral master shall in the first instance proceed on board the war-vessel with his papers; and it is doubtless generally within the discretion of the commander of a belligerent vessel to forego the right of visit on these terms. As a matter of right and common usage, however, a boat's crew may be sent

(*i*) The Eenrom, 2 Rob. 15.

(*k*) The Concordia, 1 Rob. 120.

(*l*) The Juffrau Anna, 1 Rob. 120.

(*m*) The Eenrom, *supra*.

(*n*) The Calypso, 2 Rob. 158.

(*o*) The subject of papers to be carried, and of irregularities in connexion with the same, will be found under the head "Sailing under False Papers," pp. 219—228.

off to the neutral vessel as already mentioned. The refusal by the master of a neutral vessel to permit the ship's papers to be taken on board a belligerent cruiser when demanded, to be there examined, may be deemed a resistance to the right of visit and search (*p*).

The right of visit and search implies a power, in the prize court of the belligerent to which a captured neutral vessel is sent for adjudication, to order an examination of the cargo sufficient to ascertain its character. And evidence so acquired may be employed as further proof of the culpability of the voyage (*q*).

The consequence of resistance of the right of visit and search is confiscation,—a subject which will be considered in its place (*r*).

In the same manner as the right to capture neutral vessels engaged in obnoxious trade involves the antecedent right to visit and search neutral vessels, so the right to visit and search carries with it the naturally consequent right to carry into port for adjudication vessels as to which the visit and search —both or either—have established *primâ facie* grounds for further investigation. To the consideration of this subject let us now briefly refer.

(*p*) *The Peterhoff*, *Blatch. Pr. Ca.* 464.

(*q*) *The Springbok*, *ib.* 349.

(*r*) *Vide* p. 212, *infra*, "Resistance to Visit and Search."

CARRYING OF SUSPECTED VESSELS INTO PORT FOR EXAMINATION AND ADJUDICATION.

The right of visit and search being in itself in accordance with the law of nations, no compensation is claimable by neutrals on the ground that the exercise of the right resulted in proving that there was as a fact no just cause for putting it in force. If, however, special treaty provisions be made as to the mode of execution, no doubt a belligerent commander acting in defiance of such stipulations would expose himself to a claim for indemnification on the part of the aggrieved neutral. The right of visit and search carries with it, as we have seen, the right in case of need to carry the visited vessel into port for further examination and adjudication; but this right is qualified by the condition that it must be exercised only if there be reasonable grounds for proceeding to such an extremity. The search is lawful, whether in all cases reasonable or not; but the subsequent capture may be a tortious act giving rise to a claim for costs and damages (*a*). On the other hand, if the carrying into port be caused by any act or default on the part of the neutral master, he may be mulcted in the captors' costs. The important subject of Adjudication, with the attendant subjects Costs and Damages, will be specially discussed under the general head Obligations of Belligerents (*b*).

It lies with the neutral master to prove to the reasonable satisfaction of the commander of the belligerent war-ship

---

(*a*) *La Jeune Eugenie*, 2 *Mason*, 439.

(*b*) *Vide* p. 316, *infra*.

that both voyage and cargo are in conformity with the rights and lawful requirements of the belligerent; and on the master's failure to supply proofs in all respects satisfactory, he must accept the consequence of being taken into port for further investigations. A seizure so arising is, as has been already indicated (*c*), a capture for which underwriters are liable on due notice of abandonment.

(*c*) *Vide* p. 68, *supra*.

CAPTURE AND CONFISCATION OF

CONTRABAND OF WAR.

For convenience, the consideration of this important subject has been divided under the following heads, viz.:—

Definition; a brief preamble.

Ancient Usage; showing the rule of confiscation in early times.

Modern Usage; the principles held to govern the usage nowadays.

Neutral right to carry on trade; indicating that neutrals may carry on their ordinary trade as between themselves without interference from belligerents; and that they may trade freely with belligerent ports not blockaded, but subject to the belligerent right to confiscate any contraband of war conveyed by them to the enemy.

What goods are of a Contraband Nature?—A classification of goods into three heads, viz. (a) Warlike; (b) Peaceful; (c) Equivocal; with a review of treaties bearing on the subject of classification.

Goods of Equivocal Nature. (In past times.)—A survey of the equivocal articles which have been regarded as contraband: treaties in the same connexion: the test of the quality to be ascribed to the goods.

Provisions. (In past times.)—Whether to be allowed to go free, to be pre-empted, or to be condemned as contraband. The general principle. Precedents.

Goods of Equivocal Nature, including Provisions. (Nowadays.)—The articles which in the present days of iron vessels and steam propulsion are likely to be regarded as contraband or subjected to pre-emption.

The Belligerent Destination. (Nothing can be condemned as contraband of war which is not destined for belligerent use.)—The circumstance that the destination of the ship is neutral will not render warlike goods non-contraband if their ulterior destination be hostile.

Application of the Penalty of Confiscation.—If the master be guilty of fraudulent misconduct, the ship may be condemned as well as the contraband goods. Contraband goods taint and involve in condemnation permissive goods belonging to the same owner. No freight is payable in respect of contraband goods by their captors, &c.

Summary of the above.

Insurance.—Observations generally.

Definition. — "Contraband," from *contra*, and the Low Latin *bandum*, a proclamation; the word *bandum* having come down to us as "ban," more familiar in its plural form "banns." "Contraband," therefore, that which is contrary to proclamation. The term is, however, within the meaning of the law of nations to be understood as implying a condition of war; so that in this sense, before any article can be considered contraband of war, it must appear that it has become so owing to hostilities (*d*). According to Dr. Twiss, the term was first used in 1625, when it was employed in an

(*d*) Wilbraham *v.* Wartnaby, 1 Lloyd & Wels. 144.

international treaty to describe articles which neutrals might not rightfully carry to an enemy's country in time of war.

To constitute goods contraband of war, two conditions have to be fulfilled, viz. :—

(1) The articles must be subservient to warlike uses; and

(2) They must be intended for use by a belligerent.

These several conditions will be considered presently; but it may be convenient first to briefly review the ancient and the modern usage in respect of contraband generally, and, further, to consider the position of neutrals as regards their right to carry on their ordinary commerce, notwithstanding that the nations with whom they are accustomed to trade may be engaged in hostilities as between themselves.

Ancient Usage.—The ancient practice was to forbid by proclamation all commerce whatever between neutral states and the adverse belligerent, and to deem adherents of the enemy all merchants who, disregarding the proclamation, continued to trade with his ports. Such a practice was, however, founded solely on an arbitrary right, and consequently, in course of time, it gave way to more equitable principles. According to Chancellor Kent (*e*), the ancient practice was to seize the contraband goods and keep them on paying their value; but it may be doubted whether such a gentle mode of repressing trade with the enemy, which it was originally deemed rightful to forbid absolutely, found favour to any great extent or for any considerable period. For to give and maintain practical effect to a prohibition to carry on a certain trade, measures more actively deterrent are required than the mere resort to pre-emption. Sir W. Scott, indeed, in *The Neutralitet* (*f*), remarked that the ancient practice was to

(*e*) International Law, 2nd ed., p. 338.

(*f*) 3 Rob. 295.

condemn ships found to be carrying contraband of war, and declared that it could not be denied that this practice was perfectly defensible on every principle of justice.

Modern Usage.—The principle underlying the modern application of the law of nations in relation to contraband is the right of a belligerent to prohibit and prevent the supply to the enemy by neutrals of all articles calculated to strengthen the enemy's hand, or to enable or encourage him to persevere in the prosecution of hostilities. A nation which has exhausted all peaceable means of redress, without success, has no other resource than force of arms; and in the prosecution of such a final appeal to justice the belligerent has, by universal consent, the right to demand that non-combatants shall stand aside and do nothing to stimulate the resistance of the foe. In order to reduce the latter to submission the belligerent may blockade all or any of the enemy's ports, and confiscate all supplies and property of whatever kind involved in an attempt to violate the blockade. If blockade be impracticable or inconvenient the belligerent has none the less the right to impose a qualified blockade of another kind, by which it is forbidden to neutrals to carry to the enemy any goods in the nature of warlike supplies. This is a prohibitive right so well known and understood that it goes without saying; and although it may be reasonable and proper that, on the outbreak of hostilities, belligerents should declare what are the supplies which they intend to regard as unlawful or contraband, the circumstance that no such list has been published cannot be averred by neutrals as a justification for the shipment of munitions of war to a country known to be engaged in hostilities. The public declaration of war, or the actual outbreak of hostilities, is regarded as *de facto* a notice to all the world that warlike supplies sent to either of the belligerents will be looked upon by the other as contraband.

As regards supplies distinctly warlike, there can be no doubt as to their unlawfulness, without special declaration of the fact. But there are goods of equivocal use—goods *ancipitis usûs*, as they are technically termed—which are not necessarily contraband, but become so if so considered by a belligerent. And there can be no doubt that, as a belligerent may reasonably be deemed the best judge of what supplies to the enemy constitute a danger to himself, he has the right to prohibit the supply of such articles as he, in his discretion, may deem contraband of war. A general declaration as to contraband must, however, be subject to any special treaty engagements which may have been already entered into between the declarant and any neutral powers.

Neutral right to carry on trade.—This right on the part of neutrals falls more correctly under the general head Rights of Neutrals (*g*), but some reference to the subject may fitly be made here. And let it be noted that while belligerents possess an undoubted right to prohibit neutrals from carrying the sinews of war to the enemy, such right does not extend to this, that belligerents are entitled to exercise any interference whatever in the ordinary trade of neutrals *inter se*. Thus if A. and B. go to war, it is the right of each to seize and confiscate munitions of war shipped by non-belligerent Z. to the other; but if neutrals Y. and Z. choose to trade in such articles between themselves they have a perfect right to do so, and any attempt at interference on the part of A. or of B. would be contrary to the law of nations. It is bad enough that Y. and Z. should be restricted in their ordinary dealings with B. because A. chooses to declare war against him: but it would be altogether intolerable if A. or B., quarrelling amongst themselves, should claim on that ground a right to

(*g*) *Vide* p. 345, *infra*.

interfere in the commerce between Y. and Z. In these remarks the trade between the neutrals has been assumed to be *bonâ fide*, but if it were to appear that Z., while ostensibly shipping warlike stores to Y., was really using him, with his connivance, as a conduit pipe for illicit supply to one of the belligerents, the other might reasonably decline to permit the subterfuge. Neutrals have an undoubted right to carry on their ordinary lawful trade, but this right is conditional and not absolute. That is, it is subject to the condition that it shall not interfere with the rights of belligerents to conduct hostilities to a conclusion free from any interposition on the part of neutrals. If the neutral trade operates as such an interposition, then the condition on which the trade is by the law of nations permissible is broken and it becomes unlawful. Or, rather, it is not unlawful within the strict meaning of the word, but only in the sense that it gives to belligerents the right to seize and confiscate. There are two conflicting rights, that of the neutral to carry on his ordinary trade, and that of the belligerent to prohibit such trade so far as it strengthens the hand of the enemy, and to confiscate property seized whilst being so conveyed. So that while the neutral may engage in carrying contraband goods to a belligerent, he must do so with his eyes open to the consequences if his ship should be visited and searched by the opposite belligerent. This position was clearly laid down by Lord Westbury in the case *Ex parte Chavasse, In re Grazebrook* (*h*). "In the view of international law" said his lordship, "the commerce of nations is perfectly free and unrestricted. The subjects of each nation have a right to interchange the products of labour with the inhabitants of every other country. If hostilities

(*h*) 12 L. T. (N. S.) 249. *Vide*, also, The Helen, 35 L. J. Ad. 2. With respect to the municipal prohibition of exportation of contraband goods, *vide* p. 350, *infra*.

occur between two nations and they become belligerents, neither belligerent has a right to impose, or to require a neutral government to impose, any restrictions on the commerce of its subjects." And similarly in *The Santissima Trinidad* (*i*) the United States Courts said, "There is nothing in our laws or in the laws of nations that forbids our citizens from sending armed vessels, as well as munitions of war, to foreign ports for sale. It is a commercial adventure which no nation is bound to prohibit, and which only exposes the persons engaged in it to the penalty of confiscation."

At the commencement of this chapter it was stated that to constitute goods contraband of war, two conditions have to be fulfilled viz:—

(1) The articles must be subservient to warlike uses; and

(2) They must be intended for use by a belligerent.

It has, then, first to be considered what are the goods which may be held to come within the first-named condition.

(1) **What goods are of a contraband nature?**—For present purposes merchandise may be classified under three heads, viz.:—

(a) Goods essentially of a character to be used for warlike purposes, such as arms and ammunition.

(b) Goods essentially for peaceful uses, such, for instance, as silk-stuffs, and articles of purely domestic use or of ornament.

(c) Goods capable of use either for warlike or peaceful purposes, commonly known as goods *ancipitis usûs*, such as provisions, naval stores, and money.

(*i*) 7 *Wheat.* 283.

The first and second classes present no difficulty. It is equally clear that rifles, bayonets, and rifle cartridges must be deemed contraband, and that silk dresses, lace curtains, and grand pianos must go free. The difficulty is as to the equivocal goods, the articles of twofold use. That we may the better understand the light in which such goods are to be regarded, let us briefly review some of the more important of the public declarations and treaties relative to contraband generally, from early times.

In 1625 a treaty was concluded between the Dutch and the English, known as the treaty of Southampton, declaring provisions generally, under the title "*munitions de bouche*," to be contraband; and Charles I., at the close of the year, in accordance with that treaty, published a declaration that "all ships carrying corn or other victuals, or any munitions of war, to or for the King of Spain, or any of his subjects, shall and ought to be esteemed as lawful prize." And in the following year King Charles issued a further proclamation that the articles intended by his previous declaration were "ordinance, armes of all sortes, powder, shott, match, brimstone, copper, iron, cordage of all kindes, hempe, sail, canvas, danuce pouldavis, cables, anchors, mastes, rafters, boate oars, balcks, capraves, deale board, clap board, pipe staves, and vessels, and vessel staffe, pitch, tarr, rosen, okam, corne, graine, and victualls of all sortes, of provisions of shipping, and all munition of warr, or of provisions for the same, according to former declarations and acts of State, made in this behalfe in the time of Queen Elizabeth, of famous memorie."

Twiss (*k*) regards this as probably the earliest catalogue in detail of goods deemed contraband of war, for apparently the declarations of "Queen Elizabeth of famous memorie" did not precisely specify the articles prohibited. He considers,

(*k*) Law of Nations, 2nd ed. p. 238.

indeed, that it was the Admiralty Court judgments in her reign that gave rise to the subsequent catalogue of prohibited goods. Three months' grace was allowed by Charles, and after that all vessels engaged in such prohibited trade, or returning after having delivered contraband cargoes, were liable to be seized and forfeited, with all the goods found on board. The proclamation added that this was no innovation, other states and princes on similar occasions having inflicted the like penalties. Although this proclamation covers provisions, it would appear that some difference of opinion existed, both then and subsequently, as to the propriety of including corn amongst the goods absolutely prohibited. And in the Treaty of Paris, in 1655, between France and the Hanse Towns, provisions were omitted from the list of contraband goods. The catalogue comprised in this treaty details the different kinds of military arms, accoutrements, and munitions comprehended in the treaty, and includes horses, cordage, and sailcloth. Corn, vegetables, and other food stuffs were to be regarded as lawful merchandise, unless shipped to besieged ports, in which case the provisions were to be liable to pre-emption at a fair valuation on the part of the besiegers. If the price could not be agreed upon, the master was to be allowed to retire with his ship and cargo without further interference. On the model of this treaty, it is stated, subject to the omission of cordage and sailcloth, were framed almost all the subsequent treaties in the seventeenth century relative to contraband of war. In 1713 a treaty was entered into at Utrecht between France and England, supplementing deficiencies in a similar treaty made in 1677. In this 1713 treaty was set forth a detailed list of the goods to be considered contraband. The list mentions by name all sorts of arms, ammunition, and accoutrements for men; saltpetre; horses with their furniture; and "all other warlike instruments whatever." Then follows a list of goods not to be reckoned prohibited. It includes "all sorts of cloaths," and all other woven manufactures; wearing apparel and the stuffs therefor; gold and silver, whether coined or not; metals by name; coals; grain; tobacco; provisions, including wine, salt, &c.; cotton, hemp, flax, anchors, masts, and other ships' fittings, and all other goods not worked into any warlike form. All such non-prohibited goods to be freely carried, even to the enemy's ports, always excepting ports or places under blockade or investment. The circumstance that a treaty expressly sets forth that certain named goods are not to be regarded as contraband, not unnaturally suggests that in the absence of any such agreement it might be open to doubt whether such goods are contraband or not. Some of the articles thus declared to be free are, or at any rate at that time were, certainly by the law of nations liable to be forfeited. The law of nations, in fact, may be taken to be based on the broad principle that a belligerent is entitled to prevent the conveyance of any goods to the enemy calculated to assist him in carrying on the war.

The treaty of commerce formulated in 1796 between Great Britain and the United States sets forth that under the denomination contraband of war shall be comprised all arms and implements serving for the purposes of war by land or by sea, and mentions by name as examples various arms, accoutrements, and warlike implements, including horse furniture and saltpetre. Sulphur is not specially mentioned; and it could, perhaps, scarcely be regarded as within the general head of arms and implements serving for the purposes of war. The treaty then goes on to notice under the same denomination timber for ship-building, tar or rosin, copper in sheets, sails, hemp and cordage, and generally whatever may serve directly for the equipment of vessels, unwrought iron and fir planks only excepted; all such articles to be just objects of contraband whenever attempted to be carried to an enemy.

After enumerating the goods absolutely contraband, reference is made in the treaty to the subject of "provisions and other articles not generally contraband," but liable to be regarded as such. In order to avoid inconveniences and misunderstandings likely to arise in connexion with such articles, the treaty provides that any "articles so becoming contraband according to the existing law of nations" shall, on seizure, not be confiscated; but that the owners shall be "speedily and completely indemnified" by payment of full value, together with a reasonable mercantile profit, the freight, and any demurrage incident to the detention.

The treaty concluded between Great Britain and Brazil in 1827 adopts, with one exception, the above list of goods to be deemed contraband. The exception, as pointed out by Twiss, is that whereas the 1796 treaty includes "whatever may serve directly for the equipment of vessels," the 1827 treaty with Brazil substitutes for the word "vessels" the phrase "vessels of war."

The treaty of 1796 is interesting as comprising a clearly defined list of articles to be deemed absolute contraband, whilst recognising the fact that there are other goods liable to be regarded as such, but that, as to these, they shall be the subjects of pre-emption and not of confiscation. When war was in progress against Russia in 1854, all Russian ports were invested by the allied fleets; consequently no question of contraband could well arise. In 1877, on the outbreak of hostilities between Russia and Turkey, the former power published a Decree, article VI. of which declared the following to be contraband, viz:—

> Small arms and artillery, mounted or in detached pieces; ammunition for fire-arms, such as projectiles, fuses for shells, balls, priming, cartridges, cartridge cases, powder, saltpetre, sulphur, explosive materials and ammunition, such as mines, torpedoes, dynamite, pyroxyline, and

other fulminating substances; artillery, engineering, and transport materials, such as gun carriages, caissons, cartridge boxes, campaigning forges, canteens, pontoons, &c.; articles of military equipment and attire, such as pouches, cartridge boxes, bags, cuirasses, sappers' tools, drums, saddles and harness, articles of military dress, tents, &c., and generally everything destined for military or naval forces.

These articles, when found on board neutral ships and destined for an enemy's port, to be liable to seizure and confiscation, except the quantity necessary for the use of the ship on which the seizure was made.

It is clear that the law of nations as regards contraband goods cannot be settled by a declaration on the part of any one nation, for such a declaration for war purposes might well omit from the list of contraband some articles which, in the case of another nation, might be regarded as essentially noxious. And if a list should be published enumerating, under the head of contraband of war, articles not previously commonly so regarded, the fact might create controversy and perhaps difficulties between the declarant and neutral powers. On the general principle, however, that a belligerent shall be allowed to prohibit the shipment to the enemy of all goods calculated to increase or prolong the resistance of the latter, reasonable or even indulgent latitude should presumably be permitted to such belligerent in his enumeration of the goods which he regards as coming, in his case, within this description. And if such isolated declarations are not to be looked upon as expositions of the public law respecting contraband, it is obvious that no mere international treaties can have any greater effect. This law, however, being as to its practice by no means clearly laid down, it is at least interesting to consider its application by such light as may be thrown upon it by international treaties, and especially by the public declarations of belligerents. As we have seen, some articles are so obviously contraband that even to specify them in a proclamation might seem superfluous. Others, again, are so clearly of a non-warlike character that a neutral may ship them to a belligerent without fear of the risk of confiscation. It is the third class—the goods *ancipitis usûs*—which creates the difficulty. Whether goods of this class can properly be confiscated or not will depend upon various circumstances—circumstances connected with the destination, the probable use, and especially with the place of production. The subject of such goods is important and demands special consideration.

Goods of Equivocal Nature. (In past times.)—The articles specially coming under this head, according to the views held in earlier days, would seem to be in the main the following, viz.:—

Naval stores generally, including specially tar, pitch, resin, hemp, cordage, sailcloth, tallow, masts, spars, planks, anchors, copper sheets, and the like. Naval stores being prohibited, ships suitable for warlike uses would naturally be similarly regarded. Horses, saddles, and money have also been regarded as contraband. Corn and provisions stand on a somewhat different footing, as will appear presently.

Such articles were or were not regarded as contraband according to their destination (*l*). If destined for a purely trading port of the enemy they were more probably held to be pacific goods. If, on the other hand, they were seized on their way to a governmental naval port or arsenal, they were deemed contraband, and were confiscated accord-

(*l*) Sailcloth, according to The Neptunus, 3 Rob. 108, has been universally contraband.

ingly (*m*). It was not *all* timber which was liable to confiscation: it had to be made clear that the timber was of such lengths and dimensions as to "directly serve" for shipbuilding (*n*). But articles of mixed shipbuilding use, partly innocent and partly noxious, were liable to condemnation as a whole (*o*). Masts were, in the case of *The Charlotte* (*p*) and *The Staadt Embden* (*q*), expressly declared to be contraband *per se*. In the case of *The Twende Brodre* (*r*), with a mixed timber cargo from Christiansand to St. Malo or Brest, the cargo was restored on the ground that it was not of a kind used in naval construction. But ship-timber was apparently not in all cases necessarily contraband, even if bound to a hostile military port. So at least it was decided, in 1807, by the Council of Prizes at Paris, where the Council decided against the captors on the ground that the timber was of an ordinary character, and not exclusively applicable to the building of ships of war (*s*). Tallow, again, whilst contraband to a port of naval equipment, was not so regarded if shipped to a purely mercantile port (*t*).

The subject of the contraband nature of naval stores was a fertile source of dispute between Great Britain and the Baltic Powers throughout the eighteenth century, and various special stipulations were made from time to time respecting these articles. The practice of this country was, in Sir W. Scott's time, to relax the prohibition against the shipment of pitch and tar to the enemy's country when such goods were the

---

(*m*) The Jonge Margaretha, 1 Rob. 194; *The Peterhoff, Blatch. Pr. Ca.* 463.

(*n*) The Eendraght, 1 Rob. 23.

(*o*) The Eleonora Wilhelmina, 6 Rob. 331.

(*p*) 5 Rob. 305.

(*q*) 1 Rob. 29.

(*r*) 4 Rob. 33.

(*s*) Maritime Warfare, p. 257.

(*t*) The Neptunus, 3 Rob. 108.

produce of the country from which they were exported (*u*). The reason for this leniency was that these articles formed so considerable a part of the native produce and ordinary commerce of the countries principally exporting them, that it would have been a very harsh exercise of belligerent right to subject them to confiscation. But this concession against the right of confiscation was not absolute. The goods, whilst exempted from condemnation, remained subject to the substituted milder right of pre-emption on the part of the captors if they should so elect. It might be a hardship that peaceful neutrals should be debarred from shipping to the enemy, in the ordinary course of the trade, goods forming the staple product of their country; but, on the other hand, it would equally be a hardship that a belligerent should be debarred from stopping the supply of stores directly subservient to the maintenance of hostilities by the foe. Pre-emption was a *via media* for both neutral and belligerent, but attached to this belligerent concession were the conditions—(1) *bona fides* on the part of the neutral shipper (*v*); and (2) that the latter should satisfactorily establish that the goods seized were really the produce of his own country (*x*). Hemp was not, *per se*, liable to confiscation or pre-emption, but only so if fit for naval purposes (*y*).

In *The Neptunus*, *supra*, although tallow was restored as being destined to a non-military port, sailcloth in the same vessel was condemned as being universally contraband. Copper sheets fit for the metalling of vessels have been confiscated, being a "manufactured article immediately serving for the equipment of ships of war," and therefore

(*u*) The Sarah Christina, 1 Rob. 241.
(*v*) The Sarah Christina, *supra*.
(*x*) The Twee Juffrouwen, 4 Rob. 242; The Apollo, 4 Rob. 158.
(*y*) The Gute Gesellschaft, 4 Rob. 94; The Evart Evarts, *ibid.* 354.

contrary to treaty (z). Iron in an unmanufactured state has been treated with indulgence, anchors and chains being regarded as directly contraband. On the same reasoning hemp has been more favourably regarded than cordage; and wheat (to be considered presently) than final preparations of it for human consumption. Such articles as saltpetre and sulphur suitable for making gunpowder, and all kinds of machinery for manufacturing arms or ammunition, have always been confiscated by the British Prize Courts. Lead, and the various components of explosive materials, would doubtless be subject to similar treatment. In *The Teutonia* (a) nitrate of soda seems to have been regarded as contraband. But as Sir W. Scott laid down in *The Jonge Margaretha*, *supra*, the most important distinction is whether the articles are intended for the ordinary use of life, or even for mercantile ships' use; or whether they are going with a probable destination to military use. This was the principle applied to a cargo of resin in 1747 (b). Neutral vessels may lawfully have on board such quantity of contraband as may be required for their own use, but they may not carry a larger quantity on the suggestion of the speculation of purchasing other ships (c). The master in the case cited averred that the naval stores which he had on board were wanted for another ship which he designed purchasing at Batavia. The contrary principle, if admitted, would be an endless source of fraud.

Ships of war, *i.e.*, vessels evidently built or peculiarly adapted for warlike purposes, destined to be sold to the enemy, are contraband, being, as Sir W. Scott observed in *The Richmond* (d), most powerful instruments of mischief; but

(z) The Charlotte Fox, 5 Rob. 275.
(a) L. R. 4 P. C. 171.
(b) Nostra Senora de Begona, 5 Rob. 99.
(c) The Margaretha Magdalena, 2 Rob. 138.
(d) 5 Rob. 325.

each of such cases calls for consideration in accordance with the particular circumstances. *The Richmond* was an American vessel well adapted for use as a ship of war, under a false destination, and with contraband goods concealed on board, and with the avowed intention of sale to a belligerent.

Sir W. Scott in condemning the vessel remarked that the malignant nature of such a purpose was not a little increased by the indecent levity with which the master expressed himself, viz., that the vessel "would be seen playing round the East India Company's ships in the Bay of Bengal next season." In another case, a vessel (*e*) built in America and pierced to carry fourteen guns, and despatched to the Havana for sale, was condemned as contraband, though the master had been ordered, if he could not effect a sale, to ship a cargo by her. In two somewhat similar cases (*f*) the vessels, though in the first instance condemned in the Vice-Admiralty Court at the Bahamas, were on appeal ordered to be restored, they having been actually engaged in trade, and being of a more ambiguous construction. In a fourth case (*g*) the vessel was also restored, as it appeared that the purchaser, though he had bought her as a privateer, intended to employ her in trade, and had in fact done his best to fit her for such purpose. Finding the vessel unsuitable, however, he was intending to sell her again when she was seized on the charge of being contraband.

By a convention concluded between Great Britain and Russia in 1803, it was agreed that, in addition to other named articles, the following should be deemed contraband, viz., coined money, horses, and the necessary equipments of cavalry; all naval stores, the produce of either country, to be subject to the right of pre-emption.

(*e*) The Brutus, 5 Rob. App. 1.

(*f*) The Fanny, 24 March, 1804; The Neptune, 18 July, 1804.

(*g*) The Raven, 5 Rob. App. 1.

Provisions. (In past times.)—These, though certainly coming within the description of equivocal goods, have usually been placed in a somewhat exceptional position. That there is nothing of a contraband nature in provisions *per se* is obvious,—or, rather, provisions are no more contraband than most other articles shipped for the common use of nations in a state of peace. The early writers are not unanimous on the subject of provisions, some considering them as generally contraband, others denying that this is so unless the goods are being carried to besieged places. Corn, grain, and provisions of all sorts were declared contraband by Charles I. in 1626. And Sir W. Scott, in *The Jonge Margaretha* (*h*), stated that in 1673 it was expressly declared by a person of great knowledge and experience in the English Admiralty that, by its practice, corn, wine, and oil were liable to be deemed contraband; and that in much later times many sorts of provisions, such as butter, salted fish, and rice, had been so condemned. The learned judge proceeded to say that the modern established rule was that provisions were generally not contraband; but that they might, in special circumstances, become so. Circumstances specially mentioned were the nature and quality of the port of destination, and whether the goods were presumably intended for civil or for military use. Amongst the circumstances tending to prevent condemnation was the fact that the goods were the growth of the country exporting them; or that they were in a raw or unmanufactured state. But Sir W. Scott subsequently abandoned the port-of-destination theory. Thus, in *The Charlotte* (*i*) he stated that the character of the port was immaterial; since goods sent to a mercantile port might either be there applied to the use of privateers or conveyed to a port of naval equipment. In

(*h*) 1 Rob. 192.
(*i*) 5 Rob. 305.

1793 the British Government instructed their cruisers to stop all vessels carrying corn, flour, or meal to any port in France, and to send them to a British port for pre-emption by the government. Or, as an alternative, the ships might be released on the masters giving security that they would dispose of the cargo in the ports of some country in amity with Great Britain. This action was justified on the ground that the French Government had armed almost the whole of the labouring classes in France, and that in these circumstances it was, by the modern law of nations, permissible to powers at war with that country to resort to the measure of cutting off all supplies of provisions. This reasoning was resisted by the neutral powers, Sweden, Denmark and, especially, the United States, which denied that the circumstances gave any such right of interference with the legitimate and ordinary trade of neutrals. In 1794 a treaty was drawn up between Great Britain and the United States specifying the goods to be deemed contraband as between the two nations. On the subject of provisions, it was provided that, "whereas the difficulty of agreeing on the precise cases in which alone provisions and other articles, not generally contraband, may be regarded as such renders it expedient to provide against the inconveniences and misunderstandings which might thence arise," it was agreed that such articles should not be confiscated, but should be paid for by the captors—the price paid to be the full value with a reasonable profit, the freight, and the demurrage incident to the detention.

The subject of pre-emption *versus* confiscation in the case of provisions has from time to time been hotly debated, and it cannot be said that any generally accepted conclusion has resulted as to the real position in which, by the law of nations, the matter stands. From time to time this country, acting on what it has maintained to be its rights under this law, has condemned various articles of food. Thus, cheese fit for naval use and bound to a port of naval equipment has been confiscated (*k*). In the two cases cited neither cargo was actually bound to a naval port, but both had destinations not far removed from such ports, and the question of the propinquity was in each case regarded by the Court as an element of importance in deciding as to the quality to be attributed to the cargo. In the case of *The Ranger* (*l*), ships' biscuits improperly shipped, under a proclamation permitting the carriage to Cadiz of provisions for the relief of famine, were condemned, Sir W. Scott remarking that such a shipment was a gross breach of privilege. A cargo of wine destined to Brest but under false papers to Embden was condemned by the same judge. The wine was notoriously for naval use, and his lordship remarked that, in such a case, to apply the rule of pre-emption would be to show excessive and undue indulgence, especially as the vessel was sailing under a false destination (*m*). In this case it was pleaded that the wine, having been shipped at another port of the same country, viz., Bordeaux, could not be considered contraband; but Sir W. Scott ruled that the transfer of contraband from one port to another in the same country was to be treated as an original importation. Barley and oats shipped from an enemy's port in a neutral vessel, and intended for the enemy's forces in another country, were, in *The Commercen* (*n*), condemned by the American Courts. Provisions, it was declared, might become contraband if intended for the use of the enemy's army or navy or destined for a port of naval equipment; and if the growth of the enemy's country, and destined for the use of its forces, were *contraband*, although bound for a neutral port. The circumstances in this case were peculiar. Great

---

(*k*) The Vrow Margaretha, 6 Rob. 92; The Zelden Rust, *ibid.* 93.

(*l*) 6 Rob. 125.

(*m*) The Edward, 4 Rob. 68.

(*n*) 1 *Wheaton*, 382.

Britain was at war with the United States, and also with France, and the stores in question were being carried by a Swedish vessel from Limerick to Bilboa, for the use of the allied forces in the Spanish peninsula.

During the recent hostile relations between France and China the French Government announced its intention to treat rice bound for certain of the open China ports as contraband of war. The government stated that this resolve had been come to mainly in the belief that large quantities of rice were being forwarded to these ports, and that the stoppage of the supply would materially affect the Pekin government. The British ambassador in Pekin refused to recognise the right claimed by France. The home authorities, however, decided that the exercise of the right should not be opposed by physical force, and that its legality must be determined by the French prize courts, subject to ulterior diplomatic action. But the preliminaries of peace were shortly after settled, and no case of the kind appears to have occurred (*o*). Rice, as well as butter and salt fish, had been previously condemned as contraband in 1747 and 1748. Tobacco was on the occasion of a war between Spain and the States General confiscated by the former on the ground that the article was rightly to be considered amongst victuals, since by its use the consumption of these might be prolonged. The English shippers of the tobacco in vain contended that tobacco was not a nutritive plant, and in the result the King of England granted them letters of reprisal against the subjects of the King of Spain in order that they might so make good their loss (*p*).

Goods of Equivocal Nature, including Provisions. (Nowadays.) —The precedents cited above relate for the most part to times

(*o*) Pitt Cobbett's Leading Cases, p. 226.

(*p*) Law of Nations, Twiss, 2nd ed. p. 249.

when the conditions of naval warfare differed widely from those of the present day. In most cases, therefore, the conclusions arrived at by the courts are now valuable rather as expositions of the principles by which the real quality of equivocal goods is to be tested, than as fixing, once and for all, the character of the articles then submitted for adjudication. For it is easy to see that many articles which in the days of wooden sailing vessels might be regarded as eminently capable of adaptation to warlike uses, must needs, in these times of iron steamships, be regarded from the opposite point of view: and contrariwise. In bygone days the equivocal goods declared to be contraband of war have been commonly, if not exclusively, naval stores, horses and harness, and provisions. As regards the former, tar, pitch, resin, tallow, planks, and copper sheathing were the common subjects of condemnation in cases where they were intended for a port of naval equipment. Nowadays they could scarcely be logically subjected to such a fate. Hemp, cordage, masts, and spars, although in a measure useful for iron vessels, are certainly more the attribute of those built of wood. Anchors and sailcloth are common necessaries, but it is not every anchor that will be useful to modern war-ships; and of these vessels many are quite independent of sails. So that, owing to the modern conditions of warfare, articles formerly sternly seized and ruthlessly condemned, as partaking at least as much of the nature of warlike as of peaceful goods, may now, one might well believe, be allowed to rank with permissive goods, as possessing few, if any, of the essentials of warlike stores. The recent Russian list of contraband goods already set forth (*q*) makes no mention, by name, of any of the articles just enumerated, and they would presumably no longer be held to

(*q*) Page 166, *supra*.

come within the general words "everything destined for military or naval forces."

Horses, saddles, harness, and provender, if shipped in any considerable quantity to a nation carrying on belligerent military operations, would probably be deemed at the present, as they have been in the past, military stores, and as such liable to confiscation.

PROVISIONS stand on a peculiar footing, the law of nations not being so clearly defined in respect of these as could be wished. But, broadly stated, the position appears to be approximately this:—The right to cut off food supplies altogether, with a view to starve the foe into submission, has in certain circumstances been asserted on the part of some and denied by others. The right contended for, however, has not been to condemn as contraband, but to order off or to pre-empt. Food-stuffs in an unprepared state, such as grain or flour, though liable in certain cases to pre-emption, are more favourably regarded than if in a manufactured state ready for use. Supplies of a kind specially valuable for military or naval purposes, such as ships' biscuits or Dutch cheeses, may be condemned as contraband. Food supplies of whatever kind shipped to the enemy's forces, wherever stationed, would presumably occupy a similar position. At one time great weight was attached to the destination. Thus food supplies to a port of naval equipment would probably be condemned, whilst similar goods to a non-military port would be allowed to pass. But while the case as regards goods to military ports presumably remains unaltered, modern facilities of inland communication must be held to have disposed of the theory that supplies carried to a mercantile port are to be regarded as *ipso facto* intended for mercantile uses. The principle embodied in the Declaration of Paris, that free ships make free goods, however, will, it may be supposed, be found in the future to have greatly narrowed the question of contraband,—always supposing, that is, that this item of the treaty is destined to remain an accepted principle of modern naval warfare. Formerly, owing to the restricted inland communication between the continental states, each nation was compelled to import necessaries direct. The hostile destination of the ship stamped the cargo as enemy property, and such property was liable to seizure, even in neutral vessels. So long as the Declaration of Paris holds good, enemy property can be freely carried in neutral vessels. But still more important, owing to the present network of railways on the Continent, any continental power can effect its shipping through neighbouring neutral ports and in the names of neutrals, and it will usually be a comparatively simple matter to do the national marketing in adjacent countries. So that a belligerent continental power will in future be ordinarily under no such imperative necessity to trade through its own ports.

COAL AND MODERN WARLIKE STORES AND APPLIANCES.—The articles which would appear to have taken the place of the hemp, pitch, cordage, sailcloth, and so forth, of former days, are Coal, Electric Wire and Cables, Chain Cables, Wire Ropes, Hawsers, and Netting, Ships' Plates, Marine Engines, Boilers, Shafts, &c., Fire Bars, Iron Bars and Rivets, Cement, and the like. The chief of these is coal. Coal is to the steamship what sails and sailcloth are—or were—to the sailing vessel; and if a naval power could be completely cut off from its fuel supplies, it is obvious that its fleet would be rendered useless. From this it follows that coal shipped to an enemy port may rightly be regarded as contraband of war.

To an inquiry whether the Queen's proclamation of neutrality in 1859 contemplated coal as contraband, it was replied that "The prize court of the captor is the competent tribunal to decide whether coal is or is not contraband of war, and it is obviously impossible for Her Majesty's Government as a neutral sovereign to anticipate the result of such decision. It appears, however, to Her Majesty's Government that, having regard to the present state of naval armaments, coal may in many cases be rightly held to be contraband of war, and therefore that all who engage in the traffic must do so at a risk from which Her Majesty's Government cannot relieve them" (*r*). And early in 1854 the carriage of coals to an enemy port in the Black Sea was stopped owing to a ministerial statement in the House of Commons that coals would be regarded by our cruisers as one of the articles *ancipitis usûs* not necessarily contraband, but liable to detention in circumstances warranting the suspicion that it was intended to apply the coals to the military or naval uses of the enemy. Pitt Cobbett, in his Leading Cases on International Law (*s*), says:—"In 1859 and 1870 coal was declared by France not to be contraband. According to Calvo the greater number of secondary states have expressed themselves in a similar manner with reference to this. In 1870, during the Franco-Prussian war, Great Britain held that the character of coal depended upon its destination, and refused to permit vessels to sail with it to the French fleet in the North Sea. Germany remonstrated against Great Britain's allowing its export under any circumstances" (*t*). It is impossible to forecast what view might prevail in the event of hostilities occurring in which the question became important, and was not provided for by treaty; but if a belligerent insisted on treating coal as contraband it would clearly be within his rights to do so. There might, however, be an exception to the exercise

(*r*) *Vide* Kent's Internat. Law, 2 ed. 337; and Bulletins, I. 1859, p. 1167. *Vide* also pp. 350-1, *infra*.

(*s*) *Re* The Jonge Margaretha, pp. 224-7.

(*t*) See, also, the correspondence between Earl Granville and Count Bernstorff, p. 350, *infra*. During the Franco-German war close restrictions on the sale of coal, by the national subjects, to belligerents were decreed by the United States and by Peru. (61 State Papers, pp. 665, 656-7.)

of the right in the case where a cargo of coals was shipped to a purely mercantile port with no presumption against its pacific use. Coal being an article of daily use, to condemn it absolutely and in all cases might be an extreme measure.

If at some future period petroleum or any other substance should take the place of coal as a steam or power-producing agent, such substance would doubtless be regarded as of an equivocal nature, and therefore subject to the rules governing equivocal articles generally.

By an Order in Council of 18th February, 1854, issued in anticipation of declaration of war, the following were prohibited either to be exported from the United Kingdom or carried coastwise, viz.:—

> "All arms, ammunition and gunpowder, military and naval stores, and the following articles, being articles which We have judged capable of being converted into or made useful in increasing the quantity of military or naval stores; that is to say,
>
> > "Marine engines, screw propellers, paddle-wheels, cylinders, cranks, shafts, boilers, tubes for boilers, boiler plates, fire bars, and every article (*sic*) or any other component part of an engine or boiler, or any article whatsoever which is, or can or may become, applicable for the manufacture of marine machinery" (*u*).

This, it is true, is not a public declaration of contraband, but it is useful as throwing a strong light on the class of naval stores which were in 1854 deemed by the British Government subservient to warlike uses. Two months after this prohibition the restriction on trade which it imposed was modified by a proclamation permitting the export of such articles to certain countries named, including all the British

(*u*) Bulletins, I. 1854, p. 198.

colonies, on a bond being given that the prohibited articles would be landed and entered at the port of destination.

TELEGRAPH CABLES and insulated wire suitable for submarine mining and other warlike uses would similarly be in danger of condemnation as articles of equivocal use especially subservient to warlike purposes. During the Franco-Prussian war of 1870, a vessel called *The International* (v), loaded with telegraph cables for France, was detained by the British authorities, on the ground that the contemplated shipment was contrary to the Foreign Enlistment Act (w). It was, however, shown that the undertaking for which the cables were required was of a purely commercial nature—a coastal submarine postal telegraph line—and the Court, setting aside the argument that the line when completed would equally subserve military purposes, ordered the vessel to be released. But as the Court was of opinion that the detention was, in the circumstances, warranted and justifiable, no order was made as to costs or damages.

If inland telegraph wires should ever be condemned as subservient to military uses, railway materials would seem to stand on the same footing.

There is not, and there can scarcely be formulated, a definite and comprehensive list of goods which are, and shall remain, confiscable as contraband of war, or which are liable to be so regarded. The principle governing the question is, however, very clearly defined, and time and circumstances only can show what are the articles coming lawfully within its application. As an illustration of this proposition may be mentioned the instance of the raw bulls' hides used by Spain to cover the floating batteries which that country was at one time fitting

(v) L. R. 3 A. & E. 321.

(w) For the Foreign Enlistment Act, *vide* p. 372, *infra*.

out for the purposes of attack on the fortress of Gibraltar. It was known that hides were to be used as the chief article of defence in the attack, and there can be no doubt that shipments of such articles to Algeçiras—the opposite side of the bay—would have been properly regarded as contraband of war (*x*). "The catalogue of contraband," said Sir W. Scott, in *The Jonge Margaretha* (*y*), "has varied very much, and sometimes in such a manner as to make it very difficult to assign the reason of the variations, owing to particular circumstances, the history of which has not accompanied the history of the decisions."

Any ships or vessels apparently intended to be devoted to warlike uses, or which might be regarded as specially adapted to such uses, would no doubt be regarded as of a contraband nature. It is obvious that, for purposes of transport especially, tug-boats and steam launches, their engines and appliances, might on occasion become highly necessary to a belligerent.

Condition (1)—Subservience to Warlike Uses—having now been dealt with, let us pass on to the consideration of condition (2),—

(2) **The Belligerent Destination.**—Neutrals possess, as we have seen, the right to ship warlike stores as between themselves, but they must not carry such articles to belligerents. It has by some been contended that this principle is to be literally applied, and that so long as warlike stores are shipped by a neutral to a neutral port they are absolutely free from belligerent confiscation; the question whether the property has a belligerent destination beyond such neutral port being altogether irrelevant; and that, while it must be admitted that belligerents have the right to visit and search, and, if need be, to carry into port for adjudication a neutral vessel

(*x*) Ward's Essay on Contraband, 1801, p. 248.

(*y*) 1 Rob. 192.

whose averment of neutral destination is mistrusted (z), on the facts proving to be as represented by the neutral master the vessel must be at once restored and allowed to proceed without further molestation. "Goods going to a neutral port," said Sir W. Scott, in *The Imina* (a), "cannot come under the description of contraband, all goods going there being equally lawful." But this description, with other expressions which fell from the learned judge in the same case, seem scarcely, when viewed by the context, to support the conclusion that, because the port of destination is neutral, a belligerent is *ipso facto* precluded from seizing the warlike articles. In the above case the facts were as follows:—A neutral vessel, bound from Dantzic to Amsterdam, was seized and brought in for carrying, as was alleged, warlike stores to an enemy port. But, as it proved, at the time of the capture the vessel was bound to the neutral port of Embden. For, on arriving at Elsinore, her master learnt that Amsterdam had been declared to be blockaded; whereupon he altered his course. Captors contended, however, that the *original* intention to proceed to Amsterdam with prohibited goods should be held to fix the voyage, and that the incident that the destination was subsequently altered was immaterial. But the learned judge rejected this contention. It was true, he said, that if the capture had taken place before the variation the original intention would have subjected the property to confiscation; but inasmuch as the variation had taken place before the capture, there was then no *corpus delicti*. It must be remembered that this was the point which the Court had to decide, and neither the decision nor observations leading to it should consequently be regarded as supporting the proposition that all goods going to a neutral port are *ipso facto* free from seizure. Sir

---

(z) *Vide* p. 154, *supra*. (a) 3 Rob. 167.

W. Scott's decisions on the subject of what are called Continuous Voyages (*b*) clearly show that his lordship by no means regarded the fact of an immediate neutral destination as of such sanctity as to preclude all question as to an ulterior destination towards which the neutral port might be but a first step. In the United States Courts it has been decided that the test of whether warlike articles are contraband is not solely whether they are being shipped to a neutral port, but whether they are intended for the enemy's use. *The Stephen Hart* (*c*) was the case of a neutral vessel captured by a Federal cruiser about twenty-five miles from Key West, Florida. She had on board a cargo of arms, ammunition, &c., loaded in England for Cardenas (Cuba), and the captors contended that it was contemplated to introduce these goods into the enemy's territory by breach of blockade; and they argued that if this was so, the mere fact that the vessel was neutral, and bound from one neutral port to another, would not avail as a defence against condemnation; and that if the goods were really intended for the enemy's use it was immaterial whether they were carried direct to a belligerent port or were first landed at Cardenas. In the result the cargo and—the master's conduct having been found to be fraudulent—the ship were both condemned, the Court observing that the continuous transportation of contraband goods into several intermediate voyages cannot in such cases make any part of the entire transportation a lawful transport; and that such voyages are not to be regarded as separate and distinct, but part of one unit, forming one entire transaction. "In order to constitute the unlawfulness of the transportation of contraband goods," said the Court, "it is not necessary that the immediate destination of the vessel and cargo should be to an enemy's

(*b*) As to which *vide* pp. 236—240, notably The Thomyris, p. 238, *infra*.

(*c*) Mar. Law Ca., 2 vol. 73; *Blatch. Pr. Ca.* 387. *Vide* also *The Bermuda*, 3 *Wall.* 551; *The Commercen*, 1 *Wheat. Rep.* 388.

country or port; for if the goods are contraband, and destined to the direct use of the enemy's army or navy, the transportation is illegal. . . . The proper test to be applied is, whether the contraband goods are intended for sale or consumption in the neutral market, or whether the direct and intended object of their transportation is to supply the enemy with them."

The *Springbok* (*d*) was a very similar case. The vessel was bound from London to Nassau, N. P. (Bahamas), with a mixed cargo, partly warlike, partly innocent, but all the property of one owner. It appeared that the intention was to tranship the goods at Nassau and thence to run the blockade of the Confederate ports. The whole cargo was condemned, the Court affirming the principles declared in *The Stephen Hart*; but the vessel was ultimately restored, on the ground that there was not sufficient proof that her owners knew that the ultimate destination of the cargo was a blockaded port.

Finally there occurred the case of *The Peterhoff* (*e*), which is especially interesting owing to the litigation which ensued in England in respect of policies of insurance granted on the cargo; to which proceedings reference will be made presently. The warlike stores were, in this case, shipped to the Mexican port of Matamoras, situated up the Rio Grande, forty miles from its mouth. The Rio Grande divides Texas from Mexico, Matamoras and the Texan town of Brownsville being on opposite sides of the river, at that part about sixty yards wide. The mouth of this river was not included in the general blockade of the Confederate ports, and it was found by the United States Courts that the obnoxious goods were intended to be carried to the enemy by means of lighters. The whole cargo and the ship were, in the first instance, condemned, all the claimants of the cargo having some more or

(*d*) *Blatch. Pr. Ca.* 434; 5 *Wall.* 1.
(*e*) *Blatch. Pr. Ca.* 463; 5 *Wall.* 28.

less obnoxious goods on board, and the master being found guilty of fraudulent conduct in various respects. As will presently appear, the ship and a portion of the cargo were restored on appeal to the Supreme Court, but the Court confirmed the confiscation of the distinctly warlike articles intended to be delivered to the enemy.

The above decisions make it abundantly clear that the American view of the law of nations in respect of contraband is that the point to be looked at is the ulterior destination of the warlike articles; and that from this issue the captors are not to be diverted by arguments based on the incident that the property, when seized, was in the course of transit to a neutral port. It is easy to see that the application of this principle may be, in some cases, attended by substantial difficulties, as, for instance, if the obnoxious goods are *primâ facie* shipped to what may be reasonably or plausibly alleged to be a neutral market, but it is, notwithstanding, contended by the captors that the intention was to carry the goods to the enemy *viâ* the neutral territory. But if the abstract principle be correct, the circumstance that it may occasionally be difficult of application is not to be allowed to interfere with its acceptance. That the principle as declared in the United States Courts is correct, and that it is also accepted in this country, is to be concluded from a consideration of the two suits which arose out of *The Peterhoff* seizure, viz., *Hobbs* v. *Henning*, and *Seymour* v. *London and Provincial Insurance Co.*, referred to under the head **Insurance** below.

A neutral vessel carrying contraband of war must on no account touch at an enemy's port (*f*). Nor, as was established by *The Edward* (*g*), must contraband goods be coasted from a belligerent commercial port to a port of naval equipment in the same country.

(*f*) The Trende Sostre, 6 Rob. 387.

(*g*) Page 175, *supra*.

(The subject of Continuous Voyages is considered in connexion with the offence of Engaging in the Privileged Trade of the Enemy, pp. 236—240, *infra*.)

Application of the Penalty of Confiscation.—It has already been remarked (*f*) that neutrals are within their strict rights in shipping contraband of war to belligerents; but that the exercise of such right is attended by the concurrent belligerent right of seizure and confiscation of the prohibited goods; though, in the case of ordinary provisions, the latter right is now usually softened down to that of pre-emption. The law of nations, rigorously applied, would appear to admit the principle that vessels engaged in contraband trade are themselves, as well as the contraband goods, liable to confiscation (*g*); and the Russian Government, in 1854, by proclamation adopted this principle. The milder rule of limiting the penalty of confiscation to the obnoxious article carried, together with any freight due to the ship in respect of it, may, however, be regarded as the rule now generally accepted. In cases where the right has been exercised of seizing enemy goods on board a neutral vessel, it has been usual to allow freight to the neutral vessel; but it is otherwise in the case of contraband articles carried by neutrals (*h*). Neutral owners must be made to feel that, though the ship herself may be released, to engage in the carriage of prohibited goods is still attended by the substantial disadvantages of loss of freight (where it has not been paid in advance), of time, and expenses. But if the condemnation of the goods, and the consequent confiscation of the freight, be due to deceit on the part of the shippers, the master may proceed against them for compensa-

(*f*) Page 160, *supra*.

(*g*) *Vide* 1 Rob. 288, note.

(*h*) The Mercurius, 1 Rob. 288.

tion (*i*). If the captain be found guilty of carrying false papers, or of similar misconduct calculated to defeat the rights of a belligerent, the ship will be involved in the fate of the cargo (*j*). The offence of carrying false papers, and of simulating or destroying papers, will be considered presently *per se* (*k*).

Where the ship belongs to the owner of contraband cargo, both are liable to condemnation; and the same principle has been held to apply where contraband goods appeared by the ship's papers to belong to a part-owner of the ship (*l*). The rule is that contraband contaminates any other property in the same vessel belonging to the owner of the contraband (*m*); but the application of this principle is, of course, subject to modification by treaty. Similarly, if contraband goods are carried in breach of special treaty engagements, the vessel may be condemned as well as the cargo (*n*). By the practice of the French prize courts both ship and cargo will be forfeited *en bloc* if three-fourths of the entire cargo consist of contraband. An innocent shipper and insurer of permissive goods is not to be held responsible for the shipment of contraband by other parties (*o*).

If the master carry contraband he will not be heard to aver ignorance of the contents of the objectionable packages (*p*); nor is it open to the owner of the vessel to aver ignorance of the master's act or that he acted contrary to orders; for the act of the master binds the owner (*q*). In former times the

(*i*) The Emanuel, 1 Rob. 296.

(*j*) The Franklin, 3 Rob. 217; The Edward, 4 *ib.* 68; The Ranger, 6 *ib.* 125.

(*k*) *Infra*, p. 219.

(*l*) The Jonge Tobias, 1 Rob. 329; *The Springbok; The Peterhoff*, *infra.*

(*m*) The Staadt Embden, 1 Rob. 26; *The Springbok*, *Blatch. Pr. Ca.* 434; *The Peterhoff*, *ib.* 464.

(*n*) The Neutralitet, 3 Rob. 296.

(*o*) Hobbs *v.* Henning, 34 L. J. C. P. 121.

(*p*) *The Springbok*, *Blatch. Pr. Ca.* 434; *The Peterhoff*, *ib.* 463.

(*q*) The Imina, 3 Rob. 167.

offence of carrying contraband to the enemy was not purged by successful delivery: the ship remained liable to confiscation on the homeward voyage. Nowadays, however, the vessel herself is not in ordinary cases held liable to confiscation; and, as observed by Sir W. Scott in *The Imina* (*r*), "under the present understanding of the law of nations you cannot generally take the proceeds in the return voyage. . . . If the goods are not taken *in delicto* and in the actual prosecution (of the intention) the penalty is not now generally held to attach." But where there has been misconduct on the part of the master, such as concealment of the contraband goods; or the use of papers showing a false destination; the vessel has been condemned on the return voyage, and not only the vessel, but her cargo also, though the latter was not purchased with the proceeds of the contraband goods (*s*). The soundness of these last decisions is questioned by Wheaton, who disputes the right to inflict a penalty when the offence no longer continues, arguing that if the offence is to be held to survive after termination of the actual *delictum*, it should logically be held to survive indefinitely, and not only for the return voyage. His opinion on this point is in accord with the principles laid down by the King's Advocate, Sir R. Wiseman, so far back as 1672.

Summary.—To constitute any article contraband of war two essential conditions must be fulfilled, viz. (1) the article must be adapted for warlike purposes, and (2) it must be destined for belligerent use. The circumstance that the ship is bound to a neutral port is strong presumptive evidence that the article is *bonâ fide* intended for neutral use. This presumption

(*r*) 3 Rob. 167.

(*s*) The Margaret, 1 Act. 335; The Rosalie and Betty, 2 Rob. 343; The Nancy, 3 Rob. 122.

may, however, be rebutted by the captor; but no mere unsupported allegation of a bare *intention* to deliver to the enemy will justify condemnation. The sole judge of the sufficiency of evidence, however, is in all cases the prize court of the captors. The fact that goods are not contraband of war will not necessarily ensure that they shall not be captured and brought in for adjudication. If, on restoration, the bringing-in be attributed to the fault of the shipmaster, he may be called upon to pay compensation to the captors. On the other hand, if the capture prove unwarrantable, damages may be awarded against captors. If the goods be condemned as contraband, the master cannot claim freight from the captors. If he be guilty of fraud or misconduct, the ship may be forfeited.

All articles of an essentially warlike quality are distinctly liable to confiscation if destined for belligerent use. Goods of a purely peaceful quality may be freely carried to belligerent ports not blockaded. Articles of an equivocal nature have to be considered on their merits, by the light of the facts as ascertained. It is, in short, less the goods than the disposition with which the goods are regarded. If presumably intended for warlike purposes they will probably be condemned; if for peaceful purposes, restored. The sole judge of the probable use is the capturing belligerent. His right it is also, by common consent, to say what goods are contraband and what are not, and there is no appeal against his decision. But of course if, in so deciding, he should act in a high-handed and grossly unreasonable manner, he would expose himself to the hostility of neutral powers.

The decisions of former days, on the subject of contraband, are valuable as exemplifying the principles on which prize courts proceed; but as regards the articles themselves, which called forth these decisions, the latter are at the present day worth, for the most part, very little. This is more especially the case in respect of the articles destined for maritime uses in the days when ships were built of timber, carried masts and spars of the same material, were rigged with hempen rope, and depended on canvas for their propulsion. All this is now changed. The articles which will in the future be regarded as equivocal, only the future can show. All that can be confidently affirmed on this point is that a belligerent will almost certainly regard as contraband any goods shipped to the enemy which may strengthen the hand of the latter for war. What these articles are likely to be is a question to which the answer must meantime be provided by the common sense and practical judgment of the enquirer; there is no authority to which to appeal for definite information on the subject. Many, possibly most, of the articles likely to be regarded, either absolutely or in certain circumstances, as contraband of war, have been suggested above; but on the pinch of war no doubt the list will be supplemented.

As regards provisions, they stand in an exceptional position. If made up into a form specially suitable for warlike purposes, they are likely to be condemned. So, also, with stores apparently destined for the use of forces in the field. Foodstuffs not made up, such as wheat and flour, are not likely to be condemned, unless in face of a strong presumption in favour of their warlike use. They may be ordered off from the belligerent coast, or they may be pre-empted. Generally, the tendency is rather to pre-empt than to confiscate provisions, except in the cases just indicated.

Finally, it may be observed that if the owner of permissive goods ship with them any contraband of war, or if the owner of the contraband be also owner of the vessel, the taint of the contraband will be held to permeate all the property captured belonging to the same owner, and the whole will be subjected to the same fate.

It seems improbable that the question of contraband, in any European war, will assume in the future the prominence which it occupied in the past. A belligerent is not likely to import contraband of war, at the risk of capture, if he can procure it in a neighbouring neutral market; and owing to the facilities now afforded by railway communication, this will doubtless frequently be found a matter of no great difficulty.

Insurance.

With respect to the insurance of contraband, there being, as we have seen, nothing unlawful, in the strict sense of the word, in the shipment of such articles by neutrals, there is nothing unlawful in their insurance. It is, however, within the right of a neutral government to prohibit the shipment of contraband to belligerents (*u*); and such a prohibition by this country would nullify, even if it did not in terms proscribe, any insurance of goods shipped contrary to it. But in the case of a lawful insurance, in order to secure enforcement of the contract it would have to be shown that the underwriter had either express or implied knowledge of the material facts at the time he accepted the risk (*v*). In the case of a belligerent country, all unlicensed trade with the enemy being prohibited, any insurances in protection of such trade would naturally be illegal. And any insurance of contraband in the country of the hostile belligerent, though the articles insured have been shipped by neutrals, would be incapable of being enforced (*x*); as, for example, if Great Britain were at war with France, and it was proposed to insure in England contraband goods carried by a neutral vessel from Russia to France.

In the United States it was held, in 1797 (*y*), that under an

(*u*) *Vide* as to this p. 350, *infra*.

(*v*) *The Santissima Trinidad*, 7 *Wheat.* 283; *Ex parte* Chavasse, *In re* Grazebrooke, 34 L. J. Bank. 17.

(*x*) Arnould, 5th ed. p. 699.

(*y*) *Seton* v. *Low*, 1 *Johns. Cases*, 1, confirmed by *Juhel* v. *Rhinelander*, 2 *John.* 120, 487 (*an.* 1802).

insurance on "all kinds of neutral goods," articles contraband of war may be comprised, and that all goods are lawful which are not prohibited by the positive law of the country to which the vessel belongs: further, that the insured are not bound to disclose to the underwriter that the goods are contraband of war, seeing that it is lawful for neutrals to ship contraband of war, and that the underwriter must be presumed to know that the neutral trade is very likely to consist of the same kind of articles during war as in times of peace. But it has since been decided in the British Courts, in *Ex parte Chavasse, In re Grazebrook* (z), that an insurance on contraband of war is a good insurance provided the underwriter was informed of the nature of the risk which he was undertaking, or if the circumstances were such that he might reasonably be presumed to be acquainted with the nature of the trade engaged in.

Two cases arising out of the seizure of the steamer *Peterhoff* are especially interesting in this connexion. It has already been mentioned that *The Peterhoff* was a neutral vessel carrying a cargo largely consisting of warlike or equivocal articles to the neutral port of Matamoras on the Rio Grande. Matamoras was separated from the Confederate town of Brownsville by merely a narrow stream. It came out that a packet containing papers had, in accordance with the previous instructions of the master, been thrown overboard on seizure of the vessel, and that other papers had been burnt. It was moreover averred that part of the cargo was intended to be lightered into Texas, and part to be offered in the market at Matamoras. Of the alleged contraband articles, some were distinctly for military purposes, whilst others, such as boots, horse-shoes, sapping tools, drugs, blankets, &c., would be available for similar uses. The ownership of the cargo appears to have been vested in but a few persons, and it was found that the goods of all the claimants consisted more or less of contraband articles; also, that the owner of the vessel was himself a shipper of contraband cargo. The vessel, which had been captured by a Federal cruiser off St. Thomas, was, with her cargo, declared to be confiscated.

(z) 34 L. J. Bank. 17, and p. 403, *infra*. *Vide* also Hobbs *v.* Henning, p. 404, *infra*.

It was clearly recognised by the United States Courts that a neutral vessel, laden with a neutral cargo, may lawfully trade between neutral ports in time of war, in all descriptions of merchandise, whether warlike or otherwise (*a*); and that no articles alleged to be contraband can be so unless they are going to a belligerent (*b*). On the other hand, it was stated to be equally well settled that the ulterior destination of warlike goods determines the character of the trade, and that a trade in such goods with the enemy's country, through neutral territory, is unlawful; numerous authorities, British and American, being cited in support of this doctrine (*c*). With respect to the actual destination of the warlike goods, the Court observed that there was no army or navy in Mexico at or near Matamoras to be supplied, and that there could have been no demand in Mexico for the large quantity of the other articles found on board the vessel. To sum up, the learned judge was "led to the conclusion, upon all the evidence, that *The Peterhoff*, when captured, though ostensibly on a voyage from London to neutral waters at the mouth of the Rio Grande, was laden with a cargo composed largely of articles contraband of war, which were not designed, on their departure from England, to be sold or disposed of in the neutral market of Matamoras, but were designed to be delivered either directly or indirectly, by transhipment, in the country of the enemy, and for the use of the enemy" (*d*). "It was not credible that there was a design, in good faith, to sell and dispose of the cargo in the market of Matamoras" (*e*). In these circumstances the cargo was condemned *en bloc*. The ship was likewise condemned, the owner being also an owner of contraband articles, and the master having destroyed and concealed certain papers and prevaricated generally.

The foregoing is a summary of the main features of this important case, tried by the U. S. District Court in July, 1863, as set forth at great length in Blatchford's Reports of Cases in Prize, 1861-65. This judgment was subsequently reversed, as

(*a*) *Blatch. Pr. Ca. at p.* 506.
(*b*) *Ib. at p.* 528.
(*c*) *Ib. at p.* 508.
(*d*) *Ib. at p.* 533.
(*e*) *Ib. at p.* 541.

regards the ship and part of the cargo, but it is necessary to bear the first judgment in mind, because when *Hobbs's* case, to be presently considered, came before the British Courts, *The Peterhoff* appeal had not come before the Supreme Court of the United States.

Hobbs v. *Henning* (November, 1864, and January, 1865) (*f*), was a case arising out of the above seizure. There had been no special warranty of no-contraband, but the underwriters disclaimed liability, relying mainly on the pleas (1) of concealment of material fact, and (2) of misdescription of the voyage insured. The latter defence was based on the decision of the United States Court that the real voyage was in fact to a belligerent and not to a neutral destination. Judgment was, however, given for the plaintiff, the Court deciding (1) that the goods were not contraband of war, and consequently that there had been no concealment; and (2) that the judgment of the United States Court was not intended to express that the ship's voyage was not as alleged by the master, but that the alleged destination of the cargo was false.

The decision that the goods were not contraband was directly opposed to that of the United States District Court, which condemned them for being contraband; and this case has been cited as evidence of a divergence of views, on the subject of contraband, between the Courts of this country and of the United States. But a careful examination of the decision in the British Court seems to establish that the difference between the decisions of the two Courts was one entirely as to the facts, and not as to the principle. The United States District Court held, as to the whole of the cargo, that it was not intended to be sold at Matamoras, but that it was really destined for delivery in Confederate territory. In *Seymour's* case, *infra*, the British Court held that this view of the facts, so far as the particular goods were concerned, was correct, for a contract existed under which delivery was to be made to the Confederate Government. But in *Hobbs's* case no evidence was adduced of any such arrangement, and the British Court held that the goods insured were

(*f*) 17 C. B. 818; 34 L. J. C. P. 117.

intended to be sold at the neutral port, and that they were therefore not contraband, and were wrongfully condemned as such. "The allegation," said the Court, "that the goods were shipped for the purpose of being sent to an enemy's port is an allegation of a mental process only. We are not to assume either that the plaintiff had made any contract or provided any means for the further transmission of the goods into the enemy's state, or that the shipment to Matamoras was an unreal pretence. If the goods were in a course of transmission, not to Matamoras, but to an enemy's port, the voyage would not be covered by the policy." In the view of the Court (*g*), the assured must be taken to have known of the good demand at Matamoras, and to have shipped to that port in the expectation of a profitable sale there to purchasers on behalf of the Confederate States; but that a price was the sole object in view, and that he was indifferent whether the sale were to Confederate or Federal purchasers; and that in a neutral territory he might lawfully sell to either: therefore that the plea was bad (as to intention); for, there being no warranty against contraband, it was necessary to show that the goods were contraband of war, and, as such, liable to be seized by the Federal Government: the averment of the intention that the goods should go to the Confederate States did not indicate that the goods were bound to go there, and therefore that the plea (*i. e.*, in effect, of concealment) was insufficient. (It was considered by the Court that the plea of contraband of war was intended to be a defence on the ground of concealment by the plaintiff of a material fact.) In the opinion of the Court the seizure by the Federal Government was, on the facts, so far as concerned the plaintiff's property, unlawful. But the insurance was against capture, lawful and unlawful, and the defendant, said the Court, in order to discharge himself, must show concealment by the assured. The further allegation that the ship was carrying goods and papers which involved liability to seizure, was held to be immaterial as a ground of defence; for these goods were not alleged to be plaintiff's goods, and the plaintiff was not shown to be responsible for the ship's papers, nor for any other goods than his own.

(*g*) So understood in Seymour's case, *infra*, 41 L. J. C. P. 193.

This decision was, as has been said, arrived at in 1864-5, and the American judgment in *The Peterhoff*, on appeal to the Supreme Court in 1866, amply establishes the justice of the conclusions of the British Court in *Hobbs's* case. Further, it goes to show that there is no difference of opinion between the Courts of this country and of the United States as to the principles by which the question of alleged contraband is to be tested. That the District Court had wrongly interpreted the facts in *The Peterhoff* case appears from the subsequent judgment of the Supreme Court (*h*). Said the Court: "The evidence in the record satisfies us that the voyage of *The Peterhoff* was not simulated. . . . Nor have we been able to find anything in the record which fairly warrants a belief that the cargo had any other direct destination. . . . . We dismiss, therefore, from consideration the claim, suggested rather than urged, on behalf of the Government, that the ship and cargo, both or either, were destined for the blockaded coast."

With respect to the permissive or innocent goods, the Court thought it a "fair conclusion from the whole evidence, that the cargo was intended to be disposed of in Mexico or Texas as might be found most convenient and profitable to the owners and consignees;" and that the destination in this case became specially important only in connexion with the question of the goods of a contraband nature. With respect to the equivocal goods, they had not been proved to have been actually destined to belligerent use, and they could not therefore be treated as contraband. The articles held to be contraband were artillery harness, military boots, and regulation blankets. These, said the Court, came fairly within the description of goods primarily and ordinarily used for military purposes in time of war, and made part of the necessary equipment of an army. If really intended for sale in the market at Matamoras, even these goods would have been free from liability, but all the circumstances indicated that these articles at least were destined for the use of the rebel forces then occupying Brownsville and other places in the vicinity, notwithstanding that they were primarily destined for Matamoras. This portion of the cargo was therefore con-

(*h*) 5 *Wall.* 28.

demned, and with it any part of the cargo belonging to the owner of the same goods.

As regards the ship, although the conduct of the master had been inconsistent with the frankness and good faith due from neutrals in such circumstances, yet, in face of the fact of the almost certain destination of the ship to a neutral port with a cargo for the most part neutral in character and destination, the Court decreed restitution on payment of costs and expenses.

This judgment, both for its searching and impartial examination of the facts and for its able and exhaustive review of the law, well repays perusal. The final judgment of the United States Court in *The Peterhoff* and of the British Courts in *Hobbs* v. *Henning* must be considered to set at rest, once and for all, the principles to be followed in deciding questions of contraband of war: as to which principles there would appear to be no difference of opinion between the government of this country and that of the United States.

In *Seymour* v. *London and Provincial Insurance Co.* (*i*), an insurance had been effected in London on goods per *Peterhoff* from London to Matamoras, "Warranted no contraband of war." The goods having been confiscated as above stated, the underwriters repudiated liability on the ground of misrepresentation and breach of warranty. This refusal was justified by the Court, by which it was held that the goods were intended from the beginning to go to Matamoras, not to be disposed of there as part of the merchandise of such port, but for the purpose of being transhipped across the Rio Grande, to be delivered to the Confederate Government under contract. This decision, which was on all fours with the finding of the American Court, was subsequently confirmed, the Court thinking that the special facts of the particular case clearly showed, first, that the artillery harness was destined to a belligerent state for belligerent purposes, and so, as was admitted, "in such case contraband"; and, secondly, that there had been a concealment of this material fact (*k*).

(*i*) 41 L. J. C. P. 193.
(*k*) 42 L. J. C. P. 111, *not.*

As the ownership of goods partly contraband and partly permissive taints the whole with the vice of contraband, in the case of an insurance on the permissive portion of such mixed goods, or on a neutral ship carrying contraband goods belonging to her owner, the underwriter must be either explicitly or impliedly informed of the circumstances. Otherwise, as intimated above, the insurance may be held void on the ground of concealment (*l*). But it is to be deduced from *Hobbs's* case, *supra*, that the circumstance that a Court of the alien captors has condemned property as contraband of war will not necessarily debar the assured from pleading in the Courts of this country that the condemnation was bad under the law of nations; and that it is not *de facto* a defence to a claim on the underwriters under a policy warranting no contraband (*m*).

The carriage by neutrals to a belligerent of all articles subservient to warlike uses being by the common law of nations attended by the liability to confiscation of the obnoxious cargo, it naturally follows that the transport of the enemy's troops and conveyance of his despatches will be at least as strictly prohibited. This subject we will now consider.

(*l*) Arnould, 6th ed. p. 636, reads as follows:—

"As carrying contraband articles entails the confiscation of all property on board the neutral ship belonging to the same owner, it would clearly amount to a breach of the warranty of neutrality as to such property. With regard to the ship and such portion of the cargo as belongs to different owners, it will only produce such a result when the circumstances of criminality are such as involve both ship and cargo in one common penalty; as where they show that the shipowner and the other freighters were cognizant of, and concerned in, the contraband trading."

But seeing that contraband of war may be directly shipped and insured without being so described in the policy, and yet without violating the neutral warranty, it is by no means obvious why any violation of neutral warranty should ensue in such circumstances as the above. *Vide sub* War Warranties, p. 387, *infra*.

(*m*) For examples of clauses expressly excluding risks arising from carriage of contraband of war, *vide* p. 124, *supra*.

Capture and Confiscation of property engaged in Carrying Despatches or Military Persons of the Enemy.

The transport of hostile despatches, or of military persons in the service of the enemy, is regarded as a heinous offence against the law of nations. The injury likely to result from the carriage of a cargo of contraband articles is necessarily of a limited nature; but the transport of hostile despatches may affect perhaps the whole plan of campaign: while the presence of military persons with the forces of the enemy may indefinitely increase his powers of conducting warlike operations.

What are Despatches.—"The carriage of despatches," said Sir W. Scott, in *The Atalanta* (*a*), "is a service which, in whatever degree it exists, can only be considered in one character—as an act of the most noxious and hostile nature."

"Despatches," observed the same learned judge, in *The Caroline* (*b*), "are all official communications of official persons on the public affairs of the government. The comparative importance of the particular papers," his lordship added, "is immaterial, since the Court will not construct a scale of relative importance, which, in fact, it has not the means of doing with any degree of accuracy or with satisfaction to itself; it is sufficient that they relate to the public business of the enemy, be it great or small. . . . . The true

(*a*) 6 Rob. 440.

(*b*) 6 Rob. 464.

criterion will be, are they on the public business of the state and passing between public persons for the public service?" The conveyance of the despatches of an ambassador resident in a neutral country is, however, an exception to this rule. Despatches carried from the mother country to her colonies or foreign possessions are distinctly prohibited, a belligerent having the right to assume that such despatches are hostile to himself, inasmuch as they relate to the security of the enemy's possessions; but neutrals have a right to preserve their relations with the enemy, and no such presumption of hostility exists in the case of despatches of or to ambassadors resident in a neutral country, for the purpose of preserving friendly relations between the neutral state and that of the belligerent power to which such ambassadors owe allegiance. Confidence must needs be placed in the integrity of the neutral state; and persons discharging the functions of ambassadors are peculiarly objects of the protection and favour of the law of nations (*c*). This principle was, in *The Maddison* (*d*), held equally to apply to the carrying of despatches to a consul of the enemy resident in a neutral country. And, clearly, all papers found on board a neutral vessel sailing to or from a belligerent port, although of a public nature and relating to public affairs, will not of necessity be of a contraband quality; for if the person to whom they are committed be a neutral and not invested with a public character they are not despatches, nor is the carriage of them an offence (*e*). If a neutral vessel carrying despatches from the enemy to a dependency be seized on the voyage, but the dependency have meantime ceased to be a colony of the enemy, this circumstance will absolve the vessel from confiscation (*f*).

(*c*) The Caroline, 6 Rob. 464.
(*d*) Edw. 224.
(*e*) The Rapid, Edw. 228.
(*f*) The Trendre Sostre, 6 Rob. 457.

In the familiar case of *The Trent* (g), commonly known at the time of the occurrence as the *Mason and Slidell* affair, the United States Government sought to establish the claim to an extreme exercise of belligerent rights in respect of the carriage by neutrals of hostile despatches and military persons. The case, shortly stated, is as follows:—*The Trent* was a British mail steamer bound from Havannah to England with mails and passengers. Amongst the latter were the persons named, proceeding as envoys from the Confederate States to Great Britain and France. When about nine miles from the coast of Cuba the vessel was approached by the United States cruiser *San Jacinto*, which fired a round shot in a direction obviously divergent from the course of *The Trent*, and shortly afterwards discharged a shell across her bows, the missile exploding half a cable's length from the steamer. A naval officer from the cruiser then boarded the steamer and demanded that Messrs. Mason and Slidell, with their two secretaries, should be given up. The officers of *The Trent* protested against the action of the cruiser, but ultimately, on a show of force being made, the persons indicated were allowed to be transferred to the cruiser, and they were subsequently imprisoned in a military fortress. The mail steamer proceeded on her voyage, and, on the facts becoming known in England, a demand was made to the United States Government for restoration of the prisoners and a suitable apology. In this demand the British Government was supported by France, Austria, Prussia, Italy, and Russia. It was urgently complained that this arbitrary act of the United States Government, in seizing non-combatants travelling under the protection of a neutral flag and bound to a neutral state, was unjustifiable and a breach of the common law of nations. The main contention of the captors in support of their illegal

(g) Parl. Papers, 1862, Vol. LXII.

action was, that the persons seized, and the despatches which they were believed to be carrying, were contraband of war, and therefore liable to seizure. It was not, however, attempted to justify the mode in which the alleged right of seizure had been exercised, and it was practically admitted that the steamer should properly have been brought into a United States port for adjudication. To the above contention it was replied, that whatever may be the law as regards naval and military persons, no single Admiralty decision, and no single expression on the part of any international jurist, could be cited in support of the argument that ambassadors or public officers, non-combatants, are liable to be regarded as contraband of war; and that in any case these persons were bound to a neutral destination. Further, that as to the despatches, neutral states have a perfect right to maintain friendly relations with belligerents; and that these despatches were under protection of the neutral flag and bound to a neutral destination. Ultimately the persons seized were released and allowed to proceed to their destination in a British vessel.

The interesting and important arguments arising out of this case are discussed at length in Kent's International Law, 2nd ed. pp. 357—364.

Who are Military Persons.—By naval and military persons is meant persons competent to take an active part in the prosecution of hostilities. Ambassadors or public persons holding civil appointments apparently do not, as we have seen above, come within this category, though an observation of Sir W. Scott, in *The Orozembo*, to be referred to presently (*g*), intimates a different conclusion. "As to the number of military persons necessary to subject the vessel to confiscation, it is difficult to decide; since fewer persons of high quality and character may

(*g*) *Vide* p. 210, *infra*.

be of much more importance than a much greater number of persons of lower condition. To carry a veteran general, under some circumstances, might be a much more noxious act than the conveyance of a whole regiment" (*h*).

Mail Packets: Public Vessels.—In Wheaton's International Law (*i*) the editor expresses the opinion that "the carrying of despatches can only invest a neutral vessel with a hostile character in the case of its being employed for that purpose by the belligerent, and that it cannot affect with criminality either a regular postal packet or a merchant ship, which takes a despatch in its ordinary course of conveying letters, and of the contents of which the master must necessarily be ignorant. This view, it is supposed, is not inconsistent with the text, which refers to a fraudulent carrying of the despatches of the enemy. Since the former European wars some governments have established regular postal packets, whose mails, by international conventions, are distributed throughout the civilized world; whilst in other countries every merchant vessel is obliged to receive till the moment of its setting sail, not only the despatches of the government, but all letters sent to it from the post-offices." International conventions or not, it may surely be safely assumed that the general introduction of the postal system, and the consequent institution of mail steamers, have practically extinguished the old right of confiscation for the carriage of hostile despatches. If, for example, war were to arise between France and Spain, by the strict law of nations France would have the right to stop and search every British mail steamer which she might suspect of carrying in her mail bags despatches from the Spanish Government to any of the Spanish East Indies. The

(*h*) Wheaton's Internat. Law, 2 Eng. ed. p. 580.
(*i*) 6 Am. ed. p. 567.

result of the exercise of this right would be that successive P. and O. steamers might be stopped while their scores, or even hundreds, of mail bags are got out and the contents of each examined, and on the examination proving successful, the steamer might be taken into a French port for adjudication, to the serious loss and infinite discomfort of a large complement of passengers, the peaceable subjects of various neutral powers. Such a state of affairs would raise the ire and hostility of all neutral governments, and would obviously be utterly inconsistent with the enlightened civilization of the present day. Moreover, the great facilities which now exist for communication by telegraphic cable, as well as for the forwarding of despatches by various and independent routes, must needs in most cases render it a sheer waste of time to attempt to intercept despatches by stopping and searching mail steamers. And, indeed, to search any of the floating leviathans of the present day on the chance of discovering a letter which it would be the interest of persons on board to conceal, would be little less than an absurdity. But whatever rights may still be held to exist as to the search for despatches on private trading vessels, there can, one would imagine, be no doubt that no such right exists—or that if it exists, few powers would have the hardihood to attempt to exercise it—in the case of mail or packet steamers. These vessels, being under government contract for the carriage of the mails, may in a manner be said to be public vessels. Not, it may be, vessels of war or transport, but still public vessels, as being under government subsidy, and as such exempt at any rate from the prohibition against carrying belligerent despatches; though the right of search for military persons of the enemy having a belligerent destination might still be insisted upon. But *The Peterhoff* (*j*) case, where a British

(*j*) *Vide* p. 186, *supra*.

vessel was seized by a Federal cruiser for carrying contraband of war and for the alleged intention to run the blockade of the Confederate ports, indicates that the modern view favours the recognition of the right of neutral vessels to carry mails free from belligerent examination. For although the circumstances of the voyage and cargo were in this case open to grave suspicion, and the conduct of the master was eminently unsatisfactory, a sealed postal mail bag found on board was ordered to be delivered to the attorney of the United States, out of the custody of the Court, and was given up to the British authorities unopened (*k*). It may, however, be supposed that the right to carry postal mail bags and the sanctity of their contents is now in many cases provided for by international convention.

The cases of *The Charkieh* (*l*) and *The Parlement Belge* (*m*) are interesting as bearing upon the question of public vessels; but as these were pacific cases in respect of damages caused by collision, involving the question of territorial jurisdiction of the British Admiralty Court over the property of a foreign sovereign, it is unnecessary to discuss them here. The case of *The Constitution* (*n*), a United States frigate, carrying private goods for public exhibition—against which salvage proceedings were issued in the Admiralty Court—stands on a somewhat similar footing. At one time so-called packet ships were, with certain special allowances, by statute (*o*) strictly forbidden to carry any merchandise: they were to carry "letters and packets"; and goods carried unlawfully, contrary to the statute, were to be forfeited.

The Penalty of Confiscation.—To ensure as far as practicable that contraband of war shall not be conveyed to the

(*k*) *Blatch. Pr. Ca. at pp.* 468, 532.
(*l*) L. R. 4 A. & E. 59.
(*m*) L. R. 5 P. D. 197.
(*n*) 48 L. J. (N. S.) P. D. & A. 13.
(*o*) 13 & 14 Car. II. c. 11, § 22.

enemy, a belligerent seeks to render the carriage of such articles unprofitable to the shipowner. Forfeiture of contraband goods commonly involves the shipowner in loss of freight, besides inflicting on him indirect loss by the delay attending seizure of the ship. But to confiscate despatches or to imprison military passengers would ordinarily involve no loss of freight, and the captors, in order to discourage shipowners from engaging in such prohibited traffic, therefore resort to confiscation of the ship itself. If the ship and the cargo or any of it belong to the same individual, the cargo or the part of it so owned must share the common fate. Similarly, the cargo is liable to condemnation if it appear that privity as to the offence exists between the master and the cargo-owner. Thus, in 1807, during war between this country and France, there were found in a tea-chest on board the neutral vessel *Atalanta* (*p*), on a voyage from Batavia to Bremen, despatches from the Governor of the Isle of France to the French authorities. The tea-chest was in a trunk belonging to one of the supercargoes, and on these facts the ship was condemned as well as all cargo on board belonging to the owners, and all cargo the property of the supercargo. On the conclusion of this case the Court observed that the despatches, which had been inspected, were in fact of a noxious character, "though this was a circumstance of no great consequence." In the following year an American vessel (*q*) was captured on a voyage from Bordeaux to New York, having on board a letter addressed to the Prefect of the Isle of France. The master made an affidavit that the packet was delivered to him by a private merchant as containing old newspapers and some shawls for a merchant in New York. Moreover, it was contended that the letter itself was an entirely unimportant document, unconnected with the political

(*p*) 6 Rob. 440.

(*q*) The Susan, 6 Rob. 461, note.

objects of the war. This latter objection was overruled; and as to the averment of ignorance, the Court observed that without saying what might be the effect of an extreme case of imposition practised on a neutral master, notwithstanding the utmost exertions of caution and good faith on his part (*r*), it must be taken to be the general rule that a master is not at liberty to aver his ignorance. But that if he be made the victim of imposition, practised on him by his private agents or by the government of the enemy, he must seek for his redress against them. This judgment seems to be somewhat controlled by that in the *The Rapid* (*s*), where the despatches were being carried by a neutral ship from a neutral port to a port of the enemy. It appeared that the master of the ship had received the despatch among other letters from private persons, and was ignorant of its contents, and in these circumstances the ship was released. In so deciding, the Court was in accord with the principles indicated by Sir W. Scott in *The Atalanta*, *supra*, viz., that besides the transportation there must, in order to convict the master, be a fraudulent intention on his part, and also the carrying must be in the service of the enemy. As has been already suggested, it would be utterly unreasonable to condemn a vessel carrying mails on the ground that despatches were discovered in the mail bags. In the foregoing case of *The Rapid*, the war was between England and Holland, the vessel, American owned, being bound from New York to Tonningen; and it was a decided point in the master's favour that these facts were so, and that the obnoxious article was not being carried from one port of the enemy to another. In the latter event the master is bound to exercise the utmost vigilance as to the papers he carries. The arguments in *The Atalanta* refer to several other

(*r*) *Vide* The Lisette, cited in The Atalanta, *supra*.
(*s*) Edw. 228.

decisions on this subject, of which it is unnecessary to make further mention here. It may, however, be remarked that the circumstances which in all cases justify confiscation on the one hand, or warrant release of the vessel on the other, are not so clearly defined as might be desired were this particular class of offence destined to bear the same importance in the hostilities of the future as it has borne in the past.

But whatever doubt may attend the question of the degree of delinquency on the part of the master necessary to involve confiscation of the ship, in the case of despatches, his position in the case of carrying military persons of the enemy is free from all ambiguity. The bare fact of such persons being discovered on board has been decided to afford sufficient ground for condemnation of the ship (*t*). In *The Orozembo*, three military officers of distinction were found on board, besides two persons holding civil appointments in the government of Batavia, and twelve others. Judgment having been given against the ship in the case of the military men, the Court was under no necessity to determine whether the same principle applied to the civilians. It was, however, observed that "wherever it is of sufficient importance to the enemy that such persons should be sent out on the public service at the public expense, it should afford equal ground of forfeiture against the vessel engaged in carrying them" (*u*). In *The Friendship* (*v*), a neutral vessel engaged in the transport of soldiers of the enemy, Sir W. Scott, in condemning the ship, intimated that the carrying of a few invalided soldiers or discharged sailors, taken on board by chance and at their own charge, or of a military officer travelling at his own expense as an ordinary passenger, would be entitled to be favourably looked at, but that the deliberate carrying of

(*t*) The Orozembo, 6 Rob. 430.

(*u*) See also The Henric and Alida, 1 Hay & Marriott, at p. 139.

(*v*) 6 Rob. 420.

effective soldiers undoubtedly involved confiscation of the ship, and this whether the soldiers carried be connected with immediate action in the service of the enemy or not.

In the same manner that no averment of ignorance can justify the master, so the plea of *force majeure* will not deliver him. If a neutral vessel be impressed to carry troops by a belligerent, and be seized and confiscated in consequence, the master must seek his remedy against the power by whose wrongful act he has been made to suffer. "Were an act of force exercised by one belligerent power on a neutral ship or person to be considered a justification for an act contrary to the known duties of the neutral character, there would be an end of any prohibition under the law of nations to carry contraband, or to engage in any other hostile act" (*x*).

Insurance.

The carriage of belligerent despatches or of military persons in the belligerent service being contrary to the law of nations, the act breaks a warranty of neutrality and voids the insurance. If there be no warranty of neutrality the insurance will be void on the ground of concealment of material fact, unless it can be plainly established that the underwiter was fully informed as to the nature and circumstances of the voyage at the time he undertook the insurance. The remarks *sub* Blockade (p. 123, *supra*) are somewhat pertinent to this subject.

The next neutral offence justifying capture by a belligerent which it is proposed to consider is that of Resistance to Visit and Search.

(*x*) The Carolina, 4 Rob. 256.

RESISTANCE TO VISIT AND SEARCH.

As already indicated (*y*), the right to visit and search neutral vessels in time of hostilities is inseparable from the larger belligerent right to seize and confiscate contraband of war,—or, indeed, from that, where not waived by treaty, of the capture of enemy property generally. The circumstances and manner in which the right of visit and the attendant, but not necessarily consequent, right of search are to be exercised, having already been discussed, they need not now be further reviewed.

Belligerents having a right to visit and, if thought necessary, to search neutral vessels, neutrals lie under the corresponding obligation to permit such visit and search. The penalty attaching to breach of this neutral obligation is confiscation. In applying this penalty, no regard is to be paid to the national character of the vessel or of the cargo, and the latter has to share the condemnation of the former. "The right of visiting and searching merchant ships upon the high seas," said Sir W. Scott, in *The Maria* (*z*), "whatever be the ships, whatever be the cargoes, whatever be the destinations, is an incontestable right of the lawfully commissioned cruisers of a belligerent nation. . . . . And the penalty for the violent contravention of this right is the confiscation of the property so withheld from visitation and search." Resistance to search is regarded as amounting to a forfeiture of the vessel's neutrality, and the cargo follows the fate of the ship. If, however, the vessel prove to be the property of the enemy, the cargo is not involved unless the

(*y*) P. 144, *supra*.

(*z*) 1 Rob. 340.

cargo-owner concurred in the act of the captain (*a*). There is nothing illegal in the resistance of a belligerent master. He has everything to gain and not much to lose by resisting; and in the American courts it was, in *The Nereide* (*b*), decided that his action did not bind neutral cargo not participating in it. Sir W. Scott, however, in *The Fanny* (*c*), asserted the directly contrary doctrine, declaring that the American prize courts are justly entitled to condemn property taken by an American cruiser from an armed vessel of the enemy. Three years later (in 1818), the American courts, in reviewing the judgment of *The Nereide*, affirmed the principle then laid down, and expressed the opinion that the British courts would eventually admit its justice (*d*).

If the neutral master be *bonâ fide* ignorant of the existence of hostilities, and, by consequence, that he has any neutral duties to perform, his resistance to search will not involve confiscation. This was decided by Sir W. Scott in the case of two Spanish vessels *San Juan Baptista* and *La Purissima Conception* (*e*), in which case, moreover, an award of compensation was made to the crews of these vessels, the captors having wrongfully handcuffed them.

Neutral Goods on Armed Belligerent Vessels.—The cases of *The Nereide* and *The Fanny*, just mentioned, afford instances of the shipment of neutral goods on board *armed* belligerent vessels. The American courts decided that it was no breach of neutrality to make such a shipment, and that neither the goods nor the neutral owner were to be chargeable with the consequences of the captain's resistance, unless the goods-

(*a*) The Catharina Elizabeth, 5 Rob. 232.

(*b*) 9 *Cranch*, 388.

(*c*) 1 Dods. 443.

(*d*) *The Atalanta*, 3 *Wheat. Rep.* 409.

(*e*) 5 Rob. 34.

owner concurred in the act. The British courts decided just the other way. They decided that while a neutral is entitled to put his goods on the merchant vessel of a belligerent, he is not entitled to ship by an armed belligerent vessel. And that if he does so ship he must be deemed to have showed an intention to resist visit and search, thus placing himself under enemy protection and forfeiting his neutrality. Whether the Declaration of Paris is to be deemed, as between the signatories to it, to have wiped this offence off the slate, must be left to conjecture.

Neutral Goods shipped under Convoy.—The principle laid down by the British courts, that the shipment of neutral goods by an armed vessel of the enemy is to be regarded as evidence of an intention to resist visit and search, applies equally to the placing of neutral goods under protection of convoy. Whether the convoy be that of an enemy or of a neutral, the implication is that resistance to search is intended; and the neutrality of the goods is *ipso facto* forfeited. The presumed intention to resist may never be carried into effect, but this is not material (*f*). This position may, of course, be affected by special treaty provisions, but in the absence of such provisions—and unless, again, the Treaty of Paris is to be held to have sanctioned such neutral conduct—the law will be as laid down by Sir W. Scott, in 1799, in the celebrated case of the Swedish convoy, under protection of which *The Maria* (*f*) and other vessels seized were sailing. The American Government, however, in 1810, denied the right of Denmark to seize American vessels which had sailed on the outward voyage under protection of British convoy, and after twenty years of negotiations Denmark agreed to compensate America for the seizure of the vessels. War was then prevailing between

(*f*) The Maria, 1 Rob. 340; The Elsabe, 4 Rob. 408.

Great Britain and Denmark, and several American vessels engaged in carrying naval stores between American and Russian ports had been seized by Denmark on the return voyage, in accordance with the above right, which right was maintained by Denmark as well as by this country.

Insurance.

If a vessel "warranted neutral" under the marine policy resist the right of search or sail under convoy: or if neutral goods be shipped by an *armed* belligerent vessel; this is to be regarded as a breach of warranty which voids the policy (*g*). But such illegal acts might, perhaps, in some cases, be attributed to barratry on the part of the captain and so claimed against the underwriters.

It is the duty of a neutral to submit to lawful search, and if the result of such search be that the vessel is carried to a port for adjudication, it is equally the duty of the neutral master to submit. Resistance to search involves the ship, as has been seen, in condemnation; and any attempt to resist the carrying into port by rescuing the vessel from the captors also exposes the vessel to this sentence. This subject—Attempt at Rescue—may be next reviewed.

(*g*) Arnould, 5th ed. pp. 609, 763.

ATTEMPT AT RESCUE.

Rescue, as we have already seen (*h*), is technically distinct from what is termed Recapture; the one being the action of those on board the vessel rescued, the other the result of efforts from without. If a neutral vessel be seized and taken towards port for adjudication, and the master and crew rise and attempt to rescue her from her captors, such an attempt is a breach of neutral obligation, and involves confiscation. *The Dispatch* (*i*) was a Danish vessel recaptured after a rescue effected by her crew. The Court condemned the vessel "on the ground of the parties having declared themselves enemies by this act of hostile opposition to lawful inquiry."

If the vessel be enemy property, however, the master may look upon her as already condemned, and beyond the risk of harsh usage and personal inconvenience to himself and crew, he may be said to have nothing to lose by an attempt at escape, and there is nothing unlawful in the attempt (*j*). He is, at the same time, under no obligation to make such attempt, however meritorious such conduct might be. "Seamen," said Sir W. Scott, "are not bound by their general duty as mariners to attempt a rescue; nor would they have been guilty of a desertion of their duty in that capacity if they had declined it. It is a meritorious act to join in such attempts; but it is an act perfectly voluntary, in which each individual is a volunteer, and is not acting as a part of the crew of the ship in discharge of any official duty, either ordinary or extraordinary" (*k*).

(*h*) P. 126, *supra*.

(*i*) The Catharina Elizabeth, 5 Rob. 232; *The Short Staple* v. *The United States*, 9 *Cranch*, 55; The Dispatch, 3 Rob. 278; The Washington, 2 Act. 30, n.; The Franklin, 2 Act. 109.

(*j*) The Catharina Elizabeth, 5 Rob. 232. *Vide* also *sub* (*i*) generally.

(*k*) The Two Friends, 1 Rob. 271. *Vide* also p. 63, *supra*.

A mere attempt to escape before any possession has been assumed by the captor, does not draw with it the consequence of condemnation (*l*). And if, as in *The Pennsylvania* (*m*), the captors of a neutral vessel, without putting a prize crew on board, content themselves with ordering her commander to carry the vessel into port for adjudication, without causing him to enter into a binding agreement to so proceed, and the neutral vessel, in consequence, makes her escape, such an escape, if the vessel be subsequently captured, will not be regarded as a rescue, and so involving confiscation.

"If the crew of a captured vessel, or prisoners placed on board a vessel in order to be carried to port, rise and overpower those in command of the ship and carry her into a neutral port, the neutral power cannot be required to render up the vessel to those who have thus been deprived of their right over her (*n*). It is the duty of the captors to protect their own interests, and if they fail to efficiently do so they cannot claim the interposition of neutrals to assist them" (*o*). An interesting illustration of this principle occurred during the civil war in America in 1862. A British vessel, *The Emily St. Pierre*, having been seized by a Federal cruiser for an alleged attempt to run the blockade, her crew, all but three men, were taken out of her and a prize crew of fifteen men were put on board with instructions to take the prize to Philadelphia. On the voyage the three prisoners—the master, cook, and steward, who were to have given evidence before the prize court—overpowered and secured their captors, and with the assistance of three or four consenting members of the prize crew, managed to bring the vessel to

---

(*l*) The San Juan Battista, 5 Rob. 33.

(*m*) 1 Act. 33.

(*n*) *Reid* v. *The Vere*, *Bee's Rep.* 66.

(*o*) Opinions of the Attorneys-General of the United States, Vol. III. p. 327; *L'Invincible*, 1 *Wheat.* 256.

Liverpool. Lord Russell declined to restore the vessel to her captors, as demanded by Mr. Adams on behalf of the United States, declaring that such a rescue, however punishable by the law of nations, was no offence against the municipal laws of Great Britain (*o*).

The penalty of confiscation is applied to both ship and cargo without distinction, the master being deemed to have acted as agent for the cargo (*p*). This is so, at least, in the case of neutral vessels and their cargoes; but not so as regards neutral property on an enemy vessel. In this case the master is guilty of no breach of neutral obligation in endeavouring to escape, and his action is not, therefore, to prejudice the cargo (*q*). Though if the cargo owners be found to have connived at the resistance, or the cargo belong to the owners of the ship, the case will be otherwise (*r*).

As has been already indicated, the crew of a captured neutral vessel ought not to attempt a rescue, as by so doing they expose the vessel and cargo to confiscation. And if the vessel be warranted neutral in the policy of insurance, the attempt at rescue will be deemed a breach of this warranty, and will void the policy (*s*). The crew of a captured belligerent vessel may lawfully make such an attempt, though they are ordinarily under no obligation to do so; and if the attempt be made and result successfully, the rescuers have as salvors a lien on the property salved by their action (*t*).

The next neutral offence involving confiscation is that of falsifying or destroying the ship's papers.

(*o*) An interesting account of this singularly bold and successful enterprise, with the diplomatic correspondence which grew out of it, appears in 55 State Papers, 1864-5, pp. 817—837.

(*p*) The Franklin, 2 Act. 108.

(*q*) The Catharina Elizabeth, 5 Rob. 232.

(*r*) *Vide* remarks *sub* Resistance to Search, p. 212, *supra*.

(*s*) Garrels *v.* Kensington, "The Dispatch," 8 T. R. 230.

(*t*) The Two Friends, *supra*. *Vide* also p. 135, *supra*.

CAPTURE AND, IN CERTAIN CASES, CONFISCATION OF PROPERTY INVOLVED IN SAILING UNDER FALSE PAPERS, OR IN THE SUPPRESSION OR DESTRUCTION OF PAPERS.

(With Remarks as to the Papers to be carried.)

On the exercise by a belligerent of the right of visit (*u*), probably his first demand will be to see the ship's papers. If these be promptly produced and be found in all respects in order, and there be no other circumstances warranting the detention of the vessel, she will be entitled to proceed on her course without further interference. If, however, the documents be not all produced, or if on production they bear evidence of having been tampered with, or be found in any respect contradictory—either as between themselves, or of the surroundings, or otherwise,—defective or unsatisfactory, the belligerent will be entitled to carry the vessel into port for further examination (*v*). If on adjudication it be found that the irregularities giving rise to the capture are attributable to bad faith on the part of the master, condemnation of the ship will be involved (*w*). Even if the vessel be released, the master may be ordered to pay the costs of the captors (*x*), on the ground that neutral masters are by the law of nations required to carry proper documents, and that any loss or

(*u*) *Vide* p. 144.

(*v*) The Anna, 5 Rob. 382.

(*w*) *Vide* cases cited in Wheat. Int. Law, 2nd Eng. ed. 584. *The Stephen Hart*, *Blatch. Pr. Ca.* 388; *The Springbok*, *ibid.* 434; *The Peterhoff*, *ibid.* 463; *The Louisa Agnes*, *ibid.* 107.

(*x*) The subject of costs will be dealt with in its place. *Vide* p. 325, *infra*.

charges sustained by the belligerent captors in consequence of a neutral's failure to comply with this requirement must be borne by the defaulter. And even if the master escape being required to indemnify the captors, he will probably be deemed to have forfeited all right to any compensation to which he would himself be otherwise entitled in the case of a capture not warranted by the facts. Mere irregularity resulting from inadvertence, and not accompanied by any circumstances indicating *mala fides* on the part of the master, while it may justify the bringing in of the vessel and involve the master in costs, will not necessarily entail condemnation; but irregularity accompanied by misconduct will be unfavourably construed in a prize court of the captors (*x*). It is hardly possible to define the irregularities which will justify condemnation, or at any rate warrant the bringing of the vessel into port for adjudication; each case must necessarily stand on its own merits. But if in any case a presumption of fraud or bad faith be not rebutted by the master, it will fare badly with him. Thus, the spoliation of papers is regarded as misconduct of an aggravated kind, and their destruction creates a strong presumption of enemy's property. But the spoliation of papers does not of itself create an absolute presumption of guilt, to the exclusion of further proof, for the circumstance may possibly have arisen from accident, necessity or superior force (*y*). But if, coupled with spoliation, there be unsatisfactory explanations, or vehement presumption of bad faith, or gross prevarication, it is good cause for denial of further proof. As regards the throwing overboard of papers, Lord Mansfield observed, in *Bernardi* v. *Motteux* (*z*), that while this offence is universally considered a strong presump-

(*x*) The Neutralitet, 3 Rob. 295.

(*y*) The Peacock, 4 Rob. 185; *The Stephen Hart*, *supra*; *The Springbok*, *supra*; *The Peterhoff*, *supra*; *The Pizarro*, 2 *Wheat.* 227.

(*z*) Doug. 581.

tion of enemy's property, the act does not of itself necessarily involve condemnation. Generally, if papers be destroyed, the presumption is that they related either to the ship or cargo, and that it was of material consequence to some interests that they should be destroyed; though this presumption is capable of being rebutted (*a*). Papers with which the master must needs have been acquainted, setting up a false description of cargo, clearly involve confiscation. Thus, an attempt of the master to suppress the fact of there being contraband cargo on board, by means of fictitious bills of lading, entails confiscation of the ship (*b*). In *The Sarah Christina* (*c*), goods otherwise subject to pre-emption were confiscated by reason of there being false cargo-papers on board; the Court observing, that to entitle the owner to the benefit of the rule of pre-emption a perfect *bona fides* on his part is required. And papers setting up a pretended neutral destination are regarded as evidence of bad faith on the part of the master, for which he must suffer by the confiscation of his ship (*d*).

Commenting, in *The Franklin* (*d*), on the difficulty frequently met with as regards the detection of the offence of sailing to a false destination, the Court observed that "pretences and excuses are always resorted to, the fallacy of which can seldom be completely exposed; and therefore, without undertaking the task of exposing them in a particular case, the Court had been induced to hold generally in each case, that the certain fact shall prevail over the dubious explanations."

A vessel which succeeded in delivering a contraband cargo, and was captured on the return voyage, was condemned on the ground that the success of the adventure had been ob-

---

(*a*) The Two Brothers, 1 Rob. 133.

(*b*) The Richmond, 5 Rob. 325.

(*c*) 1 Rob. 241.

(*d*) The Franklin, 3 Rob. 221; The Edward, 4 Rob. 68; The Ranger, 6 Rob. 126.

tained by means of false papers (*f*). In this case so heinous was the offence regarded that the cargo was condemned as well, notwithstanding that it had not been purchased with the proceeds of the contraband goods, and did not belong to the owner of the ship.

If some papers be produced on demand and others be withheld or concealed, it is not necessarily to be assumed that the latter are to be fully credited. "If such a rule were established as a principle of the Court," said Sir W. Scott, in *The Calypso* (*g*), "it would let in an infinity of fraud, and make it the easiest thing in the world to protect the chief bulk of property in any case by giving up some part upon the pretended disclosures contained in these concealed papers. The more reasonable rule would be, that where there is one set of papers admitted to be false, and another set coming out of the same hands, that the whole is thrown into a state of uncertainty and doubt" (*h*). "The papers alone," said Erle, C. J., in *Hobbs* v. *Henning* (*i*), "are not a breach of neutrality so as to work a forfeiture of the ship; they are only evidence from which a cause of forfeiture can be inferred. They may be evidence either of enemy's property, or of destination to a blockaded port or to an enemy's port with contraband, and so

(*f*) The Nancy, 3 Rob. 122. Also The Margaret, 1 Act. 336.

(*g*) 2 Rob. 158.

(*h*) The following extract from an "Attestation on bringing in Papers Concealed" (Story on Prize Courts, p. 209), is interesting as an illustration of the expedients resorted to for concealment on the one hand, and of determined efforts at discovery on the other:—". . . . And the day after the capture he (*i. e.*, the commander of the capturing vessel) found the parcel of papers and writings hereunto annexed, marked with the letter A, made fast to the end of a twine, and stowed away and concealed amongst the bread; that the day following he found the parcel of papers and writings hereunto also annexed, marked with the letter B, concealed in a bin of rice; and the two parcels of papers and writings, marked with the letter C, concealed in two bins of calavances."

(*i*) 34 L. J. C. P. 122.

be evidence on which the judge may find a cause of forfeiture proved; but they are in themselves no cause of forfeiture. The language of Sir W. Scott, in the case of *The Franklin*, speaking of simulated papers, and saying that 'this fraudulent conduct justly subjects the ship to condemnation,' must be taken with reference to the question before him, whether the ship should be confiscated as well as the contraband cargo; and his decision is in the affirmative, and rightly, if the ship-owner was knowingly conveying contraband to an enemy's port, of which knowledge papers indicating a false destination would raise a presumption." The Court further observed that the plaintiff had not been shown to be responsible for the ship's papers, nor for any other goods than his own.

If discrepancies be found to exist between the depositions of the master and crew on the one hand, and the ship's papers on the other, the conviction of the Court must, as a general rule, be kept *in equilibrio* till it can receive further proof; but this is not a fixed rule, and each case must be regarded on its own merits (*j*).

If a neutral master be found guilty of fraudulent misconduct as regards the ship's papers, the vessel will be subject to condemnation; and if the cargo be of the same ownership, or it appear that the cargo-owners were privy to the fraud, the cargo will presumably share the fate of the ship. So that the principles as to confiscation applicable in the case of carriage of hostile despatches (*k*), would doubtless equally apply in the case of false or irregular papers. But the circumstance that false papers relative to the cargo be found will not necessarily condemn the ship. For, as was observed by Sir W. Scott in *The Calypso* (*l*), "evidence respecting the cargo

(*j*) The Vigilantia, 1 Rob. 1; The Odin, *ibid.* 252.

(*k*) *Vide* p. 208, *supra*.

(*l*) 2 Rob. 158.

does not generally affect the ship, as it may frequently happen that the owners of the cargo will, from lust of gain, put on board false papers without the knowledge or privity of the owners of the ship. But it is a very different case when the ship and cargo belong to the same persons; although I will not say that false papers would, even in such a case, necessarily lead to condemnation of the ship."

It is the duty of the master to produce *all* his papers, and least of all to withhold his instructions (*m*). And if he have an alternative destination the fact should so appear on the papers, otherwise belligerent cruisers may be misled (*n*). General clearances (as to the East or West Indies), if not absolutely illegal, are highly objectionable: and if resorted to should be accompanied by an affidavit that the cargo contains no prohibited goods (*o*). The master, also, is required to have knowledge of his cargo. Whatever may be the rule in times of peace, in times of war the master must be prepared to answer all reasonable enquiries as to his cargo (*p*). He must not aver ignorance, but if prejudiced by imposition practised upon him, he must seek redress from those by whose action he has been made to suffer (*q*).

The Papers to be Carried.—The proofs of neutrality, and the documents hitherto held to be necessary in order to establish a vessel's neutral character, and which, in consequence, neutral masters are expected to produce when called upon to do so, are the following (*r*):—

1. **The Flag.**—This is the most obvious badge of the vessel's national character, and Sir W. Scott's remarks in

(*m*) The Concordia, 1 Rob. 120.
(*n*) The Juffrau Anna, 1 Rob. 120.
(*o*) The Eenrom, 1 Rob. 6.
(*p*) *Ibid.*
(*q*) The Susan, 6 Rob. 461, and p. 209, *supra*.
(*r*) Arn. Insce., 5th ed. p. 614.

The Elizabeth (*infra*), establish the importance attached to it in the case of the vessel, though not of the cargo (*s*). And Sir C. Robinson has subjoined a note to the case of *The Elizabeth*, stating that (*t*) in *The Vreede Scholtys* the Court laid down the distinction as to hostility of character between ship and cargo in the following terms:—"A great distinction has been always made by the nations of Europe between ships and goods; some countries have gone so far as to make the flag and pass of the enemy conclusive on the cargo also, but this country has never carried the principle to that extent. It holds the ship bound by the character imposed upon it by the authority of the government from which all the documents issue. But goods which have no such dependence upon the authority of the state may be differently considered."

For the purposes of insurance a ship warranted neutral must bear no other flag than that which was neutral on the inception of the risk. If warranted of any given national character, she must bear the flag of that and of no other nation.

2. **The Passport, Sea-brief, Sea-letter, or Pass.**—This is a certificate granted by authority of the neutral state, giving permission to the master to proceed on the voyage proposed, and declaring that while on such voyage the ship is under protection of the neutral state (*u*). It is indispensable to the safety of a neutral ship, and no vessel may disown the national character so ascribed to her (*v*). "It is the established rule," said Sir W. Scott in *The Elizabeth* (*x*), "that a vessel sailing under the colours and pass of a nation is to be

(*s*) *Vide* also The Success, 1 Dobs. 131; and The Vreede Scholtys, *infra*.
(*t*) 5 Rob. 5, *not*.
(*u*) The Vigilantia, 1 Rob. 1; The Vreede Scholtys, *supra*.
(*v*) The Vigilantia, *supra*; The Vreede Scholtys, *supra*.
(*x*) 5 Rob. 4.

considered as clothed with the national character of that country. With goods it may be otherwise." And in *The Hoop* (*y*), his lordship refused to restore the vessel to an individual laying claim to it, but whose name did not appear on the ship's pass. The pass should also contain the master's name and address; the name, ownership, description, and tonnage of the vessel; the nature and quantity of the cargo, with its origin and destination, and any other details which the circumstances of the particular case may seem to render advisable. As additional evidence of neutral ownership, the vessel is sometimes herself stamped with the nationality of the owners. Thus, *The Elize* (*z*), seized in 1854, bore branded on her deck-beams the words "Danish property," together with the royal initials.

A distinction is sometimes set up, notably in New York, between the pass or passport and the sea-letter or brief, the latter supplying more particularly the details already mentioned relative to the cargo. But, generally speaking, both terms have the same meaning (*a*).

3. **The Register, or Certificate of Registry**, showing to whom and to what port the vessel belongs; and bearing, as being signed by some officer of customs, a certain stamp of public authority. As regards insurance, this document is not indispensable in order to comply with a neutral warranty if the ship possesses other documents from which her neutral character may be decisively ascertained. So it was held in the United States, where the vessel had a sea-letter but no register (*b*).

(*y*) 1 Rob. 129.

(*z*) 24 L. T. 170.

(*a*) *Vide* cases cited Arn. Insce., 5th ed. p. 615.

(*b*) *Barker* v. *Phœnix Insce. Co.*, 8 *Johns.* 237, cited 1 Phill. Insce., No. 806; and *vide* p. 230, *infra*.

4. **The Bill of Sale.**—This document is useful in cases where the flag and the build of the vessel appear out of harmony, in order that, by its means, belligerents may be satisfied that the vessel was purchased before; or captured, legally condemned, and purchased since; the declaration of war (*c*).

5. **The Muster-roll** (rôle d'équipage), or **Ship's Articles,** as containing the names, ages, quality, place of residence, and, especially, the place of birth, of every person of the ship's company. A strong suspicion must naturally be created if the majority of the crew be found to consist of foreigners, or still more if they be enemy subjects (*d*).

6. **The Charter-party,** in the case of chartered vessels; as it serves to authenticate many of the facts on which the proof of neutrality must rest (*e*).

7. **The Log-book,** faithfully kept. In the case of a steam-ship, no doubt the engineer's log-book would also be called for by captors.

8. **The Bill of Health,** which is a certificate, properly authenticated, that the ship comes from a place where no infectious distemper prevails.

9. **Bills of Lading, Invoices, Certificates of Origin,** and any other proofs of the national character of the cargo. The "captain's copies" of the bills of lading and the invoices can no doubt be easily falsified or fabricated where fraud is intended, and they carry with them less authenticity than attaches to documents of a more official character. Nevertheless, in the absence of any circumstances indicating fraudulent intention,

(*c*) The Adriana, 1 Rob. 317; The Sisters, 5 Rob. 155; Marshall, Insce., 441; *The Mersey, Blatch. Pr. Ca.* 187; *The Stephen Hart, ibid.* 388.

(*d*) The Sisters, *supra.*

(*e*) *Ibid.*

they are valuable as evidence of the place of shipment and of destination, and probably as to the shippers and consignees. Certificates of origin were generally deemed necessary during the continuance of the French wars, in order to prove that the goods were the subject of legal transport. In *The Springbok* (*f*), the absence of invoices from on board a vessel in time of war was characterized as a suspicious circumstance.

10. **Any documents** which have to be carried in accordance with express **treaty provisions** (*g*).

Although the absence of a document ordinarily deemed requisite will not of itself involve the vessel in condemnation, it may well be that the failure to produce the document will be held to justify the captors in bringing the vessel in for adjudication.

Insurance.

"In order to be neutral within the meaning of the warranty, so as to be protected against hostile capture, the ship must be furnished with all those documents and proofs of the neutral character of herself and her cargo required to be on board either by the law of nations or by the regulations of international treaties" (*h*). A warranty of neutrality requires that the ownership of the property shall be in accordance with the warranty, and that the property shall be accompanied by the usual evidence of neutrality (*i*), or by such evidence as may be required by treaty enactments. Thus, in 1778, a ship "warranted American property," which was seized by a French privateer, and ultimately released, was proved to have sailed during a portion of her

(*f*) *Blatch. Pr. Ca.* 435.
(*g*) Pollard *v.* Bell, 8 T. R. 434.
(*h*) Arnould, 5th ed. p. 614.
(*i*) Siffkin *v.* Lee, 2 B. & P. N. R. 484.

voyage without any passport. A treaty between France and America provided that such a document should be carried, and the Court decided that the non-compliance with the treaty-requirements discharged the underwriters; the warranty not meaning merely that the ship was American property, but that she was entitled to all the privileges of the American flag, and free from all inconveniences arising from liability, owing to non-compliance with treaty, to be otherwise regarded (*k*). And in another case (*l*), where an American ship was condemned in the French Courts for not carrying a list of her crew according to the treaty model, the Court of King's Bench held this sentence to be a conclusive falsification of neutral warranty, without inquiring whether the vessel was, as a fact, neutral or not. Again, in *Baring* v. *Claggett* (*m*), where the sea-letter did not contain the master's name, as by treaty required, the Court decided that the warranty of neutrality was not satisfied, as the ship had not such a sea-letter as was required by treaty. Thus, in *Pollard* v. *Bell* (*n*), it was observed that "where a State in amity with a belligerent power has by treaty agreed that the ships of their subjects shall only have the character when furnished with certain precise documents, whoever warrants a ship as the property of such subject should provide himself with those evidences which have, by the country to which it belongs, been agreed to be the necessary proof of that character." In another case—*Bell* v. *Carstairs* (*o*)—of documents deficient in respect of treaty requirements, the underwriters were held discharged, though the sentence of condemnation also proceeded on other grounds.

And where a ship was condemned for not producing the documents required to establish her neutrality, which was warranted in the policy, the insurance was declared to be voided; though if the master had produced the documents in question, the vessel would have been subjected to condemnation on the

(*k*) Rich *v.* Parker, 7 T. R. 703.

(*l*) Geyer *v.* Aguilar, 7 T. R. 681.

(*m*) 3 B. & P. 201; and *S. C.* in error, 5 East, 398.

(*n*) 8 T. R. 434, and Park's Insce., 8th ed. 731.

(*o*) 14 East, 374.

evidence of prohibited sailing contained in the said documents (*p*).

But while a vessel must carry all documents required by treaty, and in the strict form of the requirements, a neutral shipowner is under no obligation to provide himself with every document that belligerent powers may require purely by their own private ordinances; and the want of such documents will not forfeit a neutral warranty (*q*).

Thus, where an American vessel had been condemned in a Danish prize-court on the ground that her sea passport had not been notarially certified, the defendant underwriters were called upon by the Court to show how such a requirement came within either the provisions of the general law of nations, or of any relative international treaty (*r*). Similarly, in *Le Cheminant* v. *Allnutt* (*s*), it was in effect held that condemnation on the ground that the ship had no register did not discharge the underwriters, unless they could show that the carrying of this document was necessary in the foregoing sense.

But the above implied conditions relate only to insurances effected for the shipowner, and not to those effected for cargo-owners. For Lord Ellenborough, in *Carruthers* v. *Gray* (*t*), held, that there was no implied warranty on the part of the goods-owner that the ship should be properly documented. And in another case, where the insurance was on goods, and the vessel was condemned for not being properly documented, the underwriters were held not to be discharged (*u*); and on this case being mentioned in *Bell* v. *Carstairs*, Lord Ellenborough approved it, observing that in an insurance on goods "the owner of the goods has no concern in the obtaining of the proper documents with which the vessel is to be furnished for the voyage;" the case being otherwise where the ship herself is concerned.

(*p*) Steel *v.* Lacy, 3 Taunt. 284.

(*q*) *Vide* note, Arnould, 5th ed. p. 618.

(*r*) Bell *v.* Bromfield, 15 East, 368. See also Price *v.* Bell, 1 East, 663, and Bell *v.* Carstairs, *supra*.

(*s*) 4 Taunt. 367.

(*t*) 3 Camp. 142; *S. C.* 15 East, 35. See also Hobbs *v.* Henning, 34 L. J. (C. P.) 117, 122; 17 C. B. N. S. 791.

(*u*) Dawson *v.* Atty, 7 East, 367. See also Carruthers *v.* Gray, *supra*.

Marshall and Phillips consider this distinction very questionable, but it has, in fact, been adopted by the English Courts. Arnould (*x*) is also in accord with it.

During the great French wars, trade with the Continent was carried on by means of simulated papers; but it was uniformly held by our Courts that condemnations on that ground discharged the underwriters in the absence of an express licence in the policy to carry such papers (*y*). And this, although it was notorious that the trade protected by the policy could be carried on in no other way, and that the possession of such papers actually tended to diminish the risk (*z*). The decision was the same where the fact of carrying simulated papers was apparently one at least of the efficient causes of condemnation. Looking at the terms of the sentence of condemnation, said the Court in *Oswell* v. *Vigne* (*a*), the carrying of simulated papers must be regarded as one of the grounds of forfeiture; and as the policy contained no leave to carry such papers the loss could not be charged against the underwriters. In this case the ship had been condemned by enemy captors on various grounds, and the underwriters disclaimed liability on the plea that one of these grounds was the carrying of simulated papers, for which the policy contained no permission. The Court decided, in effect, that the underwriters' contention was well founded, and that, however ungracious, in the particular circumstances, was this defence, the breach of the insurance conditions must be held to have voided the policy. Of course, if the policy contains a licence to carry simulated papers, and the ship is condemned for carrying them, the underwriters will be liable (*b*). The above cases answer an enquiry of Lord Mansfield, referred to in *Steele* v. *Lacy*, *supra*, as to the necessity for permission to carry such papers (*c*).

It has been held in the United States that the carrying of suspicious papers is a breach of neutral warranty. Thus, where

(*x*) Insce., 5th ed. p. 673.

(*y*) Arnould, 5th ed. 673.

(*z*) Horneyer *v.* Lushington, 15 East, 46, an. 1812; 3 Camp. 85. See also Fomin *v.* Oswell, 3 Camp. 357, an. 1813; 1 M. & S. 393; cf. p. 402, *infra*.

(*a*) 15 East, 70.

(*b*) Bell *v.* Bromfield, 15 East, 364.

(*c*) Arnould, 5th ed. 673, n.

certain papers relating to a former shipment, written in sympathetic ink, were found concealed in a cask on board, a mystery being in consequence thrown over the shipment, the underwriters were discharged (*d*). Concealment of papers, as justifying carrying into port for adjudication, has also been held by the United States Courts to amount to a breach of neutral warranty (*e*).

In the same country it has been held that the mixing of belligerent with neutral goods and carrying them, so disguised, as neutral, is a breach of neutral warranty, and will void the policy as to the whole of the neutral cargo (*f*).

We will now pass on to the consideration of the consequences to neutrals of engaging in the privileged trade of the enemy.

(*d*) *Carrere* v. *Union Insce. Co.*, 3 *Har. & John.* 324; 1 Phillips' Insce., No. 809.

(*e*) *Livingston* v. *Maryland Insce. Co.*, *Cranch*, 536; 1 Phillips' Insce., No. 809.

(*f*) *Phœnix Insce. Co.* v. *Pratt*, 2 *Binn.* 308; *Schultz* v. *Insce. Co. of N. Am.*, 3 *Wash. C. C. R.* 117.

CAPTURE AND CONFISCATION OF PROPERTY ENGAGED IN THE PRIVILEGED TRADE OF THE ENEMY; SAILING UNDER FLAG AND PASS OF THE ENEMY (*g*); ENGAGING IN ILLICIT TRADE.

(The "Continuous Voyage" Question.)

It was in former times common for a State to restrict to the vessels of its own subjects all carrying-trade between the mother country and its colonies, and a similar limitation was enforced as regards the national coasting trade. Thus, the coasting trade of the British Isles and possessions was, at one time, limited to British vessels, and this restriction has not been a great while abolished. (*Vide* 17 & 18 Vict. c. 5.) But the ancient barriers against a free carrying-trade have now been generally, if not entirely, removed in the case of over-seas trade, and probably in most cases of coasting traffic. But so long as such barriers existed, it was by the common law of nations deemed unlawful for neutrals on the outbreak of hostilities to engage in a trade closed to them in times of peace. If they did this, their property so employed was liable to seizure, as being devoted to service of the enemy. This principle is embodied in what is commonly known as the "**Rule of the War of 1756.**" During that war the French, finding their colonial trade, owing to the British

(*g*) Pp. 20 *et seq.*, *supra*, may be referred to for instances of fictitious transfer from hostile ownership.

maritime supremacy, entirely destroyed, removed the existing restrictions and threw the trade open to the Dutch, who were neutrals. They issued, in fact, to Dutch vessels, special licences or passes expressly authorizing them to trade between France and her colonies, while they at the same time continued the prohibition as regards all other neutrals. The British Government in consequence issued instructions ordering the seizure and condemnation of any Dutch vessels availing themselves of this privilege; the cargoes to be condemned with the ships. "It is a sound principle of the law of nations," said Sir W. Scott, in *The Rendsborg* (*h*), "that you are not to relieve the distresses of one belligerent to the prejudice of another; any advantage that you may obtain from such an act will not make it lawful. . . . . You are not, from a prospect of advantage to yourself, or from any other motive, to step in, on every outcry for help, and rescue the belligerent from the gripe of his adversary." The same principle was laid down in terms of equal clearness and force in various other cases, notably in *The Immanuel* (*i*), *Wilhelmina* (*j*), *Providentia* (*k*), *Anna Catharina* (*l*), and *The Vrow Anna Catharina* (*m*). "Vessels so engaged," observes Wheaton, "were, in the judgments of the Courts, to be considered like transports in the enemy's service, and hence liable to capture and condemnation, upon the same principle with property condemned for carrying military persons or despatches" (*n*). In the British Courts this principle has been held to apply not merely in circumstances such as those giving rise to the Rule of 1756, but to all cases in which

(*h*) 4 Rob. 121.
(*j*) 4 Rob. App. A.
(*i*) 2 Rob. 197.
(*k*) 2 Rob. 150.
(*l*) 4 Rob. 107.
(*m*) 5 Rob. 161. *Vide* also The Vigilantia, 1 Rob. 1; *The Alliance*, *Blatch. Pr. Ca.* 262; *The Julia*, 1 *Gall.* 605; 8 *Cranch*, 181; *The Aurora*, *ibid.* 203; *The Hiram*, *ibid.* 444; *The Ariadne*, 2 *Wheat.* 100.
(*n*) Int. Law, 2 Eng. ed. p. 588.

neutrals engage during war in a trade not open to them in times of peace. This general application, however, has been controverted by American statesmen, and was at one time a fruitful source of contention between that country and Great Britain. As a concession to representations in this respect, indeed, modified instructions were issued by the British Government in January, 1798, in virtue of which neutral vessels were allowed to carry on a direct commerce between the colony of the enemy and their own country (*o*). But owing to the altered conditions now, as already mentioned, prevailing, this difference of opinion is hardly likely to be a source of difficulty in the future. The Rule was, indeed, apparently entirely over-ridden in the war of 1854 by a British Order in Council, declaring that "the subjects or citizens of any neutral or friendly state shall and may, during the present hostilities with Russia, freely trade with all ports and places wheresoever situate, which shall not be in a state of blockade."

In *The Juliana* (*p*), a neutral vessel captured by the British, on a voyage between France and Senegal, then a French colony, the Court, after much investigation, decided that France had been accustomed to leave the trade of Senegal open to foreign vessels, and therefore decreed restitution of the vessel to the neutral claimants.

In *The Rebecca* (*q*), an American ship seized for carrying cargo between Surinam and Amsterdam, the Court restored the vessel, but refused to allow freight on the cargo condemned. In *The America* (*r*), where a similar vessel, bound from Mauritius ostensibly to Hamburg, was seized for proceeding to a French port, the cargo was condemned, freight

(*o*) *Vide* The Rosalie and Betty, 2 Rob. 343.
(*p*) 4 Rob. 336.
(*q*) 2 Rob. 101.
(*r*) 3 Rob. 36.

being refused. The shipowner, in claiming freight, contended that the deviation was fraudulent on the part of the master, and that it was hard that for this the shipowner should be made to suffer; but the Court held that the proof of this alleged fraudulent conduct of the master was not so clear as to warrant its acceptance in the sense claimed by the owner (*m*).

Continuous Voyages.—The colonial trade which a neutral may not carry on directly, he may not carry on circuitously. This was clearly laid down in *The William* (*n*), during the war which occurred between this country and Spain in 1800. *The William*, a neutral vessel, was bound from La Guira, a Spanish colony, to Marblehead, a port in the United States, with a cargo of sugar, &c. and cocoa, which cargo was in due course landed and entered at the custom house, and a bond was given for the payment of duties. But within ten days of the arrival at Marblehead the chief part of the cargo was reloaded and carried towards Bilboa in Spain. The vessel was captured by the British, and it was finally decided by the Court of Appeal that the mere touching at Marblehead and payment of dues there was not sufficient to establish a *boná fide* importation into America, and that the voyage was practically continuous from La Guira to Bilboa. Therefore that it was in violation of the Rule of the War of 1756; and the cocoa brought from La Guira was consequently condemned.

In the above case the landing and reshipping at Marblehead was found to be in pursuance of a preconceived design to evade the prohibition against engaging in the privileged trade of the enemy. But each of such cases has to be judged on its own merits. Thus in *The Maria* (*o*), restitution was

(*m*) *Vide* pp. 120, 189, as to owners' responsibility for master's acts.
(*n*) 5 Rob. 385, an. 1806. (*o*) 5 Rob. 365.

ordered on the ground that there had been a *bonâ fide* intention to effect a sale at the intermediate port, and consequently that the voyage was not to be regarded as continuous. And Sir W. Scott in *The Polly* (*p*), on the point as to what constituted a genuine importation (at an apparently intermediate port), said: "An American has undoubtedly a right to import the produce of the Spanish colonies for his own use, and after it is imported *bonâ fide* into his own country he would be at liberty to carry them on to the general commerce of Europe. . . . . It is not my business to say what is universally the test of a *bonâ fide* importation. It is argued that it would not be sufficient that the duties should be paid and that the cargo should be landed. If these criteria are not to be resorted to, I should be at a loss to know what should be the test; and I am strongly disposed to hold that it would be sufficient that the goods should be landed and the duties paid. If it appears to have been landed and warehoused for a considerable time, it does, I think, raise a forcible presumption on that side, and it throws on the other party to show how this could be merely insidious and colourable." This, however, was not the view taken by the Master of the Rolls (Sir William Grant) in the appeal case of *The William*, already mentioned. "If the voyage from the place of lading," said his Lordship, "be not really ended, it matters not by what acts the party may have evinced his desire of making it appear to have ended. That those acts have been attended with trouble and expense cannot alter their quality or their effect. The trouble and expense may weigh as circumstances of evidence to show the purpose for which the acts were done, but if the evasive purpose be admitted or proved we can never be bound to accept, as a substitute for the observance of the law, the means, however operose, which have been employed to

(*p*) 2 Rob. 361, an. 1800.

cover a breach of it. . . . In a fictitious importation the acts to be done are mere voluntary ceremonies which have no natural connexion whatever with the purpose of sending on the cargo to another market, and which, therefore, would never be resorted to by a person entertaining that purpose, except with a view of giving to the voyage, which he has resolved to continue, the appearance of being broken by an importation which he has resolved not really to make." It would indeed seem evident that if the original intention was to make a really continuous voyage, the mere fact that customs dues, &c., have been incurred at an intermediate port is altogether beside the question. For, the original estimate as to the balance of advantages would naturally include such charges on the debit side of the account, and if, notwithstanding, the final result promised to be satisfactory, the advantage of incurring the intermediate charges in order to secure it would be obvious. In 1801, the British Advocate-General, in an official report (*q*) on the law concerning the colonial trade, apparently quoting Sir W. Scott's decision in *The Polly*, *supra*, declared that the High Court of Admiralty had expressly decided, and that he saw no reason to expect that the Court of Appeal would vary the rules, that landing the goods and paying the duties in the neutral country breaks the continuity of the voyage, and is such an importation as legalizes the trade. But the Advocate-General, if in fact basing his remarks on the above judgment, would appear to have lost sight of the fact that it was qualified by a reference to the length of time during which the goods were warehoused; and the subsequent decision in *The William* in 1806 certainly falsified the prediction relative to the view likely to be taken by the Court of Appeal.

The Thomyris (*r*) (1808) is also an interesting case in this

(*q*) Mentioned in Maritime Warfare, p. 206.

(*r*) 1 Edw. Ad. 17. *Vide* also The Jonge Pieter, p. 260, *infra*.

connexion. A British order having prohibited all trade from the port of one enemy to that of another, certain barilla on the American ship *Thomyris* was seized in respect of an alleged breach of this order, viz., in being carried from Alicante to Cherbourg. It appeared that the goods were brought from Alicante to Lisbon, where they were put on board the neutral vessel for Cherbourg. "In all cases of this description," said Sir W. Scott, "it is a clear and settled principle that the mere transhipment of a cargo at an intermediate port will not break the continuity of the voyage, which can only be effected by a previous actual importation into the common stock of the country where the transhipment takes place." The barilla was declared to have been sold at Lisbon, but it was decided that the goods having been water-borne at the time of the alleged sale, and then transhipped, no importation could be considered to have taken place.

The Stephen Hart, *The Springbok*, and *The Peterhoff*, mentioned in connexion with the subject of contraband (pp. 186 *et seq.*, *supra*), provide an exposition of the view of the United States Courts relative to the continuous voyage question.

The prohibitions against engaging in the enemy's privileged colonial trade apply also to his privileged coasting trade. "As to the coasting trade," said Sir W. Scott in *The Emanuel* (*s*), "supposing it to be a trade not usually open to foreign vessels, can there be described a more effective accommodation that can be given to an enemy during a war, than to undertake it for him during his own disability?" In *The Johanna Tholen* (*t*), however, it was observed that whereas the penalty formerly enforced by this country against neutral vessels so engaged was confiscation, it has in later times been reduced to a forfeiture of freight. But this mitigated penalty is applicable only in cases where the trading has

(*s*) 1 Rob. 300.

(*t*) 6 Rob. 72.

been open and undisguised. Where it has been aggravated by concealment or subterfuge, such as the carrying of false papers (as in this case), the stricter penalty of former times has been enforced.

"Sailing under the enemy's licence is deemed, *per se*, an efficient cause of condemnation" (*u*).

Illicit Trade.—Neutrals possess, it is true, the right to carry lawful merchandise the property of belligerents, but annexed to this right is the implied condition that such traffic shall be engaged in openly, without subterfuge. Any underhand or fraudulent conduct on the part of a neutral, with the view of evading belligerent rights, will expose both ship and cargo to condemnation. Of this, the case of *Darby* v. *The Brig Ernstern*, in the United States Courts (*x*), is an exceptional but well-defined instance, the ship and cargo being both condemned on the ground that neutral subjects cannot, consistently with neutrality, combine with enemy subjects to wrest from their adversary advantages acquired by the rights of war, and so, in effect, take part with the enemy. During the hostilities occurring in 1782 between this country and the United States, Dominica capitulated to the latter power, which thereupon prohibited all commerce between the island and Great Britain. To evade this prohibition, one Mason, a British subject, arranged with an Ostend firm to ship goods from London *viâ* Ostend. This firm bought in London the brig *Ernstern*, which was loaded by Mason for Ostend. On arrival there the Ostend firm supplied her with false and colourable papers, assumed the ownership of the cargo, and disguised it under neutral garb in order to

(*u*) Story's Prize Courts, p. 70, cases cited.
(*x*) 2 *Dall.* 34.

screen it from capture. These precautions were, it would seem, quite superfluous, as an Act of Congress had already extended protection to enemy goods on neutral ships. The vessel was seized and detained, and ultimately, in the peculiar circumstances, condemned, the American Court deciding that the vessel had exceeded the rights accorded to neutral vessels. "Can such conduct," it was inquired, "consist with neutrality? Can there be a more flagrant violation of it? Does it not aim to wrest from France and the United States the advantages they acquired by the conquest of Dominica? And does it not evince a fraudulent combination with British subjects, and a palpable partiality?"

The Commercen (y) is another leading case in the American Courts in relation to unlawful trade. During the progress of hostilities between Great Britain and the United States, a Swedish vessel, whilst carrying a cargo of English oats and barley for use by the British forces in the Spanish peninsula, was captured by an American cruiser. The direct effect of this voyage, said the Court, was to aid the British hostilities against the United States; and a vessel engaged in carrying stores for the exclusive use of the British forces must, to all intents and purposes, be deemed a British transport. The cargo being confiscated, freight was denied to the neutral carrier—a penalty which was declared to be, in the circumstances, a very lenient administration of justice.

Confiscation.—To engage in the privileged trade of the enemy, with the necessary consequence of mitigating, so far as he is concerned, the inconveniences to which it is the right, as well as the policy, of his adversary to subject him, is an offence involving confiscation of neutral property so engaged.

(y) 1 *Wheat. Rep.* 382. Also p. 175, *supra.*

As we have seen, there is not complete unanimity touching the propriety of classifying such an objectionable traffic as an offence against the law of nations, and the penalty of confiscation is not enforced with the strict severity observed in some other cases. Thus, in the leading case of *The Immanuel* (z), in 1799, though the ship and cargo were of the same ownership, the cargo only was condemned. *The Immanuel*, a Hamburg ship, whilst on a voyage from Hamburg to St. Domingo, a French possession, shipped some goods at Bordeaux, and Sir W. Scott, in condemning these goods, intimated that, until better instructed by the judgment of a superior tribunal, he would hold himself not to be authorized to restore goods, although neutral property, passing in direct voyage between the mother country of the enemy and its colonies. The Hamburg goods, on the other hand, were restored; and also the ship, but without freight or expenses. The learned judge, in restoring the ship, remarked that if the goods had been contraband, the ship would have been liable to confiscation, but that this was a case where a neutral might more easily misapprehend his own rights, and where he acted without the notice afforded by former decisions on the subject. In *The Johanna Tholen* (a), however, the King's Advocate, in his reply, laid down a clear distinction between cases of open and undisguised traffic, and cases attended by concealment of purpose and falsification of documents. "In such cases, the course which this Court has pursued in various instances has been to resort to the more strict principle of former times, and to hold the vessel herself subject to confiscation." Cases on this point are *The Edward* (b), *The Hoffnung* (c), *The Ebenezer* (d), *The George*

(z) 2 Rob. 186.

(a) *Supra.*

(b) 4 Rob. 68.

(c) 2 Rob. 162.

(d) 6 Rob. 250. See also The Carolina, 3 Rob. 75; and The Mars, 6 Rob. 79.

Thomas (*e*), and *The Volant* (*f*). And application of the same principle involved, as we have just seen, the condemnation of the brig *Ernstern* in the United States Courts.

Insurance.

The engaging in the enemy's privileged trade constitutes a breach of neutral warranty. Thus in *Berens* v. *Rucker* (*g*), Lord Mansfield intimated that if a neutral vessel traded to a French colony with all the privileges of a French vessel, it must be deemed to have been adopted and naturalized, and to be liable to condemnation as an enemy's ship. "There can be no doubt," says Arnould (*h*), "that an insurance effected in this country, being at the time a belligerent power, to protect neutral trading of this exceptional character, would be treated as wholly illegal and void by our Courts, on the ground that 'trading to an enemy's colony, with all the privileges of an enemy's ship, causes a neutral vessel to be regarded as an enemy's ship, and renders her lawful prize.'" If illegal trading be carried on by the master without the authority of his owners, and the vessel be confiscated in consequence, the circumstances may be such that the loss may be attributed to barratry (*i*).

The last of the Belligerent Rights against Neutrals to be considered is that of Pre-emption.

(*e*) 3 Rob. 233.

(*f*) 4 Rob. App.; 1 Act. 171.

(*g*) 1 W. Black. 314. See also The Immanuel, and The Anna Catharina, *supra*, and The Dree Gebrœders, 4 Rob. 232.

(*h*) Mar. Insce. 5th ed. 701.

(*i*) Arnould's Insce. 5th ed. 763.

PRE-EMPTION.

The belligerent right to pre-empt or "requisition" the property of neutrals may be resorted to either as a modified form of the harsher right of confiscation, or on the principle that necessity knows no law, and that consequently in a moment of peril the paramount right of self-preservation justifies the appropriation of whatever comes ready to hand either as a weapon of offence or a means of defence.

Under the head Contraband of War (*k*), the articles generally subject to pre-emption in lieu of confiscation, and the circumstances in which the right is to be applied, have already been considered. It may, however, be convenient for present purposes to briefly recapitulate them. Certain articles, then, of equivocal nature, that is, equally applicable either to peaceful or to warlike uses, have in bygone days, in lieu of the confiscation to which the latter quality condemned them, been sometimes placed on an exceptional footing.

Chief amongst these articles are provisions. There seems to be no definite rule governing the circumstances in which such goods are liable to pre-emption, and the subject has from time to time been by turns hotly debated and regulated by international treaty. This will sufficiently appear on reference to the subject of Contraband generally, pp. 156—200. Broadly stated, provisions in a made-up or manufactured state, ready for consumption and suitable for naval or military purposes, have been regarded as contraband if destined for a naval or military port of the enemy, or if presum-

(*k*) Pages 173—179, *supra*.

ably intended for warlike purposes. Foodstuffs not made up ready for consumption, such as grain and flour, and provisions generally, destined for non-military ports of the enemy not invested, have been by some held to be subject to pre-emption, on the ground that such goods, though not subject to condemnation as contraband, are nevertheless objectionable as tending to defeat the possibility of starving the enemy into submission: and that it is therefore permissible either to pre-empt them or to order them off from the enemy coast. Naval stores apparently intended for the enemy's warlike uses have been regarded as contraband and subject to condemnation accordingly, but pitch and tar, when the produce of the country exporting them, were, in Sir W. Scott's time, subjected to the milder right of pre-emption. The reason for this relaxation of the stricter belligerent right was that these articles formed such a considerable part of the ordinary export trade of the countries producing them that their wholesale confiscation would have exposed such neutral powers to exceptional injury. The treaty of commerce arranged between this country and the United States in 1796 provided, as regards provisions and other articles which, though not generally contraband, may be so regarded, that whenever these should by the existing law of nations be regarded and seized as contraband, they should not be confiscated, but the masters or owners of the vessels should be paid the full value of the articles, with a reasonable mercantile profit, plus freight and demurrage. The reason expressly given for this stipulation is that it is "expedient to provide against the inconveniences and misunderstandings" likely to arise from the difficulty of agreeing on the precise cases in which such goods become contraband. But to entitle a neutral owner to the benefit of the milder rule of pre-emption it has always been necessary that he shall have acted strictly *bonâ fide* (*l*). As to

(*l*) The Sarah Christina, 1 Rob. 241.

the price to be paid by the pre-emptors, it is to be based on the principle of reasonable compensation. Although famine prices may be prevailing at the port of the vessel's intended destination, the belligerent captor is not to be held liable to indemnify on that basis (*m*). The owner is to receive a reasonable indemnification and a fair profit, having regard to the original cost and expenses, and the captor is under no obligation to take these cargoes on the terms on which the enemy would be content to purchase them; and the same principle is to be observed in awarding costs and damages against captors adjudged to have made a wrongful seizure (*n*). In *The Zacheman* (*o*), where a cargo of tar from Sweden to Rochefort had been brought in for inquiry whether it was intended for government purposes or not, and with a view to exercise of the right of pre-emption (substituted by treaty with Sweden for that of confiscation), the British Government ultimately refused to purchase. On this the neutral owners claimed damages for the delay, and Sir W. Scott decided that three weeks' demurrage should be paid by the government, observing that the Admiralty must understand that it was due to the owners that such matters should not be kept subject to long negotiation, but that a conclusion must be come to promptly. Naval stores laden on neutral vessels before declaration of hostilities, and intended for an enemy port, are liable to be seized in port of loading and pre-empted (*p*).

Section No. 38, in the Naval Prize Act, 1864, deals with the subject of pre-emption as follows:—

> "Where a ship of a foreign nation passing the seas laden with naval or victualling stores intended to be

(*m*) The Haabet, 2 Rob. 174.

(*n*) The Sarah Christina, *supra*.

(*o*) 5 Rob. 152.

(*p*) The Maria Magdalena, Hay & Marriott, 250. *Vide* also The Vryheid, *ibid.* 188; and Mar. Warfare, pp. 253, 254.

carried to a port of any enemy of Her Majesty is taken and brought into a port of the United Kingdom, and the purchase for the service of Her Majesty of the stores on board the ship appears to the Lords of the Admiralty expedient without the condemnation thereof in a Prize Court, in that case the Lords of the Admiralty may purchase, on the account or for the service of Her Majesty, all or any of the stores on board the ship; and the Commissioners of Customs may permit the stores purchased to be entered and landed within any port."

In former times, it was no doubt, on occasion, quite within the range of possibility to bring the enemy to terms by cutting off his food supplies. But matters now stand on a very different footing. Well-nigh the whole of Europe is a network of railway communication, and not only is each country intersected, but the communication is carried uninterruptedly into neighbouring states; so that the expedient of pre-emption as a means of cutting off supplies from the enemy will presumably not be largely resorted to in the future.

The above remarks relate more particularly to the pre-emption of neutral property destined for enemy uses, and seized with the primary object of preventing such use. The requisitioning of neutral property by belligerents altogether irrespective of its intended use or destination, stands on a different footing; viz. that based on the principle of self-preservation or urgent necessity. This peculiar belligerent right, for present purposes—and perhaps not altogether incorrectly—included under the head Pre-emption, is technically known by the name *Droit d'angarie*, *jus angariæ*, or Angary (*q*). "By virtue of urgent necessities of war," says

(*q*) ἀγγαρεύω: "to press one to serve as a courier." A Roman system of impressment, in force of which the supply and maintenance of horses was compulsory on the roads of the Empire in order to secure the constant transmission of imperial despatches: a government postal system.

Beawes (*r*), "vessels are frequently detained to serve a prince in an expedition; and, for this, have often their lading taken out, if a sufficient number of empty ones are not procurable to supply the state's necessity, and this without any regard to the colours they bear, or whose subjects they are; so that it frequently happens that many of the European nations may be forcibly united in the same service at a juncture when most of their sovereigns are at peace and in amity with the nation which they are obliged to serve. Some have doubted of the legality of the thing, but it is certainly conformable to the law both of nations and nature, for a prince in distress to make use of whatever vessels he finds in his ports, that are fit for his purpose and may contribute to the successes of his enterprise; but under this condition, that he makes them a reasonable recompense for their trouble, and does not expose either the ships or the men to any loss or damage."

The right has been described as less a right than an abuse of that power which a sovereign disposes of in places within his dominion; but, both by treaty and by special agreement, it has been recognised as a necessary incident of war. An instance in which the right was, two centuries ago, exercised by this country will be found in the footnote on p. 255, *infra;* but a recent and therefore more important example occurred in the Franco-Prussian War of 1870. Lying in the Seine, near Duchair, were eleven merchant vessels, and these were all seized and sunk by the Prussian troops in order to block the channel against the approach of certain French warships. Amongst the ships thus requisitioned were six English colliers, which, in accordance with permission previously obtained from the Prussians, had come up to Rouen to discharge their cargoes. This operation had, in fact, been

(*r*) Lex Mercatoria, quoted in Mar. Warfare, p. 213.

completed, and the vessels were about to return with a ballasting of cliff-chalk for the Tyne, when the crews were ordered ashore, the ballast-ports were enlarged, and the vessels sunk, the Prussian officer declaring that he took the vessels (for which he gave receipts) as a military requisition. On representations being made to Prince (then Count) Bismarck with respect to this arbitrary destruction of British property, he replied that the measure, however exceptional, was justified on the ground of necessity. "It did not," he said, "overstep the bounds of international warlike usage, and was, so far as a neutral state was concerned, entirely a matter of indemnification for the damage done." At another stage of the negotiations, the Count had, it is true, stated that he found that the law officers held that a belligerent had a full right, in self-defence, to the seizure of neutral vessels in the rivers or inland waters of the other belligerent, and that compensation to the owners was due by the vanquished power, not by the victors; adding, that if conquering belligerents admitted the right of foreigners to compensation for the destruction of their property in the invaded state, they would open the door to new and inadmissible principles in warfare; and that claims for indemnity were submitted to him daily by neutrals holding property in France, which he could never admit: but that he valued the friendship and goodwill of England too highly to accept this interpretation of the law in the case which had arisen, and that he preferred to give full satisfaction to the people of England.

With all respect for the opinion attributed to the German law officers, and to Count Bismarck's illustration in connexion with it, the case of foreigners domiciled in the conquered country, the fortunes of which they must be held to have deliberately elected to share, stands on a very different footing from that of neutrals present on the waters of the belligerent state for a purely temporary purpose, especially when, as in this case, the British vessels were within the belligerent dominion by express permission of the invaders. But be this as it may, the Prussian Government having both frankly expressed their regret at the occurrence, and their perfect willingness to indemnify the sufferers if the British Government would accept the duty of fixing the amount of compensation, the difficulty was thus amicably arranged, the question of compensation being referred to the Board of Trade.

Compensation was ultimately awarded as follows:—

(1) Estimated market value of the ships as fixed by Lloyd's surveyors, less 15*l.* net proceeds of ship's boats sold by the masters. The Prussian Government voluntarily agreed to pay, in addition, the sum of 25 per cent. on such values as a compensation to the owners in respect of any loss to them consequent on a forced sale. The Board of Trade considered this allowance extremely liberal, and beyond the merits of the case.

(2) The chalk ballast to be valued at 3*s.* 6*d.* per ton, that is, those vessels which were already ballasted to be dealt with on that basis. Vessels not loaded to be allowed 2*s.* 6*d.* per ton—the loading charges being calculated at 1*s.* per ton. The owners claimed 10*s.* per ton, the famine value at Newcastle, where the price had been sent up in consequence of the non-arrival of the vessels with the expected supplies. But on the basis of the official report, the allowance was fixed at the ordinary market price there.

(3) Claims for owners' loss of employment of the vessels, and for masters' and crews' loss of employment, were rejected. As regards the second item, it was observed that the crew were presumably engaged for the voyage out and home, and that they were consequently liable to be dismissed on their return to the Tyne without right to compensation.

(4) Claims for loss of effects were rejected, as it was evident that the men were allowed ample opportunity to land

their effects. Excessive claims were put forward, in some cases for loss of watches and chains, cash, and nautical instruments, though, as it appears, the claimants, notwithstanding their alleged precipitate departure, had contrived to carry ashore with them cumbrous articles of clothing. It was, however, agreed to allow a small gratuity as against the possible value of any portion of clothes which might have been lost.

(5) Expenses incurred by Her Majesty's Government in sending the crews home were allowed, as well as the outlay for consular fees and protests. Also travelling and subsistence money and cost of valuations.

(6) Interest was allowed at 5 per cent. from 1st January, 1871 (instead of from 21st December, 1870, as claimed) to end of April, 1871.

The total allowance was 7,088*l.* 8*s.* 5*d.* (minus the value of the boats, 15*l.* 2*s.* 0*d.*), or less than one-third of the sum for which claims were originally put forward (*s*).

There were also, it may be mentioned, seized by the Prussians during the same war, between six and seven hundred Swiss railway carriages and some Austrian rolling stock, which were devoted to military uses throughout a considerable period of the war (*t*).

The seizure of the Genoese corn-ship by the Venetian war-galleys, to which reference has already been made (*u*), although apparently unconnected with the existence of any hostilities, is interesting as an instance of the right of pre-emption arising out of urgent necessity. "There was a famine at Corfu"—this is the history of the seizure as tersely given by Roccus (Note LX.)—and on this fact the seizure was justified.

(*s*) State Papers, 1870-1, vol. 61, pp. 575—612.

(*t*) Pitt Cobbett's Leading Cases, p. 254.

(*u*) P. 39, *supra*.

Insurance.

As has already been pointed out under the head "Embargo and Reprisals" (*v*), a seizure of neutral property with the view not of confiscation, but of paying for or ultimately restoring it, is, within the meaning of the marine policy, to be regarded rather as an arrest than as a capture (*w*). The ordinary wording of the policy, it is true, admits liability for the one as much as for the other, but it would seem that the right to abandon to underwriters may, in certain cases of arrest, be less obvious than in cases of capture. The seizure of the Genoese corn-ship, mentioned above, was held not to be a capture but an arrest, during which the captain remained in charge of his ship; and as this arrest was, so far as the vessel herself was concerned, merely temporary, the Genoese Rota-Court decided that the shipowners were not entitled to abandon to underwriters. Arnould, referring to the corn, observes that a question has been raised whether in similar cases the assured can recover as for a loss by arrest and detention; but, he observes, "I have no doubt that in point of strict law the assured is entitled to recover as for a total loss, deducting, however, the money paid him by the arresting government from the amount of his claim under the policy" (*x*). Later, referring to the ship, he says, "Of course, if the arrest creates only a temporary obstruction of the voyage, without giving rise to any permanent loss of control over the ship, it cannot give any right to abandon." Perhaps a distinction may reasonably be drawn in such a case between the ship and the cargo, for it may well be a foregone conclusion that the ship will be released—and this without unnecessary delay—and that the cargo will be retained. This being so, the reason for abandonment of the ship seems less obvious. But, as regards the cargo, as it has passed away from the owners for good and all, owing to the operation of a peril insured against, they are presumably entitled to recover as for a total loss, after notice of abandonment. But if, before commencement of the proceedings,

(*v*) P. 39, *supra*.

(*w*) *Vide* Rodocanachi *v.* Elliott, 28 L. T. Rep. 844.

(*x*) 5th ed. p. 755.

the arresting government should have paid over the value of the cargo appropriated, then the amount recoverable from underwriters would presumably be any deficiency as between the amount of such payment and the sum insured. Which, it may be supposed, is what Arnould intended by his above observation relative to the corn.

The wages and provisions of the crew while the ship is under arrest are not chargeable against the underwriters on the ship. The shipowner is deemed to have taken into his conclusions the possibility of detention, and to have calculated his freight accordingly. The period of detention is considered as part of the voyage, and the shipowner cannot look to his underwriter for expenses outside the contract of insurance. Nor does the arrest break up the voyage under the charter-party, or dissolve the contract of affreightment. "Subject to the rights of the captor, and so long as these rights remain unestablished by a sentence of condemnation as to ship or cargo, or both, the original contract of affreightment is binding on both parties." (Maclachlan on Shipping, 2nd ed., p. 460; but *vide* p. 425, *infra*, with respect to the effect of unlivery by order of the Court.)

Having now considered the rights of belligerents (1) against the enemy, and (2) against neutrals, let us proceed to discuss the third class of belligerent rights, viz., Municipal (in contradistinction to International) Rights.

VI.

BELLIGERENT MUNICIPAL RIGHTS.

Restraint, Seizure, and Destruction of Property of the National Subjects.

It has been seen above (*a*) that there is conceded to belligerents the right in case of pressing necessity to "requisition" neutral property within the belligerent dominion, subject to the condition that property so seized shall be duly paid for. There is, therefore, nothing surprising in the fact of a state resorting in case of need to similar measures as regards property of its own subjects, of whatever nature consisting. Thus it is related that Peter the Great laid

(*a*) P. 244, *supra*.

waste some eighty leagues of his own territory in order to check the advance of Charles XII. of Sweden, and in 1812 the city of Moscow was, as is commonly believed, set on fire by the Russian authorities with a view to rendering the position of the French invaders untenable. Just as the Prussians sank the English colliers at Rouen in 1870 in order to prevent the French war-ships coming up the Seine, so in 1667 Charles II. sank vessels in the Thames in order to stay the progress of the Dutch fleet towards London (*b*), and seized English vessels for conversion into fire ships. "Receiving," writes Pepys in his diary, "every hour almost letters from Sir W. Coventry calling for more fire-ships; and an order from council to enable us to take any man's ships; and Sir W. Coventry, in his letter to us, says he do not doubt but at this time (under an invasion as he owns it to be) the king may by law take any man's goods." Emerigon, in his Treatise on Insurances (§ XXXII.), writes: "By the Roman law the owners of vessels were obliged to furnish their vessels for the transport of corn, and for other public necessities. It is the same with us. . . . Not only may the King take the ships of his subjects for the service of the state; he has besides authority to employ in the same

(*b*) Pepys's Diary is instructive reading on this point. On 14 June, 1667, he writes:—"At night come home Sir W. Batten and Mr. Pen, who can only tell me that they have placed guns at Woolwich and Deptford, and sunk some ships below Woolwich and Blackwall, and are in hopes that they will stop the enemy coming up. But strange our confusion! that among them that are sunk they have gone and sunk without consideration the 'Franclin,' one of the King's ships, with stores to a very considerable value that hath been long loaded for supply of the ships; and the new ship at Bristoll, and much wanted there. And nobody will own that they directed it, but do lay it on Sir W. Ryder. They speak also of another ship loaded to the value of 80,000*l.* sunk with the goods in her, or at least was mightily contended for by him, and a foreign ship that had the faith of the nation for her security; this Sir R. Ford tells us. And it is too plain a truth that both here and at Chatham the ships that we have sunk have many, and the first of them, been ships completely fitted for fire-ships at great charge."

manner foreign vessels found in his ports: in which the law of nations is not violated. The practice of Europe, says Vattel, conforms with this maxim. And again he remarks: Sovereigns who thus take national or foreign vessels for their service, never fail to pay them a suitable freight." It goes, indeed, without saying, that if the ships or goods of the national subjects be utilized or destroyed by the state in protection of the nation, the subjects whose property is thus forcibly seized must be duly indemnified.

Insurance.

It has been indicated above, *sub* "Embargo and Reprisals" (*c*), that seizures of which the motive is not confiscation as prize, but rather appropriation and payment of value, are to be regarded as "arrests," and not as "captures." "There appears to be no doubt," says Arnould (*d*), "that if a British ship be arrested or seized by the British Government, from any state necessity, or detained in port by a British-laid embargo, this is a loss for which the underwriters are liable as a detention within the meaning of the policy" (*e*). He observes also that (*f*) "an arrest takes place whenever the government of a country to which a ship belongs, or any other friendly power, with the design not to make prize (for then it would be a capture), but to restore the ship and goods, or to pay the value of them to their owners, seizes ship and goods for state purposes, either in port or at sea." And in a recent case (*g*), the Court, in accepting this definition, observed that Arnould stated it "in the clearest possible way." That underwriters are liable for losses arising from such arrests was decided by the Courts in a case where a British vessel was seized by the British Government, and con-

(*c*) P. 39, *supra*. *Vide* also *sub* "Pre-emption," p. 252.

(*d*) Mar. Insce., 5th ed. p. 753.

(*e*) Dictum of Lord Alvanley in Touteng *v.* Hubbard, 3 B. & P. 291, 302. *Vide* p. 42, *supra*.

(*f*) 5th ed. p. 751.

(*g*) Crew, Widgery & Co. *v.* Gt. Western S.S. Co., T. L. R. p. 738.

verted into a fire-ship (*h*), and in another, where a vessel was seized and taken in tow by a British man-of-war, and damage was thereby caused to her cargo (*i*).

In *Aubert* v. *Gray* (*j*), already referred to in connexion with the subject of Embargo (p. 45, *supra*), it was definitely decided by the Court that the assured is not to be identified with and deemed responsible for the acts of his own government so long as peaceful relations exist between such government and the government of the underwriter. This was a case where the assured was a Spaniard who had effected insurance in England, and the loss was caused by the act of the Spanish Government. But any question whether the embargo or arrest was effected by the home or by a foreign government will, so far as concerns the underwriters, apparently be immaterial (*k*).

In connexion with this subject, the remarks *sub* Embargo (pp. 39—48, *supra*) may be usefully referred to.

As regards the effect of arrest, detention, or embargo on the contract of affreightment, the point has already been touched upon *sub* Pre-emption (p. 252), *supra*. Chap. XIII.—Effect of War on Contract—is also interesting in the same connexion.

Let us now look at the belligerent municipal right of prohibiting all intercourse with the national foe,—a condition which may be said to be almost necessarily attendant on the existence of hostile relations.

(*h*) Green *v*. Young, 2 Lord Raym. 840; Salk. 444.
(*i*) Hagedorn *v*. Whitmore, 1 Stark. 157.
(*j*) 3 B. & S. 163.
(*k*) Arnould, 5th ed. p. 754.

PROHIBITION OF TRADE WITH THE ENEMY.

It has been explained above (*k*) that when war has once been entered upon, every individual of the nations engaged is considered to be involved in it, and that the effect of this taint of hostilities is to stop all peaceable intercourse as between the subjects of the nations so opposed; and that, as a natural consequence, all trading with the common enemy becomes at once illicit to the subjects of the belligerent state. For it is obvious that there cannot consistently exist at one and the same time a condition of open hostility between two nations at large, and a state of peaceful—that is, friendly—intercourse as between the subjects of such nations as individuals. While the times have presumably for ever passed away when the persons and property of enemy subjects domiciled in the belligerent country can be seized on the outbreak of war (*l*), the condition remains that trade with the foe, whether by land or by water, must absolutely cease immediately on the close of friendly relations. In the last formal declaration of war issued by this country, viz., in 1762, against Spain (*m*), British subjects were thenceforth strictly forbidden to "hold any correspondence or communication with the King of Spain or his subjects." And on declaration of war against Russia in 1854, it was ordered that "no ships or vessels belonging to any of her Majesty's subjects be permitted to enter and clear out for any of the ports of Russia till further order." No such express declarations are, however, neces-

(*k*) *Vide* p. 13, *supra*.
(*l*) *Ibid.*
(*m*) *Vide* Twiss's Int. Law, p. 65.

sary, the doctrine being well settled by the English Courts that there cannot exist at the same time a war for arms and a peace for commerce. For this reason all contracts made with the enemy during war are utterly void (*n*), and such contracts existing prior to the outbreak of hostilities are suspended until the resumption of peaceful relations. (For further consideration of this subject, see under Effect of War on Contract, p. 412.) The prohibition of friendly intercourse covers not merely trade as generally understood, but also communications and transactions of whatever kind; such, for example, as the negotiation of bills, or the remission of funds to the enemy's country (*o*).

In the leading case of *Willison* v. *Patteson* the circumstances were as follows:—

One Varlet, of Dunkirk, was debtor to Michelon of the same place, and in this capacity he transferred to the latter certain cambrics held by Patteson & Co. of London, the defendants, who were notified accordingly. Michelon drew against Patteson, who accepted the drafts, which Michelon had endorsed over to Willison, a Scotchman resident at Dunkirk. During these transactions war prevailed between England and France. The defendant Patteson having failed to honour his acceptance, Willison, on restoration of peace, sued him on the drafts. The Court, in deciding against the plaintiff, observed that that cannot be done indirectly which cannot be done directly; and that Michelon could neither during war bring an action for money had and received against the holder of his funds here, nor by drawing on his debtor produce the same effect. The bill was a contract; and no contract could be enforced in a British Court which is made during the war by an alien enemy.

(*n*) Willison *v*. Patteson, 7 Taunt. 439; Ogden *v*. Peele, 8 D. & R. 1; Bell *v*. Reid, 1 M. & S. 731; Esposito *v*. Bowden, *infra*, p. 416.

(*o*) Willison *v*. Patteson, *supra*.

In *Antoine* v. *Morshead* (*p*), however, where a British subject, prisoner of war in France, drew a bill in favour of fellow prisoners, also British subjects, on his son in England for his own subsistence whilst in captivity, and the bill was endorsed in favour of a French banker, who obtained its acceptance, it was held that this was not a trading with the enemy, and that the plaintiff, on peace being proclaimed, was entitled to sue for payment by the acceptor. An element in this case was that the bill was drawn by a British subject on a British subject.

Prohibitions against commercial intercourse are not to be evaded by any artifice or device, such as by means of partnerships with or the interposition of third parties (*q*). In *The Jonge Pieter* (*r*), goods purchased in England and shipped for Embden, with ultimate destination Amsterdam, an enemy port, were seized by a British cruiser as being shipped in breach of the prohibition of trade with the enemy. The goods were claimed as the property of a neutral, a merchant in America, for whose account the shipment was declared to have been made by his agent in London. The Court found that, in the absence of sufficient evidence in support of this allegation, the ownership must be deemed to be vested in the British shipper; and, as the goods were destined for the enemy *viâ* neutral territory, judgment was given in favour of the captors. "Without the licence of government," said Sir W. Scott, "no communication, direct or indirect, can be carried on with the enemy." So also in *The Samuel* (*s*), where a British subject employed a neutral to purchase for him in the country of the enemy, the neutral was held to be merely the agent.

(*p*) 6 Taunt. 237.
(*q*) Kent's Int. Law, 2nd ed. p. 186.
(*r*) 4 Rob. 79.
(*s*) 4 Rob. 284; 8 Term R. 548.

In *The Nayade* (*t*), England and Portugal being at war with France, a cargo shipped at Lisbon for Bordeaux was seized by a British cruiser. The property was alleged to belong to a Prussian subject resident in Lisbon, but the Court declared that there was nothing in this case to distinguish it from that of any other Portuguese merchants trading with the enemy. In another case (*u*) a shipment of tobacco had been made from Virginia to Bordeaux, described as the property of J. Bell, the shipper. It appeared, however, that J. Bell was a member of the firm J. & W. Bell, established both in America and in England, and the captors claimed that the shipment, so far as it belonged to W. Bell, the partner resident in England, was lawful prize. W. Bell having failed to produce satisfactory evidence in disproof of his interest in the property, the Court condemned a moiety of it as the property of a British subject trading with the enemy.

In *The Indian Chief* (*v*), a cargo had been shipped at Batavia (a possession of the enemy) on behalf of a Mr. Miller, an American subject and consul in Calcutta, who protested against the captors' claim on the ground that, being resident in Calcutta, and a neutral subject, and American consul, he did not come within the law against trading with the enemy. The Court held that, being domiciled in Calcutta, which was in possession of the British, he must be held to be a British subject, and that a consul engaged in commerce derived no such special protection from his official position.

In another case it was decided that the property of a British representative, resident in the enemy's country, is not protected from seizure, however beneficial to this country the

---

(*t*) 4 Rob. 251.
(*u*) The Franklin, 6 Rob. 127.
(*v*) 3 Rob. 22.

commerce may be (*w*). On the other hand, the citizen of a belligerent country, domiciled in a neutral country, may lawfully trade with the enemy of his native country (*x*). The trade must not, however, be in articles contraband of war (*y*).

The leading case on trading with the enemy is that of *The Hoop* (*z*), a neutral vessel which, at the end of the last century, sailed with a cargo from Rotterdam, ostensibly, in order to deceive the French cruisers, to Bergen, but really for a British port. This case affords an instance of the strict severity with which the law is administered as regards the offence now under consideration, and is, moreover, especially instructive owing to the numerous relative precedents cited in the judgment. The British owners of the cargo had, it appeared, for some time traded extensively with Holland, and on the occupation of that country by the French, a special licence was granted to them to continue this trade. Being, however, subsequently officially, but erroneously, informed by the Commissioners of Customs of Glasgow that goods could in future, according to a recent Act of Parliament, be brought from the United Provinces without special permit, the above shipment was thereupon made without such permit, and was seized and submitted for adjudication. Sir W. Scott, in giving judgment for the captors, observed that by a general rule in the maritime jurisprudence of this country, all trading with the public enemy, unless with the permission of the sovereign, was interdicted and involved confiscation, and he cited numerous cases illustrative of the strictness with which this rule had been enforced in the past. "In my

(*w*) Ex parte Baglehole, 18 Ves. jun. 528; 1 Rose, 271.

(*x*) The Danous, 4 Rob. 255, note.

(*y*) The Neptunus, p. 270, *infra*.

(*z*) 1 Rob. 196.

opinion," he observed, "no principle ought to be held more sacred than that commercial intercourse cannot subsist on any other footing than that of the direct permission of the state." Further:—"In all cases of this kind which have come before this tribunal, they have received an uniform determination. The cases which I have produced prove that the rule has been rigidly enforced, where Acts of Parliament have, on different occasions, been made to relax the navigation laws, and other Revenue Acts, when the government has authorized, under the sanction of an Act of Parliament, a homeward trade from the enemy's possessions, but has not specifically protected an outward trade to the same, though intimately connected with that homeward trade, and almost necessary to its existence; that it has been enforced where strong claim, not merely of convenience, but almost of necessity, excused it on behalf of the individual; that it has been enforced where cargoes have been laden before the war, but where the parties have not used all possible diligence to countermand the voyage after the first notice of hostilities; and that it has been enforced not only against the subjects of the Crown, but likewise against those of its allies in the war, upon the supposition that the rule was founded on a strong and universal principle which allied states in war had a right to notice and apply mutually to each other's subjects. Indeed, it is the less necessary to produce these cases, because it is expressly laid down by Lord Mansfield (*a*) that such is the maritime law of England."

The Bella Guidita (*b*) is another instance of the rigid application of the principle under consideration. Here, goods were sent in a neutral vessel from England to Grenada, a British possession, which possession, although seized, had apparently not been definitely appropriated, by

(*a*) In Gist *v.* Mason, 1 Term R. 86. (*b*) 1 Rob. 207.

the French. Special circumstances existed, moreover, in countenance of such a shipment, but, notwithstanding, the vessel was confiscated as being employed in illicit intercourse with the enemy.

The case of *The Abby* (*b*) is somewhat exceptional. A British vessel sailed for a friendly port in the West Indies, but war was shortly afterwards declared against the country owning the port. On arrival off the coast the vessel was captured, as being engaged in trade with the enemy. But before this occurred the port had been captured by the British, so that at the moment of capture the vessel, although her master was not aware of the fact, was trading with a British and not with a hostile possession. The Court, in ordering the release of the vessel, observed that to justify condemnation there must be the act of trading to the enemy's country, as well as the intention. If the destination, however, had been known to be hostile when the vessel sailed, such a sailing might have been a sufficient act of illegality. In *The Anna Catharina* (*c*), Sir W. Scott laid it down that a contract existing between a person domiciled in a place which had passed by conquest into the possession of Great Britain, and a foreign government at war with Great Britain, became illegal; but that this illegality ceased on transfer of the contract to a neutral.

In the American Courts the rule against trading with the enemy is applied with equal strictness. This was exemplified in *The Rapid* (*d*), where an American citizen, having purchased goods on British territory, deposited them on an island near the frontier, within the British dominion. On the outbreak of hostilities between Great Britain and the

(*b*) 5 Rob. 251, referred to also on p. 272, *infra*, *q. v.* *Vide* also The De Bilboa, 2 Rob. 133.

(*c*) 4 Rob. 107.

(*d*) 8 *Cranch*, 155. *Vide also The St. Lawrence*, *ibid.* 434.

American States he sent a vessel—nearly a year after the purchase—to the island, and removed the goods. The vessel was captured with her cargo, and both were condemned, the Court observing that to admit a citizen to withdraw property from a hostile country a long time after the commencement of war, on the pretext of its having been purchased before the war, would lead to the most injurious consequences, and hold out temptations to every species of fraudulent and illegal traffic with the enemy. In the same country it has been held that if a belligerent vessel takes on board a cargo from an enemy's ship under pretence of ransom, this is a trading with the enemy. And the vessel may be seized on her return voyage, after having discharged her cargo (*e*). Also, that a vessel which is captured by the enemy, but released, and on leaving the port of the captors ships a cargo from the enemy's country, must be held to have been engaged in trade with the enemy (*f*).

Immediately on the breaking out of hostilities, a citizen may remove to his own country, with his property (*g*). But it is permitted to no person to leave his own country in order to fetch from the enemy country property belonging to him (*h*). In *The General C. C. Pinckney* (*i*), a resident in the Confederate States bought a vessel, loaded her with his property, and with papers issued by the enemy brought her through the blockade. The ship and cargo were captured and condemned, but were restored on appeal, the claimant having succeeded in establishing to the satisfaction of the Court that he had left Charleston, S. C., with the intent to withdraw from the enemy's country with his effects. In

(*e*) *The Lord Wellington*, 2 *Gall.* 103.

(*f*) *The Alexander*, 8 *Cranch*, 169.

(*g*) *Vide* p. 16.

(*h*) The Rapid, *supra*.

(*i*) *Blatch. Pr. Ca.*, 278, 668.

similar cases it was laid down by the Court that a citizen temporarily resident on hostile soil is entitled, on the breaking out of hostilities, to a reasonable time to close his business connexions, collect his effects, and withdraw from the enemy's country (*i*). But in *The Gray Jacket* (*j*), where the removal was undertaken nearly two years after the outbreak of war, condemnation was decreed.

In *The Ocean* (*k*), a British-born subject settled as partner in a house of trade in Flushing was about to terminate his business relations there and return to England, when war broke out between the two countries, and he, in common with other British subjects resident in Holland, was for some time forcibly detained. Sir W. Scott considered that it would be going further than the law required to hold in this particular case that the claimant was precluded, and that, on sufficient proof being made of the property, restitution might be decreed.

Sir C. Robinson, in a note to the last-mentioned case, commenting on the hardship to which British subjects are sometimes exposed, owing to the difficulty of removing their goods from the enemy country immediately on the outbreak of hostilities, advises persons so situated to protect themselves by obtaining a special pass from the British Government. In *The Dree Gebroeders* (*l*), Sir W. Scott, in condemning the property seized, observed that "pretences of withdrawing funds are at all times to be watched with considerable jealousy, but that when the transaction appears to have been conducted *bonâ fide*, cases of this kind are entitled to be treated with considerable leniency." This was a case where a

(*i*) *The Evening Star*, *ibid.* 582; *Fifty-two bales of cotton*, *ibid.* 644; *The Sarah Starr*, *ibid.* 650; *The John Gilpin*, *ibid.* 661; *The Pioneer*, *ibid.* 666.

(*j*) 5 *Wall.* 342, 369.

(*k*) 5 Rob. 91.

(*l*) 4 Rob. 234.

native of Great Britain, settled in America, had, for reasons alleged, temporarily returned to England. While in England he took a house for his wife, and then crossed over to France to collect some debts there. Some of the proceeds of such collection he invested in a cargo of butter, which he shipped for Lisbon. On its seizure by a British vessel, he claimed its release on the ground that he was an American subject. The Court decided that the claimant's mercantile connexion with America was held by such a mere thread that this plea could not be entertained. This was an independent and voluntary speculation in the enemy's trade, not to be regarded as originating in any purpose of remitting funds to America *viâ* England.

The case of *The Jonge Pieter* (*m*) affords an instance of the condemnation of goods which, though shipped to a neutral port, were intended to be transmitted to the enemy's country. For if a trade be illegal in itself, no subterfuges in carrying it out will avail to remove from it this taint. In reply to a letter addressed to the Privy Council for Trade previous to the actual outbreak of hostilities in 1854, it was stated on 14th March, 1854, that, in the event of war, "every indirect attempt to carry on trade with the enemy's country will be illegal." And a few days afterwards (on 25th March), Lord Clarendon, in reply to the inquiry of a deputation of merchants engaged in trade with Russia, whether Russian produce brought over the frontier by land to Prussian ports, thence to be shipped to England, would be liable to British confiscation, stated that the question would turn upon the true ownership and destination of the property. And that such property, if shipped *bonâ fide* as neutral property, would not be liable to condemnation, whatever its destination; but if it should still remain enemy's property, though shipped

(*m*) *Supra*, p. 260.

from a neutral port in a neutral vessel, it would be condemned, whatever its destination. Further, that such property, "if it be British property, or shipped at British risk, or on British account, will be condemned if it is proved to be really engaged in a trade with the enemy, but not otherwise. The place of its origin will be immaterial, and if there has been a *bonâ fide* and complete transfer of ownership to a neutral (as by purchase in the neutral market), the goods will not be liable to condemnation, notwithstanding they may have come to that neutral market from the enemy's country, either overland or by sea." Moreover, that "circumstances of reasonable suspicion will justify capture, although release, and not condemnation, may follow; and ships with cargoes of Russian produce may not improbably be considered, under certain circumstances, as liable to capture, even though not liable to condemnation." And in a supplementary letter of 12th April, it was, *inter alia*, added that "It will be equally illegal for a British subject to trade with the enemy, whether he sends or receives the goods by sea or overland, and whether a blockade of the enemy's ports does or does not exist." But the above definite conclusions, both as regards enemy goods in neutral vessels, and trading with the enemy (by other than British vessels to enemy ports), were completely reversed by a proclamation dated only three days later, viz., on 15th April, 1854, that—

> "All vessels under a neutral or friendly flag, being neutral or friendly property, shall be permitted to import into any port or place in her Majesty's dominions all goods and merchandise whatsoever, to whomsoever the same may belong, and to export from any port or place in her Majesty's dominions to any port not blockaded any cargo or goods, not being contraband of war, or not requiring a special permission, to whomsoever the same may belong."

Also that with certain named exceptions, viz., carriage of contraband, &c.,

> "All the subjects of her Majesty, and the subjects or citizens of any neutral or friendly state, shall and may, during and notwithstanding the present hostilities with Russia, freely trade with all ports and places, wheresoever situate, which shall not be in a state of blockade, save and except that no British vessel shall under any circumstances whatsoever, either under or by virtue of this order, or otherwise, be permitted or empowered to enter or communicate with any port or place which shall belong to or be in the possession or occupation of her Majesty's enemies."

On the outbreak of the Franco-German war, France permitted German vessels which had left Germany for French ports before the declaration of war to proceed and discharge unmolested, but if the vessels were bound to neutral ports they remained subject to capture (*m*).

The Declaration of Paris has formulated the principle that an enemy's permissive goods carried under the neutral flag shall be exempt from capture; and if in the future the above general permission to trade should be re-established, the existing prohibitions against trading with the enemy will be greatly narrowed.

If two countries, acting conjointly, carry on war against a third, it is equally illegal for subjects of either of the former to engage in trade with the common foe. Accordingly, either belligerent may seize and confiscate the property of subjects of his ally on finding it engaged in such trade. It would obviously be absurd for one of the allies to strictly apply the principles of warfare against, whilst the subjects of

(*m*) Wheat. Int. Law, 2nd Eng. ed. 377. *Vide* State Papers, vol. 60, for diplomatic correspondence on this subject.

the other ministered to the needs and comfort of, the common enemy. Though, of course, it would be open to the allies to make mutual concessions in this respect, by granting special licences so to trade, if a joint agreement should be come to in this sense. *The Nayade* (n) has already furnished an instance of the application of this principle, but a leading case on the subject is *The Neptunus* (o), which arose during the war between this country and Holland early in the present century. The vessel belonged to a subject of Sweden, one of the allies of Great Britain, and was seized by a British cruiser whilst on a voyage between Sweden and Amsterdam. It was claimed against the captors that a modified permission had been granted by the Swedish Government to trade with the common enemy in innocent articles; but Sir W. Scott, in decreeing condemnation, observed that while it is of no importance to other nations how much a single belligerent chooses to weaken and dilute his own rights, it is otherwise when allied nations are pursuing a common cause against a common enemy. "Between them it must be taken as an implied, if not an express, contract, that one state shall not do anything to defeat the general object."

The cargo carried was pitch and tar—naval stores which, if not actually contraband, were clearly of a contraband nature. "In no instance," said the learned judge, "can the penalty of confiscation be applied with more propriety than in this first case which occurs, in which the parties exporting these articles to the enemy are British subjects domiciled in Sweden. It has been decided, both in this Court and in the Court of Appeal, that though a British subject resident abroad may engage generally in trade with the enemy, he cannot carry on such a trade in articles of a contraband nature. The duties of allegiance travel with them, so as to

---

(n) P. 261, *supra*.

(o) 6 Rob. 403.

restrain them from supplying articles of this kind to the enemy."

In *The Benjamin Franklin* (*p*), it was decided that a British pilot cannot sue in these Courts for wages alleged to be due to him for piloting a neutral vessel into a port of the enemy.

A comparatively recent instance of trading with the enemy is afforded by *The Neptune* (*q*), a Russian vessel sold to a British subject during the progress of hostilities between this country and Russia. The vessel having arrived at Grimsby, under protection of the British Order in Council of 29th March, 1854, was there dismantled and laid up, and in this condition was sold. The purchase was adjudged illegal as being within the prohibition of trading with the enemy.

The property of the subject of a belligerent state which is shipped by him, or for his account, on board a ship of the enemy, is liable to confiscation as being shipped in violation of the law against trading with the enemy (*r*).

It has been held that the inhabitants of a state placed under the protection of a belligerent are at liberty to carry on commerce with the enemy. By a Treaty of Paris of 1815, the Ionian Islands were constituted a free and independent state under the exclusive protection of Great Britain. In the case of *The Ionian Ships* (*s*), it was held that the trade carried on with Russia during the Crimean war by the Ionian Islanders was not illegal, they not being either British subjects, allies in the war, or enemies of Russia (*t*).

(*p*) 6 Rob. 350.

(*q*) 26 L. T. 110.

(*r*) Wheat. Int. Law, 2 Eng. ed. 530.

(*s*) 2 Spinks' Ec. & Ad. 212. *Vide* also The Leucade, *ibid.* 229.

(*t*) Pitt Cobbett's Leading Cases, p. 113.

Insurance.

Trading with the enemy being, unless specially licensed (*u*), illegal, contracts entered into with a view to support such trading are also illegal and void. And a policy, though legal in its inception, may become invalid by what is tantamount to a declaration of hostilities between the government of the assured and that of the assurer (*v*). But in the case of an insurance, the parties to which are subjects of the same state, it would appear that the policy would not be *ipso facto* voided by declaration of war, after sailing of the ship, between the government to which such parties owe allegiance and the country to which the vessel has sailed on the voyage insured. For in *The Abby* (*x*), bound from a British port to Demerara, war occurred a few days after the sailing of the vessel, which was captured by a British cruiser on arriving off the coast of Demerara. Sir W. Scott, in giving judgment against the captors, remarked that at the time of the ship's sailing Demerara could not be considered as the colony of the enemy. "It would be impossible for me," he declared, "to say, therefore, that it was an illegal trade at that time, as a trade to the colony of the enemy, because there was no state of hostilities. . . . Soon after the sailing of the vessel the declaration of hostilities took place; and if the ship had been taken on a voyage to a colony now become an enemy, the Court would have required it to be shown that due diligence had been used to alter the voyage, and to exonerate the claimant from the charge of an illegal trading with the enemy. . . . . Where a country is known to be hostile, the commencement of a voyage towards that country may be a sufficient act of illegality; but where the voyage is undertaken without that knowledge, the subsequent event of hostilities will have no such effect." Judgment was given for the claimant on the ground (1) that there was *no intention* to trade illegally (on the vessel's sailing; the destination then being neutral); and (2) that there was *no illegal act* (on arrival; the British having, in the meantime, occupied the colony). It was added that if the colony

(*u*) *Vide* Kensington *v.* Inglis, p. 290, *infra*.

(*v*) Arnould, 5th ed. p. 725, *q. v.*

(*x*) *Supra*, p. 264.

had remained hostile, the Court would have expected the claimant to have exonerated himself from the intention of trading with the enemy after the knowledge of hostilities; but as the colony had not remained hostile, such proof became unnecessary.

The illegality of insurances to protect trade with the enemy was definitely decided in *Potts* v. *Bell* (*y*). In this case a British subject had shipped, by a neutral vessel from the enemy's country, goods purchased of the enemy during hostilities, and it was held that all insurances in protection of such trading are void. But as we have seen above (*z*), a British subject regularly domiciled abroad may lawfully trade with the enemies of Great Britain in permissive goods, and this decision consequently does not apply to insurances effected in this country by a person so situated (*a*). On the other hand, if a British subject be domiciled in a country with which Great Britain is at war, he will *pro hac vice* be regarded as an enemy subject (*b*), and insurances in protection of his property connected with such domicile will be *ipso facto* void.

The principle that no insurances may be effected in support of trade with the national foe does not relate to neutral property. "It is nowhere laid down," said Lord Mansfield in *Gist* v. *Mason* (*c*), "that policies on neutral property, though bound to an enemy's port, are void."

In *Hagedorn* v. *Bazett* (*d*), where goods, the property of various independent persons, had been shipped by an agent, and insured under one policy, and it turned out that one of such principals was an enemy, the insurance was held to be good, except so far as concerned the enemy property, in respect of which it was declared to be void.

In *Wright* v. *Welbie* (*e*), where an insurance had been effected

---

(*y*) 8 T. R. 548.

(*z*) *Vide* p. 17, *supra*.

(*a*) Arnould, 5th ed. p. 691.

(*b*) *Vide* p. 19, *supra*.

(*c*) 1 T. R. 88.

(*d*) 2 M. & S. 100. Conf. Parkin *v.* Dick, p. 309, *infra*.

(*e*) 1 Chitt. 49. For further references to these cases, *vide* Arnould's Insce. 5th ed. 691-4.

to "any port or ports in the Baltic," it was held that the insurance was legal until it was proved that the ship was destined for one of the ports which was hostile—a decision equally applicable in a case where the vessel had leave to touch at ports in a particular sea, some of them hostile and some not (*f*). When Napoleon I. overran the Continent and occupied many of the ports, our Courts decided that all such ports should be regarded as neutral, so long as they continued to preserve the forms of an independent neutral government (*g*). On the same principle, Corfu was held to be neutral, though occupied by the Russians, so long as it continued to hoist the Ionian flag, appoint a port-admiral, &c. (*h*). And similarly, though in 1811 political relations had ceased to exist between this country and Prussia, Lord Ellenborough held that, in the absence of open hostility between the two states, an insurance from a British to a Prussian port was not to be considered illegal (*i*). Again, whilst Hamburg was occupied by the French, an insurance was effected in this country on the property of certain persons domiciled in Hamburg, and the question arose whether such persons could in the circumstances be regarded as neutrals. It was held that, inasmuch as the city still possessed the forms of its own government, it must be regarded as a neutral port, although in hostile occupation (*k*).

It is for the government of the country to determine in what relation any other country stands towards it. If, therefore, during war, the official orders recognise the non-hostility of certain ports, trading with such ports must be regarded as legal, and insurances to protect the trading will consequently be valid (*l*).

Although illegal trading operates as a voidance of insurance, yet if the trading be entered upon by the master without the knowledge or permission of his owners, and the vessel be con-

---

(*f*) Muller *v*. Thompson, 2 Camp. 610.
(*g*) *Vide* Hagedorn *v*. Bell, 1 M. & S. 459-60.
(*h*) Donaldson *v*. Thompson, 1 Camp. 429, an. 1808.
(*i*) Muller *v*. Thompson, 2 Camp. 610, an. 1811.
(*k*) Hagedorn *v*. Bell, 1 M. & S. 450.
(*l*) Arnould, 5th ed. pp. 694-5.

demned for the illegal trading, the loss will be attributable to barratry, and the underwriters will become liable accordingly. This was decided by Lord Ellenborough in *Earle* v. *Rowcroft* (*m*), a leading case on barratry. The vessel had sailed from Liverpool to the west coast of Africa, there to trade, and thence to the West Indies. After being two days at the British settlement of Cape Coast Castle, the master, hearing that profitable trade could be transacted at the neighbouring Dutch port of D'Elmina, proceeded there and traded. The Dutch flag was flying at D'Elmina, and the master, having a letter of marque on board against the French and Dutch, well knew that he was trading with the enemy. On being informed that an English frigate was in sight, he made sail back to Cape Coast Castle in order, as he said, "to prevent mischief." The vessel was, however, captured: and hence these proceedings. On the facts the Court found that the confiscation of the ship was due to barratry of the master.

Insurances on enemy property, and against the risk of British capture, are also void as being opposed to the national war policy. "The question is," said Lord Alvanley in *Furtado* v. *Rogers* (*n*), "whether it be competent to an English underwriter to indemnify persons who are engaged in war with his own sovereign from the consequences of that war; and we are all of opinion that on the principles of the English law it is not competent to any subject to enter into a contract to do anything which may be detrimental to the interests of his own country; and that such contract is as much prohibited as if it had been expressly forbidden by Act of Parliament." In this case it was decisively laid down that "insurances effected on behalf of an alien enemy, though made previously to the commencement of hostilities, and therefore legal in their inception, could not cover a loss by British capture after war had broken out; and that no action could be brought upon them in our Courts, even after the restoration of peace" (*o*). Two important cases illustrating the illegality of insurances to protect enemy property are *Bristow* v.

(*m*) 8 East, 126.

(*n*) 3 B. & P. 191, 198. And see cases cited in Arnould's Insce., 5th ed. p. 131, note.

(*o*) Arnould's Insce., 5th ed. p. 131.

Towers (*p*), in which it was decided that no action can be maintained on a policy on an alien enemy's property, though of British manufacture and exported from this country; and *Brandon* v. *Nesbitt* (*q*), in which it was held that an insurance effected on behalf of an alien enemy is void, though the goods be shipped before the war commenced. In another case (*r*), where goods were shipped by a neutral vessel on French account, and exported after the outbreak of war, it was held that the insurance was void, and therefore did not avail to protect against their capture by a co-belligerent. All such insurances, said Lord Ellenborough, should be considered as having engrafted upon them such a proviso as the following, viz.:—"Provided that this insurance shall not extend to cover any loss happening during the existence of hostilities between the respective countries of the assured and assurer."

Where war breaks out after the occurrence of a loss insured against, the rights of the assured under the policy are postponed till the resumption of peaceful relations between the countries, and the plea that the assured is an alien enemy will serve only as a temporary bar to the proceedings (*s*).

Whether it is also illegal to insure against British capture of a British merchant ship has not been decided; but it may be concluded from the opinion expressed in *Lubbock* v. *Potts* (*t*), that the illegality exists only in the case of insurances on foreign vessels (*u*). Broadly stated, however, the offence which would justify the condemnation of a British ship in the British Courts would no doubt invalidate any relative insurance.

The next subject for consideration is the granting of special licences, and the conditions and consequences of their use and misuse respectively. The remarks *sub* Insurance in relation to Special Licences are in some measure apposite in connexion with the subject Trading with the Enemy, above.

(*p*) 6 T. R. 35. (*q*) *Ibid.* 23. (*r*) Brandon *v.* Curling, 4 East, 410.

(*s*) Flindt *v.* Waters, 15 East, 260, 266. *Vide* also "Effect of War on Contract," p. 412, *infra*.

(*t*) 7 East, 449; also Glaser *v.* Cowie, 1 M. & S. 52. *Vide* also Page *v.* Thompson, 8th ed. Park's Insce. 175.

(*u*) *Vide* Owen's Mar. Insce. Notes and Clauses, 2nd ed. p. 21, for clauses in connexion with British capture.

Issue of Special Licences to Trade with the Enemy; Passports and Safe-Conducts.

A special licence, says Kent (*v*), "is the assumption of a state of peace to the extent of the licence, and the act rests in the discretion of the sovereign authority of the state, which alone is competent to decide how far considerations of commercial and political expediency may, in particular cases, control the ordinary consequences of war"—a generalization founded on the dictum of Sir W. Scott in his judgment in *The Cosmopolite* (*x*).

The following is an example of a special licence (*y*) :—

> "George the Third, by the Grace of God, of the United Kingdom of Great Britain and Ireland King, Defender of the Faith, &c. To all commanders of our ships of war and privateers, and all others whom it may concern, Greeting. Our will and pleasure is, that you permit John Whitton to export on board the Papenburgh ship "*St. Anton.*" N. Wilkens, master, from the port of Liverpool to any port of Holland, with liberty to touch at Tonningen to obtain fresh clearances, one cargo of rock salt, to whomsoever the said cargo may appear to belong, and notwithstanding all the documents which accompany the same may represent it to be destined to any other neutral or hostile port; and that if the said vessel so laden and documented be detained, and brought in by any of our ships of war or privateers, the same shall be forthwith liberated, if proceeding against for adjudication, upon a claim being given for the same by or on the behalf of the said John Whitton, and bail being given to answer adjudication, and shall be finally restored

(*v*) Internat. Law, Abdy's 2nd ed. p. 381.

(*x*) 4 Rob. 11.

(*y*) Story's Prize Courts, by Pratt, 171.

upon satisfactory proof being made that such cargo was really shipped by or under the directions of the said John Whitton or his agents, for the purpose of being exported to Holland, and thereupon the said vessel shall be permitted to proceed on her voyage. This, our licence, to remain in force for four months from the date hereof. Given at our Court at St. James's, the 6th day of June, 1807, in the forty-seventh year of our reign.

By His Majesty's command.

(Signed) HAWKESBURY."

John Whitton }
Licence. }

Varieties of the same instrument permit the vessel to bear "any flag except the French"; to bear the French flag "only until she is two leagues distant from her foreign port of clearance, or the neighbouring coast"; the vessel not to be navigated by French seamen; not to proceed to any blockaded port; and so forth. As regards this last provision, it may be observed that Sir W. Scott declared in *The Byfield* (z), that a licence expressed in general terms, to enable a ship to enter or leave an enemy's port, did not apply to a port under blockade. To authorize trade with such a port there must be an express provision in the licence. This decision, though not altogether in harmony with that of the same learned judge in a previous case (a), may apparently be accepted as establishing the law on the subject (b).

It is stated that in 1811 there were granted 8,000 English licences, and that in 1808 and 1809 the system was carried to a still greater extent (c). Without a licence all trading with the enemy is, as has been already set forth (d),

(z) Edwards, p. 188.
(a) The Hoffnung, 2 Rob. 162.
(b) *Vide* Twiss's Law of Nations, pp. 228—230.
(c) Wheaton's Int. Law, 6th ed. Introd. p. xxi.
(d) Pp. 258 *et seq.*, *supra*.

absolutely prohibited, and where such licences are granted they are construed with great strictness. This strictness is, however, not to be carried to the extreme of pedantic accuracy, nor is every small deviation to be held to operate as a vitiation of the fair effect of the licence (*e*). In *The Juffrow Catharina* (*f*), a licence had been given for the importation of certain raw materials from France, and under this permission a shipment was made of certain lace. The article, it seems, had been ordered before the outbreak of hostilities, and could not, owing to peculiar circumstances, be countermanded. The Court stated that it would have been a more guarded proceeding on the part of the British merchant to have applied for a licence for this special importation, but that there were considerations to induce a favourable view of his claim. But at the same time the Court wished it to be understood that by a decree in his favour the necessity of obtaining a licence was not in any way relaxed. Thus in another case (*g*), where the claimant had exported under a licence specially enumerating various articles, certain barilla not included amongst them, Sir W. Scott condemned the shipment. "It seems absolutely essential," said his Lordship, in *The Cosmopolite* (*supra*), "that that only shall be done which the grantor intended to permit; whatever he did not mean to permit is absolutely interdicted; and the party who uses the licence engages not only for fair intention, but for an accurate interpretation and execution. When I say an accurate interpretation and execution, I do not mean to exclude such a latitude as may be supposed to conform to the intentions of the grantor, liberally understood."

In a case where the person to whom the licence had been

(*e*) The Cosmopolite, *supra*, p. 277.

(*f*) 5 Rob. 141.

(*g*) The Vriendschap, 4 Rob. 96. See also Shiffner *v*. Gordon, 12 East, 302.

granted had been incorrectly described in it, it was held that this misdescription was in the circumstances immaterial, the conditions on which the authority had been granted having been duly complied with (*h*).

"Another material circumstance in all licences is the limitation of time in which they are to be carried into effect; for as it is within the view of government, in granting these licences, to combine all commercial and political considerations, a communication with the enemy might be very proper at one time, and at another very unfit and mischievous" (*i*). But if the voyage be by unavoidable accident delayed beyond the time for which the licence was granted, the breach of the time-limit—provided the person licensed be clear of all fraud or laches—will not render the voyage illegal (*k*). Sir W. Scott laid it down as a general rule that "where no fraud has been committed, where no fraud has been meditated, as far as appears, and where the parties have been prevented from carrying the licence into execution by a power which they could not control, they shall be entitled to the benefit of its protection, although the terms may not have been literally and strictly fulfilled" (*l*). But the circumstances in which the strict terms of the licence have been departed from must not be of the making of the person licensed. Thus in *The Twee Gebroeders* (*m*), where a licence had been granted to carry a cargo from Bordeaux, and the person licensed thought fit to treat it as available from another port—St. Martin—the licence was vitiated, and ship and cargo were condemned, Sir W. Scott remarking that parties cannot be permitted to

(*h*) Lemecke *v.* Vaughan, 1 Bing. 473.

(*i*) The Cosmopolite, *supra*. *Vide* also Vandyck *v.* Whitmore, 1 East, 475.

(*k*) Schrœder *v.* Vaux, 15 East, 52.

(*l*) The Good Hope, Edw. Cases on Licences, 6. And see Evereth *v.* Tunno, 1 B. & A. 142.

(*m*) 1 Edw. 95.

take licences for one purpose and apply them to another; and that in such a case it would be going beyond the powers of the Court to extend its protection.

In like manner, the use of the licence must be strictly limited to the persons for whose benefit it was granted. "The great principle in these cases," said the same learned judge, "is, that subjects are not to trade with the enemy without the special permission of the government; and a material object of the control which government exercises over such a trade is, that it may judge of the particular persons who are fit to be entrusted with an exemption from the ordinary restrictions of a state of war" (*n*). In this sense the holder of a licence must be prepared to substantiate, if required, that he is its *bonâ fide* holder. Thus, in *Barlow* v. *Mackintosh* (*o*), where the vessel had been seized as being engaged in trade with the enemy, the underwriters denied that the assured was entitled to the protection of the licence on which he relied, and Lord Ellenborough gave judgment in their favour, unless the plaintiff should prove his title to the document. The licence was "general," in that it specified neither the name of the ship nor of the shipper, and it was to remain in force for six months from date. The voyage protected was between London and Holland; and as the licence was more than three months old when the plaintiff made use of it, the Court observed that it might already have served for three voyages to Holland; it might have dropped out of the pocket of the person entitled to it and been found by the plaintiff, who must, in these circumstances, connect himself by other evidence than the mere possession of the document; otherwise there was a natural suspicion, a preponderance of

(*n*) The Jonge Johannes, 4 Rob. 263. See also The Aurora, *ibid.* 418; and Barlow *v.* Mackintosh, 12 East, 311.

(*o*) *Supra.* See also Rawlinson *v.* Jansen, 12 East, 223.

probability, that the licence had been used before to cover an antecedent voyage, and against the lawful use of it on this occasion.

It must not, however, be understood from the foregoing that a general licence is available only to the parties to whom it was originally granted; for in *The Louise Charlotte de Guldenoroni*, the holders had purchased the document in market overt, and there was no suggestion that such a proceeding was improper. In *The Acteon* (*p*), where a licence had been issued in London available from America, and had been disposed of in America, Sir W. Scott observed, that "if the licence was *general*, which it appeared to have been, it could be of no consequence who were the individuals who acted under it, provided they complied with the conditions annexed to it." But in another case (*q*), where there was granted to a manufacturer a special licence for himself and others to ship certain gunpowder, and he sold the powder to a third party, it was held that the condition that the merchant exporter should give certain security was not complied with, notwithstanding that the manufacturer gave the security, the said manufacturer not being the merchant exporter within the meaning of the licence.

And if the licence contain a condition which is only *colourably* complied with, it will be voided (*r*).

The fraudulent alteration of a licence destroys its validity, even where the person claiming its protection is innocent of the fraud. This was decided by Sir W. Scott in a case (*s*) where the date of the licence had been altered; which licence he pronounced to have become in consequence a mere nullity.

A general licence must be construed strictly, in the sense

(*p*) 2 Dods. 53. See also Butler *v.* Allnutt, 1 Stark. 222.

(*q*) Camelo *v.* Britten, 4 B. & A. 184.

(*r*) Gordon *v.* Vaughan, 12 East, 302, note.

(*s*) The Louise Charlotte de Guldenoroni, 2 Dod. 308.

that it cannot be understood to extend to protect the property of an enemy. Thus, where a licence had been granted for the purpose of bringing certain gum from the enemy's colony of Senegal, and the master of the vessel, in order to oblige the French governor, who had befriended him, took on board some gum the property of this individual, the Court held that such property was not protected by the licence (*t*).

A licence must also be construed strictly in the sense that, if granted to a British merchant as such, this merchant cannot use it in his capacity of a domiciled subject of the enemy state (*u*). Thus, a licence had been granted to one Ravie, of Birmingham, "for the importation of certain goods from Holland into this country," and the question arose whether it could operate to protect a shipment made by him in person, in Holland, and under papers describing his firm as "Ravie & Co., of Amsterdam." The Court held, that whereas the licence had been granted to Ravie as a British subject to import goods from Holland, he had practically, in the capacity of a Dutch merchant, exported goods from Holland. He had no right to engraft the character of a Dutch exporter on a licence granted to him as a British importer. He was a merchant of both countries, and must be liable to be considered as a subject of both.

A licence to trade with the enemy will cover the enemy's ship carrying the goods licensed to be conveyed. This was illustrated in *Kensington* v. *Inglis* (*x*), which case establishes that an insurance on an enemy's vessel is, in such circumstances, lawful.

To authorize trade with the enemy, and to exempt his property from the effect of hostilities, is a very high act of

(*t*) The Josephine, 1 Act. 313.

(*u*) The Jonge Klassina, 5 Rob. 297. And see the reference to this case, *sub* Domicile, p. 17. See also The Rose in Bloom, 1 Dods. 57.

(*x*) P. 290, *infra*.

sovereign authority; and such a licence, to be effectual, must come from those who have a competent authority to grant this protection. In *The Hope* (y)—the leading case on the subject—an American vessel, carrying provisions from the United States to Peninsular ports occupied by British troops, on being seized claimed to be protected by a licence granted by the British consul at Boston, in conjunction with a letter from the admiral on the Halifax station. Sir W. Scott pronounced the documents in question to be insufficient, as coming from persons vested with no competent authority to grant them. It was quite clear, said his lordship, that no consul in any country, particularly in an enemy's country, is vested with any such power in virtue of his station; and that the admiral was also without this authority. But inasmuch as the British Government had by a special Order in Council confirmed the acts of its officers, the property was ordered to be restored. In other cases (z), where similar irregularities had not been ratified by the government, condemnation was decreed. In America it has been specifically determined that the President is the only functionary who can grant a licence to trade with the enemy (a).

When allies are jointly engaged in waging war, it is illegal for one of them to authorize trade with the enemy, unless with the previous consent of the other. An implied contract exists that neither state shall do anything to defeat the object common to both; and it is a recognised principle of the law of nations that one of conjoint belligerents may seize and confiscate the property of any subjects of the other engaged, without the consent of the co-allies jointly, in trade with the enemy.

If a licence to trade be on the condition that a bond in a

(y) 1 Dods. 226. See also Johnson *v.* Sutton, Doug. 254.
(z) For which, see Wheaton's Int. Law, 2 Eng. ed. p. 473.
(a) *Ibid.* p. 474.

penalty be given that the goods shall be exported to the places specified; if the bond be not given, then the licence becomes void, and the voyage illegal (*b*).

A licence must be so intelligibly worded as not to keep the parties in the dark as to its extent. Thus, where a licence had been granted to the ports of the Vlie, Sir W. Scott held that Amsterdam was included, and that it was no material deviation to have entered this port by another passage (*c*).

In *Fenton* v. *Pearson* (*d*), it was decided by Lord Ellenborough, that where a licence in effect legalized purchase from and sale by an enemy, it also impliedly legalized the enemy's right by his agent here to stop the goods *in transitu* after their arrival, on the insolvency of the vendee. "To maintain the contrary," said his lordship, "would be to hold out to Europe that this country would allow foreigners, by the royal licence, to send their goods to this country, and then take the goods without paying for them."

"Dispensations from the general prohibition to trade with the enemy, that affect whole classes of cases, as dispensations by licence affect individuals, are granted from time to time, as the exigencies of the case shall require, by the sovereign, with the advice of the Privy Council, and are promulgated by proclamation, as Orders in Council. 'The fundamental principle on which this new system of commercial policy is founded,' said Lord Brougham, in his great speech on Orders in Council and the Licence Trade (March 3, 1812), 'has always professed itself to be a retaliating principle.' The power to make these Orders of Council, and to grant licences in pursuance of them, being derived from special Acts of Parliament, is of a limited nature, and cannot be extended

(*b*) Vandyck *v*. Whitmore, 1 East, 475.

(*c*) The Juno, 2 Rob. 117.

(*d*) 15 East, 419. Also Morgan *v*. Oswald, 3 Taunt. 568.

further than the Acts themselves permit. The construction of licences granted by virtue of the King's prerogative will, in general, be applicable to licences founded on these statutes" (*e*). The royal proclamation of 15th April, 1854, referred to on p. 268, affords an instance of such a general dispensation.

By an Order in Council (*f*) at the commencement of the war with Russia, six weeks' grace was allowed in which Russian vessels in British ports could load and depart, free from molestation. In *Clementson* v. *Blessig* (*g*), the plaintiff supplied for shipment to a firm in Odessa certain goods which had been contracted for before the declaration of war. The goods were provided in time to be lawfully shipped under the above order, and the sale was held to be good.

Where there is neither licence nor dispensation, a case may still arise which the Court will place on the footing of being protected, as, for example, if the circumstances of the alleged trading be such that, if a licence had been applied for, it would undoubtedly have been granted. Thus, one Gregory, British consul at Barcelona, had purchased a quantity of wine for the sole purpose of supplying the British fleet in the Mediterranean. On hostilities occurring between this country and Spain, Gregory was forced to leave his domicile, and he left behind him, in his private store, a quantity of this wine. After a considerable interval of time, an opportunity occurred to get possession of the goods, which were shipped on his behalf to Leghorn. On the voyage, they were captured on the ground of unlicensed trading with the enemy. Sir W. Scott, in decreeing restitution, observed that the claimant had purchased the wine solely for the supply of the British fleet before the outbreak

(*e*) Maritime Warfare, p. 372.

(*f*) *Vide* p. 53, *supra*.

(*g*) 11 Ex. 135.

of hostilities, and that he had not in any other manner acted as a merchant, a situation which very much distinguished this case from cases in other respects analogous. The claimant had himself retired from the country, and had made application to get his wines consigned to the original purpose, but without effect. Great difficulties lay in the way of his applying for or using a licence, the goods being deposited secretly. The conditions of this case might be taken as virtually amounting to a licence, inasmuch as, in the peculiar circumstances, the British Government, had it been applied to, must have granted it. It had been further urged against the claimant that he had not disposed of his house; but it was nothing more than his own mansion, and not a house of trade (*h*).

Finally, when peace has been concluded, a licence becomes inoperative, having no subject matter to act upon, and it cannot be acted upon on hostilities being so resumed as to constitute a new war. A licence must be referred to the state and condition of affairs existing when it was granted (*i*).

Passports and Safe-conducts.—Whereas a licence is granted for purposes of trade, passports and safe-conducts are granted in favour of individuals, and ordinarily include a permission to transport baggage and effects; with, also, on occasion, a provision for the safe passage of the servants and household of the person protected. The person named in the passport must not transfer the pass, but if the safe-conduct be for effects, those effects may be removed by others besides the owner, provided such persons be not, for any reason, objectionable within the territory of the power granting the permission. Such power is morally bound to make good any

(*h*) The Madonna delle Gracie, 4 Rob. 195.

(*i*) The Planter's Wensch, 5 Rob. 22.

damage or loss arising out of a disregard of the pass on the part of the subjects or forces against whom it was intended to operate as a protection. On the other hand, the party to whom it was granted must act strictly within it as regards the purpose, place, and time for which it was granted. It is usual to enumerate with precision every particular branch and extent of the indulgence, and any breach of these conditions will be at the peril of the grantee. If a safe-conduct be given for a stated period, the party protected must leave the enemy's country before the time expires, but if detained by sickness or other unavoidable circumstance the permit will still extend to protect him. It is stated that a safe-conduct may be revoked by him who granted it; but if the grantee have obtained the privilege by purchase, and not gratuitously, he is entitled to indemnity against all injurious consequences of the revocation, and he is also to be allowed time and liberty to depart in safety (*j*).

Persons domiciled in a state which, owing to outbreak of hostilities between it and the country to which they owe allegiance, has become the country of an enemy, should, if they desire to remove, lose no time in applying for a special pass, to enable them to do so. This point has already been touched upon, pp. 264, 265.

The effect of a ransom from the enemy is equivalent to a safe-conduct on the part of the state granting the ransom, and its allies (*k*). The subject of Ransom generally will be considered presently (*vide infra*, p. 296).

(*j*) *Vide* Kent's Internat. Law by Abdy, 2nd ed. pp. 379—381.

(*k*) *Miller* v. *The Resolution*, 2 *Dall.* 15.

Insurance.

There is little to say on this point which has not already been conveyed in treating of the subject of insurance, under the head Prohibition of Trade with the Enemy (*l*). Broadly stated, the position seems to be this:—Where the trade is lawful, an insurance in support of it is good and valid; where it is unlawful, such an insurance becomes *ipso facto* void. If the trade be duly licensed the insurance will be protected; if there be no licence, or the licence be for any reason found not to avail to cover the adventure insured, then, the trade being unlawful, the contract of insurance entered into to protect it will stand on no higher ground. For wherever a man makes an illegal contract, the courts of justice will not lend him their aid to compel a performance (*m*).

In *Usparicha* v. *Noble* (*n*), where a native Spaniard domiciled in England had, under a British licence, shipped goods to Spain, with which country England was at war, it was held that such commerce was fully legalized, notwithstanding that the consignees were alien enemies. The latter could not sue in respect of such licensed traffic in the British Courts: only the person actually licensed could do this; but the commerce itself was to be regarded as legalized for all purposes of its due and effectual prosecution. This being so, to say that the person licensed could not insure, Lord Ellenborough observed, would be to convert the licence itself into an instrument of fraud and deception. "The Crown, in licensing the end, impliedly licenses all the ordinary legitimate means of obtaining that end. . . . Whatever commerce of this sort the Crown has thought fit to permit . . . must be regarded by all the subjects of the realm, and by the Courts of law, when any question relative to it comes before them, as legal, with all the consequences of its being legal." The fact that the trade is contrary to the laws of the other belligerent state cannot be pleaded as a defence to a claim under the policy. "It will not be contended," said the

(*l*) *Vide* p. 272, *supra*.

(*m*) Delmada *v.* Motteux, B. R. Mich. 25 Geo. 3.

(*n*) 13 East, 332, an. 1811.

learned judge, "to be illegal to insure a trade carried on in contravention of the laws of a state at war with us, and in furtherance of the policy of our country and its trade." And the principle thus clearly laid down was adopted in subsequent cases (*o*).

Where a licence had been granted to trade with the enemy, the cargo to be brought from the enemy's country in his ships to our colonial ports, it was held that not only was the insurance on the cargo shipped for the benefit of British subjects incidentally legalized, but that an insurance on the enemy's ship was also valid; and that it was competent for the British agent of both parties, in whose name the insurance was effected, to sue upon the policy in time of war, the trust not contravening any rule of law or public policy, and there being no personal disability in the plaintiff on the record to sue. The alien enemy could, however, by no means sue in his own name (*p*).

If part of a cargo be licensed and therefore legal; and part unlicensed; the insurance, unless the contract be indivisible, will hold good so far as the licensed interest is concerned. Thus, in *Pieschell* v. *Allnutt* (*q*), where the owners were licensed to import a cargo of corn and many other enumerated articles (not including books), "and no other articles whatever"; and the master took on board sundry cases of books not the property of the assured and not covered by the policy; and the vessel was lost: the Court observed that if the ship and cargo had been libelled in the Court of Admiralty the books would have been condemned and the ship and other goods restored; and that if they ought to be restored, there seemed to be no reason why they should not be insured. The circumstance of the books being on board, said the learned judge, did not render the whole of the adventure illegal, nor the insurance void. And in another case (*r*), where the licence was for the purpose of impor-

(*o*) *Vide* Flindt *v.* Scott, Flindt *v.* Crokatt on appeal (1814), 5 Taunt. 674; and Bazett *v.* Meyer (1814), *ibid.* 824, overruling Menett *v.* Bonham (1812), 15 East, 477; Flindt *v.* Crokatt, *ibid.* 522; Flindt *v.* Scott, *ibid.* 525.

(*p*) Kensington *v.* Inglis, 8 East, 273.

(*q*) 4 Taunt. 792.

(*r*) Butler *v.* Alnutt, 1 Stark. 222.

tation of specific articles, not including the particular drugs forming part of the cargo insured, Lord Ellenborough held that the consequence was that such drugs would not be within the protection of the licence; but that it would be very dangerous if the introduction of a single article not specified in the order were to vacate the licence altogether. Where, again, an insurance had been effected on gunpowder shipped under a licence, and it turned out that the quantity exported exceeded the limits of the licence, the insurance was supported to the extent of the quantity for which the licence had been obtained (*s*). But where, in *Camelo* v. *Britten* (*t*), certain gunpowder was shipped under a licence, but the conditions of the licence were not complied with, the policy was held to be void in respect of other goods besides the gunpowder, on the ground that the insurance was one entire contract.

The granting of licences to cartel or truce ships not being ordinarily connected with any question of trade, the subject may be considered under a special head.

(*s*) Keir *v*. Andrade, 2 Marsh. 196.
(*t*) *Supra*, p. 282.

GRANT OF

LICENCE TO CARTEL-SHIPS.

Cartel is the name given to an agreement for the exchange of prisoners of war, and a cartel-ship is one employed in carrying out such an agreement. It is usual, in order to promote the objects of a cartel, for a commissary of prisoners to reside in the enemy's country, and it is competent for him to grant a pass or safe-conduct to ships engaged in effecting these exchanges. The intercourse between belligerents involved in this traffic is of a very peculiar nature, and it is indispensable that it be conducted with the most scrupulous regard to the original purpose. "The conduct of ships of this description," said Sir W. Scott, in *The Venus* (*u*), "cannot be too narrowly watched. The service on which they are sent is so highly important to the interests of humanity, that it is peculiarly incumbent on all parties to take care that it should be conducted in such a manner as not to become a subject of jealousy and distrust between the two nations." *The Venus*, a British vessel, had gone to Marseilles, under cartel for the exchange of prisoners. After discharging his prisoners, the master took on board certain goods for which freight was to be paid. Whilst on a voyage to Port Mahon, the vessel was seized by a British cruiser on the ground of trading with the enemy. The learned judge, in condemning the vessel, would not say that if the master had taken on board a few articles for his own petty profit, the ship would necessarily be subjected to confiscation; but where, as in this

(*u*) 4 Rob. 355. *Vide* also The Rose in Bloom, 1 Dods. 60; and The Carolina, 6 Rob. 336.

case, goods were shipped so as to call forth remonstrances on the part of the ship's officers, it was too much to say that the offence was imputable only to the master. Cartel-ships were under a double obligation not to trade, and it was not without the consent of both belligerent governments that vessels engaged in this service could be permitted to take in any goods whatever. The prohibition against trade equally applies to the conveyance of passengers for hire.

In *The La Rosine* (*x*), the Court condemned as a droit of admiralty some goods put on board a French cartel-ship by a British manufacturer, the ship lying at Dover with her sails set, ready to return to France.

In the absence of any special stipulation on the point, it is, in general, immaterial whether the ship sent on a cartel mission be a ship of war or a private vessel. A ship going to be so employed is not *ipso facto* protected whilst proceeding to the port at which her engagement is to commence, but, if necessary, she should be provided with a pass by the commissary of prisoners in the enemy's country (*y*). But even if a ship *bonâ fide* engaged in a cartel mission be found to be provided with no letter of cartel, she ought not to be condemned, and the protection of her mission should extend, as in other cases, to the return voyage (*z*).

"All contracts made for equipping and fitting cartel-ships are to be considered as contracts between friends, and consequently to be enforced in the tribunals of either belligerent. Such vessels are considered neutral licensed vessels, and all persons connected with their navigation, upon the particular service of which both belligerents have employed her, are neutral in respect of both, and under the protection of both (*a*). Persons put on board a cartel with their own con-

(*x*) 2 Rob. 372.

(*y*) The Diafjie, 3 Rob. 143.

(*z*) *Ibid.* and La Gloire, 5 Rob. 192.

(*a*) *Crawford* v. *The William Penn*, *Peters' Rep.* 106.

sent, by the government of the enemy, to be carried to their own country, are bound to do no act of hostility. Therefore, a capture made by such persons of a vessel of their own country from the enemy, is not a recapture in contemplation of law, and gives them no title to salvage, and the former owner no title to claim the vessel" (*b*).

The officers and crew of a cartel ship are bound to commit no act in violation of the conditions of cartel. Thus, in the above case (*The Mary*), where certain English prisoners of war made their escape, in breach of parole, and regained possession of their vessel, which had been captured by the Dutch, the crew of *The Mary* were, on the arrival of that vessel in Holland, immediately thrown into prison. The recaptured British vessel, on the other hand, was ordered to be delivered to his Majesty, to be by him disposed of as his sense of justice towards the injured (Dutch) government might direct.

The Treaty of Paris (30th March, 1856), provided that all prisoners of war should be immediately released. This indeed has, according to Twiss's International Law (1 ed. p. 126), been the universal practice of Christian powers, at the end of a war, since the Treaty of Munster in 1648 (*d*).

(*b*) The Mary (Folger), 5 Rob. 201; Maritime Warfare, p. 66.

(*d*) "But here (at White Hall) he (Sir G. Downing) and Sir William Doyly were attending the Council as Commissioners for sick and wounded, and prisoners: and they told me their business, which was to know how we shall do to release our prisoners; for it seems the Dutch have got us to agree in the treaty (as they fool us in anything) that the dyet of the prisoners on both sides shall be paid for before they be released: which they have done, knowing ours to run high, they having more prisoners of ours than we have of theirs; so they are able and most ready to discharge the debt of theirs, but we are neither able nor willing to do that for ours, the debt of those in Zeland only amounting to above 5,000*l.* for men taken in the King's own ships, besides others taken in merchantmen, who expect, as is usual, that the King should redeem them; but I think he will not, by what Sir G. Downing says. This our prisoners complain of there; and say in their letters, which Sir G. Downing showed me, that they have made a good feat that they should be taken in the service of the King, and the King not pay for their

The treatment to be accorded to the crews of captured merchant ships is a matter of doubt. In the Franco-Prussian war such persons were treated by the French as prisoners of war, on the ground, presumably, that to allow them to return to their own country would be to supply their government with means to augment the national naval power. Prince Bismarck, however, objected to this course, and seized, as a measure of retortion, forty notables of Dijon, Gray, and Vesoul (*e*).

The cases of *The Virginius*, where, in 1874, the Spanish Government summarily executed certain British subjects found on board a Cuban insurgent vessel; and of *The Cagliari*, where, in 1857, the Neapolitan Government imprisoned British subjects found on board a vessel seized by rebels; may be referred to for information as to the view held by this country of any irregularity in dealing with British subjects seized on the ground of being engaged in hostilities against an alien power (*f*).

Somewhat allied to the subject of cartel-ships for the release of prisoners, is that of ransoming property from the enemy. This subject, therefore, may now be considered.

---

victuals while prisoners for him. But so far they are from doing thus with their men as we do to discourage ours, that I find in the letters of some of our prisoners there, which he showed me, that they have with money got our men, that they took, to work and carry their ships home for them; and they have been well rewarded, and released when they come into Holland: which is done like a noble, brave, and wise people."—Pepys's Diary, 30 Aug. 1667.

(*e*) Edinb. Review, July 1884, 263.

(*f*) Pitt-Cobbett's Leading Cases: The Virginius, p. 89; The Cagliari, p. 87. *Vide* also pp. 435—6, *infra*.

PERMISSION OR PROHIBITION OF RANSOM.

"It was formerly the general custom to redeem property from the hands of the enemy by ransom, and the contract is undoubtedly valid when municipal regulations do not intervene" (*g*). So far as this country is concerned, municipal regulations do intervene, both as regards the ransoming of property captured *by* the enemy, and the restoration of property captured *from* the enemy. The Act, 17 Vict. c. 18, cited as "The Prize Act, *Russia*, 1854," deals with ransom of property *from* the enemy as follows:—

§ XLII. "It shall not be lawful for any of her Majesty's subjects to ransom, or to enter into any contract or agreement for ransoming, any ship, vessel, goods or merchandise belonging to any of her Majesty's subjects, which shall be captured by any of her Majesty's enemies; and all contracts and agreements which shall be entered into, and all bills, notes, and other securities which shall be given by any person for ransom of any ship, vessel, goods or merchandise, contrary to the provisions of this Act, shall be absolutely null and void."

§ XLIII. imposes a penalty of 500*l.* for breach of the provisions of this Act, "unless it shall appear that the circumstances of the case were such as to justify the said ransoming."

And with respect to restoration *to* the enemy:—

§ XLIV. provides that any commander of any of her Majesty's war-ships agreeing for the ransoming or restoring of any ship or goods taken by any of her Majesty's ships, shall suffer such penalty as the Court shall adjudge, "unless it shall appear to such Court that the circumstances of the case were such as to have justified the same."

(*g*) Kent's Internat. Law, 2 Eng. ed. p. 251.

The Act 27 & 28 Vict. c. 25, however, cited as "The Naval Prize Act, 1864" (*h*), so provides for the ransom of property captured *by* the enemy, that it shall be deemed legal or illegal to effect such ransoms according as an Order in Council shall declare. § 45 runs as follows:

"Her Majesty in Council may from time to time, in relation to any war, make such orders as may seem expedient, according to circumstances, for prohibiting or allowing, wholly or in certain cases, or subject to any conditions or regulations or otherwise, as may from time to time seem meet, the ransoming, or the entering into any contract or agreement for the ransoming, of any ship or goods belonging to any of her Majesty's subjects, and taken as prize by any of her Majesty's enemies.

"Any contract or agreement entered into, and any bill, bond, or other security, given for ransom of any ship or goods, shall be under the exclusive jurisdiction of the High Court of Admiralty as a Prize Court (subject to appeal to the Judicial Committee of the Privy Council), and if entered into or given in contravention of any such Order in Council, shall be deemed to have been entered into or given for an illegal consideration.

"If any person ransoms, or enters into any contract or agreement for ransoming, any ship or goods, in contravention of any such Order in Council, he shall, for every such offence, be liable to be proceeded against in the High Court of Admiralty, at the suit of her Majesty in her office of Admiralty, and on conviction to be fined, in the discretion of the Court, any sum not exceeding five hundred pounds."

(*h*) The Act will be found in the Appendix.

In the absence of an Order in Council, it is to be presumed that the law stands as is expressed in §§ 42—44 of the Act of 1854, already quoted, viz., that all ransom is *primâ facie* illegal. This principle is in accord with the general policy of the European powers, but it would seem that in the United States, ransoms have never been prohibited by Congress.

The precise nature of the circumstances which shall "appear to the court to be such as to justify" the ransoming, cannot be laid down. Sir W. Scott, in *The Ships taken at Genoa* (*i*), in declaring that "even ransoms, under circumstances of necessity, are still allowed," forbore to enlarge upon this text, and the circumstances of the particular case are not such as to be very valuable as a precedent. Lord Keith, on the capitulation of Genoa, seized some five hundred vessels lying in the harbour, leaving it to the owners of each vessel to show that their property was neutral and had not broken the blockade which had been established for a considerable time. On the subsequent evacuation of the port, Lord Keith demanded the sum of 500,000*l.*, as an equivalent for all ships in the port. "To carry all the ships away was impossible, yet he had a right to take away the value of all, as having a right to the possession," said the learned judge. On the Genoese declaring their inability to raise any such sum as that demanded, Lord Keith agreed to accept 17,000*l.*, and this was paid to him. Three years afterwards the Genoese raised the plea that the terms of the capitulation, exempting property generally from seizure, exempted the ships, and that the seizure was consequently illegal. Sir W. Scott held, as to this, that ships are a species of property *sui generis*, and are not included by mere general terms, however comprehensive. The claimants having raised the further plea that the trans-

(*i*) 4 Rob. 388.

action constituted a ransom (though it is not easy to see how such a plea, even if successful, could benefit them), and that ransom was prohibited by British law, his Lordship delivered himself as above, adding, however, that the money-proceeds must go to the Crown, the Prize Act giving to captors only ships, goods, &c., afloat,—whereas this was a sum of money.

The above is an instance, it should be noted, of restoring, for a money-payment, property captured *from* the enemy, a transaction to be more favourably regarded than the ransom of property captured *by* the enemy; for while in the latter case there may always be the possibility or even the probability of a recapture by British cruisers, in the former the acceptance of a money equivalent (it should be an equivalent) operates to practically defeat any such chance of recapture on the part of the enemy.

The American Courts, in *Jecker* v. *Montgomery* (*k*), when referring to the duty of captors to bring in their prizes for adjudication, gave utterance to remarks useful as throwing some little light on the subject of justification of ransom. "There are cases," said Mr. Justice Taney, "where, from existing circumstances, the captors may be excused from the performance of this duty, and may sell or otherwise dispose of the property before condemnation. And where the commander of a national ship cannot, without weakening inconveniently the force under his command, spare a sufficient prize crew to man the captured vessel, or where the orders of his government prohibit him from doing so, he may lawfully sell or otherwise dispose of the captured property in a foreign country, and may afterwards proceed to adjudication in a Court of the United States." It must, however, be remembered that ransom is apparently not illegal by United

(*k*) 13 *Howard*, 115.

States law. Under the present greatly altered conditions of naval warfare, in which seamen and marines have been largely supplanted by machinery and machine guns, it will necessarily be a difficult matter to spare men for the navigation of prize ships to the extent practised in former days. So that unless the circumstances justifying release to the enemy, for ransom money, should be liberally regarded by Orders in Council, captors will often have to choose between letting their prizes go scot free on the one hand, or wantonly destroying them on the other. Possibly the framers of the 1864 Act had this contingency in view when they decided to provide for a relaxation of the stringency of the Act passed in 1854.

But it was formerly a common practice to ransom British ships taken by the enemy, by delivering to the captor what was called a **ransom bill.** This secured to him the price agreed upon, and operated both as a bill of sale to the original owners and as a protection to the ship against other cruisers of the enemy during the remainder of her voyage. A hostage was likewise delivered to the captor as security for the punctual payment of the stipulated sum. Actions at common law were formerly maintained upon ransom bills (*l*); but inasmuch as ransom has since become unlawful, no action can now be supported by such bills. Moreover, it was in *Anthon* v. *Fisher* (*m*) decided that an alien enemy cannot sue for any right claimed to be acquired by him in actual war: and, as we have seen above, persons who have given such a ransom bill are *primâ facie* liable to heavy penalties. Previous to this the case of *Ricord* v. *Bettenham* (*n*) had established the contrary. In this case the master of an English vessel,

(*l*) Park's Mar. Insce. 8th ed. p. 154.

(*m*) 2 Doug. 649, an. 1781. See also The Hoop, 1 Rob. 196; also Antoine *v.* Morshead, 6 Taunt. 237, an. 1815.

(*n*) 3 Burr. 1734, an. 1765.

on obtaining a release from the French privateer which had captured his vessel, gave to the Frenchman a ransom bill, and at the same time handed over his mate, Bell, as a collateral security. The unfortunate hostage having died in prison, the defendants pleaded that the plaintiff had by this event lost his right of action; that, being at the time of the contract an alien enemy, he himself could not sue on the bill, and that the action should have been brought by the mate. The Court, however, found for the plaintiff, presumably on the ground that such a contract was valid among the other nations of Europe, and was not discharged by the death of the hostage, who was merely a collateral security.

Emerigon (p. 377), treating on this subject, writes as follows:—"The ransom bill is lawful and binding in itself. It is only for greater precaution that the captor fortifies himself with a hostage, whose person thus becomes both surety and pledge for the promise made. If this hostage has the baseness to escape by flight, or should he come to die, the promise would not the less exist." Lord Mansfield also, in *Cornu* v. *Blackburne* (*o*), emphatically declared his opinion that the contract was "worthy to be sustained by sound morality and good policy, and as governed by the law of nations and the eternal rules of justice." Sir W. Scott, however, in a subsequent case (*p*), observed that "even in cases of ransom . . . . the ransom could not be put in suit on the part of the enemy: proceedings were always carried on against the owner in the name of the hostage suing for his liberty"; but this observation is scarcely in accord with the decision in *Ricord's* case, *supra*.

The ordinary procedure in case of ransom is as follows:— The captor, on restoring the captured vessel to the master, takes from him a ransom bill, in which the master binds

(*o*) 2 Doug. 641, an. 1781.

(*p*) The Rebecca, 5 Rob. 102, an. 1804.

himself and owners to pay a certain sum of money at a future day named in the bill. This bill or contract is usually made in duplicate, one copy, retained by the captor, being termed the ransom bill; whilst the other, kept by the master, serves him as a pass or safe-conduct against further molestation on the part of other vessels of the country to which the captor is subject (*q*), and its allies. As a hostage or collateral security for due payment of the bill, the master of the vessel released delivers up to the captor some member of the ship's company, generally—as in *Ricord* v. *Bettenham*, *supra*—the mate of the ship. The vessel is then allowed to proceed on the voyage prescribed, and the safe-conduct will avail to protect her so long as she is found within the course prescribed, and within the time limited by the contract. If driven out of her course by stress of weather or other unavoidable circumstances, such a departure is not to be deemed a breach of the contract. But if the vessel be captured a second time and condemned for breach of the conditions of safe-conduct, the debtors under the ransom-bill will be discharged, and the first captors will have to be paid off by the second. If the vessel should be lost by a peril of the sea before arrival, the ransom is still due, for all that the captor undertook was that she should not be captured by cruisers of his own nation or of the allies of his country. In case, however, the ransom contract should provide that a loss by perils of the sea shall be deemed a discharge of the debtors, such a provision should cover only actual total losses. Otherwise there might be a temptation to fraudulent stranding with a view to saving the cargo at the expense of the ship.

If the captor should himself be taken, with the ransom bill in his possession, the bill becomes a part of the prize of

---

(*q*) *Miller* v. *The Resolution*, 2 *Dall.* 15.

his captors, and the debtors under the ransom bill become, so it is said, thereby discharged (*r*). It is not, however, quite clear why this should be so, absolutely. If it had been the ship which had been recaptured before the ransom was arranged, the recaptors would have been entitled to salvage; and it would seem reasonable that the recaptors should also be rewarded for their meritorious action, which in a similar manner benefited the debtors under the ransom bill. But if the ransom bill and hostage shall have been placed beyond the reach of the (second) captors the bill will still hold good against the debtors under it (*s*).

If the master of a ship shall give a bill for a greater sum than the property ransomed is worth, the owners can abandon the property to the holders of the bill, as in the case of a bottomry bond (*t*). For any deficiency arising, on sale, between the proceeds realised, and the amount of the ransom plus the expenses of the hostage, the master is liable to be personally sued, as he had no right to bind the property in a larger sum than its value. But if, after sale of the property, and exhaustion of remedy against the master, there should still be a shortfall, the Court of Admiralty will refuse to let the proceeds be paid over until the hostage shall be released (*u*).

A captor has the right to release the prize against delivery of a ransom bill, immediately he effects the capture. The position, as regards ransom, seems to be this: If the master of the captured vessel chooses to accept the terms of the captors, and buy his freedom by a bill on his owners, unless prohibited by the law of his country, he can do so. If he declines to compound, and prefers to take his chance in

---

(*r*) Wheaton's Internat. Law, 2 Eng. ed. p. 475.
(*s*) Cornu *v.* Blackburne, 2 Doug. 640.
(*t*) The Gratitudine, 3 Rob. 258.
(*u*) Yates *v.* Hall, 1 Term R. 80.

adjudication proceedings, he can do so. If he should think that the adjudication will probably go against him, he will doubtless compound. If, on the other hand, he has confidence in the justice of his cause, he will probably abide the issue of proceedings in the Court of the captors. But he will clearly understand that, whether the capture be good or bad, if once he compounds, all question of adjudication becomes thereby closed; and, however improper the seizure may prove to have been, he and his owners will still be bound by the bill. And this principle will hold good whether the vessel seized be the property of belligerents or of neutrals (*v*).

Insurance.

So long as ransom from the enemy is prohibited by British law, money paid as ransom to the country's enemies cannot be recovered under the marine policy. The ransom contract being illegal, no contract in support of it can be legal. On seizure of the vessel, the assured would be entitled to abandon to his underwriters, but if the captors be bought off, the ship, being in safety, cannot be abandoned. And if a ransom should be procured by the master, the ransom bill would still be incapable of enforcement in the British Courts. If, however, the master, instead of giving a bill, barratrously purchase the release of the vessel by making over the cargo, or part of it, to the captor, the value of cargo so lost would presumably be recoverable under the policy as being a loss caused by barratry of the master (*x*). If the insurance be on alien belligerent property, this country not being engaged in any hostilities, the British enactments against ransom from the enemy would naturally be inapplicable (*y*).

(*v*) See *Maissonnaire* v. *Keating*, 2 *Gall.* 337. Other leading United States decisions, *re* Ransom, are *The Lord Wellington*, 2 *Gall.* 104; *Gerard* v. *Ware*, *Peters' C. R.* 142; *Moodie* v. *Brig Harriett*, *Bee's Rep.* 128.

(*x*) But cf. Cory *v.* Burr, p. 79, *supra*.

(*y*) See note, Arnould, 5th ed. p. 849.

The law against ransom will be strictly interpreted. This was illustrated in *The Themis* (z). The vessel had been captured and carried into Bergen, where she was condemned by the French consul. She was then bought at public auction by the plaintiff's agent; and for the money so expended plaintiff claimed under the policy. It was, however, held by the Court that such a condemnation—viz., by a French consul in a neutral port—was contrary to the law of nations, and therefore void. And that, this being so, the property never was divested from the original owner, and the money paid as for the re-purchase, being in the nature of a ransom, could not be recovered. The circumstance that the purchase was effected at an auction and on land was held to be immaterial, the Acts of Parliament prohibiting ransom being in general terms.

If the prohibitions against ransom were to be removed, no doubt money thus paid in order to procure the restoration of the ship would be treated as general average, as in the case of ransom paid to pirates or other plunderers (a). Indeed, in Magens's Essay on Insurances (vol. 1, p. 290), there is set forth a general average statement drawn up at Leghorn in 1748 "by way of a gross average for the ransom of a cargo of wheat from London in the last war."

The ransom of prisoners has been referred to *sub* Licence to Cartel Ships, p. 292.

The last of the belligerent municipal rights to be considered is the right to prohibit the exportation of articles subservient to warlike uses. This right we will now examine.

(z) Havelock *v.* Rockwood, 8 T. R. 268.
(a) Abbott on Shipping, Part III. cap. VIII.

PROHIBITION OF EXPORT OF ARTICLES SUBSERVIENT TO WARLIKE USES.

Export of warlike stores and materials may be prohibited by a belligerent, either on account of an assumed necessity to secure all such articles for the national use, or in order to make sure that there shall be no possibility of their being captured by or conveyed to the enemy. The Act 16 & 17 Vict. c. 107, s. 150, provides that—

> "The following goods may, by Proclamation or Order in Council, be prohibited either to be exported or carried coastwise: arms, ammunition, and gunpowder, military and naval stores, and any articles which her Majesty shall judge capable of being converted and made into or made useful in increasing the quantity of military or naval stores, provisions, or any sort of victual which may be used as food by man; and if any so prohibited shall be exported from the United Kingdom or carried coastwise, or be water-borne to be so exported or carried, they shall be forfeited."

On 18th February, 1854, in anticipation of war with Russia, an Order in Council, referring to the above Act, was issued, declaring that—

> "All arms, ammunition, and gunpowder, military and naval stores, and the following articles, being articles which are judged capable of being converted into or made useful in increasing the quantity of military or naval stores; that is to say, marine engines, screw propellers, paddle wheels, cylinders, cranks, shafts, boilers, tubes for boilers, boiler plates, fire bars, and every article (*sic*)

or any other component part of an engine or boiler, or any article whatsoever, which is, or can or may become, applicable for the manufacture of marine machinery, are prohibited either to be exported from the United Kingdom, or carried coastwise."

A letter dated three days subsequently, addressed by the Treasury to the Commissioners of Customs, comments on the circumstance that it had become known to the government that extensive shipments of warlike stores were being made to Russian ports (*b*). And instructions are given that while any such shipments, whether made directly or indirectly, are to be prevented; where satisfactory proof is given of a destination other than Russian, such goods shall be cleared in the usual way, subject to a compliance with the formalities laid down. The letter finishes as follows:—

"I am, in conclusion, to add that it is with regret that my Lords feel it to be their duty to impose any restriction whatever upon trade, but they are confident that all respectable traders will willingly submit to the small additional trouble which these regulations will impose upon legitimate and fair trade, when the object is to prevent, by all the means in their power, unprincipled persons from contributing, through our own arts and manufactures, arms and ammunition to be used against her Majesty's forces, or those of her allies."

On 17th April another Order was issued removing the restriction against the carrying coastwise, and permitting export within certain defined geographical limits, on the condition that the exporters gave a bond that the goods should be landed at the port of destination, and that they ultimately produced certificates of such landing and entry. If, however, the Commissioners of Customs should have reason to suspect the existence of a clandestine intention to transmit

(*b*) A Royal Proclamation of 8 Feb. 1855, declares as traitors all British subjects assisting H. M. enemies. 46 State Papers, 542.

the articles to places other than those indicated by the applicants, permission to export was to be refused. An Order of 24th April, referring to applications received, intimated that the prohibition of export was removed in the case of all goods except gunpowder, saltpetre, brimstone, arms and ammunition; and that marine engines and boilers and the component parts thereof should be prohibited from export only when destined for ports within certain geographical limits indicated in the Order.

In the event of this country becoming involved in hostilities with a maritime power, it is not improbable that the export of coal will be either prohibited or placed under such special restrictions as may prevent its finding its way into the hands of the enemy (*a*).

Insurance.

All insurances upon goods forbidden to be exported or imported by positive statutes, by the general rules of our municipal law, or by royal proclamation in time of war, are absolutely void (*b*). If a ship, though neutral, be insured on a voyage prohibited by an embargo laid on in time of war by the prince of the country in whose ports the ship happens to be, the insurance—*i.e.*, if effected within the dominions of such prince—is void (*c*). Thus, in *The Bella Juditta* (*Delmada* v. *Motteux*) (*d*), where a neutral vessel, calling at Cork, took away goods the export of which had been prohibited, the insurance was declared void. "To break an embargo," said Lord Mansfield, "is undoubtedly a criminal act, and whenever a man makes an illegal contract, this Court will not lend him their aid." But an insurance upon goods, the exportation or importation of which is forbidden by the laws of other countries, is

(*a*) *Vide* references *sub* Coal in Index, *infra*.

(*b*) Park's Insce., 8th ed. 538.

(*c*) *Ibid.* 503.

(*d*) *Ibid.*

valid, the foundation of the contract, so far as the subjects of this country are concerned, not being illicit (*e*).

At the same time, as in the case of such goods the effect of the prohibition may be to expose them to confiscation, this liability constitutes a material enhancement of the risk, and the insurance will accordingly be void, unless the underwriter was informed, or should be presumed to have been aware, of the facts, when agreeing to the insurance (*f*).

Where an open insurance was effected on "goods" to be hereafter declared, and it subsequently proved that part of the interest insured consisted of prohibited articles, shipped without special licence, the whole insurance was held to be void, the policy being regarded as an indivisible contract (*g*). And an insurance effected in conjunction with traffic designed to fraudulently contravene municipal regulations will also be held void. Thus, in *Gibson* v. *Service* (*h*), a bond had been given on behalf of a British vessel that her cargo of arms and ammunition should be expended in trade on the coast of Africa, but the vessel proceeded to the Congo, and there, in pursuance of previous arrangement, transhipped cargo to the (neutral) American ship *Washington*, to be carried to Charlestown, S. Carolina. An insurance had been effected in England on *The Washington* at and from the African coast to Charlestown, and this insurance was held to be void, as being in protection of a traffic declared to be illegal by the laws of the country where the insurance was made. The connivance of the neutral master at a fraud on the laws of this country was deemed a sufficient ground of condemnation of the vessel. The arrangement was described as a fraudulent agreement planned here and carried out in Africa.

In *Johnson* v. *Sutton* (*i*), where an insurance was effected on a cargo of goods exported to New York, in direct contravention of an Act of Parliament, the underwriters were discharged.

(*e*) *Ibid.* 548.

(*f*) Arnould's Insce., 5th ed. 682.

(*g*) Parkin *v.* Dick, 11 East, 502; conf. Hagedorn *v.* Bazett, p. 273, *supra.* See also Gordon *v.* Vaughan, and other cases cited in Arnould's Insce., 5th ed. 687.

(*h*) 1 Marshall's Rep. 119.

(*i*) Doug. 254.

"Prohibition of Export" is the last of the Belligerent Municipal Rights on which it has seemed necessary to comment; and with this subject ends our consideration of Belligerent Rights generally. Rights against the Enemy, Rights against Neutrals, and Municipal Rights have in turn been dealt with, and it now only remains to review those Obligations by which, under the law of nations, Belligerents are held to be bound.

VII.

BELLIGERENT OBLIGATIONS.

RESPECT OF NEUTRAL TERRITORY.

CHIEF amongst the obligations by which a belligerent is bound is that of respecting the sanctity of all land and water within the jurisdiction of neutral states. "The rights of war," writes Wheaton (*a*), "can be exercised only within the territory of the belligerent powers, upon the high seas, or in a territory belonging to no one." All property lying within the zone of neutral jurisdiction is, in this sense, deemed to be neutral, whether the actual ownership of such property be neutral or belligerent. It was by Bynkershoek contended that an enemy attacked outside of neutral territory might, if he should flee within the neutral jurisdiction, be pursued across the border; "but," says Chancellor Kent (*b*), quoting Vattel and other learned writers, "there is no exception to the rule,

(*a*) Internat. Law, 2 Eng. ed. p. 497.
(*b*) Internat. Law, 2 Eng. ed. p. 306.

that every voluntary entrance into neutral territory, with hostile purposes, is absolutely unlawful."

The maritime territory of every state extends to the ports, harbours, bays, mouths of rivers, and adjacent parts of the sea enclosed by headlands belonging to the same state. The general usage of nations superadds to this extent of territorial jurisdiction, along all the coasts of the state (*c*), a distance of a marine league, the range formerly ascribed to cannon shot, from the shore. The range of modern projectiles has far outgrown the limit thus ascribed to the artillery of former times, but this definition of the territorial jurisdiction over the coastal waters is, notwithstanding, still maintained. Obviously the range of projectiles is no real test of the question of jurisdiction; for a case may well be imagined where, owing to the narrowness of a channel or to the great and ever increasing power of gunnery, the states divided by the channel could both send projectiles completely across it. In *The Anna* (*d*), a Spanish vessel captured by a British privateer near the mouth of the Mississippi, the vessel was claimed by the American ambassador in England, on the ground that the seizure had taken place within three miles of United States territory. It was proved that the capture had, in fact, been effected within three miles of some small mud islands forming a kind of portico to the main land. On this, Sir W. Scott decreed restitution; holding that the three mile limit must be reckoned from the islands, these being the natural appendages of the coast on which they bordered. "Captors," said his lordship, "must understand that they are not to station themselves in the mouth of a neutral river for the purpose of exercising the rights of war from that river; much less in the very river itself. They are not to be standing on and off,

(*c*) Wheat. Int. Law, 2 Eng. ed. p. 237.
(*d*) 5 Rob. 373.

overhauling vessels in their course down the river, and making the river as much subservient to the purposes of war as if it had been a river of their own country."

Inclosed parts of the sea along the British coasts—that is, bays, called the "King's Chambers," cut off by lines drawn from one promontory to another—have immemorially been held to be within the British jurisdiction; and a similar jurisdiction is asserted by the United States over such bays on the American coasts.

In *The Twee Gebroeder* (e), it was argued against the condemnation of the ship, that the capture was invalidated by the previous passage of the capturing vessel over neutral waters, *animo capiendi;* but Sir W. Scott held that the act of a war-vessel passing over neutral territory without violence was not considered a violation of the rights of that territory. In another case (*f*), a British cruiser stationed in neutral waters had sent boats off to, and had captured, some Dutch ships lying out of the jurisdiction; and the same eminent judge held that no proximate acts of war could be allowed to originate within neutral dominions, and he decreed restitution accordingly. The cases of *The Chesapeake* (*g*), *The Wachusett* (*g*), and *The Caroline* (*h*), may also be referred to in this connexion.

The Franconia (*Reg.* v. *Keyn*) (*i*), tried in 1876 before thirteen learned judges, of whom seven held to one opinion, and six to another, raised the question of criminal jurisdiction over foreigners on foreign vessels within the three mile limit; and the judgment of Cockburn, L. C. J., in this case, is a highly instructive review of the authorities and statutes touching the three mile limit generally. This question of

(*e*) (Capt. Northolt), 3 Rob. 336.

(*f*) The Twee Gebroeder (Alberts), 3 Rob. 162.

(*g*) Wheat. Int. Law, 2 Eng. ed. pp. 498-9.

(*h*) Parl. Papers, 1843, Vol. LXI. See also The Grange (1793), Am. State Papers, Vol. I. p. 77.

(*i*) L. R. 2 Exch. Div. 63.

criminal jurisdiction, it may be here observed, has since been dealt with by 41 & 42 Vict. c. 73.

But a capture within the neutral jurisdiction is not *ipso facto* void. It is good as between the belligerents, and can be called in question only by the aggrieved neutral state. On this subject Sir W. Scott declared that "it is a known principle of this (Admiralty) Court that the privilege of territory will not itself enure to the protection of property, unless the state from which that protection is due steps forward to assert the right" (*j*)—a doctrine also upheld by the United States Courts. But if the captured vessel shall at the outset have used force in its defence, the master will be deemed to have foregone his right of appeal to the protection of the neutral state (*k*). The neutral state, may, however, none the less claim restitution of the vessel—indeed, it is asserted that it is the duty of a neutral to do so—not by way of compensation to the unsuccessful belligerent, but in vindication of its own rights (*l*).

Not only is it unlawful for a belligerent to engage in hostile acts within the dominions of neutral states, but it is also contrary to the law of nations for the commander of a belligerent vessel to enlist the subjects of such states to serve on his vessel, unless with the licence of their sovereign. And any such unlawful augmentation of forces will infect subsequent captures made by the vessel thus illegally reinforced. Belligerents are under the obligation to respect the municipal laws and proclamations of neutral states generally, but it will be more convenient to merge further

(*j*) The Purissima Concepcion, 6 Rob. 45; *The Anne*, 3 *Wheat.* 447. See also *The Sir Wm. Peel*, 5 *Wall.* 585.

(*k*) The General Armstrong, *vide* Cobbett's Cases, p. 162; *The Anne*, 3 *Wheat.* 435.

(*l*) La Amistad de Rues, Cobbett's Cases, 190.

reference to this and any other items of such obligation in the consideration of those neutral municipal laws themselves, viz., *sub* Neutral Rights and Obligations, p. 345, *infra*.

(The subject of Admission of Belligerent Warships to Neutral Ports will be specially considered *sub* Neutral Rights and Obligations (*m*). As regards prisoners on board a belligerent vessel in neutral waters, *vide* p. 58, *supra*.)

The special belligerent obligation with which we have now to deal is that of subjecting prizes to the adjudication of a properly constituted prize court of the captors.

(*m*) *Vide* p. 375, *infra*.

ADJUDICATION OF PRIZES

(with a consideration of the Principles governing the Award of

COSTS AND DAMAGES).

In 1745, during the course of hostilities between this country and France, subjects of Prussia proceeded to employ neutral vessels to carry their own merchandise, whilst Prussian vessels loaded cargoes on account of France. On this, British cruisers intervened and seized fifty-one Prussian vessels thus engaged, and these vessels were subsequently condemned. By way of reprisal, the King of Prussia confiscated certain funds lent to the State by British subjects; and to report on questions arising out of the seizure and the consequent reprisal, a commission was appointed by the British Government. Amongst the findings of this commission were three which are material to the present consideration: viz. (1) That before appropriation there must be condemnation; (2) That the only tribunal competent to condemn is the court of the captor; and (3) That all proofs in the matter should, in the first instance, be taken from the vessel seized (*n*). The municipal laws of the European states commonly provide that prizes made by vessels cruising under their flag shall be brought into one of the national ports for adjudication; and condemnation can be adjudged only by a competent prize court of the captors. The court of an ally has no jurisdiction; but, on the other hand, a prize court of the captors

(*n*) *Vide* Pitt Cobbett's summary of the case of The Silesian Loan: Leading Cases, p. 95.

may lawfully sit in the territory of an ally: but not in the territory of a neutral state, so long as the neutral government is *de facto* still existing. Allies, being co-belligerents, are so far identified that the court of the one can condemn a prize lying at the time in the territory of the other (*o*). A prize cannot be condemned whilst within neutral jurisdiction, though under control of the captors; for a prize can never be said to be absolutely reduced into the possession of the captors until they shall have brought it safely into one of their ports or into a port of their ally. This principle has not always been strictly maintained by the British Courts, but it may apparently be considered to have been finally decided by Sir W. Scott, in *The Henrick and Maria* (*p*). In this case the learned judge, on the ground of previous British irregularities, confirmed a foreign condemnation based on the authority of such exceptions, whilst at the same time vindicating the justice of the principle that there can be no legal condemnation so long as the prize is within neutral jurisdiction. Chancellor Kent (*q*), however, observes that the United States Court "has followed the English rule, and has held valid the condemnation, by a belligerent court, of prizes carried into a neutral port and remaining there. . . . . And though the prize was in fact within a neutral jurisdiction, it was still to be deemed under the control, or *sub potestate*, of the captor." And Story (p. 77) also observes that "a condemnation of a prize ship, while lying in a neutral port, by a regular Court of Admiralty in the hostile country, is clearly valid." Owing, however, to the increasing tendency of municipal regulations to restrict the admission of prizes into neutral ports, the question of belligerent rights as to prizes lying in such ports is reduced in importance. Thus, in 1861,

(*o*) *Vide* Arnould's Marine Insce., 5th ed. 628.

(*p*) 4 Rob. 43. *Vide* Arnould, 5th ed. p. 629, note.

(*q*) Int. Law, 2nd ed. p. 250.

it was, both by the British and the French Governments, proclaimed that the ports of these states were to be closed to prizes of parties engaged in the American civil war.

The case of *The Polka* (q), arising out of the Anglo-Russian war, though an apparent exception to the principle laid down by the Courts, must rather be regarded as confirming it. The circumstances were very peculiar. Lying in the Russian port of Libau were sundry vessels, presumably Russian, completely dismantled and without papers. These vessels were seized by British captors, who, finding them in a condition which rendered them unfit to perform the voyage to England, carried them into Memel. In these circumstances the vessels were condemned, and, by consent of the Prussian Government, were ordered to be sold at Memel. But the Court wished it to be expressly understood that this case was decided in its own peculiar circumstances, and was not to be considered as a precedent for the condemnation of a prize whilst lying in a neutral port.

The port of the captors to which the prize is to be brought is that which the captor shall find in the circumstances most convenient (r). But the captor is not justified in selecting any port he pleases, and the convenience of the claimant, in proceeding to adjudication, has been decided to be one of the first things to which the captor's attention should be directed (s).

If a neutral subject acquire a vessel condemned by an irregular court of the captors, and peace ensue before recapture, the defect in the neutral title will be cured by the intervention of peace, which completely bars the title of the former owner (t).

(q) 1 Ec. & Ad. Rep. (Spinks), 447.

(r) Instructions to Navy; Story on Prize Courts, p. 254.

(s) The Wilhelmsberg, 5 Rob. 143; *The Lively and Cargo*, 1 *Gall.* 318; The Washington, 6 Rob. 275.

(t) The Schoone Sophie, 6 Rob. 140.

The right to all captures has from the earliest times vested primarily in the sovereign, and no captor can have any interest in a prize except that which he receives from the bounty of the state. The common practice, however, is to distribute the proceeds of prizes, when condemned, amongst the captors, whether the capturing vessels be public warships or privateers (*u*).

"Head-money" is a payment in the nature of prize bounty to the officers and crews of ships of war actually present at the taking or destroying of any *armed* ship of the enemy. By the Naval Prize Act, 1864, s. 42, it is to be calculated at the rate of 5*l.* for each person on board the enemy's ship at the beginning of the engagement.

On the outbreak of war a royal proclamation is issued, of which the effect is to charge the High Court of Admiralty with the duty of adjudicating in cases of prize. But until final condemnation by this Court, the Crown can, by virtue of its prerogative, restore a prize to the enemy from whom it has been captured, without regard to the rights or claims of the captors (*x*). And, by ancient law of the Admiralty, captors may by any misconduct on their part forfeit their rights of prize,—a penalty frequently enforced for fraud, misconduct, or improper deviation from the regular course of proceedings (*y*).

Hostile vessels seized within the British dominions are either droits of Admiralty or the property of the Crown, according to the circumstances in which they entered port. "It appears," said Sir W. Scott (*z*), in *The Marie Françoise*,

(*u*) *Vide The Emma, Blatch. Pr. Ca.* 561, for effect of seizure by non-commissioned transport.

(*x*) The Elsebe, 5 Rob. 181.

(*y*) *Vide* Story on Prize Courts, p. 32. Also Naval Prize Act, 1864, s. 37 (in Appendix).

(*z*) 6 Rob. 282. *Vide* also The Gertruyda, 2 Rob. 218.

"from the tenor of this order (*a*), that the distinction between the admiral and rights of the Crown is founded on this:—that when vessels come in not under any motive arising out of the occasions of war, but from distress of weather, or want of provisions, or from ignorance of war, and are seized in port, they belong to the Lord High Admiral; but where the hand of violence has been exercised upon them, where the impression arises from acts connected with war, from revolt of their own crew, or from being forced or driven in by the King's ships, they belong to the Crown. This is the broad distinction which is laid down in the Order in Council, and which has since been invariably observed."

In times of war the various national courts of prize, established for adjudicating on captured property, proceed according to the law of nations, and not according to municipal law. But experience shows that such courts of belligerents do not by any means necessarily take always the same strict view of the principles governing questions of condemnation or of restitution.

In cases where, owing to the impracticability of carrying it into a port of the captors, or otherwise, the captured property has been lost, destroyed, or sold (*b*), the Court may, at the instance either of the captors or of the neutral or national claimants, still proceed to adjudication (*c*).

Captors must proceed to adjudication without unnecessary delay, the failure to do so being attended by the liability to pay costs and damages. Moreover, in case of undue delay, any person claiming an interest in the captured property may obtain a monition against captors to proceed in the adjudica-

(*a*) *I. e.*, an Order in Council of Charles II., for which *vide* Maritime Warfare, p. 380.

(*b*) *Vide* p. 55, *supra*.

(*c*) The Peacock, 4 Rob. 185; The Falcon, 6 Rob. 194; The Pomona, 1 Dods. 25. See also The L'Eole, 6 Rob. 220; and The La Dame Cecile, *ibid.*

tion. On their continued failure to do so, or inability to show cause why the property should be condemned, it may be restored to the claimants proving an interest in it. But if the capture be justified, instead of restoration being decreed the prize may be condemned to the State,—a result which may also occur if the captor be found guilty of misconduct (*d*).

The Statute of Limitations does not apply to prize causes; so that captors may at any time during the existence of the prize commission be required to proceed to adjudication, for the purpose of obtaining an award of damages against them (*e*). But claimants will not be allowed to demand adjudication after a great lapse of time (*f*).

The obligation to bring vessels in for adjudication exists as between belligerent captors and neutral claimants, but is not to be extended to cover the case where the seizure has been of enemy property. Enemies have no *locus standi* in a prize court under the law of nations, unless in virtue of a flag of truce or analogous conditions; and under this law property which is plainly that of an enemy can be destroyed immediately on seizure. This principle was freely acted upon by the Confederate cruiser *Alabama* in the American civil war. If, however, neutral property be for any reason thus destroyed, restitution must be made (*g*).

If the persons interested in captured property be of opinion that no grounds exist to justify condemnation, it is

---

257; also The Betsey, 1 Rob. 93; The Der Mohr, 3 Rob. 129; The George, *ibid.* 212; The William, 4 Rob. 215; The Purissima Concepcion, 6 Rob. 45; *The Anna Maria*, 2 *Wheat.* 327.

(*d*) *The Bothnea*, 2 *Gall.* 78; The Triton, 4 Rob. 78; *Miller* v. *The Resolution*, 2 *Dall.* 1.

(*e*) The Mentor, 1 Rob. 179; The Huldah, 3 Rob. 235.

(*f*) The Susanna, 6 Rob. 48; The Mentor, *supra.*

(*g*) The Felicity, 2 Dod. 386. But cf. The Ludwig and The Vorwärts, p. 357, *infra.*

open to them to enter their claim in due time before the proper Court. In their absence the claim can be made by the master of the vessel or by others on their behalf. The claim must be supported by a sworn affidavit, which must be framed without any examination of the ship's papers; though the Court will, on application, consider the propriety of making an order authorizing the examination of such papers as directly relate to the claim (*i*). And no claim will in ordinary circumstances be admitted which is in direct opposition to the ship's papers and to the preparatory examinations (*j*). When the neutrality of the ownership does not sufficiently appear, the claimant is often indulged with time to submit affidavits to supply the deficiency. The *onus probandi* lies on the claimant, and if he fails in his proof condemnation ensues. If no claim be put forward, the general rule, except where there are strong grounds for belief that the property is that of an enemy, is to defer condemnation till a year and a day have elapsed from the time of the return of the monition. But if no claim has then been interposed, condemnation goes as of course, and the question of former ownership is for ever precluded.

If the property be proved to be that of an enemy, condemnation will be decreed forthwith. Until condemnation has been decreed by a regularly constituted prize court of the captors, the property in the prize is not changed, and a neutral vendee or a recaptor must show documentary evidence of such condemnation in order to support his title against a claim by the original owner (*k*). In short, until

(*i*) The Port Mary, 3 Rob. 233.

(*j*) The Vrow Anna Catharina, 5 Rob. 15, 19; The La Flora, 6 Rob. 1.

(*k*) Le Caux *v.* Eden, Doug. 613, 616; Goss *v.* Withers, 2 Burr. 683; The Flad Oyen, 1 Rob. 135; The Santa Cruz, 1 Rob. 50; The Fanny and Elmira, Edw. 117; The Ceylon, 1 Dod. 105; The L'Actif, Edw. 185; The Nostra Signora de los Angelos, 3 Rob. 287.

legal adjudication has taken place, captured property is deemed to be held by the government of the captors in trust for the rightful owners, whoever they may ultimately prove to be.

In *The Kierlighett* (*l*), where an English vessel had been condemned by the French consul at a Norwegian port, and had been recaptured after sale to a neutral purchaser, the Court declared the condemnation bad and the sale consequently invalid. The neutral claimant then petitioned for an allowance to be made to him for amelioration of the vessel whilst in his possession. The Court, not considering that he had acquired the vessel under a title notoriously bad, directed that the registrar should report on the *quantum* of amelioration, but exclusive of ordinary repairs, against which the use of the vessel was to be set off.

If the proceedings be prolonged or the cargo be of a perishable nature, an interlocutory sale may be ordered; but it is a settled rule of the Court not to deliver a cargo on bail, unless with the consent of all parties, until the case has been fully heard (*m*). Nor may bulk be broken until final judgment, unless in cases of urgent necessity or by decree of the Court. When the cargo is discharged under order of the Court, the proceeding is usually deemed to have been effected for the benefit of all parties. If the discharge has been on the application of captors and condemnation has ensued, the expense falls on the captors. If, on the other hand, restitution be awarded, the Court usually charges it on the cargo (*n*).

The jurisdiction of the Court of the capturing nation is conclusive upon the question of property in the thing

---

(*l*) 3 Rob. 96. *Vide* also The Nostra de Conceicas, 5 Rob. 294.

(*m*) The Copenhagen, 3 Rob. 178. Naval Prize Act, 1864, ss. 26—31 (in Appendix).

(*n*) The Industrie, 5 Rob. 88.

captured (*o*). Its sentence forecloses all controversy respecting the validity of the capture as between claimant and captors, and those claiming under them, and terminates all ordinary judicial inquiry upon the subject-matter. For all captures made by the belligerent cruisers the captors are, until adjudication, answerable only to the government of the state to which they are subject, and whose commission they bear. Neutrals have till that time no right of complaint, any loss or inconvenience to which they may have been exposed by the acts of such cruisers being regarded as the inevitable result of the belligerent right of capture. But when once the tribunals of the captor's country have pronounced their decision, the capture and condemnation become the acts of the state, and for any wrongful acts so endorsed the state is responsible to the government of the claimant. But aggrieved neutral subjects cannot appeal to their own government till they have resorted to the superior Courts of the captors, and the sentence has been finally confirmed (*p*). For a capture adjudged unjustifiable, captors are personally liable to the claimants (*pp*).

On a prize being brought in by captors, they are required to give notice to the district judge, or to the prize commissioners, in order that the captured crew may be examined in accordance with the standing interrogatories (*q*). These interrogatories, which are most minute and searching, are administered to the witnesses separately, and not in presence of each other, in order to prevent any fraudulent concert between them. So that if during the voyage the vessel should have been engaged in any unlawful or hostile act of which the captors have no knowledge or suspicion, the fact is pretty sure to come out in the examination. Any illegality

(*o*) The effect of judgments by alien tribunals is referred to *sub* War Warranties, p. 389, *infra*.

(*p*) Wheaton's Internat. Law, 2 Eng. ed. 456—461.

(*pp*) *Vide* The Ostsee, p. 325, *infra*. *Vide* also pp. 55 and 57, *supra;* and cf. Flanagan *v.* Hulme, *Times*, 15 July, 1889.

(*q*) Set forth at length in Story on Prize Courts, pp. 244—254.

so ascertained can be pleaded by the captors as ground for condemnation, although the particular suspicion which caused them to seize the vessel may prove to have been ill-founded.

"The general rule of law is that, on all points, the evidence of the claimants alone shall be received in the first instance. The evidence must, of course, be received with caution, and duly tested, but the rule is to take the original evidence of the claimants as conclusive, unless impeached" (*r*). A witness cannot, according to the general rule of prize court procedure, claim a right to modify or enlarge his testimony when once it has been completed and submitted to the Court (*s*). It is, however, within the rights of the Court to admit such a request (*t*). A prize commissioner has no right to put to a witness interrogatories other than the standing interrogatories, except such as may have been specially framed for the particular case by the Court (*u*).

For a more detailed history of the rules and procedure adopted by the Courts in prize adjudication, reference may be made to Story's exhaustive treatise on the Principles and Practice of Prize Courts. The Naval Prize Act, 1864, may also be profitably studied in this connexion (see Appendix).

Costs and Damages.—The principles governing the award of costs and compensation are clearly and comprehensively set forth in the learned judgment of the Privy Council in a case arising out of the hostilities against Russia, in 1854 (*x*). *The Ostsee*, a neutral vessel, having been seized by *H.M.S. Alban*, Captain Otter, and, on adjudication, released, the claimants prayed for compensation on the ground that the capture had

(*r*) The Haabet, 6 Rob. 54.

(*s*) *The Peterhoff, Blatch. Pr. Ca.* 345.

(*t*) *The Stephen Hart, ibid.* 387.

(*u*) *The Peterhoff, ibid.* 463.

(*x*) The Ostsee, Schact *v.* Otter, Spinks' Prize Cases, 1854-6.

been unjustifiable. Dr. Lushington, in rejecting this claim in the Admiralty Court, delivered himself thus:—"During the seventeen years that Lord Stowell (Sir W. Scott) presided in this Court, and administered the law of nations with regard to war, I believe that, out of the many ships and cargoes brought before him, he condemned the captors in costs and damages in only about ten or a dozen cases—not one in a thousand. And Lord Stowell, also, as I right well remember, laid it down that he would not condemn the captors in costs and damages upon evidence given before him, without giving them the opportunity of justifying their conduct, and of stating, if they thought fit, the grounds on which they made the capture. As far as I recollect, there are only three cases of restitution with costs and damages." In the particular circumstances the Court declined to award costs and damages. From this judgment the claimants appealed to the Privy Council. The Rt. Hon. T. Pemberton Leigh, in delivering the judgment of the Court, said:—"It is agreed on all hands that the restitution of a ship and cargo may be attended, according to the circumstances of the case, with any of the following consequences:—

1. The claimants may be ordered to pay to the captors their costs and expenses; or
2. The restitution may be, as in this case, simple restitution without costs or expenses, or damages to either party; or
3. The captors may be ordered to pay costs and damages to the claimants.

These provisions seem well adapted to meet the various circumstances, not ultimately affording ground of condemnation, under which captures may take place.

(1.) A ship may, by her own misconduct, have occasioned her capture; and in such a case it is reasonable that she should indemnify the captors against the expenses which her misconduct has occasioned. Or,

(2.) She may be involved, with little or no fault on her part, in such suspicion as to make it the right or even the duty of a belligerent to seize her. There may be no fault either in the captor or the captured; or both may be in fault; and in such cases there may be *damnum absque injuriâ*, and no ground for anything but simple restitution. Or,

(3.) There may be a third case, where not only the ship is in no fault, but she is not by any act of her own, voluntary or involuntary, open to any fair ground of suspicion. In such a case a belligerent may seize at his peril, and take the chance of something appearing on investigation to justify the capture; but if he fails in such a case, it seems very fit that he should pay the costs and damages which he has occasioned."

His lordship then proceeded to deliver an exhaustive and instructive summary of opinions of the text-writers, and of cases in precedent—some twenty in number—of which he declared the result to be, "that in order to exempt a captor from costs and damages in case of restitution, there must have been some circumstance connected with the ship or cargo affording reasonable ground for belief that one or both, or some part of the cargo, might prove, upon further inquiry, to be lawful prize." What should amount to probable cause, could not be exactly defined; but if the Court should find in any case in favour of such grounds of capture, the captors would be justified, although the Court should acquit without ordering further proof. In order to subject captors to damages and costs, it is not necessary to prove vexatious conduct on their part, nor will honesty of mistake exempt them from liability to compensate the neutral sufferer by their action; for costs and damages are not the punishment of captors, but the compensation of the injured party.

If the captors' mistake arises from the proceedings of their own Government, they are none the less liable to the captured, but they have a claim, on their part, to be indemnified by the Government (y). In this case (*The Ostsee*), the vessel had been seized for a supposed breach of blockade, whereas it was clear from her papers that she had committed no such breach. If, as was alleged, there was a confusion with respect to the blockades in the Baltic, the circumstance could nevertheless afford no answer to the claim of a neutral, innocent of all fault. With respect to the captors' contention that having acted *bonâ fide* they ought to be indemnified by her Majesty's Government, it was, said the Court, sufficient to say that in this case there appeared to be no blame whatever imputable to the Government. They had in no way contributed to the capture or done anything to mislead the naval officers. Whether naval officers who have acted wrongfully as regards neutrals, but without wilful misconduct, should be indemnified against the consequences of their acts, by the Crown authorities, was held not to be for the Court to decide. The Court had only to administer justice as between the claimants and the captors. Further, it was not for the Court to discuss the question of liability as between the admiral who had given general orders, and Captain Otter who had acted under them; and public ships and privateers, it was declared, must both be held to be governed by the same principle as regards their liability to pay damages for captures effected without probable or reasonable cause. The Court, moreover, was not in this decision laying down rules merely for the British navy; for whatever was held in the English prize courts to excuse a British officer, would, it was observed, be held by foreign Courts to excuse captors members of such foreign nations.

(y) *Vide* Routh *v.* Thompson, 11 East, 428.

Upon the whole, said the Court, the captors must be held liable, —amount of damages to be fixed by the registrar in the usual way. So far as any claim for demurrage was concerned, three weeks of the delay had to be attributed to the fault of the claimants in rejecting captors' offer of restitution, accompanied by payment of claimants' expenses. The Court observed, in conclusion, that judgment seemed to have passed in the Court below without much examination of the principles and the authorities; and that the cases in which, during the late war, restitution was attended with costs and damages, turned out to be more numerous than was supposed. (It may be added that the damages—1,223*l.* as against 1,961*l.* claimed—were, with interest at 4 per cent., subsequently paid by the Government.)

It is very clear that where there have been reasonable grounds for carrying a vessel into port for examination, no claim for costs or damages will be allowed against the captors.

Whether in any case the grounds are to be deemed reasonable or not will depend upon the actual circumstances (*z*). And where a capture has arisen from a reasonable misapprehension or mistake, a claim for compensation will similarly be refused. Thus, in the case of the four Dutch vessels (*a*) seized by boats sent from a warship lying in neutral waters, although restitution was ordered, costs were refused, as the seizure had not been made with any intention to violate neutral territory. In the United States Courts, where a vessel had been captured in consequence of her firing on her subsequent captors under the mistake that they were pirates, the Court refused compensation, observing that no case had been cited to prove that where a capture was in itself justifi-

(*z*) *Vide* Story's instances of "probable cause," Prize Courts, p. 36. Also The Leucade, 2 Spinks' Ec. & Ad. Rep. 229.

(*a*) The Twee Gebrœder, p. 313, *supra;* The Gauntlet (1870), L. R. 4 P. C. 184. But *vide* also The Actæon, 2 Dods. 52.

able, the subsequent detention for adjudication had ever been punished by damages (*a*).

In *The Glen* (*b*), where a capture was declared to have been made without reasonable cause, costs and damages were awarded. And reprehensible conduct on the part of captors will, where restoration is decreed, involve a similar award (*c*).

The circumstance that the captured vessel has been lost or destroyed without being brought into a port of the captors will not operate as a stop against the adjudication necessary in order to obtain an award against captors, for proceedings may be instituted notwithstanding (*d*).

Where property is sold at a loss, and restitution is subsequently decreed, captors' liability will be limited to the sale proceeds (*e*).

The prize courts will also award damages for all personal torts, not confining the judgment to the actual wrongdoer, but granting a decree, in the case of privateers, against the owners of the vessel (*f*). And where the captured crew have been grossly ill-treated, a liberal recompense will be adjudged (*g*). Owners, said the Court, in *The Die Fire Damer* (*gg*), ought not to put their vessels in charge of persons capable of outrageous behaviour.

"Whenever the captors are justified in the capture, they are considered as having a *bonâ fide* possession, and are not responsible for any subsequent losses or injuries arising to the property from mere accident or casualty; as from stress of

(*a*) *The Marianna Flora*, 11 *Wheat.* 1.

(*b*) *Blatch. Pr. Ca.* 375.

(*c*) The Anna, p. 312, *supra*; The Jane Campbell, *infra*.

(*d*) *Vide* p. 320, *supra*.

(*e*) The Two Susannahs, 2 Rob. 152.

(*f*) *The Anna Maria*, 2 *Wheat.* 327.

(*g*) The St. Juan Baptista, 5 Rob. 33; The Die Fire Damer, 5 Rob. 357; *The Jane Campbell*, *Blatch. Pr. Ca.* 101.

(*gg*) 5 Rob. 357.

weather, recapture by the enemy, shipwreck, &c. They are, however, in all cases bound for fair and safe custody, and if the property be lost from the want of proper care, they are responsible to the amount of the damage; for subsequent misconduct may forfeit the fair title of a *bonâ fide* possessor, and make him a trespasser from the beginning; therefore, if the prize be lost by the misconduct of the prize-master, or for neglecting to take a pilot, or to put on board a proper prize-crew, the Court will decree restitution in value against the captors. But although, in general, irregularity of conduct in captors makes them liable for damages, yet in case of a *bonâ fide* possession, the irregularity, to bind them, must be such as produces irreparable loss; as, for instance, such as may prevent restitution from an enemy who recaptures the property" (*h*).

"In cases of illegal capture, vindictive damages are not usually given, unless where the misconduct has been very gross, and left destitute of all apology. Great indulgence is allowed to errors, and even improprieties of captors, where they do not appear to have acted with malignity and cruelty (*i*). If a captor destroys a ship of an enemy protected by the licence of his own government, he or his government is responsible for the loss occasioned by such destruction (*k*); but when the captor acts *bonâ fide* in pursuance of his rights, in an ignorance, honest and invincible on his part, of a foreign fact not governed by his own domestic law, but dependent on transactions with which he is unavoidably unacquainted till actually communicated to him, he will be protected by the Court" (*l*).

(*h*) Story on Prize Courts, p. 36 (with cases cited).

(*i*) *The Lively and Cargo*, 1 *Gall.* 29; *The Anne*, 3 *Wheat.* 435; *The George*, 1 *Mason*, 24.

(*k*) The Felicity, 2 Dod. 381; The Actæon, *ibid.* 52; but see The Ostsee, *supra*, *re* liability of Government.

(*l*) The John, 2 Dod. 339; Maritime Warfare, p. 305.

Great and unnecessary delay in bringing the prize to adjudication will be chargeable against the captors, as in *The Madonna del Burso* (*m*), where Sir W. Scott condemned them in costs and damages. But no demurrage will be allowed to the claimants in respect of any time lost owing to their own neglect or misconduct (*n*). In *The Elize* (*o*), where the vessel was seized whilst in port at Leith under the erroneous belief that she had broken blockade, costs and damages were ordered against the capturing revenue officers, apparently on the ground that they could have ascertained the facts before going to the length they did. But such costs and damages were to be calculated only up to the time when the captors voluntarily tendered restitution, which the claimants had refused unless costs and damages were paid; the Court observing that claimants should have accepted the vessel whilst reserving the question of costs and damages. In *The Primus* (*p*) (1854), where an enemy ship had been condemned and the neutral cargo released, the Court refused costs against captors, observing that "at the time the owners of the cargo put it on board there was imminent risk of war, and they must abide by the consequences of their act." The claimants had applied to have their costs paid out of the sale proceeds of the ship.

If the master of a non-commissioned vessel should make a capture, and it turn out illegal, the claim will be against him personally and not against the owners, unless the wrongful act have been committed within the scope of the ordinary authority of the latter (*q*).

(*m*) 4 Rob. 169. See also The San Juan Battista, and The Purissima Concepcion, 5 Rob. 33; The Corier Maritimo, 1 Rob. 287; The Susanna, 6 Rob. 51; The Peacock, 4 Rob. 185; The Anna Catharina, 6 Rob. 10.

(*n*) The Ostsee, *supra;* The Elize, 24 L. T. 170.

(*o*) *Ibid.*

(*p*) 24 L. T. 34.

(*q*) Story on Prize Courts, p. 75.

In *The La Amistad de Rues* (r), it was decided by Story, J., that in awarding damages, claims for loss of market or probable profits cannot be considered. And in *The Alabama Case* (the Geneva Award, 1872), it was unanimously held by the arbitrators that prospective earnings were to be excluded, seeing that they depended upon future and uncertain contingencies. Claims for indirect or consequential damages were also excluded (s). In *Kulen Kemp* v. *Vigne* (t), where sentence of condemnation had been reversed on appeal, the Court, for reasons which do not appear, ordered the expenses of reclaiming the ship and cargo to be a charge upon the cargo.

During the Franco-German war two merchant vessels of the enemy were captured by a French cruiser, and as it was impracticable to carry the vessels into port, the captors burnt them. A claim was presented by English owners of cargo on board, but was rejected by the French Courts. "This decision," says a writer in the Edinburgh Review, for July 1884 (p. 263), "is important, as it affirmed that the third article of the Paris Declaration did not guarantee neutrals from damages caused by the legitimate capture of an enemy's vessel, or by the military acts which accompanied or followed the capture. This seems to be going a little too far, as the captors should in justice have been held bound to compensate the neutrals for any damages which may have been caused. In any case, nothing but the most absolute necessity should justify the destruction of a prize."

"In cases when further proof is directed," says Story (u), "costs and expenses are never allowed to the claimant. Nor where the neutrality of the property does not appear by the

(r) 5 *Wheat.* 385.

(s) *Vide* p. 364, *infra*, for further reference to this case.

(t) 1 T. R. 304.

(u) Prize Courts, p. 95, with cases cited.

papers on board and the preparatory evidence; nor where papers are spoiled or thrown overboard, unless the act be produced by the captors' misconduct, as by firing under false colours; nor where the master or crew, upon the preparatory examinations, grossly prevaricate; nor where any part of the cargo is condemned; nor where the ship comes from a blockaded port; nor if the ship be restored by consent, without reserving the question of costs and expenses. But in all these cases it is in the discretion of the Court to allow the captors their costs and expenses; and, in general, wherever the captors are justified in the capture, their costs and expenses are decreed to them by the Court, in case of restitution of property. Therefore they are allowed where the original destination was to a blockaded port, although changed on hearing of the blockade; where ships, even of our own country, are captured sailing under false papers; where the nature of the cargo is ambiguous as to contraband; and, generally, in all cases of false papers; and in all cases where further proof is required. In cases where the captors' expenses are allowed, the expenses intended are such as are necessarily incurred in consequence of the act of capture; such are the expenses of the captors' agent, but not insurance made by the captors, nor expenses of transmitting a cargo from a colony to the mother country. And property restored to the claimant is not to be charged with any expenses of agency, or for taking care of it, unless made a charge by the Court. And the expense of an unlivery or delivery of the property which is restored, is to be borne by the captors or releasing party, and not by the property, unless it is so directed by the Court. In general, where the property is condemned, the expenses of unlivery and warehousing, &c. fall on the captors; and where it is restored the Court will apportion them in its discretion on the captors and on the cargo."

In *The Ocean Bride* (*x*), the ship had, on the eve of the Crimean War, been colourably sold to a Russian merchant at Archangel in order to prevent capture by the Russians. On her return to England she was seized, but restored; the Court, in the special circumstances, approving the colourable sale. Costs were, however, awarded to captors.

In *The Hoop* (*y*), where the cargo was condemned on the ground that it had been carried from Holland contrary to British prohibition, and without licence, but in circumstances which exonerated the concerned from any charge of wilful misconduct, freight and expenses were allowed to the master, and the expenses of the claims were also ordered to be paid out of the cargo.

In *The Maria Powlona* (*z*), where the claimant, after accepting restitution without any reserve of rights as regards damages, demanded compensation, the Court decided that he must take the inconvenience with the convenience of restitution, and that he had put himself out of Court by thus accepting the offer of restitution.

In *The Catharine and Anna* (*a*), where the ship and cargo, of very considerable value, had been restored on payment of captors' expenses, the Court refused to include amongst the latter a sum of 270*l.* incurred for fire insurance. The claimants had themselves insured against fire, and the captors had incurred a similar charge without previous reference either to them or to the Court.

Whilst a prize is in the custody of the Marshal of the Court, he is responsible for its safe keeping. In *The Hoop* (*b*), a claim was made against this official for a boat and cable removed from the ship, and the Court decreed compensation and costs; observing that the credit of the Court was con-

(*x*) 24 L. T. 99.
(*y*) 1 Rob. 196, and p. 262, *supra*.
(*z*) 6 Rob. 236.
(*a*) 4 Rob. 39.
(*b*) 4 Rob. 145.

cerned in the safe keeping of the property under its protection. And in *The Concordia* (c), the Court, the cargo having been restored, held the captors liable for a deficiency of cargo alleged to be due to their embezzlement.

In *The Rendsborg* (d), a prize valued with her cargo at nearly 100,000*l.*, the charges of the Marshal were objected to as being excessive, and the Court, in a judgment which criticised the items in detail, ordered them to be considerably reduced.

Insurance.

If an insurance be warranted free from capture and seizure, it is obvious that the underwriters will not be liable for costs consequent on capture, for it is a matter of indifference to them whether the interest insured be condemned to the captors or not. Or rather, it is to underwriters' advantage to have their liability prematurely terminated by a loss which they have not undertaken to cover; and, this being so, the question of costs subsequent to capture is clearly no concern of theirs. Similarly, where the policy undertakes the risk of capture, but the insurance has been invalidated by some breach of the law of nations, or of the conditions on which the policy was granted (e). But in ordinary cases, where the risk of capture is covered under the policy, expenses reasonably incurred by the assured in order to obtain restitution of his property seized by a belligerent are, on the judgment in *Berens* v. *Rucker* (*f*), recoverable from underwriters. In this case a neutral vessel had been seized by a British privateer, and brought into Portsmouth, on the ground of being engaged in illicit trade of the enemy. On the refusal or delay of the claimants to furnish information demanded, judgment was pronounced against them by default, and against

(c) 2 Rob. 102.

(d) 6 Rob. 142.

(e) *Vide* as to this *sub* Void Insurances, p. 405, *infra*.

(*f*) 1 Black. 313.

this decision they appealed to the Lords Commissioners of Prizes. But in the circumstance that considerable time would necessarily elapse before the appeal could be heard, the market also being high, and some of the cargo perishable, the claimants agreed to pay captors 800*l.* and costs in order to obtain a reversal of the sentence. For plaintiff's share of this payment, and for the costs of the litigation generally, action was brought against the underwriters. Lord Mansfield, in giving judgment for the plaintiff, observed that, although, as a fact, the sentence of condemnation was unjust, an appeal would have been hazardous, the delay certain, and no costs or damages would have been given which had accrued subsequent to the sentence. For, such damages are ordinarily attributed to the fault of the judge, and not of the parties; so that even in case of a total reversal of the sentence, the costs would have sat heavy on the plaintiffs. Therefore, the question whether plaintiffs had acted *bonâ fide* and uprightly, as men acting for themselves, and upon a reasonable footing, so as to make the expenses of this compromise attach to the insurers, was to be answered in the affirmative. The insurers were, therefore, in the circumstances, to be held to answer this average loss, which had been submitted to in order to avoid a total loss.

If a vessel be captured and brought in for adjudication, and the services of the master and crew be given with the object of securing restitution generally, their wages and provisions, and all relative charges, will have to be treatéd as a general average charge. But if the capture be in respect solely of the ship or solely of the cargo, the other being in no danger of confiscation, the expenses in question would then, it may be supposed, be *primâ facie* chargeable against the interest for whose benefit they have been incurred (*g*).

Costs adjudged against a claimant on restoration of the property would apparently be similarly recoverable, either on the reasoning that they have attached as a consequence of the operation of a peril insured against, viz., capture; or that they must needs be paid in order to release the property from the captors' lien.

(*g*) The Hiram, 3 Rob. 180; Liddard *v.* Lopes, 10 East, 526.

Obviously, if underwriters have undertaken the risk of loss by capture, they will be liable for expenses necessarily or reasonably incurred in order to obtain the restoration of the property seized. Whether the expenses have or have not been reasonably incurred will depend upon the facts; but in these days of rapid communication, the assured will in most cases be able to learn the views of the underwriters before embarking in expenses of which the wisdom may be matter of opinion.

PAYMENT OF FREIGHT TO NEUTRAL CARRIERS.

(With Considerations as to Freight generally.)

Enemy Goods in Neutral Vessels.—It is a general rule under the law of nations, that a neutral carrier of goods the property of a belligerent is entitled to be paid the freight on such goods in the event of their capture by the enemy. A belligerent has the right (in the absence of treaty engagements to the contrary) to seize and confiscate enemy property found on board a neutral vessel, but he must take the property *cum onere* (*h*),—that is, with the usual liens upon it which would have to be discharged by the consignee before he could take delivery. This rule, however, does not apply to mere rights of action, such as bottomry bonds, &c., by which the captor is not affected (*i*). Neutrals are fully within their rights in carrying the goods of belligerents, and even in carrying the goods of a belligerent to the enemy of the latter, however illegal such traffic may be as regards the subjects of the belligerents themselves (*k*). And although belligerents possess on their part the co-existent right to seize and carry into port for adjudication, this right must not be so extended as to operate as a punishment to the lawful carrier. Therefore, if a belligerent seizes enemy goods which are being carried by a neutral for freight, the belligerent must pay such freight or balance of freight (so long as its amount be reasonable: as to which, see below) as would be payable to the carrier on

(*h*) *Vide* p. 90, *supra*.

(*i*) See the cases cited in Hazlitt & Roche's Maritime Warfare, p. 306.

(*k*) The Hoop, 1 Rob. 196, 219; The Wilhelmina, 2 Rob. 101, note.

delivery of the goods at their destination. As between the owner of the goods and the carrier, delivery to a captor is to be looked upon as a delivery under the contract of affreightment, although effected short of the agreed destination; the captor being regarded as standing, by the rights of war, in the place of the consignee (*l*). This is the general rule as regards captors' liability, but there are exceptions to it.

Thus, if the goods seized be contraband of war, no freight will be payable to the carrier (*m*), for, as already observed (*n*), neutral masters must be made to understand that the engagement in a prohibited traffic is attended by the risk of deprivation of freight if the goods be seized. But it is reasonable to suppose that neutrals who engage in such transactions with their eyes open to its contingencies will, in most cases, take care that the freight, or the greater part of it, shall be payable on shipment, and not on delivery. The neutral carrier was deprived of his freight on enemy provisions—barley and oats—in *The Commercen* (*o*); but in this case the goods were being conveyed for the use of the enemy's forces, and the voyage was declared to be illicit on the part of a neutral. For the modern tendency is, on seizure of provisions on the way to a hostile destination, to allow the master his freight. In *The Neptunus* (*p*), where the quantity of contraband goods proved to be very small, viz., a little sailcloth, the cargo being tallow, the Court allowed freight and expenses. And where part of the cargo has been condemned as contraband and the remainder ultimately restored, freight may be decreed as a charge on

---

(*l*) The Copenhagen, 1 Rob. 289; The Hoop, *ibid.* 196.

(*m*) The Mercurius, 1 Rob. 288; *The Commercen*, 1 *Wheat.* 382. And see Story on Prize Courts, p. 93.

(*n*) P. 188, *supra*.

(*o*) *Vide* pp. 175, 241, *supra*.

(*p*) 3 Rob. 108.

the cargo restored (*r*). An averment on the part of the master that he was ignorant of the nature of the goods will not be entertained (*r*).

If goods be carried by a neutral between an enemy country and the privileged colonies of such country, no freight will be allowed by the Court of the captors (*s*), on the ground that the neutral is devoting himself to the service of the enemy (*t*). So, too, if the cargo be condemned on account of the vessel being engaged in the enemy's coasting trade (*u*).

The neutral carrier is entitled to his expenses as well as to his freight; but if he should have been guilty of fraud or unfair dealing he forfeits all right to compensation. And in flagrant cases such conduct may involve the confiscation of his ship and even of the innocent portion of the cargo, a result which may also ensue where the ship belongs to the owner of the contraband articles. Sailing under a false destination or with false papers is an especially heinous offence. No freight will be allowed in such cases, or where there has been a spoliation of papers (*x*); or where the ship herself has been the ground of the capture (*y*). (For the subject of offences on the part of neutrals generally, involving confiscation, *vide sub* Belligerent Rights against Neutrals, scheduled on p. 144, *supra*.)

When a decree is made that the freight shall be a charge on the cargo, application may be made to the Court for the sale of so much as is necessary for this purpose (*z*). In general, where a ship and cargo are restored, with a decree

(*r*) The Oster Risoer, 4 Rob. 199.

(*s*) The Immanuel, p. 242, *supra*.

(*t*) *Vide* p. 233, *supra*.

(*u*) The Atlas, 3 Rob. 299; The Johanna Tholen, 6 Rob. 72.

(*x*) The Rising Sun, 2 Rob. 104; The Madonna del Burso, 4 Rob. 169, 183.

(*y*) The Fortuna, Edw. 56. And see the numerous citations in Kent's Int. Law, 2 Eng. ed. p. 339 *not.*, as to forfeiture generally.

(*z*) The Vrow Margaretha, 4 Rob. 304, note.

that the freight shall be a charge on the cargo, if the proceeds of the cargo are not sufficient to pay the freight, the captors are not responsible for the deficiency (*a*). Where the cargo is adjudged lawful prize, but the ship is ordered to be restored and the freight is decreed a charge on the cargo,— if, owing to the neglect or fault of captors or their agents, the cargo be lost, captors are liable to the master for the freight (*b*). Where the freight of the neutral and the expenses of the captors are both decreed to be a charge on the cargo, and the proceeds are insufficient to discharge both, priority of payment of the freight is, in ordinary cases, allowed by the Court, as a lien that takes place of all others (*c*). (Story on Prize Courts, p. 94.)

But the freight to be paid must be reasonable in amount. If it be excessive, notwithstanding that the contract might in existing circumstances have been fair as between shipper and carrier, the captor is liable to pay only such amount as would ordinarily be due for carrying similar goods (*d*). For though, owing to the state of war and the attendant risks of carriage, an extravagant rate of freight might well be charged to the shipper, it would be unreasonable to require the captor to pay such an exceptional sum, due to the carrier as being in a great measure in the nature of an encouragement to him to use his best efforts to defeat the captor's vigilance.

Where the goods have once been unlivered by order of the Court, the whole freight for the voyage is due, and the owner of the goods, even in case of restitution, cannot require the ship to reload them and carry them to the original port of destination, for by the separation the ship is exonerated (*e*);

(*a*) The Haabet, 4 Rob. 302.
(*b*) The Der Mohr, *ibid.* 315.
(*c*) The Bremen Flugge, *ibid.* 90.
(*d*) The Twilling Riget, 5 Rob. 82.
(*e*) The Hoffnung, 6 Rob. 231; The Prosper, Edw. 72.

but it would be otherwise if there had been no unlivery (*f*). (Story on Prize Courts, p. 92.)

Where ship and cargo are both restored, without any authoritative unlivery of the cargo having taken place, the original contract of affreightment is not dissolved; and the parties to that contract are again at large, after a temporary inability, to fulfil their obligations and enforce their rights (*g*). (*Vide* Effect of War on Contract, p. 412, *infra*.)

To entitle the neutral carrier to freight at the hand of the captor, he must bring the goods to such port as the latter may select. And if on arrival at the port so selected the captor should find it desirable to carry the cargo to some other safe port, the neutral master, it is stated, is bound to convey it thither. For this fresh undertaking, however, a special contract must be made between captor and carrier. If the latter refuse to proceed as required, it is, according to the *Consolato del Mare* (§ 5), the captor's right to sink the vessel, though without causing loss of life. But this extreme measure must be resorted to only when the whole, or at least the greater part, of the cargo is enemy's property. The same ancient code contains other provisions of interest in this connexion.

Insurance.

So far as freight stands in a position differing, in respect of marine insurance, from that of other insurable interests liable to capture, such exceptional position has already been commented upon, pp. 46 and 70, *supra*. Freight is, of course, an indifferent subject for insurance against risks of capture, seeing that abandonment of the ship to the underwriters on the body of the vessel carries with it the right to freight being earned, thereby

---

(*f*) The Copenhagen, 1 Rob. 289.

(*g*) Maclachlan's Laws of Merchant Shipping, p. 418.

defeating any expectation of salvage to which the underwriters on freight might otherwise be entitled.

The above subject of payment of freight by belligerent captors completes the consideration of Belligerent Obligations scheduled on p. 311. Having thus gone over the obligations as well as the rights of belligerents, we will turn in the next place to consider the position occupied by neutrals during the prevalence of hostilities.

VIII.

NEUTRAL RIGHTS AND OBLIGATIONS,

TREATED UNDER THE FOLLOWING HEADS, VIZ. :—

Neutral Rights and Obligations—Generally.

The scheme of neutral rights has as a broad foundation the general principle that the existence of war between certain states shall not be allowed to operate in restriction of the ordinary trade and commercial relations of nations standing aloof from the hostilities (*h*). On the other hand, peaceful nations, in order that their right to be regarded as neutrals may be respected, are under the obligation to preserve a strict impartiality towards the belligerents, and to studiously refrain from any action calculated to promote, directly or indirectly, the warlike purposes of the one to the detriment of the other. This does not import, for example, that a neutral power must refuse to allow a belligerent to purchase warlike stores within the neutral jurisdiction; but that a permission to effect such purchases shall be impartially granted or denied to both belligerents. It may, it is true, very likely be the case that such a permission may be valueless to one of the belligerents and all-important to the other; but this is a matter in which the neutral state is not concerned. The neutral must show impartiality, and if this impartiality should benefit the one belligerent and prejudice the other, this is not the affair of the neutral.

Whilst admitting the general right of neutrals to maintain friendly commercial relations with belligerents, the modern tendency would seem to be to include amongst the negative obligations of neutrals the abstention from equivocal traffic in which, in bygone days, their right to engage was not questioned. And there is, moreover, a growing disposition to consider it the obligation of neutral governments to restrain their subjects from engaging in so-called illicit transactions; transactions for which, as it was formerly understood, the sole penalty was the seizure and confiscation, by an aggrieved belligerent, of the articles to which, by the law of nations, exception could properly be taken. Notwithstanding that the law of nations is on this point so well established as to be practically beyond dispute, there is a sort of evolution now in progress which seems to have created an

(*h*) Ex parte Chavasse, In re Grazebrook, 34 L. J. N. S. Bk. p. 17.

apparent overlapping of rights and obligations. For now and again one nation upholds the right to do or permit that which another asserts that the doer is under obligation to refrain from or to restrain. Instances of this will appear presently in reference to the controversy which arose between this country and Germany during the Franco-Prussian war, relative to the supply, by British merchants, of contraband of war to France; and, more especially, in the history of *The Alabama* claims. In such circumstances, therefore, it has been thought better, for present purposes, not to attempt to deal separately with the rights and the obligations, but to consider them under one and the same head. They are, indeed, so interwoven the one with the other that it is quite impracticable, if not impossible, to discuss them separately without a degree of repetition inconsistent with the conciseness aimed at in this work. These rights and obligations may, moreover, be appropriately classified under two distinct heads—the mercantile and the political; but while some fall clearly within the one and some clearly within the other category, others can with nearly equal propriety be ascribed to either. The difficulties which are thus presented render impracticable, therefore, any accurate classification of the rights and obligations under their several heads, so that the arrangement followed below must be regarded rather as for the convenience of the reader than as aiming at a technical accuracy which is unattainable.

Let us first look at the matter from the view in which the predominant element is that of trade and commerce.

NEUTRAL RIGHTS AND OBLIGATIONS—MERCANTILE.

Trade with Belligerents, and generally.—As between themselves neutrals have, of course, the right to carry on their ordinary trade, of whatever it may consist (*i*), and no question of contraband of war can arise as between neutrals. For supposing, for example, that France and Spain were mutually at war, it would obviously be absurd for either belligerent to claim that the fact should prevent this country or Germany from continuing to supply torpedo boats or guns to, say, Italy or Greece. Either belligerent would have the right to carry into port for adjudication (*j*) the vessels carrying these warlike materials, if there should be grounds for believing the neutral destination to be assumed, and the transit to be really intended to end within the dominions of the other belligerent; but on the papers being found in order, the vessels would be allowed to proceed to their destination without further molestation. As has appeared above (*k*), if the grounds for seizure were found on adjudication to be reasonable, no costs would be awarded against the captors, or the captured vessel might even be required to pay captor's costs. If, on the other hand, the seizure were found to be unjustifiable, costs, and perhaps damages, would be adjudged against the captors.

And not only may neutrals carry on their ordinary trade as between themselves, but they may likewise carry the goods of one belligerent to the enemy, and, as will be presently set forth, carry the goods of belligerents generally.

(*i*) *Vide* the brief remarks in this connexion on p. 160, *supra*.

(*j*) *Vide* p. 154, *supra*.

(*k*) *Vide* p. 325, *supra*.

Neutrals are under the obligation to respect the rights of belligerents as recognised by the law of nations, but these obligations need not be discussed here, seeing that they have already been reviewed from their corresponding aspect of Belligerent Rights. These obligations are as follows, viz.:—

	PAGE
The obligation to respect blockades	**104**
to submit to visit and search	**212**
not to carry contraband	**156**
,, ,, belligerent despatches or troops	**201**
,, ,, false papers, and to carry proper and usual papers	**219**
not to attempt a rescue	**216**
not to engage in belligerent privileged trade, or sail under belligerent flag or license	**233**
not to ship by armed belligerent vessels, or to sail under convoy	**213, 214**

On the subject of contraband generally, it may here be repeated (*l*) that there is nothing in itself illegal in the shipment of contraband to belligerents; only, if neutrals choose to carry prohibited goods to a belligerent, they must understand that if these goods be seized by the adverse belligerent, the goods will be confiscated, together with any freight which may attach to their safe delivery (*m*). And fraudulent conduct on the carrier's part may involve forfeiture of the ship, in addition. This, then, is the position: If a neutral engage in trade contraband of war, he has no right to complain to his government if the goods be seized in consequence. On the other hand, belligerents have no right to complain that the subjects of a neutral government are shipping contraband to the enemy. Their remedy is against the shipper—or,

(*l*) *Vide* p. 160, *supra*.

(*m*) *Vide* p. 188, *supra*.

rather, against the goods—not against the government. It is a matter between the shipper or carrier and the belligerent; and the neutral government has a right to wash its hands of the whole matter, and to turn a deaf ear alike to the complaint of the subject whose goods are seized and of the belligerent who seizes them. This, at any rate, is the view, based on the law of nations, commonly taken by the neutral government, though the aggrieved belligerent is nowadays apt to look at the matter from a different light. Thus, the subject gave rise to a long correspondence between Great Britain and Germany during the progress of the Franco-German war, as will be seen from the following:—

Exportation and Carriage of Contraband of War.—In a letter from Earl Granville to Count Bernstorff (*n*), written from the Foreign Office, 15th September, 1870, dealing with the Prussian complaint relative to the exportation of arms to the French, Earl Granville said—

> "You demand that the export to France of arms, ammunition, coal, and other contraband of war should be prevented; and you have observed that Her Majesty's Government have declared that the law empowered the Executive to take this step:
>
> There is no doubt that the Executive has, under the Customs Consolidation Act of 1853, the legal power to prohibit the export of contraband of war; but the highest authority can be adduced to show that such exportation is not forbidden by our municipal law, and it has not been the practice to prohibit it except where the interests of this country, as in the case of self-defence, are directly and immediately concerned in the prohibition; and even in some of these cases, such

(*n*) State Papers, Vol. LXI. p. 764.

as in the Crimean war, considerable doubts arose during its continuance, whether the prohibition, when actually attempted to be enforced, was as disadvantageous to the enemy as it was inconvenient to ourselves."

One reason given against any such prohibition was that the effect of it would be that arms, &c., would be shipped with a colourable neutral destination; and that such subterfuges could only be detected, if at all, by interfering with the trade of neutrals.

Dealing with the argument that coal should be considered contraband, it was in the above letter enquired where the line was to be drawn between coal and such equivocal goods as, for example, cloth, leather, and quinine, than which no cargoes would have been more useful to the Southern States in the American War. Moreover, as it was pointed out, Article XI. of the Treaty of Commerce between Great Britain and France expressly provided that the contracting parties should not prohibit the exportation of coal.

In his reply to this letter, Count Bernstorff (*n*) referred to a letter alleged to have been written in 1825 by the Duke of Wellington to Mr. Canning, which, it was observed, proved that England as a neutral had repeatedly prohibited the export of arms, by an Order in Council, "according," in the words of the renowned Duke, "to the usual practice." And, further, the Count quoted enactments to show that Earl Granville's declaration, that the exportation of contraband was not forbidden by British municipal law, could only mean that a positive declaration of the Government was required in order to bring into force the power with which it is invested. He also pointed out that a check might be placed on colourable shipments to neutrals by the exaction of

(*n*) State Papers, Vol. LXI. p. 828.

security on the part of the shippers. The correspondence on this subject is at great length, and may be described as an endless diplomatic chain of apparently unanswerable argument on the one hand, and of equally convincing reply and counter-argument on the other. From this point of view it affords, indeed, most instructive reading, but as each argument seems in turn to have been demolished by the reply, it is difficult to evolve from the correspondence any definite conclusion. As regards the allegations against Great Britain, similar complaints appear to have been called forth by the action of the United States. But on this, as on nearly every other point of the law of nations from its maritime aspect, the views of Great Britain and of the United States are in strict accord. As regards the United States, arms were exported thence on a large scale, with the avowed object of sale to the French Government. The French Government being in need of this class of supplies, a refusal to permit shipment of the latter would, no doubt, have produced forcible remonstrances on the part of France, on the ground that such a prohibition was an act of partiality towards Germany.

But while a neutral government is, as it is held, under no obligation to prevent its subjects from continuing to ship to belligerents goods, whether contraband of war or otherwise, which it is part of the ordinary trade of such subjects to supply (*o*), the neutral government should not itself be a party to the like transactions. Thus, in 1825, whilst Spain was at war with her revolted subjects in Mexico, the Swedish Government offered for sale six warships. These vessels were bought by a Swedish firm, which transferred them to a London house, the financial agents of the revolted subjects. There being no doubt as to the object of the purchase, the

(*o*) *Vide* Bell *v.* Reid, 1 M. & S. 727; De Tastet *v.* Taylor, 4 Taunt. 238.

Spanish Government made representations to the Swedish Government, pointing out the disloyal act into which Sweden had been unwittingly betrayed, and urging cancelment of the sale to the Swedish firm. Several of the European powers having supported the Spanish demand, Sweden ultimately cancelled the sale, so far as concerned three of the vessels still within the national jurisdiction. The original sale by the Swedish Government was, no doubt, a purely commercial transaction, but on the facts becoming known to the selling government it could not, consistently with neutrality, refuse to prevent the vessels passing over to the enemy of Spain. Nor must a neutral power permit the sale of coal out of the government stores to a belligerent (*p*).

Clearly it is within the right of neutrals, as of belligerents (*q*), to pass such municipal laws as may be deemed generally expedient; and the right may be exercised in respect of prohibition of export of warlike stores, either because such stores may be required by the neutral government, or because it is desired to abstain from any action likely to create ill-will on the part of either belligerent (*r*). But that there is, according to the view of this country, no obligation on neutrals to prohibit export of contraband, has just been demonstrated. The provisions of special treaty engagements may, however, sometimes be found to require the observance of particular rules not by the public law of Europe rendered obligatory.

There is nothing in the law of nations to impose on a neutral state the obligation to prevent its subjects from send-

(*p*) Twiss's Internat. Law, pp. 468, 469.

(*q*) As instanced on p. 306, *supra*.

(*r*) On the outbreak of war between France and Germany, the sale of contraband of war to belligerents was forbidden to Peruvian subjects by the national government. 61 State Papers, 656, 657.

ing to belligerents vessels specially adapted for warlike uses, any more than contraband articles of a more ordinary kind. An instance of this principle is supplied by *The Independencia del Sud*, an armed vessel sent out with a cargo of munitions of war from Baltimore for sale at Buenos Ayres to the *de facto* government, at that time engaged in hostilities with Spain. The vessel, subsequent to her purchase by the revolted colony, effected the capture of a Spanish vessel, and carried into the port of Virginia certain goods taken out of this vessel. The Spanish owner of this property thereupon claimed that it should be restored to him by the United States Government, on the ground that the capture had been effected in circumstances which involved a violation of the neutrality of the United States. It was pleaded by the claimant in support of this demand (1) That the capturing vessel had been originally equipped, armed, and manned as a vessel of war in the United States; and (2) that during her cruise she had illegally augmented her force whilst in an American port. The first plea was at once dismissed by Justice Story, who, in delivering the judgment of the Supreme Court, declared, in effect, that the vessel was ordinary contraband of war, of which the neutral power was under no obligation to prevent the despatch to a belligerent. "It was a commercial adventure which no nation was bound to prohibit, and which only exposed the persons engaged in it to the penalty of confiscation." The original outfit, therefore, was in no sense illegal. With respect to the second plea, however, the learned judge found that there had been an illegal augmentation of the vessel's force in an American port, whereby there was both an infraction of the country's municipal law and a violation of the law of nations. "It has never been held," said Justice Story, "that an augmentation of force or an illegal outfit affected any captures made after the original cruise was terminated. By analogy to other cases of violation of public law, the offence may be well deemed to be deposited at the termination of the voyage, and not to affect future transactions. But as to captures made during the same cruise, the doctrine of this Court has long been established, that such illegal augmentation is a violation of the law of nations as well as of our own municipal laws; and, as a violation of our neutrality, by analogy to other cases, it infects the captures subsequently made with the character of torts, and justifies and requires a restitution to the parties who have been injured by the misconduct. It does not lie in the mouth of wrongdoers to set up a title derived from a violation of our neutrality."

So that, according to a strict interpretation of the law of nations, there would seem to be nothing more required of a neutral state, as regards the prohibition of export of armed vessels to belligerents, than in the case of any other warlike articles; but the result of *The Alabama* claims (*s*), to be referred to presently, is by no means in harmony with this principle.

The position of neutral subjects engaging in the transport of contraband of war generally has already been considered under the head Belligerent Rights against Neutrals, pp. 156—200.

Carriage of Belligerent Goods.—That neutrals may in time of war carry on their ordinary trade with belligerents has already been seen, and amongst such lawful trade is included the carriage of goods the property of belligerents (*t*). This right exists, however, without prejudice to the countervailing belligerent right to seize goods so carried, the right of seizure being attended by the obligation to pay freight on the goods

(*s*) *Vide* p. 364, *infra*.
(*t*) Barker *v.* Blakes, 9 East, 283.

seized, to the neutral carrier. Neutrals may carry belligerent goods, but they must in so doing take their chance of the attendant inconvenience of being carried into port for adjudication. This is the position under the common law of nations; but it is, of course, materially modified by the principle embodied in the Declaration of Paris, that "free ships make free goods."

In *The Mary Clinton* (*u*), it was held, in the United States, that a neutral friend to both belligerents may not ship the property of the one to the use of the other; but whether the Court intended this decision to be accepted as expressing a general principle, or only as applicable to the special circumstances of the case under adjudication, cannot be certainly affirmed. There would seem to be no doubt, however, that a neutral is fully entitled to carry the (permissive) goods of one belligerent to the other without contravening neutral obligations, and without any regard to the fact that in so doing he may be conducing to an illicit trade between the subjects of hostile states.

If the carrier should be found guilty of conduct inconsistent with neutrality, such as attempting to screen from lawful capture the goods carried, or otherwise to mislead or baffle the captor, he will be held to have forfeited his right to freight, and may be further punished by the confiscation of his ship, as already explained (*x*).

Also, neutrals must not engage in the privileged or colonial trade of belligerents,—that is, in any trade which in time of peace is limited to the belligerent subjects (*y*); nor may they sail under the licence or pass of belligerents (*y*).

Resistance of visit and search is a breach of neutrality in-

(*u*) *Blatch. Pr. Ca.* 556.

(*x*) *Vide* "Enemy Goods in Neutral Vessels," p. 88, and "Payment of Freight to Neutrals," p. 339, *supra*.

(*y*) *Vide* p. 233.

volving confiscation (z), and the same penalty attaches to an attempt at rescue of the ship from the lawful captors (*a*).

For the effect of blending neutral and belligerent goods, see the subject next following.

Shipment by Belligerent Vessels.—Just as it is lawful for a neutral to carry the goods of belligerents, so it is permissible to him to ship his own goods by vessels the property of belligerents (*b*). As has been well said, "The rule that the goods of an enemy, found in the vessel of a friend, are prize of war; and that the goods of a friend, found in the vessel of an enemy, are to be restored; is believed to be a part of the original law of nations, as generally, perhaps universally, acknowledged. This rule is founded on the simple and intelligible principle that war gives a full right to capture the goods of an enemy, but gives no right to capture the goods of a friend" (*c*). But this right does not extend to permit neutrals to ship by an armed belligerent vessel, for this is held to be tantamount to a resistance of the right of visit and search (*d*). Nor, for the same reason, may the shipment be made under convoy (*e*).

As has been mentioned above (*f*), if a captor finds himself unable to carry his prize into port he may destroy it, but that, before resorting to this extreme exercise of the rights of war, he should satisfy himself that the property, if taken before the Court, would be condemned. In the Franco-Prussian war two German vessels, *The Ludwig* and

(z) *Vide* p. 212.

(*a*) *Vide* p. 216.

(*b*) *Vide sub* Declaration of Paris, p. 27, *supra*.

(*c*) Marshall, C. J., in *The Nereide*, 9 *Cranch*, 418.

(*d*) *Vide* p. 213, *supra*.

(*e*) *Vide* p. 214, *supra*.

(*f*) *Vide* p. 55, *supra*.

The Vorwärts (*o*), were captured and burnt by the French cruiser *Desaix*. The owners of neutral (British) goods on board the vessels, claimed compensation before a prize court at Bordeaux, relying especially on the Third Article of the Declaration of Paris, which declares that neutral goods on enemy's vessels shall be free from capture. But the Court, holding that the act of destruction was justified by *force majeure*, declined to award compensation. The Declaration of Paris, said the Court, exempted from confiscation neutral goods on an enemy's vessel, and entitled the owners to the proceeds in the event of sale; but it gave to neutrals no right to compensation for damages resulting from the lawful capture of the ship, or from any justifiable proceedings of the captors. Irrespective of the Declaration of Paris, innocent neutral goods on belligerent vessels have always been regarded as exempt from capture; and it would certainly seem that in such a case as the foregoing this principle of the law of nations would have been better supported by an award of compensation.

For if a belligerent has no right to capture the lawful goods of a friend, the mere fact that their destruction by him is to be attributed to the exigencies of war, seems scarcely a sufficient reason for refusing to entertain the demand of the friend for compensation. It is, indeed, not easy to see on what logical grounds the principles governing such a case are to be distinguished from those applicable in cases of pre-emption (*p*).

If a belligerent vessel carrying neutral goods be captured and condemned by the enemy, the latter can carry the goods to their destination, and earn the freight due thereon (*q*); though it does not appear that the captor is under any obli-

(*o*) Dalloz, Jurisprudence Générale, 1872, iii. 94.

(*p*) *Vide* p. 248, *supra*, sinking of British vessels in the Seine.

(*q*) *Vide* p. 67, *supra*.

gation thus to complete the voyage. Apparently a neutral, if he chooses to ship by a belligerent vessel, must run the risk of having his goods landed for his own account at a port short of their destination (*r*).

And if the neutral goods be so shipped as to be blended with enemy goods on the same vessel, or if enemy goods be fraudulently included in a claim for the restoration of neutral goods, the fate of condemnation will attach to both alike (*s*). But if a neutral and a belligerent subject be engaged in a joint adventure, and the property be captured, the share of the neutral will be restored, whilst that of the belligerent may be condemned (*t*).

With respect to the effect of resistance to search, as regards neutral goods on a belligerent vessel, reference may be made to the subject "Resistance to Search," p. 212, *supra*.

Transport of Belligerent Troops.—The Foreign Enlistment Acts, to be mentioned presently, are silent on the subject of transport of belligerent troops by neutral merchant vessels. So far, therefore, as municipal restrictions are concerned,

(*r*) The following instructions are given to Lloyd's agents as regards neutral goods in enemies' vessels: "If the country in which the agent resides is at war with any other country, and a captured vessel of that other country should be brought into any port within the agent's district, he should watch the proceedings of the prize court, and endeavour to prevent any sale of the cargo, either before or after the condemnation of the vessel as lawful prize.

"In reporting the circumstance to Lloyd's, he should point out particularly what steps it will be necessary for the owners of the goods to take, whether in any local marine court, or in the central court of prize, to obtain possession of their goods, and should specify the documents which the Court will require for establishing the ownership of the goods, and for proving that the owners belong to a neutral country."

(*s*) *Penhallow* v. *Doane*, 3 *Dall.* 54; The Eenrom, 2 Rob. 9; *The Betsey and George*, 2 *Gall.* 377; *The St. Nicholas*, 1 *Wheat.* 417; *The Phœnix Insce. Co.* v. *Pratt*, 2 *Binney*, 308; *The Fortuna*, 3 *Wheat.* 236.

(*t*) *Vide* p. 18, *supra*.

such traffic is presumably not unlawful. But, as has already been pointed out (*u*), neutrals who thus lay themselves out to promote the warlike aims of a belligerent, do so at the risk of seizure and confiscation of the offending vessel by the foe of the belligerent whom it is sought to assist.

Purchase from Belligerents.—Under "Domicile and Ownership" (*x*) reference has already been made to the sale, by belligerents to neutrals, of belligerent property *in transitu*. It may, however, be here repeated that sales by belligerents to neutrals must be absolute and unconditional, and that any sale effected with the object, or with the effect, of placing belligerent property beyond the reach of lawful capture is, by the law of nations, null and void. So, also, if goods be consigned by a neutral to a belligerent, any reservation of interest in the property in favour of the neutral shipper will in like manner be disregarded. To follow a different principle would, it is obvious, enable belligerents so to transfer or postpone their interests in property otherwise the lawful subject of condemnation, that the right of capture would be liable to become of purely nominal value. All such transfers or reservations, therefore, in the presence of actual or impending hostilities, are looked at by the prize courts of the captors with the closest scrutiny, and presumably with a bias against the neutral claimant. But if the transfer shall have taken place in such circumstances as to rebut any presumption of bad faith, the property will be deemed to be neutral. The onus of proof, however, will in all such cases lie upon the claimant.

The purchase of belligerent vessels within the belligerent jurisdiction, *flagrante bello*—and, indeed, the purchase of belligerent vessels at all during war—is by some nations

(*u*) Pages 207 *et seq.*, *supra*.

(*x*) P. 15, *supra*.

declared to be altogether illegal, and is always subject to great suspicion. As has been indicated (pp. 22 *et seq.*, *supra*), the strictest proof will be required as to the *bona fides* and unconditional nature of the sale in all such cases; and if after the purchase the vessel be found to be so employed as to support the presumption that the belligerent seller still has an interest in the property, the sale will be regarded as merely colourable. If in any case the neutral purchaser appears to be permanently resident in the country of the belligerent sellers, the circumstance will of itself create a suspicion as to the character of the sale. The right to purchase vessels from a belligerent is, however, strictly limited to merchant vessels, the purchase of a ship of war being invalid.

(For further consideration of the subject of purchase of belligerent vessels reference may with advantage be made to Story's Practice of Prize Courts, p. 63.)

Insurance.

There would appear to be no direct legal decision whether it is lawful for a belligerent subject to insure neutral property on board a merchant vessel belonging to the adverse belligerent. It might be argued that such a shipment advances the interests and prosperity of the enemy, and that it is, therefore, repugnant to the national policy that the national subjects should effect insurances in support of such a trade. On the other hand, the trade is perfectly lawful to the neutral, neither belligerent having any right to object to it; therefore it would seem to follow that it may be insured by the subjects of either belligerent without detriment to the national war policy. This view is certainly encouraged by the observations of the Court in *Gist* v. *Mason* (*y*), and *Barker* v. *Blakes* (*z*), in which it was held that policies on neutral property destined to an enemy's port, are not unlawful. In the latter case a neutral vessel, carrying a

(*y*) 1 T. R. 88. (*z*) 9 East, 283.

mixed enemy and neutral cargo bound to an enemy port, had been brought in for adjudication; and the underwriter on the neutral cargo disclaimed liability for the consequent charges, on the ground that the insurance was illegal. "If a neutral ship," it was argued, "act in aid of the enemy by protecting his goods, and it be lawful for a British ship to seize the neutral and bring her into port for the purpose of search, and the event justify the seizure, it is as much against public policy to suffer a British subject to insure against such seizure and the necessary consequences of it as to insure against the capture of an enemy's ship." The Court, in disclaiming this view, observed that "The indemnity sought under the policy was not an indemnity to an enemy or to a neutral forfeiting his neutrality by an act hostilely done by him against the interests of Great Britain, but an indemnity to a neutral, as such, against the consequences of an act innocently and allowably done by him in the exercise of his own neutral rights." Further, "It has never yet been held a breach of implied duty in subjects of either state to lend their assistance, by insurance or otherwise, to such rival or exclusive commerce or interests of the other." On the principle of this declaration it would seem to follow that if neutral goods bound to an enemy port can be lawfully insured, neutral goods (lawful goods on a lawful voyage) on an enemy ship can be insured with equal propriety.

Having thus endeavoured to sum up the position as regards the Rights and Obligations of Neutrals, viewed more especially from a mercantile aspect, let us now review the same subject from a standpoint from which the predominating considerations are more especially political.

Neutral Rights and Obligations—Political.

Generally.—It is very difficult, if not impossible, to propound any universally-accepted comprehensive definition of the principles which, by the law of nations, must be held to govern the conduct of neutrals towards belligerents. It is on all hands admitted that the conduct of a neutral must be that of strict impartiality; but it is impossible to define the precise limits which such conduct, in order to be considered impartial, must on no account overstep. The publicists themselves are, to begin with, not in accord on the theory of the shipment of contraband. One contends that a neutral may carry to both belligerents articles of the same character, and that it is not his concern if they use them to each other's hurt. Another submits that it would be absurd for a nation claiming to be neutral to, at one and the same time, assist two nations at war with each other; and holds that no assistance should be given to either. A third suggests the view that if both belligerents be regarded as friends of the neutral, all commerce of whatever kind may be carried on with both indiscriminately; whereas, on the other hand, if each be regarded as the enemy of a friend, the neutral must exclude from his shipments to both all those articles from which, in war, harm may accrue to a friend.

But as a matter of law and practice, as we have seen, the neutral is held to be under no obligation to prohibit the exportation of contraband of war, it being understood that such articles are liable to seizure and confiscation by the belligerent to whose adversary they are being carried. It may apparently be accepted as sanctioned by the public law of Europe that a neutral nation need not forbid the shipment of contraband, whatever arguments against such traffic may be based on the claims of friendship or the obligations of international courtesy. Therefore, vessels specially adapted for warlike purposes may, with other contraband articles, legitimately be conveyed to belligerents. And if such vessels may be carried to the port of a belligerent, for sale or delivery to him, what logical distinction can be made between such a delivery and sale, and a sale and delivery effected to a belligerent purchaser at the neutral port of outfit? Especially as it is within the rights of neutrals to sell to belligerents in the neutral territory warlike stores generally (*y*). Thus, in 1721, on a complaint being made by Sweden that British subjects had built ships of war and sold them to the Czar, the judges expressly advised the House of Lords that the king of England had no power to prohibit the sale of such ships to foreigners—that is, presumably, according to the municipal law then in force. Subsequently to this decision, municipal enactments were passed both in the United States and in Great Britain prohibiting the national subjects from, *inter alia*, fitting out vessels to aid one belligerent against another at amity with the states passing these enactments. It is not necessary for the purposes of this work to discuss the causes which led to these municipal enactments, nor to comment upon the cases which came before the Courts, chiefly of the United States, in connexion with evasions or alleged evasions of them. A valuable summary of these is provided in the treatises of Dr. Wheaton (*z*) and Chancellor Kent. For present purposes it is sufficient to refer to the above Acts as they now stand.

The "Alabama" Case.—Previous to the passing of the American Foreign Enlistment Acts of 1794 and 1818, and of the British Act of 1819, there seems to have been no obliga-

(*y*) *Vide* p. 346, *supra*.

(*z*) *Vide* especially the notes of the learned editor of 2 Eng. ed. of Wheat. Inter. Law, pp. 511-519.

tion under the law of nations binding neutrals to prohibit, for example, the supply or the equipment of warships for the use of belligerents. Municipal enactments take effect, of course, simply between the government passing them and the national subjects, and have, as such, nothing whatever to do with the rights or obligations existing under the law of nations as between such government and any other state. The circumstance—to take one instance—that Sweden complained of the action of Great Britain in the matter of the supply of warships already mentioned, seems to suggest that at that time there was at any rate room for a difference of opinion as to the obligations of neutrals in this respect. The subsequent passing of municipal Acts forbidding neutral subjects from engaging in such undertakings, and cases in which the government, especially of the United States, took action to enforce the provisions of the Acts, no doubt tended to foster the belief that neutrals were by the law of nations bound generally to observe the principles underlying these Acts. To this belief must doubtless be attributed the view of British obligations taken by the United States in *The Alabama* case. Briefly told, the history of the claims "generically known as *The Alabama Claims*," is as follows:—

In the early part of 1862 there was being built in England a vessel undoubtedly intended for warlike uses, and on the 15th May she was launched. Very shortly afterwards the American minister in England wrote to Lord Russell that the vessel was about to depart for the service of the Confederate Government. The law officers of the Crown hereupon advised that if sufficient evidence could be obtained to justify proceedings under the Foreign Enlistment Act, such proceedings should be taken as early as possible. A difference of opinion arose on the point of evidence, and meantime the vessel sailed. She was then unarmed; but shortly afterwards a tug put thirty or forty men on board—the vessel being then off Moelfra Bay—and two vessels, from Liverpool and from London severally, carried an armament out to her at the Azores, where she was fully equipped as a vessel of war. The British authorities had no knowledge that the armament thus shipped from England had any connexion with the vessel in question, viz., *The Alabama*. This vessel, during the American civil war, wrought, under a commission of the Confederate Government, great havoc amongst the shipping of the Northern States; and for the damages so sustained the American Government urged that compensation was due from this country. Prolonged diplomatic controversy ensued without any satisfactory result; until in 1871 it was on both sides finally agreed by the Treaty of Washington to submit the matter to the decision of a mixed tribunal, consisting of five arbitrators, to be severally nominated by the United States, Her Britannic Majesty, the King of Italy, the President of the Swiss Confederation, and the Emperor of Brazil; the conference to be held at Geneva. The adjudication was to be based on the principles of the following three rules, "and by such principles of international law not inconsistent therewith as the arbitrators should determine to have been applicable to the case":—

"A neutral government is bound—

First, to use due diligence to prevent the fitting out, arming or equipping, within its jurisdiction, of any vessel which it has reasonable ground to believe is intended to cruise or to carry on war against a power with which it is at peace; and also to use like diligence to prevent the departure from its jurisdiction of any vessel intended to cruise or carry on war as above, such vessel having been specially adapted, in whole or in part, within such jurisdiction, to warlike use.

Secondly, not to permit or suffer either belligerent to

make use of its ports or waters as the base of naval operations against the other, or for the purpose of the renewal or augmentation of military supplies or arms, or the recruitment of men.

Thirdly, to exercise due diligence in its own ports and waters, and, as to all persons within its jurisdiction, to prevent any violation of the foregoing obligations and duties.

Her Britannic Majesty has commanded her high commissioners and plenipotentiaries to declare that Her Majesty's Government cannot assent to the foregoing rules as a statement of principles of international law which were in force at the time when the claims mentioned in Article I. arose; but that Her Majesty's Government, in order to evince its desire of strengthening the friendly relations between the two countries, and of making satisfactory provision for the future, agrees that, in deciding the questions between the two countries arising out of those claims, the arbitrators should assume that Her Majesty's Government had undertaken to act upon the principles set forth in these rules.

And the high contracting parties agree to observe these rules as between themselves in future, and to bring them to the knowledge of other maritime powers, and to invite them to accede to them."

It is particularly to be noted that the British Government, whilst giving adhesion to the above rules, declined to admit that they were in force, by the law of nations, when the claims arose; and that the contracting powers agreed to adopt the rules in future, and to invite other powers to do the same. On the subject of these rules Mr. Boyd, the learned editor of Wheaton's International Law (*a*), delivers

---

(*a*) 2 Eng. ed. p. 521.

himself thus :—"What does this amount to? Simply that England agreed that her liabilities should be judged of by rules which she admits were not in force at the time the acts she is charged with were done. It is useless to rake up a past quarrel, but it is much to be regretted that the noble spectacle of two great nations referring their disputes to a peaceful tribunal, should be marred by the tribunal being bound to act in a manner contrary to all the known principles of justice. To consent to be judged by *ex post facto* rules is a sacrifice which few care to make, and which when made is not likely to call forth imitation. Another fault of the treaty lay in its containing no definition of 'due diligence,' and thus the arbitrators were thrown upon general principles to ascribe a meaning to the term."

A writer in the "Edinburgh Review" of July, 1884 (p. 279), describes the rules as "a gross departure from the established principles of the law of nations, adopted apparently for a particular purpose; and so far from having been adopted by other nations, they have fallen into merited oblivion, and been acceded to by no other state." Adding, that this "extraordinary transaction is probably the only instance in history in which a great nation broke the law of nations in a sense directly adverse to its own interest, and entered a court of arbitration only to invite a condemnation which might have been self-imposed." Quoting from Mr. Wharton's Commentaries on Law, published in Philadelphia in 1884, the writer remarks that Mr. Wharton repudiates the three rules altogether. Now that the war is over, says Mr. Wharton, "political opinion in the United States has swung back to its old bearings" (*b*). That the rules did not embody the law of nations as then understood is evident; and a mere agreement, on the part of certain nations, to be governed by

(*b*) For these, see *The Santissima Trinidad*, 7 *Wheat*. 283.

these rules in the future, must be regarded as nothing more than a private compact as between the nations parties to it.

In the result, four out of the five arbitrators, the British representative (Sir Alexander Cockburn) dissenting, signed an award, of which the following is an extract:—

> "Whereas, with respect to the vessel called *The Alabama*, it clearly results from all the facts relative to the construction of the ship, at first designated by the No. '290' in the port of Liverpool, and its equipment and armament in the vicinity of Terceira, through the agency of the vessels called *The Agrippina* and *The Bahama*, dispatched from Great Britain to that end, that the British Government failed to use due diligence in the performance of its neutral obligations; and especially that it omitted, notwithstanding the warnings and official representations made by the diplomatic agents of the United States during the construction of the said No. '290,' to take in due time any effective measures of prevention, and that those orders which it did give, at last, for the detention of the vessel, were issued so late that their execution was not practicable;
>
> "And whereas, after the escape of that vessel, the measures taken for its pursuit and arrest were so imperfect as to lead to no result, and therefore cannot be considered sufficient to release Great Britain from the responsibility already incurred;
>
> "And whereas, in despite of the violations of the neutrality of Great Britain committed by the '290,' this same vessel, later known as the Confederate cruiser *Alabama*, was on several occasions freely admitted into the ports of colonies of Great Britain, instead of being proceeded against as it ought to have been in any and every port within British jurisdiction in which it might have been found;

"And whereas the Government of Her Britannic Majesty cannot justify itself for a failure in due diligence on the plea of the insufficiency of the legal means of action which it possessed;

"Four of the arbitrators, for the reasons above assigned, and the fifth for reasons separately assigned by him, are of opinion,

"That Great Britain has in the case failed, by omission, to fulfil the duties prescribed in the first and the third of the Rules established by the Sixth Article of the Treaty of Washington."

The responsibility of the British Government for the acts of certain other vessels was also left to the decision of the Convention, and the following conclusion was arrived at in respect of these, viz.:—

The Florida, built at and issuing from Liverpool, and subsequently, notwithstanding her alleged breach of neutrality, freely admitted into ports within the British jurisdiction, and treated as a belligerent cruiser:—The British Government to be held responsible. (The circumstances in this case were somewhat similar to those in that of *The Alabama.*)

The Shenandoah, issuing from London, and converted into a cruiser off Madeira, and subsequently enlisted men at Melbourne:—The Government not liable for acts prior to arrival at Melbourne, but liable for her acts after departure from that port.

The Tuscaloosa (tender to *Alabama*)
The Clarence
The Taconey and *The Archer* (tenders to *Florida*) } :—These vessels, being accessories, must follow the lot of their principals.

The Retribution, *Georgia*, *Sumter*, *Nashville*, *Tallahassee* and *Chicamauga* :—The Government not responsible.

The Sallie, Jefferson Davis, Music, Boston and *V. H. Joy*:—Excluded from consideration for want of evidence.

As regards the damages, the following conclusions were arrived at:—

Costs of pursuit of the Confederate cruisers, being part of the general war expenditure:—Disallowed.

Prospective earnings, inasmuch as they depend in their nature upon future and uncertain contingencies:—Disallowed.

Double claims, *i.e.*, on behalf of owners and on behalf of underwriters, in respect of the same losses:—Disallowed.

Claims for freight to be disallowed so far as they exceeded *net* freights. On these conclusions, the Convention awarded a lump sum of fifteen millions five hundred thousand dollars as compensation, such amount being held to cover the losses sustained, and a reasonable allowance for interest. Date of award, 14th September, 1872.

The so-called "indirect claims" were dismissed by the arbitrators at the outset of the proceedings. They were for: (1) The enhanced rates of insurance in the United States occasioned by the cruisers in question; (2) The transfer of the maritime commerce of the United States to England; and (3) The prolongation of the civil war.

For a reference to the "Reasons" of Sir Alexander Cockburn for refusing to sign the award relative to *The Alabama*, see Kent's International Law, 2nd ed. p. 468.

This arbitrator's comments on the subject of the "due diligence" required to be shown by a neutral power in the prevention of outfit of vessels for belligerent use, and similar conduct, are especially worthy of perusal. A convenient summary of the American claims and the British rejoinders in the cases of the various vessels above mentioned, will be found in Pitt Cobbett's Leading Cases, pp. 191—199. A *résumé* of the Geneva Arbitration and Award is supplied in the same work, pp. 199—204.

The Foreign Enlistment Act.—The diplomatic controversy arising out of *The Alabama* claims having called attention to important defects in the British Foreign Enlistment Act of 1819, a commission was appointed to report on the Act, and, as a result of their deliberations, a new statute, entitled the "Foreign Enlistment Act of 1870" (*c*), repealing the former Act, was passed by both Houses. The principal provisions of the Act, which extends to all the British dominions, are as follows:—

§ 4. *Illegal Enlistment.*—Penalties provided in the case of any British subject accepting, without permission, any engagement in the military or naval service of a state at war with another state at peace with this country; or, in the case of any person in the British dominions inducing any other person to enter into such an engagement (*d*).

§ 5. Similarly, in the case of any such persons going on board any ship with a view to accepting such engagement, or inducing any other person, &c.

§ 6. Similarly, for, by misrepresentation, inducing any person to leave the British dominions to enter into foreign naval or military service, as above.

§ 7. Similarly, in the case of any master or owner of a ship knowingly having on board persons voluntarily or by misrepresentation proceeding abroad to accept engagements as above.

§ 8. *Illegal Shipbuilding and Illegal Expeditions.*—Penalties provided in the case of any person in the

(*c*) 33 & 34 Vict. c. 90.

(*d*) There is, under the common law of nations, no prohibition against the enlistment of neutral subjects into the military or naval service of belligerents.

British dominions building, without licence and knowingly, any ship to be employed in the service of a belligerent state, as above; or equipping or despatching any such vessel.

Unless such building, &c., shall be in pursuance of a contract made before the commencement of the hostilities; in which case he shall furnish all relative particulars to the Secretary of State, and shall guarantee that the vessel shall not be removed without licence until the termination of the hostilities.

§ 9. Any ship built or delivered to any such belligerent state, or to the agent thereof, shall be deemed to have been so built, &c., with a view to such delivery; the burden of proof of innocent intent to lie on the builder, &c.

§ 10. *Illegal Equipment.*—Penalties provided in the case of any person in the British dominions adding without licence to the number of guns, or exchanging the guns, or being concerned in the augmentation of the warlike force of any ship at such time in the warlike service of a belligerent state, as above.

§ 11. *Fitting-out Expeditions.*—Penalties provided in the case of any person in the British dominions being, without licence, concerned in the fitting out of any warlike expedition to proceed against the dominions of any friendly state.

§ 14. *Illegal Prize.*—During a war, in which this country is neutral,—if any prize captured within the British dominions, or captured by any ship built, equipped, commissioned, or despatched, or the force of which may have been illegally augmented, as above, be brought by or on behalf of the captors within the British dominions,—it shall be lawful for the original owner of such prize to apply to the Admiralty Court to seize and detain it; and the same shall, on due proof of the facts, be restored.

§ 21 gives power to the officials designated to seize and detain any ship liable, as above, to be seized.

§ 30 (Interpretation clause) gives a comprehensive meaning to the term "ship," and states that "equipping" shall include the furnishing a ship with any tackle, apparel, furniture, provisions, arms, munitions, or stores, &c.

The above Act is set forth at length in the appendix to the treatises on International Law by Wheaton and Kent. The former work comprises also the American Act, entitled the "Act for the Punishment of certain Crimes against the United States" (1818) (*e*).

As regards the first Foreign Enlistment Act passed by Great Britain, and the first of such Acts passed in the United States, both seem to have owed their introduction

(*e*) In Kent's Internat. Law (2 Eng. ed. p. 288), attention is drawn to two or three features by which the American is distinguished from the British Act, as follows:—

"The first is that by the American Statute the owners or consignors of armed vessels sailing out of the United States are to give a bond to the United States, with sufficient sureties, prior to clearing out, in double the amount of the value of the vessel and cargo on board, not to employ them to cruise or commit hostilities against the subjects, citizens, or property, of any friendly power. The second is, that the collectors of customs are authorized and required to detain any vessel manifestly built for war purposes, and about to depart from the United States, when circumstances render it probable her owner intends to cruise or commit hostilities, until the President's decision thereon be had, or until a bond be taken. Whilst the third is, that by the British Act, the enlistment of troops and the armament of ships within the British dominions are not, as in the American Act of Congress, prohibited absolutely, but only if they take place without the leave and licence of the Crown, signified by an Order in Council, or by a Proclamation."

The municipal regulations of the nature of Foreign Enlistment Acts established by other powers are summarised in Pitt Cobbett's useful work, "Leading Cases on International Law," pp. 181—183.

much more to a desire to provide protection for the neutral than to any sense, on the part of the neutral, of obligation towards belligerents. All such acts should, indeed, be regarded as strictly municipal, and not as being intended to in any way interpret the obligations of neutrals towards belligerents.

So recently as 1887 proceedings were set on foot under the British Act. One Sandoval, a foreigner temporarily resident in England, had bought certain guns and ammunition in England which he sent to Antwerp. At Antwerp these articles were put on board *The Justitia*, which then, with Sandoval on board, sailed under the British flag ostensibly for Trinidad. Subsequently a foreign flag was run up in place of the British, and the vessel, on arriving at a Venezuelan port, took in tow a flotilla of boats filled with armed men. After shelling a Venezuelan custom house at long range and engaging a Venezuelan cruiser—in the latter of which enterprises *The Justitia* got the worse of it—the vessel retired to San Domingo. The defendant, Colonel Sandoval, was subsequently arrested in England for violating clauses 8 and 11 of the above Act of 1870, of which offence he was found guilty. The Court, observing that any future case would be visited with much severer punishment, passed a sentence of one month's imprisonment, 500*l.* fine and the costs of the proceedings (*f*).

Hospitality to Belligerent Warships.—The permission to belligerent vessels of war to enter neutral ports; or the refusal of such permission; or the granting of a qualified permission; is a matter in the sole discretion of neutral powers, and the granting or refusal, as the case may be,

---

(*f*) Reg. *v.* Sandoval, 16 Cox's C. L. C., Pt. III., described as the first case occurring under the Act; but *vide* The Gauntlet, and The International, p. 382, *infra*.

of permission, is not to be construed as an unfriendly act towards either belligerent. But this axiom is subject to the principle that neutrals must act impartially; they must not permit to the one belligerent a privilege which they deny to the other. In the absence of any neutral proclamation a belligerent is entitled to assume that the hospitality of the neutral ports will be extended to him, as in times of peace. A neutral, whilst permitting the entry of the public armed vessels of belligerents, may by proclamation deny admission to privateers. Thus, during the war with Russia in 1854, the various neutral Baltic and Mediterranean powers issued proclamations forbidding privateers to enter their ports unless under stress of weather, Sweden prohibiting such vessels even from remaining in her roadsteads. In the same war, the latter power, with Norway, in a proclamation conceding permission to belligerent warships to enter its ports generally, reserved to itself the right to refuse admission to certain military ports named in the notice. A similar note was issued by Denmark (*g*).

But the general denial of the right of entry of armed belligerent vessels would presumably not be held to apply in the case of a vessel seeking a neutral port for succour when in distress; as, for instance, to escape from pressing dangers of the seas, to effect necessary repairs, to obtain medical assistance or to supply an urgent need of water or provisions; hospitality being regarded in such cases as the common duty of humanity. But a vessel entering in such circumstances would be required to depart as soon as her wants had been supplied.

The right of neutrals to permit or prohibit the entry of belligerent warships, or to regulate the admission of these vessels, extends equally to the prizes seized by belligerent

(*g*) Twiss's Internat. Law, p. 447.

vessels; and leave may be granted or refused to belligerents to sell their prizes in the neutral ports. Some there are who hold, and the modern tendency seems to be in support of this view, that the granting of this privilege is inconsistent with the conditions of strict neutrality; but it can hardly be doubted that a *bonâ fide* possessor of property may traffic with it in every country where the sovereign does not choose to establish a different rule (*h*). In the American Civil War, Great Britain issued injunctions prohibiting the armed vessels of either belligerent from carrying their prizes into British ports, and similar instructions were issued by France and Spain. It was, moreover, subsequently declared that the British prohibition applied not only to captured vessels but also to prize cargoes transhipped to armed vessels. And no warship was to be supplied with coal more than once in three months, and any coal supplied was to be only sufficient to carry the ship to the nearest port of her own country. Any vessel putting in for supplies or repairs was to be required to depart within twenty-four hours, or so soon as her wants had been supplied (*i*).

Belligerents have the right to convert their prizes into warships after condemnation, and any vessels so converted would be entitled to share the privileges extended to warships generally. If converted without condemnation, it is an open question how such vessels should be regarded by neutrals (*j*).

In 1854 both Spain and Portugal published stringent decrees against affording facilities to the belligerents (*k*), on the part of the national subjects; and on the outbreak of hostilities between France and Germany in 1870, H. M.

(*h*) Kent's Internat. Law, p. 313.

(*i*) London Gazette, 15 Dec. 1863. On this subject generally, *vide* Wheat. Int. Law, 2 Eng. ed. 505-6.

(*j*) *Vide* Wheat. Int. Law, 2 Eng. ed. 506.

(*k*) 44 State Papers, 12 April, 1854.

Government issued a circular letter declaring that belligerents would not be allowed to bring their prizes into British waters except under pressure of necessity. Belligerent vessels disregarding this notice were to be immediately ordered to quit, and, if necessary, compelled to do so by force (*l*).

If the capture of a prize shall have been effected in violation of, or after illegal augmentation (*m*) of the crew of the capturing vessel within, the neutral territory, the neutral power should, in the event of the vessel being brought within the neutral territory, require its restoration to the original owner, regardless of any decree of condemnation passed upon it by a prize court of the captors, and notwithstanding, as it is asserted, that the prize may have been previously taken *infra præsidia* of the captors' country (*n*). If the neutral power, on being applied to, should improperly decline to exercise its right to restore a vessel captured in violation of neutral rights, the government of the injured belligerent is entitled to demand compensation from the neutral (*o*). In other cases of prize carried into neutral ports, the neutral power has no right to inquire into the propriety of the capture (*p*).

A summary of a Declaration on the part of the United States Government, of the American views, so far as they relate to the privilege of asylum within neutral waters, is to be found in Twiss's Law of Nations in Times of War, pp. 453, 454.

(*l*) State Papers, vol. 61, 1093. Declarations of neutrality were also issued by the United States, Peru, &c., that of the latter power prohibiting the sale of contraband of war, and placing restrictions on the sale of coal. *Vide* State Papers, vol. 61, pp. 656, 665, &c.

(*m*) *Vide* p. 62, *supra*.

(*n*) Wheat. Int. Law, 2nd Eng. ed. 504. For the Belligerent Obligation "Respect of Neutral Territory," *vide* p. 311, *supra*.

(*o*) The General Armstrong, Ortolan, Diplom. de la Mer, 2, p. 300.

(*p*) *Vide* pp. 62, 317, *supra*, for remarks relative to the sale of prizes within neutral territory.

The Twenty-four Hours Rule.—It is an established rule of the law of nations that when warships belonging to adverse belligerents shall be in a neutral port together, on one of such vessels putting to sea, that of the adverse belligerent shall not be permitted to leave for twenty-four hours following. Thus, in 1759, when a British fleet had entered Cadiz where a French warship was, at the time, lying at anchor, the governor of Cadiz sent a requisition to the English admiral to permit the French vessel—Great Britain being then at war with France —to sail at least twenty-four hours before the departure of the British fleet; and the admiral at once acceded to this request. During the American Civil War this rule was on one occasion evaded by the Northern States in the following manner:—The Confederate cruiser *Nashville* having put in to Southampton, the Federal corvette *Tuscarora* stationed herself off the port, but within the neutral limits. So soon as the *Nashville* got ready to sail, the agents of the *Tuscarora* notified the latter vessel, which thereupon put to sea. This prevented the departure of the *Nashville* for twenty-four hours, and before that time had elapsed the *Tuscarora* would have again returned to her moorings. By repeating this manœuvre whenever the *Nashville* was reported to be getting ready for sea, the latter was prevented from leaving port at all. To guard against similar devices in other cases, it was provided by a British Order in Council that any belligerent vessel entering a British port during hostilities should, in the absence of valid reason to the contrary, be required to depart within twenty-four hours after entrance (*q*).

A neutral power has also the right to prohibit belligerent vessels from lying in wait for the enemy's vessels at the mouths of the neutral rivers or harbours (*r*); or from sending

(*q*) Pitt Cobbett's Leading Cases, p. 199; 55 State Papers, 816.

(*r*) The Anna, p. 312, *supra*.

out boats from the neutral port to attack an enemy's vessels lying outside the neutral jurisdiction (*s*).

Augmentation of Forces of Belligerent Vessels.—According to the law of nations, as it would seem, a neutral state may, without any breach of her neutrality, permit belligerent vessels to be equipped or to augment their forces within the neutral territory; but belligerents have no right to assume this permission. That is to say, if a belligerent thus augments his force without express permission he is guilty of a violation of neutral rights. This was clearly laid down in the United States by several decisions on the American Act of 1794 (*t*). This principle, however, is apparently not to be carried so far that belligerent vessels shall not equip themselves to the same extent as would be permissible to merchant vessels; but that they must not go beyond this limit. If, notwithstanding, a belligerent vessel should be illegally equipped or fortified, and should thereafter—that is, during the succeeding cruise—effect captures, the neutral power has the right, or rather is under the obligation, to seize and restore any of such prizes which may be brought within the neutral jurisdiction; and the offenders, moreover, may be subject to penalties. But so far as the owners of the vessel thus captured and restored are concerned, there the matter ends. The restitution is made in justification of neutral rights, and not as rectifying a wrong done to the belligerent nation to which the prize belonged: so that no damages will be awarded against the captors (*u*). In 1828 when conflicting claims arose to the throne of Portugal, England prohibited any equipment of vessels in her ports on

(*s*) The Twee Gebrœders, p. 313, *supra*.

(*t*) *E.g.*, *Brig Alerta* v. *Blas Moran*, 9 *Cranch*, 365. And *vide* p. 354, *supra*.

(*u*) *La Amistad de Rues*, 5 *Wheat.* 385.

the part of either belligerent; and an armament having notwithstanding been smuggled out of Plymouth in the interests of one of the claimants, a naval force was sent in pursuit of it, and prevented the squadron from engaging in hostilities at the island of Terceira, as had been contemplated. But, as appears above, the Foreign Enlistment Acts, both of this country and of the United States, definitely prohibit, on the part of the neutral subjects, any abetting of such augmentation of forces (*x*), and provide for the restitution of prizes as already mentioned.

Neutrals are entitled to insist that their territory shall be respected by belligerents, and the latter are under the obligation to observe this requirement (*y*). It has been held in the United States that a foreign vessel guilty of a breach of municipal laws may be pursued on the high seas, and brought back for adjudication; but such a right could scarcely be maintained. So recently as 1857, the Neapolitan Government seized and condemned a Sardinian merchant vessel—*The Cagliari*—whose officers were alleged to have taken part in excesses on Neapolitan territory, and imprisoned her crew, amongst whom were two Englishmen. It was found on the facts that, as no war existed at the time, the seizure of the vessel was altogether illegal; and an indemnity of 3,000*l.* was ultimately paid to the British Government on behalf of the two Englishmen wrongfully detained and imprisoned (*z*).

Assistance to Belligerents.—If the subjects of a neutral state render assistance to a belligerent, the fact, it is to be

(*x*) See §§ 10 and 14 of the British Act, p. 373, *supra*. For cases deciding what constitutes illegal equipment, see Wheaton's Internat. Law, 2 Eng. ed. pp. 512—519.

(*y*) *Vide* p. 311.

(*z*) For remarks on this (Cagliari) case, and on The Virginius (1873), and Huascar (1877), see Wheaton's Internat. Law, 2 Eng. ed. pp. 169—173; also p. 435, *infra*.

apprehended, does not by the law of nations taint the neutral state with any violation of neutral duties. Indeed, if the state should itself render such assistance, short of taking any step which might reasonably be interpreted as an actual interference in the hostilities, this action would not be any breach of neutrality so long as the state was ready to impartially render similar aids to both belligerents without distinction. And, as we have seen (*a*), no municipal enactments limiting or prohibiting such assistance should be regarded as an admission of obligation imposed by the law of nations. As between the neutral state and its subjects, however, any such enactments become of material importance. An instance of this was supplied by *The Gauntlet*, in 1870 (*b*). A Prussian merchant vessel, captured by a French man-of-war, was driven, whilst in charge of a prize crew, to take shelter in the Downs, and an English tug was engaged by the French consul at Dover to tow her to Dunkirk. This the tug did, and was in consequence proceeded against for breach of the Foreign Enlistment Act (*c*). Judgment was given by the Admiralty Court in favour of the tug, but this decision was reversed on appeal to the Privy Council, which held that the engagement to tow the prize with her prisoners and crew, into French waters, was despatching a ship within the meaning of the section, and the tug was declared to be forfeited to the Crown.

The case of *The International* (*d*), which does not appear to have been carried beyond the Admiralty Court, may also be considered in this connexion. The vessel belonged to an English company which, during the Franco-Prussian war, had contracted with the French Government to lay certain submarine cables on the French coast. The undertaking

(*a*) *Vide* p. 365, *supra*.
(*b*) L. R. 4 P. C. 184.
(*c*) *Vide* § 8, p. 372, *supra*.
(*d*) L. R. 3 A. & E. 321.

was purely commercial in its design, but the steamship was detained by the British authorities on the ground that she was engaged contrary to the provisions of the Foreign Enlistment Act,—for, it was argued, the proposed lines of telegraph could be made available to promote military purposes on the part of France. The ship was, however, on an application of the owners, released by the Admiralty Court. The possibility that the cable might be used for military purposes did not, the Court decided, divest the transaction of its primary commercial character, or clothe with a military or naval character within the meaning of the Act the service to be rendered. But as, in the opinion of the Court, there was a reasonable and probable cause for the detention, no order was made as to costs or damages (*e*).

By the law of nations a neutral power is permitted to fulfil pre-existing treaty engagements, such as the furnishing of limited succours to another nation in case its territory should be invaded by a third nation, without being deemed guilty of a breach of neutral obligations. Thus, in 1788, Denmark furnished certain ships and troops to Russia, in her war with Sweden, in accordance with the conditions of a previous treaty, and Sweden accepted the Danish declaration of amity, declaring, however, at the same time that the practice was inconsistent with the practice of the law of nations. On this point the learned editor of Wheaton's International Law (*f*) gives the following pertinent extract from Sir R. Phillimore's work :—"There remains the grave question whether a state has any right to stipulate in time of peace that, when the time of war arrives, it will do the act of a belligerent and yet claim the immunity of a neutral,"—and

(*e*) For other cases, see Burton *v.* Pinkerton, 36 L. J. Ex. 137; Reg. *v.* Carlin (The Salvador), L. R. 3 P. C. 218; Reg. *v.* Corbett, 4 Fos. & Fin. 555.

(*f*) 2 Eng. ed. by Boyd, p. 495.

the conclusions as to this inquiry are, as might be supposed, against such a proposition.

With respect to loans made to belligerents by neutrals:—If the loan be made by or with the consent or collusion of the neutral government, the act would, it appears, be regarded as a violation of neutrality. But private loans made by neutral subjects, without the cognizance of their government, would no doubt stand, as regards their legality, on the same footing as the shipment of contraband of war by individuals. Much would, however, depend on the circumstances in which the loan was made (*g*).

Insurance.

The obligations implied under a warranty of neutrality will be set forth presently under the head "War Warranties" (*h*). With respect to the effect of municipal regulations on the legality of insurance, it should be observed that no shipment or traffic prohibited by British municipal law is capable of insurance within the national jurisdiction.

As regards the subject of marine insurance in connexion with the rights of neutrals, it may here suffice to remark generally that any traffic lawfully open to neutrals would appear to be *primâ facie* capable of insurance by them (*i*); although, as it need scarcely be observed, there may, owing to the existence of hostilities, be peculiar circumstances or risks allied to the traffic which it may be advisable to expressly communicate to the underwriter at the time of effecting the insurance, in order to preclude any subsequent question as to the perils contemplated by him.

As we have already seen (*k*), a neutral may lawfully carry the

(*g*) *Vide* p. 413, *infra*.

(*h*) *Vide* p. 386.

(*i*) *Vide* remarks on p. 357, *supra*, relative to neutral goods on enemy ships; and on p. 193, *supra*, relative to the insurance of contraband shipped by neutrals to the enemy.

(*k*) *Vide* p. 355, *supra*.

goods of belligerents, subject to the risk of capture where the Declaration of Paris or other treaty does not secure immunity to belligerent goods under the neutral flag. As regards freight payable on delivery of permissible belligerent goods, the captor must pay it to the carrier (*l*).

Neutrals may also ship by belligerent merchant vessels, though in so doing they must take their chance of the vessel being captured. Should this contingency occur, the captors may, if they so elect, carry the goods to their destination and so earn the freight; or, as it would seem, they may land them for account and risk of the neutral owner (*m*).

The position in respect of neutral goods pre-empted by belligerents, or placed under arrest or embargo, has been detailed on pp. 244—253, *supra*. The subject of costs incurred by neutrals with the view to procure the restoration of their property wrongfully seized by belligerents has been briefly reviewed on pp. 336 *et seq.*

With this Chapter ends our Summary, for mercantile purposes, of the Law of Nations from its maritime aspect, during time of war. It now only remains to set before the reader a brief review of those mercantile considerations not already dealt with which are specially interesting in the same connexion. What these considerations are will appear on reference to the explanatory remarks on pp. 6—7, *supra*.

(*l*) *Vide* p. 339, *supra*.

(*m*) *Vide* p. 358, *supra*.

IX.

WAR WARRANTIES.

"**Warranted Neutral.**"—A warranty of neutrality of a vessel implies that she is owned by a neutral state, and that she shall be navigated with due respect to the obligations imposed upon neutrals by the common law of nations. To act contrary to this law is to break the warranty and void the insurance. The obligations in question have already been considered in their several places, and reference to the relative considerations of marine insurance has been made at the same time. The obligations as regards the shipowner are these:—

(i) To respect blockades .... p. 104

(ii) Not to carry contraband of war; *i.e.* articles intended for the warlike uses of belligerents.............. 156

(This obligation is, however, of a qualified kind, the penalty for its breach being ordinarily confined to loss of freight of the confiscated articles. See the remarks below relative to the insurance of contraband of war generally.)

(iii) Not to carry despatches or military persons of a belligerent state............................. 201

(iv) Not to resist visit and search 212

(v) Not to sail under convoy or to ship by armed belligerent vessels................................ 213

(vi) Not to attempt a rescue 216

(vii) Not to falsify, destroy, or suppress shipping papers, or carry false papers 219

(viii) To carry and exhibit all usual shipping papers...... 224

(ix) Not to engage in the privileged trade of a belligerent state, or in any trade deemed by the law of nations illicit 233

With respect to the obligations of the cargo owner, as a general principle he is held not to be bound by the act of the master, unless the former be the owner of both ship and cargo, or cognisant in fact, or by presumption, of the intended violation of the law; or the master be his agent. If the circumstances of the breach point to the conclusion that it has been attempted in accordance with design antecedent to the voyage, the cargo will be held bound; but if, on the contrary, the breach spring out of an unforeseen emergency, then the cargo will be deemed *primâ facie* innocent of the offence (*a*). Whether in any case loss or damages arising out of such breaches of the law can be attributed to barratry of the master will depend upon the circumstances.

With respect to the insurance of contraband of war, neutral subjects may, as has been indicated (*b*), ship and insure such goods without breach of the neutral warranty,—for though the contraband articles are subject to confiscation, the fact of their shipment by individuals does not technically involve a breach of neutrality. But if there be an express warranty against contraband, a breach of this warranty on the part of the assured will of course void the insurance (*c*). And the policy may also be voided on the ground of concealment of material fact, if it should appear that the underwriter was not informed of the intention to ship contraband, and the circumstances were not such as to charge him with implied knowledge of this intention (*d*).

The principles on which has to be decided the question of ownership of property *in transitu* have already been considered under the head Domicile (*e*). Further illustrations in Arnould's treatise on Marine Insurance (5th ed., pp. 611—614) indicate that a warranty of neutrality is strictly construed by the Courts. A neutral warranty is complied with if the property be neutral at the commencement of the risk, and a subsequent declaration

(*a*) The Vrow Judith, 1 Rob. 150; The Imina, 3 Rob. 169; The Rosalie and Betty, 2 Rob. 343, 351; The Alexander, 4 Rob. 93; The Elsebe, 5 Rob. 173; The Shepherdess, 5 Rob. 262.

(*b*) Pp. 160, 188, 200, *supra*.

(*c*) *Vide* Seymour *v.* Lo. and Prov. Insce. Co., p. 199, *supra*. *Vide* also p. 403, *infra*.

(*d*) P. 193, *supra*.

(*e*) P. 15, *supra*.

of hostility will not release the underwriter; this is a risk which he must be held to have taken upon himself (*f*); except that if hostilities should occur between the governments of the assured and of the insurer, the insurance then becomes void as being contrary to the war policy of the country of the insurer (*g*).

If a ship, not in fact neutral, be so warranted, the contract is void from the commencement, and the underwriter will be discharged, whatever may be the cause of the vessel's loss (*h*).

It has been explained above (*i*) that false or simulated papers must not be carried, unless under express licence in the policy. In the same place reference has been made to the consequences of carrying suspicious papers, and belligerent property under a disguise of neutrality.

Neutral goods are not liable to seizure on the fact of shipment by belligerent merchant vessels, so long as such vessels are unarmed and not under convoy; consequently such a shipment is no breach of a neutral warranty of the goods (*j*).

The warranty of neutrality may be explicit, as "warranted neutral ship and neutral property"; "warranted neutral": or it may be implied in the description of the vessel, as, for instance, "a Danish brig," "the Swedish ship *Sophia*," such wording amounting to a warranty that the vessel has the national character thus ascribed to her (*k*). A vessel so described must carry shipping papers in accordance with any relative subsisting treaties (*l*). It is, in fact, a standing condition of the neutral warranty that the vessel shall be properly documented, both in accordance with the general requirements of the law of nations, and of any special treaties operating in a particular case (*m*). The papers generally regarded as necessary proofs of nationality have already been enumerated (*n*). Failure in this respect

---

(*f*) Eden *v.* Parkinson, 2 Doug. 732.

(*g*) *Vide* Arnould's Insce., 5th ed. p. 610, note.

(*h*) Woolmer *v.* Muilman, 4 Burr. 1419; 1 Blac. R. 427; Fernandes *v.* Da Costa, Park's Insce., 8th ed. p. 407.

(*i*) P. 231.

(*j*) Arnould, 5th ed. p. 622.

(*k*) Arnould, 5th ed. p. 589.

(*l*) Baring *v.* Claggett, 3 B. & P. 201; *S. C.*, 5 East, 398; Lothian *v.* Henderson, 3 B. & P. 499.

(*m*) *Vide* p. 228, *supra*.

(*n*) *Vide* p. 224, *supra*.

constitutes a breach of neutrality, and voids the policy *ab initio;* a result which is also involved by a breach of any other of the neutral obligations set forth above (*o*). But if a merely transitory breach, involving no loss or injury, should occur, it has been suggested (*p*) that this should not necessarily absolve the underwriter from a subsequent loss in no way consequent on the breach. For instance, if a master should improperly refuse to produce the necessary documentary proofs of nationality to a belligerent cruiser, such conduct would be a breach of neutral warranty; and if the ship should be condemned in consequence, the underwriter would be discharged; but that if she should be released, and be subsequently lost by perils of the seas, the assured should not be deprived of his indemnity on the mere ground of the previous breach.

In every policy effected on the shipowner's account, the condition is implied that the vessel shall carry the proper proofs of her nationality, quite apart from any question of neutral warranty (*q*). But failure to comply with this requirement absolves the underwriter only when the vessel is condemned on the ground of want of proper documents (*r*). And as has already been indicated, it would appear that the underwriter is discharged only when his contract is with the shipowner, not when it is with the cargo-owner (*s*).

In considering a foreign condemnation, the grounds of which are not explicitly defined, the Court will examine the sentence as a whole, in order to arrive at the real grounds of the judgment (*t*). It is held in the United States that whether the grounds of the condemnation by the foreign tribunal be good or bad, the finding of such Court is to be accepted as evidence in actions on policies of insurance. The French Courts decline to accept such judgments as conclusive evidence, and in the British Courts foreign judgments are to be regarded as con-

---

(*o*) *Vide* p. 386.

(*p*) *Vide* Arnould's Insce., 5th ed. p. 535, and note.

(*q*) *Vide* Arnould's Mar. Insce., 5th ed. p. 668.

(*r*) Price *v.* Bell, 1 East, 663, 673.

(*s*) *Vide* p. 230, *supra.*

(*t*) Kindersley *v.* Chase, Park's Insce., 8th ed. 743. *Vide* also Arnould's Insce., 5th ed. 631, note.

clusive only as to the points which they profess to decide (*u*); and the Courts must be satisfied that the ground of the condemnation is such as to forfeit neutrality according to the law of nations, and not, for example, merely according to some national municipal law. A condemnation of the latter kind is not conclusive as discharging underwriters (*v*).

"**Warranted to sail with Convoy.**"—It was decided in *Hibbert* v. *Pigou* (*x*) that by convoy is meant a naval force under the command of a person appointed by the Government of the country; the sailing under the protection of a man-of-war not forming part of a convoy not being a compliance with the warranty. The vessels in the convoy receive sailing orders from the admiral, in order that they may know the signals for the places to which they are to steer in case of dispersion by storm or any other just cause. "Generally speaking," said Buller, J., following the judgment of Lord Mansfield in this case, "unless sailing instructions are obtained, the warranty is not complied with; the captain cannot answer signals; he does not know the place of rendezvous in case of a storm; he does not in effect put himself under the protection of the convoy, and therefore the underwriters are not benefited." In the above case the vessel was lost in a violent storm which occurred *after she had joined* the convoy, but inasmuch as the warranty to "depart with convoy" was absolute, and the vessel had not actually and technically so departed, the underwriters were held discharged. This was an insurance on ship. The underwriters and the insured were, in the words of Lord Mansfield, equally innocent, but the only question for the Court to decide was whether the warranty to "depart with convoy" had or had not been literally complied with. It should, perhaps, be observed that Willes, J., expressed some dissent from such a stringent interpretation of the warranty.

The case of *Smith* v. *Readshaw* (*y*) (1781) seems to have

(*u*) Bolton *v.* Gladstone, 5 East, 155. But cf. Hobbs *v.* Henning, p. 196, *supra*.

(*v*) Pollard *v.* Bell, 8 T. R. 434; Mayne *v.* Walter, 8th ed. Park's Insce., p. 730. *Vide* also cases cited in Arnould, 5th ed. pp. 618, 632—634, on this subject generally.

(*x*) 8th ed. Park's Insce., p. 694. See also Smith *v.* Readshaw, *ibid.* p. 708.

(*y*) 8th ed. Park's Insce., 708; Lilly *v.* Ewer, Doug. 72 (1779).

decided that if a ship be warranted to sail with convoy, the warranty must be understood to relate to the whole voyage, and that if, as a fact, the convoy only goes a part of the way, this is not a convoy for the voyage. But this conclusion must presumably be regarded as reversed by the judgment in *D'Equino* v. *Berwicke* (z) (1795), when Buller, J., dealing with an argument advanced by counsel for the defendant underwriter, delivered himself thus:—

"If Government thought a convoy to the Cape was a sufficient protection to the East India trade, and the usage was for the East India ships to sail with a convoy only to the Cape, and no other convoy was appointed to the East Indies, I should hold that the warranty was complied with; though I agree that if there were another convoy to the East Indies, it would be otherwise."

And if the vessel be separated from the convoy by stress of weather or other circumstances beyond the master's control, the underwriters also remain liable (a).

In *Le Thullier's Case* (b) it was decided that the warranty to depart with convoy, in the case of a vessel sailing from London, must be held to mean that the vessel was to join the convoy in the Downs; for that there never was a convoy from the port of London. And in a somewhat similar case (c) it was decided to be no deviation for a vessel to depart from the direct course in order to seek convoy, the captain having acted fairly and *bonâ fide*. And if a ship duly sails with convoy, and after being driven back to port sails subsequently without convoy, there is no breach of warranty (d).

With respect to sailing instructions, in *Victoria* v. *Cleeve* (e), where the vessel insured was captured shortly after joining the convoy, it was contended on behalf of underwriters that there had been a breach of warranty, inasmuch as at the time of the capture the vessel had obtained no sailing instructions. But as

(z) 2 H. Black. 551. *Vide* also De Garey *v.* Clagget, 8th ed. Park's Insce., 708.

(a) Jeffreys *v.* Legendra, 3 Lev. 320.

(b) 2 Salk. 445.

(c) Gordon *v.* Morley, 2 Stra. 1265. See also cases cited in Arnould's Insce., 5th ed. p. 501, note.

(d) Laing *v.* Glover, 5 Taunt. 49.

(e) 2 Stra. 1250.

it appeared that there had been no default of the master in seeking such instructions, and that the failure to obtain them was actually due to violence of the weather, judgment was given for the plaintiff. In a case where failure to join convoy or to obtain the necessary sailing orders is attributable to neglect or default on the part of the master, the underwriter will be discharged (*f*).

In *Williams* v. *Shee* (*g*), where a vessel stopped behind to complete her loading instead of leaving with the convoy, this was held to be a deviation which voided the policy. Where a vessel, however, becomes separated from convoy by storm, and is captured whilst out of the direct course, but seeking to resume it, the underwriters are not discharged (*h*).

In *Christie* v. *Secretan* (*i*), the broker stated that the ship would sail under convoy, and this representation, in the absence of evidence of further conversation on the subject, was held to be binding.

"Cables cut away or anchors slipped to avoid being separated from convoy are not the subject of general average contribution in this country, though they are so on the continent, and in the opinion of Mr. Phillips it would be so in the United States" (*j*). Expenses consequent on waiting for convoy are not ordinarily to be treated as general average, but if the circumstances be such as to make the delay, or the protection of a man-of-war an exceptional necessity, the case would apparently be otherwise (*k*).

Under the Convoy Act of 1798, now expired, stringent provisions were made against sailing without convoy, leaving convoy, sailing without proper signalling flags, omitting to destroy sailing instructions in the face of imminent risk of capture, &c. It might be supposed that a penalty for wilfully leaving convoy was a superfluous provision, but naturally the speed of the convoy would be reduced to the capacities of the dull sailers, and there is always a temptation for the master of a

(*f*) Taylor *v*. Woodness, Park's Insce., 8th ed. p. 707.

(*g*) 3 Camp. 469.

(*h*) Harrington *v*. Halkeld, Park's Insce., 8th ed. p. 638.

(*i*) 8 T. R. 192.

(*j*) Arnould's Insce., 5th ed. p. 830.

(*k*) *Ibid.* 844.

fast vessel, impatient of the slow progress made, to spread all sail, and set the risk of capture, on the one hand, against the certain advantage of being first in the market, with the saving of wages and provisions, on the other.

The Naval Prize Act, 1864, § 46, provides that if any person, while in command of a ship under convoy, wilfully disobeys the commands of the commander of the convoy, or without leave deserts the convoy, he shall be liable to a penalty not exceeding 500*l.*, and imprisonment not exceeding one year. (*Vide* Appendix, p. 449.)

In Arnould's treatise on marine insurance (*l*), the following are enumerated as being the five requisites essential in respect of the warranty to sail with convoy, viz.: (1) The sailing must be with the regular convoy appointed by government; (2) from the place of rendezvous appointed by government; (3) it must be convoy for the voyage; (4) under proper sailing instructions received from the officer in command; and (5) the vessel must depart with convoy, and continue with it till the end of the voyage, unless separated by necessity (*m*). But the proposition that the vessel must continue with convoy to the end of the voyage should be read in conjunction with *D'Equino* v. *Berwicke*, mentioned above.

It may be convenient to observe in this place that crew's wages and provisions whilst a vessel is awaiting convoy or change of convoy, or whilst taking refuge in port in order to avoid imminent risk of capture, are not recoverable in general average. Seeing that such delays may, however, be on occasion indefinitely prolonged, this contingency will, no doubt, be kept in view by shipowners when entering upon contracts of affreightment.

RETURN FOR ARRIVAL: FOR SAILING,—WITH CONVOY.—In *Simond* v. *Boydell* (*n*), an insurance had been effected on sugar from Grenada to London, "to return eight per cent. if the ship sails with convoy and arrives." The vessel having got aground in the Downs, some of the sugar was washed overboard and other was damaged. The underwriters claimed that no return was due in respect of the value of the sugar which did not, within

(*l*) 5th ed. p. 608.

(*m*) But see as to (5), D'Equino *v.* Berwicke, p. 391, *supra.*

(*n*) Doug. 255.

the meaning of the policy, arrive. Lord Mansfield decided that the clause must be held to refer to the arrival of the ship, and not merely of the cargo. If it had been meant that no return should be made unless *all* the goods arrived *safe*, the clause should have been ". . . . if the ship arrive *with all the goods*," or ". . . . if the ship arrive *safely with all the goods*." "It is amazing," said the learned judge, "when additional clauses are introduced, that the merchants do not take some advice in framing them or bestow more consideration upon them themselves. I do not recollect an addition made, which has not created doubts on the construction of it." In this case, however, as in others, the ambiguity was in favour of the merchants; for the rule of law is in parallel cases to construe such ambiguities of construction against the grantor of the contract.

In another case (*o*), where a similar clause had been employed in an insurance on freight, and the vessel was captured, and subsequently recaptured and delivered up against payment of salvage, the Court gave a similar judgment, ordering payment of return on the whole amount insured. If the clause was intended to bear the meaning which the underwriters claimed for it, the Court observed, it should have had added to it "safely from the enemy," or some such words.

"Every arrival of the ship at her port of destination," said Lord Kenyon, "would not be an arrival within the fair construction of this memorandum; such, for instance, as an arrival in the possession of an enemy at a neutral port; or an arrival at her port in England as the property of other persons after a capture. But in order to satisfy the meaning of the memorandum, it should be an arrival at her destined port in the course of her voyage." In *Horncastle* v. *Haworth* (*p*), the ship had arrived but was captured in port before her discharge was completed. The policy contained a return-clause as above, and the underwriters were held liable for the return, notwithstanding their payment of total loss. In another case (*q*), however, where it was provided that a return should be made "for convoy," and the assured claimed the return as well as a total loss, it was

(*o*) Aguilar *v.* Rodgers, 7 T. R. 421.
(*p*) 2 Marshall's Insce., 681. See also Dalgleish *v.* Brooke, 15 East, 295.
(*q*) Langhorn *v.* Allnutt, 4 Taunt. 511.

found by the jury that no return was due, on the ground that the assured "had a right, in case of a total loss, to add the whole amount of the premium to his invoice and so would recover it in that shape, included in the total loss,"—a proposition which seems to call for some explanation (*r*).

If a return for sailing with convoy be stipulated for, and, owing to breach of warranty, *e.g.*, sailing out of date (*s*), the policy become invalid, the return will apparently be recoverable, notwithstanding that, as in the case cited, a local risk before sailing has been incurred under the policy.

In *Stevenson* v. *Snow* (*t*), where the voyage was from London to Halifax, Nova Scotia, warranted to depart with convoy from Portsmouth, and the vessel arrived at Portsmouth after departure of the convoy, the underwriter, who refused to continue the insurance, was ordered to make a return of premium in respect of the risk not run by him. "These contracts," said Lord Mansfield, "are to be taken with great latitude; the strict letter of the contract is not to be so much regarded as the object and intention of it." Equity implies a condition "that the insurer shall not receive the price of running a risk, if he run none." "Wherever there is a contingency in the voyage, the risk may be divided" (*u*). But the principle affirmed by Lord Mansfield is not to be applied in a case where a vessel has been insured for twelve months, and is captured shortly after the making of the contract (*x*). And where the insurance is "at and from," and the risk is entire, no return is claimable (*y*).

(*r*) The following is the custom of Lloyd's in respect of a provision for return of premium "and arrival":—

"When the words 'and arrival' follow the stipulation for a return of premium on a policy on goods, the particular average, but not the special charges, is deducted from the amount insured, to arrive at the amount on which the return is taken." *Report as to the customs of Lloyd's, issued by the Association of Average Adjusters.*

(*s*) Meyer *v.* Gregson, 3 Doug. 402; and see Arnould's Insce., 5th ed. 1065, note.

(*t*) 3 Burr. 1237; 1 Black. 318.

(*u*) Gale *v.* Machell, Park's Insce., 8th ed. 797. See also Long *v.* Allen, 4 Doug. 276.

(*x*) Tyrie *v.* Fletcher, Cowp. 666.

(*y*) Moses *v.* Pratt, 4 Camp. 296.

In *Kellner* v. *Le Mesurier* (z), where the clause provided for separate returns in respect of portions of the voyage, "or ten per cent. if with convoy for the voyage and arrives," it was held that the words "and arrives" controlled the provision as a whole. Therefore, the vessel having been captured in the last stage of the voyage, no return was payable in respect of the earlier stages, for which a return would otherwise have been claimable.

In *Dudley* v. *Duff* (a), a return had been provided for, "if the vessel sailed with convoy from the coast of Portugal and arrived." The vessel sailed under convoy from Oporto for the general rendezvous at Lisbon, but having lost the convoy before arrival at the rendezvous, she ran for England, and arrived. Held, that the vessel having sailed from some part of the coast of Portugal under convoy and arrived, the assured were entitled to the return (b).

"**Warranted free from Capture.**"—*Vide* as to this important warranty, *sub* "Capture," pp. 68—84, *supra*. The clause is subject to considerable variations (c), both in wording and effect. The more usual form runs as follows :—

> "Warranted free from capture, seizure and detention, and all the consequences thereof, or of any attempt thereat,"—or

> "Warranted free from capture, seizure and detention, and from all consequences of hostilities or warlike operations, whether before or after declaration of war."

For such varieties as "Warranted free from capture in port"; "in port of discharge"; "in port of loading"; "Warranted free from confiscation"; "Warranted free from American condemnation," reference may be made as above (p. 81).

If a vessel insured free of capture be seized and carried into port for adjudication, and eventually allowed to resume her

(z) 4 East, 396. And see Leevin *v.* Cormac, 4 Taunt. 438, note.

(a) Arnould's Insce., 5th ed. 1076.

(b) For a consideration of the subject of Return-premium generally, reference is recommended to Arnould's Marine Insce., 5th ed. pp. 1057 *et seq.*

(c) *Vide* Owen's Marine Insce. Notes and Clauses, 2nd ed. p. 19.

voyage, this interruption of the voyage would not, according to *Scott* v. *Thompson* (*d*), be regarded as a deviation. In the case cited, the insurance included the risk of capture, and the vessel was detained six weeks. The Court held that where the deviation was necessitated by superior force there was no ground for distinction between a policy confined to particular risks and a general policy embracing all risks.

Implied Warranty of Seaworthiness.—In *Wedderburn* v. *Bell* (*e*), where a missing ship was found not to have been efficiently provided with sails, Lord Ellenborough said:—"A person who underwrites a policy upon a vessel has a right to expect that she will be so equipped with sails, that she may be able to keep up with the convoy and get to her port of destination with reasonable expedition. She must be rendered as secure as possible from capture by the enemy, as well as from the danger of the winds and waves. But here the vessel appears to have been deficient in sails, on which her speed might materially depend; and if so, the risk thereby being greatly increased, the policy never attached." It appeared that the sails for use in stormy weather were in good condition, but that the maintop-gallant sails and studding sails, useful in light breezes, were rotten and practically unserviceable. From this case it would seem that an equipment which will fulfil the implied warranty of seaworthiness in time of peace, may be regarded as insufficient if there be a risk of hostile capture.

(*d*) 1 B. & P. N. R. 181. *Vide* also Arnould's Insce., 5th ed. p. 503, note.

(*e*) 1 Camp. 1.

X.

MISREPRESENTATION AND CONCEALMENT.

"On the true principles of equity and justice, for the sake of that consensus indispensable to a contract, concealment or misrepresentation by the assured, whether wilful or not, of any such facts as might reasonably be supposed to have influenced the underwriter in taking the risk or fixing the rate of premium, will avoid the policy" (*a*). The technical distinction between representation and warranty, and the general principles of law in connexion therewith, need not be entered upon here: for information on such points reference should rather be made to treatises on marine insurance generally. The object of this chapter is to indicate the points—other than those relating to marine insurance generally, in times of peace—upon which insurers should, in time of hostilities or apprehended hostilities, give accurate and full information to underwriters.

Misrepresentation.—In *Reid* v. *Harvey* (*b*), where the insurer knew that the vessel had sailed without convoy, and nevertheless secured as a condition of the insurance a provision for return for sailing with convoy, thereby leading the underwriter to believe that there was a prospect of her so sailing, this was held to be a fraudulent misrepresentation which voided the policy.

In *Edwards* v. *Footner* (*c*), where a representation was made that the ship was to sail with convoy and a certain armament, and this representation was not substantially complied with, the policy was held to be void.

(*a*) Arnould's Insce., 5th ed. 507.

(*b*) 4 Dow's Rep. 97.

(*c*) 1 Camp. 530. See also Pawson *v.* Watson, 2 Cowp. 785.

"If, with the intention to deceive, the owner of a ship states to the underwriter that he believes the ship to be neutral, knowing nothing on the subject, and having no reason to believe either way, the better opinion would seem to be that the representation, if false, would avoid the policy" (*d*). "Every misrepresentation," said Lord Eldon in *Sibbald* v. *Hill* (*e*), "is fatal to a contract which is made under such circumstances and in such a way as to gain the confidence of the other party, and induce him to act when otherwise he would not."

In *Seymour* v. *London and Provincial M. I. Co.* (*f*), an insurance had been effected on goods "warranted no contraband of war." The vessel was herself destined to a neutral port on the borders of belligerent soil. The interest insured was condemned as being actually intended for enemy use, and the British Court approved of the decision of the belligerent prize court. The policy was declared void on the grounds of misrepresentation and breach of warranty.

In *Macdowell* v. *Fraser* (*g*) the assured, owing to an erroneous computation as to dates, represented the ship to be safe in the Delaware on 11th December. It turned out that on the 9th December she had been lost by running against a *chevaux de frise* placed across the river, and the misrepresentation was held to have voided the policy.

In *Christie* v. *Secretan* (*h*), where the broker spoke of the ship as an American, but said he was directed not to warrant anything; this was held to be a representation binding the assured to have the vessel documented as American. In another case (*i*), however, where the broker had stated to the underwriter, when the insurance was opened, that the ship was an American, and on closing the policy observed only that it "was an insurance on goods by *The Hermon*," without a word as to the national character of the ship, Lord Ellenborough held that the first conversation had been qualified and controlled by what followed,

---

(*d*) Arnould's Insce., 5th ed. 520.

(*e*) 2 Dow's P. C. 263.

(*f*) 41 L. J. C. P. 193; and p. 199, *supra*.

(*g*) Doug. 247, 260. See also Arnot *v*. Stewart, 5 Dow, 274.

(*h*) 8 T. R. 192.

(*i*) Dawson *v*. Atty, 7 East, 367.

and that the ship was not represented to be an American so as to require documents of nationality. (See Arnould's Insurance, 5th ed. p. 540, note, for the learned author's comment on this, as he calls it, remarkable decision.)

In *Woolmer* v. *Muilman* (*k*), where the insurance was effected with the warranty "Neutral ship and property," the interest being in fact not neutral, the policy was held to be void, though the loss was due to perils of the sea. For, the fact that the loss, in parallel cases, is in no way connected with the circumstances of the warranty or misrepresentation, is not material. And this is so whether the misrepresentation be wilful, or whether it be due to ignorance, accident, or mistake. A misrepresentation, if fraudulently made, whether it be material or not, will void the policy. This, however, will not be so if the representation, though not strictly, be substantially fulfilled, where there is no moral fraud (*l*). But a warranty must be in all cases strictly complied with (*m*).

Concealment.—"Concealment, in the law of insurance, is the suppression of a material fact within the knowledge of one of the parties which the other has not the means of knowing or is not presumed to know. A material fact in this connexion is one which, if communicated to the other of the parties, would induce him either to refrain altogether from the contract, or not to enter into it on the same terms" (*n*).

If a person intending to insure should receive a report of such a nature as to materially affect the risk to be covered, he must acquaint the underwriter with it. Otherwise the insurance may be held void on the ground of the concealment, even though the report subsequently prove to be unfounded (*o*).

"The assured," said Lord Mansfield in *Carter* v. *Boehm* (*p*), "need not mention what the underwriter ought to know; what

---

(*k*) 3 Burr. 1419; 1 Black. 427. See also cases cited in note, Arnould's Insce., 5th ed. 515; and Fernandes *v.* Da Costa, Park's Insce., 8th ed. 407.

(*l*) Pawson *v.* Watson, 2 Cowp. 785.

(*m*) De Hahn *v.* Hartley, 1 T. R. 345.

(*n*) Arnould's Insce., 5th ed. 545.

(*o*) *Vide* cases cited in Arnould's Insce., 5th ed. 563, note.

(*p*) 3 Burr. 1905; 1 Black. R. 593.

he takes upon himself the knowledge of; or what he waives being informed of. . . . The underwriter is bound to know every cause which may occasion political perils; from the rupture of states, from war, and the various operations of war." This was an insurance on a so-called fort in Sumatra. On its being captured by a French ship of war the underwriters objected that they had not been informed of its deficiency of defensive power, and that, owing to certain circumstances, the French might seek to take it. The Court held that the underwriters, having asked no questions, took upon themselves the knowledge of the state of the place; and that the chances of the French making a visit to it were a matter of mere speculation. Judgment for the plaintiff.

In the above trial the learned judge observed that in the case of an insurance on a privateer, the underwriter need not to be told of the secret enterprises contemplated. For from the nature of the contract he waives this information. But "any circumstance within the knowledge of the assured, and not equally within the knowledge of the underwriter, which affects the national character of the subject insured, and therefore exposes it to capture or detention, must be disclosed to the underwriters" (*q*). But ignorance of an exceptional circumstance, though material to the risk, will apparently excuse the assured in respect of his failure to communicate such information to the underwriter. As where a vessel insured, warranted Portuguese, was condemned by a French Court on the ground that she carried an English supercargo, contrary to a recent French ordinance, of which the insurer and the underwriter were both ignorant (*r*). "If both parties were ignorant of the ordinance," said Lord Mansfield, "the underwriter must run all risks. It must be a fraudulent concealment of circumstances that will vitiate a policy." In the United States it has been held that new or shifting ordinances of foreign states, by which the property is exposed to seizure, must be disclosed to the underwriter if the insurer knows of them; for the underwriter cannot be presumed to be necessarily aware of such ordinances (*s*). And in the same country it has been held that failure to disclose that the property insured belongs to a

(*q*) Arnould's Insce., 5th ed. 559.

(*r*) Mayne *v.* Walter, Park's Insce., 8th ed. 431.

(*s*) *Vide* cases cited Arnould's Insce., 5th ed. 560.

house established and doing business in a belligerent state will defeat an insurance effected in a neutral country "for whom it may concern." Also, that not disclosing that enemy property embarked in a neutral ship has been covered as the property of a neutral, is a material concealment (*t*).

According to Arnould (*u*), if it be the established custom for vessels, in order to deceive the enemy's cruisers, to sail on certain voyages with false papers, it is unnecessary to specially communicate the fact to the underwriter when proposing insurances on such voyages. The decisions on which the learned author relies in support of this proposition, however (*Planché* v. *Fletcher*, 1 Doug. 251, An. 1779; *Barnewell* v. *Church*, 1 Caine, 217, An. 1803), seem to be at variance with the later judgments in *Horneyer* v. *Lushington* and *Fomin* v. *Oswell*, cited on p. 231, *supra*.

In *Bates* v. *Hewitt* (*x*), *The Georgia*, a notorious Confederate cruiser, after being laid up for some time at Liverpool, was sold to the plaintiff at public auction, and converted by him into a merchant ship (*y*). The circumstances were well known at the time, but plaintiff, when effecting the insurance, did not call the underwriter's attention to them. It was admitted that the fact of the vessel having been in the Confederate military service, which rendered her liable to be seized by the United States Government, was a circumstance material to the risk. The vessel was, immediately on leaving Liverpool, seized by a Federal war-ship and condemned. It was found by the jury that the underwriter, when accepting the risk, was not aware that the vessel had the above antecedents, though he possessed abundant means of identifying her. The Court held that the plaintiff was not excused from communicating to the underwriter the above material fact, and that the insurance was consequently void.

In *Sawtell* v. *Loudon* (*z*), it was decided that if a vessel be sailing without convoy, and be not within the exception of the convoy statutes, this is a material circumstance to be disclosed to

---

(*t*) *Vide* cases cited, Arnould's Insce., 5th ed. 560.

(*u*) *Ibid.* 567.

(*x*) L. R. 2 Q. B. 595.

(*y*) With reference to such a sale it may be remarked that on 8 Sept. 1864, a notification was issued that no ship of war belonging to either of the American combatants should be allowed to enter, remain, or be in any British port for the purpose of being dismantled or sold. 54 State Papers, 850.

(*z*) 5 Taunt. 359.

the underwriter. In this case the policy expressly gave leave to seek, join, and exchange convoy, and the underwriter, in granting it, remarked that a vessel of the same name was reported to be sailing without convoy. Subsequently the broker was informed by his principal that the report related in fact to the vessel insured, but he failed to acquaint the underwriter with this information, and it was held that the fact, being material, should have been so communicated.

In *Da Costa* v. *Scandret* (*a*), where an owner insured his ship on hearing a report that a vessel resembling it had been captured, and did not communicate this report to his underwriter: in *Durrell* v. *Bederley* (*b*), where the owner of a privateer, having heard it rumoured that some French frigates had made a capture which might well be his vessel, caused her to be insured without mentioning in his order for the insurance the rumour and relative facts; and in *Beckthwaite* v. *Nalgrove* (*c*), where the plaintiff concealed from his underwriter that he had received information that two or three French privateers were in the neighbourhood of the Cape of Good Hope, thus, apparently, constituting special danger to his vessel; the concealment was held to be fatal to the policy.

In *Campbell* v. *Innes* (*d*), there being, as it would seem, a prospect of hostilities between this country and the United States, an insurance was effected on a ship from London to America "against all risks, American capture and seizure included." After the vessel had sailed, information was received that the American Government had declared war, and on the vessel arriving at her destination she was seized under a municipal act prohibiting the importation of British goods, the owner being, as it proved, an American subject. It was decided that this fact as to ownership, being material to the risk, should have been communicated to the underwriter, for whom judgment was given accordingly.

With respect to the carriage of contraband of war, the fact that an insurance on neutral goods is intended to include

(*a*) 2 Peere Wms. 170. *Vide* also Seaman *v*. Fournereau, 2 Stra. 1183.

(*b*) Holt, N. P. 283.

(*c*) Cited in 3 Taunt. 41.

(*d*) 4 B. & A. 423.

contraband articles being material to the risk, it must be communicated to the underwriter when the insurance is proposed to him. Or, failing such express communication, it must be shown that the underwriter might reasonably be presumed to know the nature of the trade engaged in (*e*).

In *Hobbs* v. *Henning* (*f*), a vessel, *The Peterhoff*, was bound from London to Matamoras, a neutral port on the borders of the Confederate territory. There was no warranty against contraband, and the goods were condemned in a Federal prize court as being contraband of war. The British court held that the goods were not by the law of nations contraband of war although unlawfully confiscated as such: that there was no concealment on the part of the assured, and that, the insurance being against capture (lawful or unlawful), the underwriters were liable.

In the United States it was, at the close of last century, held that an insurance on "all kinds of lawful goods" covers contraband articles (*g*). But the Courts, in thus deciding, laid some stress on the circumstance that, if this were not so, some similar case would doubtless have been decided in the British Courts; and, since then, the latter Courts have decided, in effect, that this declaration of the law must be qualified as above explained.

Similarly, if it be intended to attempt a breach of blockade, in order to render the insurance valid the underwriter must either be expressly informed of such intention, or else it must be shown that the fact was within his knowledge when he entered upon the insurance (*h*).

If the imposition of a foreign embargo or municipal prohibition should affect the interest proposed for insurance, the underwriter must be acquainted accordingly (*i*).

(*e*) Arnould's Insce., 5th ed. 699; *Santissima Trinidad*, 7 *Wheat.* 283; *Ex parte* Chavasse, *In re* Grazebrook, 34 L. J. Bkcy. 17. *Vide* also p. 387, *supra*.

(*f*) 17 C. B. 818; 34 L. J. C. P. 117; and p. 196, *supra*.

(*g*) *Vide Seton* v. *Low, and Juhel* v. *Rhinelander*, p. 193, *supra*.

(*h*) P. 123, *supra*.

(*i*) Arnould's Insce., 5th ed. 682.

XI.

VOID INSURANCES.

All insurances on voyages expressly prohibited by the common, statute, or maritime law, or which contravene the war policy, of the country of the insurer, are void *ab initio*. For the purposes of this work, however, consideration of the subject may be confined to its relation to a condition of war. "Where a voyage is illegal," said Tindal, C. J., in *Redmond* v. *Smith* (*a*), "an insurance upon it is invalid, for it would be singular if, the original contract being invalid and incapable to be enforced, a collateral contract founded upon it could be enforced."

Trading with the enemy being illegal unless expressly licensed, insurances to protect such trade will consequently be also void. This has already been explained under the head "Prohibition of Trade with the Enemy" (*b*). If the trade be expressly licensed, the licence must be granted by the proper authority, and it must be strictly complied with, otherwise the voyage will be illegal, and any relative insurance void (*c*).

Engaging in the enemy's privileged trade—that is, in any trade confined, in times of peace, to the subjects of the enemy country—is unlawful unless permitted by proclamation, and, being unlawful, insurances to protect such traffic are void (*d*).

Ransom from the enemy being prohibited, no insurance can be made on ransom-money (*e*), so long as the prohibition is maintained.

(*a*) 7 M. & Gr. 457, 474.
(*b*) P. 272, *supra*.
(*c*) P. 289, *supra*.
(*d*) P. 243, *supra*.
(*e*) P. 304, *supra*.

If the exportation or importation of certain articles be declared prohibited, insurances on goods shipped contrary to the prohibition will necessarily be void (*f*).

Insurances against British capture or embargo, or on enemy property, being contrary to the national war policy, are illegal and void (*g*).

Insurances are also void on trades or voyages prohibited by law or proclamation in this country. Thus, in *Johnson* v. *Sutton* (*h*), where an insurance had been effected on goods from London to New York, and it proved that one-half of the cargo, including the goods insured, was shipped without licence, all unlicensed trade with New York having been expressly prohibited, the voyage was held to be illegal, and the insurance consequently void.

But if, as in the exceptional case of *Atkinson* v. *Abbott* (*i*), there be no intent to evade a prohibition, the voyage will not be held illegal, though involving the payment of a penalty. In this case, clearances to a Danish port having been prohibited, the vessel, with intent to supply the British fleet with provisions, had sailed under a false clearance to a neighbouring neutral port.

If a voyage be one and entire, the whole is rendered illegal by an illegality at the commencement or in the course of the voyage. For illustrations in this connexion, reference may be made to Arnould's Insurance, 5th ed., pp. 676—679. In the same valuable treatise, pp. 673—680 and 1061-5, the question is discussed as to return of premium in respect of illegal insurances generally.

(*f*) P. 308, *supra*.

(*g*) Pp. 275, 308, *supra*. Consequently, such a clause as the following would invalidate any policy in which it was incorporated:—

"Against all war risks whatsoever, including British as well as foreign capture, seizure, and detention, and the consequences of any attempt thereat, as well as by any vessels of war, letters of marque, privateers, or pirates." Owen's Marine Insce. Notes, 2nd ed. p. 21. *Vide* also on p. 42, *supra*, note.

(*h*) 1 Doug. 254.

(*i*) 11 East, 135.

XII.

INSURABLE INTEREST OF CAPTORS.

"PRIZE," said Sir W. Scott in *The Elsebe* (*k*), "is altogether a creature of the Crown. No man has, or can have, any interest but what he takes as the mere gift of the Crown; beyond the extent of that gift he has nothing." In the same case the Court decided that up to the period of final condemnation by the Court of Admiralty, the Crown could, by virtue of its prerogative, restore a prize to the enemy from whom it had been captured, without any reference to the captors; though these instances were of rare occurrence, and rightly so. "A capture at sea," said the same learned judge in *The Rebekah* (*l*), "made by a force upon the land . . . . as, if a ship of the enemy was compelled to strike by a firing from the castle of Dover . . . . that ship would be a droit of Admiralty, and the garrison must be content to take a reward from the bounty of the Admiralty, and not a prize interest under the king's proclamation." On the outbreak of war it is usual for a prize proclamation to be issued, ordering reprisals on the enemy's ships, goods, and subjects, and declaring that the proceeds of property so seized by the ships of war shall be for the benefit and encouragement of the officers, seamen, and marines on board the vessels effecting the captures, after final condemnation as lawful prize of war. "In all cases of prize," as Sir W. Scott expressed it, "the words of the royal proclamation are the title-deeds of flag officers, and no naval officer can by law claim an interest in prize unless it falls clearly within the provisions of the proclamation in force for the time

(*k*) 5 Rob. 181.

(*l*) 1 Rob. 235.

being" (*m*). The Prize Proclamation issued in 1854 makes special provision for the case where a capture is due to the conjoint action of the land forces and sea forces, or to the fleet in conjunction with the vessels of an ally; but declares that in other cases the net proceeds of property captured and condemned shall be for the officers and men manning the capturing vessels, or vessels adjudged to be joint-captors therewith. The shares of prize-money attaching to the several ranks and grades of officers and men are set forth in detail, beginning with flag officer or commodore and ending with the ship's boys and supernumeraries; and the title to share in the prize is elaborately dealt with generally. The Prize Act, 1864 (*n*), deals with the various questions arising in connexion with prize captures, but the apportionment of prize proceeds is left to be the subject of proclamation on the outbreak of war.

The first occasion on which the question arose as to captors' right to insure prizes proceeding to port for adjudication was that known as *The Omoa Case* (*o*). In this case a conjoint detachment of sea and land forces had captured the fort of Omoa, with two Spanish vessels lying under its protection. An insurance was effected on one of these vessels on behalf of the officers and crews of the naval detachment, at and from Omoa to London. The vessel having been lost on the voyage, a question arose whether the officers and crews of the capturing vessels had such an insurable interest as entitled them to recover. Two issues were raised, viz.:—(1) whether the sea officers had an insurable interest under the then Prize Act; and (2) whether possession would entitle them to insure, upon the bare contingency of a future grant from the Crown. Lord Mansfield decided as to the first, that under the wording of the Act the circumstance that this was not a capture by the naval forces solely did not lessen the right of the navy: that wherever a capture had been made by a King's ship or a privateer, the Crown had always given a grant of it after condemnation: that in this case the possession was in the assured: and that a certain expectation of receiving from the Crown the property captured gave them an interest in

(*m*) Mar. Warfare, 399.

(*n*) For which, *vide* Appendix.

(*o*) The Omoa case, Le Cras *v.* Hughes, Park's Insce., 8th ed. 568.

the arrival. It being thus decided that the captors had an insurable interest under the Prize Act, a decision upon the second question became unnecessary. But in the subsequent case of *Lucena* v. *Crawford* (*p*), Lord Mansfield's deduction based on the fact of possession and the contingency of future grant failed to receive general endorsement, Lord Eldon declaring that expectation, however well founded, was not interest, and that that which was wholly in the Crown, and which it was in the power of His Majesty to give or withhold, could not belong to the captors so as to create any right in them. This was the celebrated case where a fleet of Dutch merchantmen had been captured and provisionally carried to St. Helena, under an Order in Council directing that all Dutch vessels bound to and from the ports of Holland should be brought into this country, Holland being then in possession of the armies of the French Republic. Four of the vessels thus seized having been lost on their way to this country, a question arose as to the right to insure them claimed by the members of a Commission appointed for the disposal of Dutch property thus brought to England. This case, which was for more than eight years under litigation, and in the House of Lords gave rise to "one of the most elaborate and ingenious legal discussions ever raised upon a maritime point of law," is discussed in Arnould's Insurance, 5th ed., pp. 93—97. For the purposes of this work it is sufficient, after this reference, to say that the final result of the case must now be considered to be contained in the judgment of Lord Eldon, just mentioned, although his Lordship's judgment was not that delivered by the majority of the House of Lords. And in *Routh* v. *Thompson* (*q*), where in consequence of a royal proclamation on the eve of hostilities with Denmark an armed vessel carried into Lisbon a Danish vessel; and after declaration of hostilities the captors effected an insurance on the vessel; it was held that they had no insurable interest, as they could claim nothing as of right. "Can a man," inquired Lord Ellenborough, "who has no right, legal or equitable . . . . effect an insurance merely because he has a chance that some collateral benefit may come to him if the ship and cargo should arrive in safety? The de-

(*p*) 2 B. & P. N. R. 323; The Hoop may also be referred to, 1 Rob. 196.
(*q*) 11 East, 434.

claration must aver an interest in the subject insured, and that interest must be proved. And how can it be said that these captors have any interest either in the ship or freight, when the ship is altogether the King's?" In this case, it is true, the seizure had been effected before declaration of hostilities; but the circumstance does not appear to affect his Lordship's argument. Again, in *De Vaux* v. *Steele* (*r*), it was decided by Tindal, C. J., that the chance of receiving a bounty from the French Government on the successful termination of a fishing voyage did not constitute an insurable interest. (This decision is not connected with any question of captors' interest, but is mentioned as being in opposition to the statement of the law as declared in *The Omoa* case, above.) So that if Lord Mansfield's judgment in the latter case is to be followed in the future, it will presumably be so only where the expectation is founded on a long and uniform course of practice of the Crown to make the grant, and no instance can be given to the contrary (*s*).

In the above case of *Routh* v. *Thompson*, it was further pleaded that the fact of possession rendered captors liable, either to the Crown or to the foreign owner, for costs and damages in respect of the capture and custody of the ship, and that they had, therefore, an interest in her safety. Lord Ellenborough, however, held that this argument—which had been previously adopted by Lord Kenyon in *Boehm* v. *Bell* (*t*), and approved by Lord Eldon in *Lucena* v. *Crawford*—was inapplicable to the present case, because a formal declaration of hostilities had intervened before the loss, at once vesting the right of ownership in the Crown, putting an end to all claim on the part of the foreign owners, and freeing the captors, as agents for the Crown, from all liability for acts done within the scope of their authority, which it did not appear that they had in any degree exceeded (*u*).

But if an insurance be effected for the captors "and such as it may concern," the Crown may subsequently ratify the insurance. It would seem, indeed, from the case of *Stirling* v.

(*r*) 8 Scott, 637; 6 Bing. N. C. 358, 370, 371.

(*s*) Arnould's Insce., 5th ed. 92.

(*t*) 8 T. R. 154, 161.

(*u*) Arnould's Insce., 5th ed. 98.

Vaughan (*x*), that the captors, as servants and agents of the Crown, have an implied authority to insure on behalf of the Crown, and, consequently, the right to recover on an averment of interest in the Crown. For the Crown has in all cases an insurable interest in ships lawfully detained and captured under the laws of war (*y*).

It is important to note that in H. M. Prize Proclamation, 1854, it was announced that the net produce of all Russian prizes taken by British war-ships

> "Shall be for the entire benefit and encouragement of "our flag officers, captains, commanders and other commis-"sioned officers in our pay; and of all subordinate warrant, "petty, and non-commissioned officers, and of the seamen, "marines and soldiers on board our said ships and vessels "at the time of the capture, after the same shall have been "to us finally adjudged lawful prize" (*z*).

As regards Fire insurance, see *The Catharine and Anna*, briefly referred to on p. 335, *supra*.

(*x*) 11 East, 619.

(*y*) Arnould's Insce., 5th ed. 99.

(*z*) 46 State Papers, 1855, p. 40. *Vide* also p. 319, *supra*.

XIII.

THE EFFECT OF WAR ON CONTRACT.

On the outbreak of hostilities, all peaceful relations between the subjects of the states at enmity come immediately to an end. As a consequence, all contracts in opposition to this principle entered into during, or, as it may be supposed, in contemplation of hostilities, are absolutely void and incapable of enforcement at any time. Contracts existing prior to, and not made in contemplation of, the outbreak of war, are not extinguished absolutely, but are held in suspense until the resumption of friendly relations, when they revive (*a*). The only exceptions to this general principle are (1) contracts in support of trade with the enemy authorized by special licence or by proclamation—as to which *vide* p. 289, *supra;* and (2) contracts of necessity, such as ransom contracts, when not prohibited by the state, as to which *vide* p. 296, *supra.*

Under the head Prohibition of Trade with the Enemy (*b*), the illegality of contracts designed to support such a trade has already been considered. The effect of Embargo and Blockade will be reviewed below, but further reference may also be made to the remarks already suggested under these heads (*c*). The subject Prohibition of Export may likewise be referred to in this connexion (*d*).

Partnerships between the subjects of the adverse states are, on occurrence of hostilities, absolutely extinguished, on the reasoning that it is impossible for the partnership relations to be

(*a*) *Ex parte* Boussmaker, 13 Ves. 71.

(*b*) P. 258, *supra.*

(*c*) Pp. 36, 104, *supra.*

(*d*) P. 306, *supra.*

resumed, on the return of peace, at the point at which they were broken off on the outbreak of war (*e*).

But the law of nations, which prohibits all intercourse between subjects of belligerent states, does not apply to transactions taking place entirely in the territory of one belligerent—as where a creditor, residing in one of the states at war, has an agent in the other state to whom the debtor could pay the money, such agent having been appointed before the war broke out. In such a case the payment by the debtor to this agent is lawful, and it does not follow that the latter will violate the law by remitting the amount to his alien principal (*f*). So, at least, it was declared by the United States Court in *Ward* v. *Smith* (*g*); but as this dictum, if accepted literally, would seem to sanction the existence of business relations with the national foe, it may be doubted whether such a wide meaning should be accorded to it.

It has recently been held in America that a statute of limitations does not run against the creditor, who has become an enemy of the debtor, while the war lasts (*h*).

As regards public loans, the contract to pay interest to all holders of the national stock or securities should, in strictness, on the above principles, be held in abeyance, so far as alien enemies are concerned, until the resumption of peace. As a matter affecting the national honour, however, even if the bonds themselves contain no express stipulation (*i*) as to the payment of interest during hostilities, nothing should be allowed to interfere with the prompt and regular discharge of an obligation founded on the national good faith (*k*).

Any agreement which contemplates action hostile to a friendly state is unlawful and incapable of enforcement. Consequently, no assistance will be afforded by the Courts to persons who set about to raise loans for subjects of a friendly state, to enable them to prosecute war against their sovereign (*l*).

(*e*) *Griswold* v. *Waddington*, 15 *Johns. Rep.* 57. And *vide* 4th ed. Pollock on Contracts, 279, and note.

(*f*) Wheat. Int. Law, 2 Eng. ed. p. 378.

(*g*) 7 *Wall.* 452.

(*h*) Wheat. Int. Law, 2 Eng. ed. p. 378.

(*i*) *Vide* p. 51, *supra*, note.

(*k*) *Vide* on this subject Twiss's Law of Nations, pp. 110—114.

(*l*) De Wutz *v.* Hendricks, 2 Bing. 316. *Vide* also Pitt Cobbett's Leading Cases, pp. 167—171; also p. 384, *supra*.

All mercantile transactions contrary to the national war policy are bad in law. Consequently, all contracts founded on or designed to support such transactions are also void. (*Vide sub* Void Insurances, p. 405, *supra.*)

Contracts of affreightment and ocean carriage being sometimes entered into at a considerable period before their actual performance can be commenced, such contracts are especially liable to be interfered with by the outbreak of hostilities. Instances of this will appear below.

The Contract of Affreightment.—The effect of war or hostilities on the contract of carriage must obviously depend largely on the terms and conditions of the contract itself. Without discussing the various and varying conditions of bills of lading and charterparties, it will suffice for present purposes to state generally the main features of the contract of affreightment as represented by the form of charterparty in common use, namely:—

> The shipowner on the one side, and the charterer on the other, mutually contract—The shipowner to carry a cargo to or from a certain port, at an agreed remuneration by way of freight: The charterer to provide a cargo, and, subject to its right delivery, to pay the freight for its carriage. Penalty for default on the part of either contractor to be the estimated amount of freight; Except: If the reason for the shipowner's non-performance be the operation of certain causes or perils beyond his control, then he shall not be liable for the breach. Whether this stipulation shall equally avail to protect the charterer in respect of a breach caused by one of the same perils will depend upon the wording of the agreement (*m*). The perils enumerated are ordinarily, The Act of God: The Queen's Enemies: Fire and other Perils of the Seas. Following the exception "The

(*m*) See as to this, and as to the contract of carriage generally, Carver's "Carriage by Sea," which has been especially valuable for reference in the present connexion. Foard's "Law of Merchant Shipping" (*sub* Dissolution of Charter-parties, &c.), may also be usefully referred to for cases cited other than the leading decisions here mentioned.

Queen's Enemies," there also very frequently occurs the exception "The Restraint of Princes and Rulers."

The contract is conditional on the shipowner (or charterer) not being prevented from performing it by one of the enumerated contingencies; but it is otherwise absolute: there is no provision for part payment or part performance. The charterer must provide the whole amount of the cargo which he undertook to supply (*n*): the shipowner must transport such cargo the whole of the distance which he undertook to carry it. The Courts of this country will not award freight *pro ratâ itineris*, though, as will appear presently, this general principle can scarcely be regarded as a certainty beyond the reach of exception.

If the contract cannot be fulfilled without trading with the Queen's enemies, it is *ipso facto* dissolved. In *Reid* v. *Hoskins* (*o*), defendant had chartered a vessel to proceed to a Black Sea port, there to receive a cargo of tallow. Before the time when he should have begun to put the cargo on board, war was declared between Great Britain and Russia. On this he refused to fulfil his contract, on the ground that he could not do so without trading with the enemy. The same reason, he averred, would have prevented the plaintiff shipowner from receiving such a cargo. Judgment for the defendant, but plaintiff to be entitled to a verdict if he could prove that by any previous default of the defendant the contract had been in any respect broken before it was dissolved by war.

In *Avery* v. *Bowden* (*The Lebanon*) (*p*), a vessel was chartered to load at Odessa. On her arrival there, war was imminent between England and Russia. The charterer provided no cargo during the first twenty of the forty-five lay-days, although called upon to do so, and the vessel ultimately left empty, before the running days were expired, but after declaration of war. The Court held that prior to the declaration of war no cause of action had accrued to the shipowner: the language in which a cargo was refused was not such an absolute renunciation of the contract as would have warranted the master in sailing; and when

(*n*) For decisions in this connexion, *vide* Carver's Carriage by Sea, Cap. IX.

(*o*) 25 L. T. 161; 26 L. J. Q. B. D. 5.

(*p*) 25 L. J. Q. B. 49; 26 *ibid.* 3.

war was declared the contract was dissolved, as it could not have been fulfilled without trading with the Queen's enemies.

Esposito v. *Bowden* (*q*) is an important case arising in very similar circumstances. Defendant had chartered a vessel to receive a cargo of grain at Odessa, to be carried to Falmouth for orders. While the vessel was on her way to the loading port war was declared against Russia, and on her arrival defendant refused to provide a cargo, on the ground that he could not do so without trading with the Queen's enemies. The plaintiff shipowner contended on the other hand that defendant might have bought a cargo from British subjects, and that it would have been meritorious to have brought such a cargo away; and that grace had been specially allowed by British proclamation during a period within which a cargo so purchased might have been shipped and brought away. Judgment was, in the Court of Queen's Bench, given for the plaintiff, and against this verdict defendant appealed. The Exchequer Chamber reversed the judgment appealed against, the Court indicating the view that all goods in the country of an enemy must be deemed enemy goods, and as such incapable of exportation except under special licence; and holding that even if plaintiff's contention to the contrary could be maintained, the passing of the (so-called British) goods through the Russian custom-house, and paying export duties, would have constituted a trading with the enemy and so have rendered the transaction illegal; and that with respect to the period of grace allowed by the British Order in Council, the contract had been previously dissolved by the declaration of war, and was not revived by the Order in Council.

If a shipowner carries a cargo in circumstances which convict him of the offence of trading with the enemy, the Courts will not assist him in a claim for freight so earned. Freight is "the reward which the law entitles a plaintiff to recover for bringing goods lawfully into this country upon a legal voyage" (*r*).

A contracting party must not abandon the contract on any mere apprehension that the place of loading is about to become

(*q*) 27 L. J. Q. B. 217; 24 *ibid.* 10; 7 E. & B. 763.
(*r*) Muller *v.* Gernon, 3 Taunt. 394.

hostile. In *Atkinson* v. *Ritchie* (*s*), a shipowner had contracted to load a cargo at St. Petersburg, and when half loaded, on hearing a rumour that an embargo was about to be placed on all British vessels within the jurisdiction, he sailed away. This event did, in fact, take place six weeks afterwards. Against the shipowner's plea that performance of the contract had been prevented by "restraint of princes," the Court decided that the restraint must be actual and operative, and not merely expectant and contingent. And on the shipowner's further plea that he owed it a duty to the state to withdraw his property from the grasp of the enemy, the Court decided that to warrant this public duty superseding the private obligation, an actual change in the political relations of the two countries should have taken place. The shipowner was consequently condemned in damages in respect of his non-delivery of the cargo contracted for. And in *Osgood* v. *Groning* (*t*), where the master had landed his cargo at an English port, and declined to proceed to his destination in the North Sea on the ground that his vessel would be exposed to the risk of capture and confiscation by the enemy, the Court decided that no freight was due, the contract not having been fulfilled. In a subsequent action this decision was justified on the ground that the plaintiff might reasonably have been required to proceed on the voyage.

It has been stated above that the contract of carriage must be performed unless its completion be prevented by the intervention of the named contingencies. It is, however, to be understood that, apart from any express or implied exception as to trading with the Queen's enemies, as a matter of course neither of the contractors shall be required to proceed with the agreement if its performance should subsequently be rendered unlawful by his government. If, therefore, after the contract has been lawfully made, and before its execution, hostilities should occur between the state to which the ship or cargo belongs and that in which the cargo is to be supplied or to which it is to be carried, whereby one of the contracting parties is precluded from performing his agreement, the contract is *ipso facto* dissolved. Similarly if commerce between such countries be prohibited.

(*s*) 10 East, 530. (*t*) 2 Camp. 466.

For example: A merchant in London charters a Danish vessel to load a cargo at a Turkish port. If war should occur between England and Turkey, it would be unlawful for the British charterer to supply the cargo in Turkey. If the hostilities were between Denmark and Turkey, it would be unlawful for the Danish ship to transact business at the Turkish port. If between England and Denmark, the contract would become unlawful to both parties. The contract may in all such cases be said to be dissolved by *force majeure*. A good illustration of the application of this principle is furnished by *Baily* v. *De Crespigny* (*u*), where defendant had covenanted that no building should be erected on a certain paddock, and plaintiff proceeded against him for breach, inasmuch as a railway station had been built upon it. The Court held that defendant had been discharged from his covenant by the operation of an Act of Parliament giving compulsory powers of purchase to the railway company, in the exercise of which powers the land had been acquired and built upon by the company. The Act of Parliament had put it out of his power to perform his covenant, and on the principle of the maxim "*lex non cogit ad impossibilia*," he was entitled to judgment.

"The law compelleth not impossibilities"; the question remains—What does the law understand by the relative term impossibility? This can hardly be reduced to a definition, but may in a great measure be deduced from judgments. In *Medeiros* v. *Hill* (*x*), a shipowner had refused to proceed to fulfil his contract on the ground that the port of destination was blockaded, and that the voyage was therefore illegal. The Court held that the mere act of sailing to a blockaded port without premeditated intent to break the blockade if it should be found to continue on the vessel's arrival off the port, was no offence against the law of nations; that when the contract was made the fact of the blockade was known, and that the contracting parties must be taken to have entered into the charterparty with equal knowledge of its existence; and that there was no

(*u*) L. R. 4 Q. B. D. 180. *Vide* also Barker *v.* Hodgson, 3 M. & S. 267. With respect to joint inability to perform contract, *vide* Carver's Carriage by Sea, §§ 228, 229.

(*x*) 8 Bing. 231 (an. 1832). *Vide* also Barker *v.* Hodgson, 3 M. & S. 267.

evidence of any intention on either side to break it: therefore, that no difficulty attending the performance of the contract could be set up as an excuse for its non-performance.

In *Metcalfe* v. *Britannia Ironworks Co.* (*y*) a vessel had been chartered to proceed from Middlesborough to Taganrog, "or as near thereto as she could safely get," freight being due on right delivery at destination. On arrival at Kertch further progress was blocked by ice, navigation being closed for the winter, and the master there terminated the voyage. On a demand for freight it was held that none was due, there having been no voluntary acceptance by charterer at the substituted port. The stoppage at Kertch was no breach of the contract, because the master could get no further; but the landing cargo there was a breach. He might have waited till the navigation reopened; for the charter-party did not say, ". . . . as near thereto as he could safely get *at that time*." Between a blockade by ice and a blockade by proclamation there would seem to be in principle no great difference; time will dissolve them both.

In *Hadley* v. *Clarke* (*z*) a vessel was under charter to carry a cargo from Liverpool to Leghorn. Whilst awaiting convoy at Falmouth an embargo was laid on all vessels sailing to Leghorn, and the vessel in consequence remained at Falmouth. She lay there, in fact, for more than two years, when she returned to Liverpool and landed her cargo. A few weeks afterwards the embargo was taken off. The shippers sued the shipowners for breach of contract, and judgment was given against the latter, the Court declaring that the contract was not dissolved by the embargo, which was a restraint of a merely temporary character. The Court observed that in such a case the verdict must needs inflict a hardship on one of the parties. The law was, however, clear, and the shipowner, had he so desired, could have protected himself by a clause in the contract of affreightment (*a*).

In the leading case, *Touteng* v. *Hubbard* (*b*), Lord Alvanley "had no difficulty in subscribing to the doctrine laid down in

(*y*) L. R. 2 Q. B. D. (1876-7) 423.

(*z*) 8 T. R. 259.

(*a*) *Vide* also in this connexion *sub* Discharge Short of Destination, p. 423, *infra*.

(*b*) Pp. 42, 256, *supra*.

Hadley v. *Clarke*, that a common embargo does not put an end to any contract between the parties, but is to be considered as a temporary suspension of the contract only, and that the parties must submit to whatever inconvenience may arise therefrom, unless they have provided against it by the terms of their contract;" and that the voyage in *Touteng* v. *Hubbard* "might equally have been defeated by the act of God as by the act of the state; as if the ship had been weather-bound until the fruit season was over; and yet in that case the merchant would have been bound to fulfil his contract. The principle of *Hadley* v. *Clarke* is this:—that an embargo is a circumstance against which it is equally competent to the parties to provide as against the dangers of the sea; and therefore if they do not provide against it they must abide by the consequences of their contract." And referring to the cases cited, his lordship observed that the principle which they established appeared to be that if a party contract to do anything, he shall be bound to the performance of his contract, if from the nature of that contract it is capable of being performed, and legally may be performed. But where the policy of the state intervenes and prevents execution, the party will be excused.

But in *Geipel* v. *Smith* (*c*) it was held that "where circumstances have arisen which show that, without any default of the parties, a contract cannot be carried out as contemplated within a reasonable time, the shipowner is excused from going to the port of loading at all." In this case a British vessel had been chartered to load a cargo of coal in England to be carried, restraint of princes and rulers excepted, to Hamburg. Before anything had been done towards performance of the contract, Hamburg was blockaded by the French, and the shipowner thereupon refused to receive the cargo, alleging that it was impossible to fulfil the charter within a reasonable time except by running the blockade, and that to attempt this would be to disregard the royal proclamation of neutrality. The Courts supported this defence, holding that an effective blockade of the port of discharge not merely excuses delay in the carrying out of a contract, but *after a reasonable time* it relieves the parties, *the contract being*

(*c*) L. R. 7 Q. B. D. 104.

altogether executory, from the performance of it. If in this case the impediment had been in its nature temporary, the plea might have been considered bad, but a state of war must be presumed to be likely to continue so long as to defeat and destroy the object of such a commercial adventure.

In *Adamson* v. *Newcastle Insurance Association* (*d*) the charterparty contained a clause "in the event of war, blockade or prohibition of export preventing export," the charterparty to be cancelled. On arrival of the vessel at Constantinople the master learned that the loading port—Galatz—was blockaded by Russia; and considering that there was no reasonable probability of its being opened in time for him to perform his contract, he loaded a cargo at Constantinople instead. The majority of the Court held that, having regard to the special clause, on the closing of the port the agreement was *ipso facto* terminated. Lush, J., dissenting, was of opinion that on the blockade the clause made the charter *voidable* by either side, but not *ipso facto* void. This case, like that of *Metcalfe* v. *Britannia Ironworks Co.* (*e*), emphasises the importance of accuracy and unambiguity in the language of contracts of affreightment. Similarly, in *Avery* v. *Bowden* (*f*) (*The Rolla* (*g*)), where a vessel had been chartered to proceed to Odessa, but "in case of war having commenced" on the vessel's arrival at Constantinople, cargo to be loaded there instead; and war had so commenced between Russia and Turkey; the Court was called upon to decide what was intended by the special provision relative to war. It was finally decided that such a war was contemplated as would make it unlawful for a British ship to proceed from Constantinople to Odessa; and that the war which did occur was not such a contingency as entitled the master to demand a cargo at Constantinople.

Delay consequent on Hostilities.—If in the course of performance of his contract the master, in order to avoid imminent risk of capture, should deviate from the regular course or detain his vessel in neutral waters, this deviation or delay will not support

(*d*) 4 Q. B. D. (1879) 462.
(*e*) P. 419, *supra*.
(*f*) 25 L. J. Q. B. 49.
(*g*) 26 *ibid*. 3.

an action for damages; but it will lie upon the master to justify such an apparent breach of contract. In 1870 the German vessel *San Roman* (*h*), under charter from Vancouver's Island to the United Kingdom, put into Valparaiso to repair. Whilst there the master learned of the war which had broken out between his country and France, and as several French cruisers were in the neighbourhood of the port, he decided to remain where he was. He remained at Valparaiso for three months after completion of his repairs. At the end of that time the fear of capture, owing to the departure of the enemy's cruisers, not being then imminent, he again put to sea. For damages caused by this three months' delay charterers sued the shipowners. The Court held that the master was excused, on the principle that "an apprehension of capture founded on circumstances calculated to affect the mind of a master of ordinary courage, judgment and experience, would justify delay." The charter-party excepted the act of God, the Queen's enemies, and restraints of princes and rulers. If, however, the delay had been found not to be warranted by the facts, these exceptions would presumably not have availed to protect the shipowners. On the other hand, it seems not unreasonable to suppose that even without such protective provisions the master would have been justified for delay reasonably incurred, either on the ground that he was entitled to take necessary measures to defeat an imminent danger which threatened the fulfilment of his contract and the safety of his ship and cargo; or that his obligations as a German subject required him not to expose the national property to the risk of almost certain capture by the enemy.

"It seems obvious," said Mellish, L. J., in *The Teutonia* (*i*), "that if a master receives credible information that if he continues in the direct course of his voyage his ship will be exposed to some imminent peril; as for instance, that there are pirates in his course, or icebergs or other dangers of navigation; he must be justified in pausing and deviating from the direct course, and taking any step which a prudent man would take for the purpose of avoiding danger." It should be noticed that the

(*h*) L. R. 3 A. & E. 583; 5 P. C. 301. *Vide* also The Patria, L. R. 3 A. & E. 436; The Express, *ibid.* 597; The Heinrich, *ibid.* 424.

(*i*) L. R. 4 P. C. 171.

phrase "the Queen's enemies" existing in an alien charter-party is, on the authority of *Russell* v. *Niemann* (*j*), to be construed to mean the enemies of the sovereign power to which the shipowner is subject.

In an action under a time-charter, where the ship had been detained for breach of blockade, Lord Ellenborough decided that freight must be paid during the delay, "in the same manner as if it had arisen from contrary winds or from an embargo" (*k*).

Convoy.—In the absence of any stipulation otherwise, any loss or inconvenience consequent on the vessel having to wait for or with convoy must doubtless be borne by the party on whom it falls: wages, provisions, and demurrage by the shipowner; loss of market and of interest, and any deterioration consequent on the delay, by the owner of the goods. Similarly, in the case of delay caused by embargo, blockade, ice, or other circumstances not attributable to the ship or cargo.

In *Lannoy* v. *Werry* (*l*), where it had been agreed that the merchants should pay certain sums for each day the vessel should *wait for convoy* above the space of twenty days in the whole, the Court decided, in effect, that the words "wait for" meant "wait for or with." Considerable delay had been caused after joining convoy by detention of the latter at Lisbon and Falmouth.

And in *Marshall* v. *De la Torre* (*m*), where the charter allowed in all forty-one days for awaiting convoy at Portsmouth and discharging at Barcelona, and owing to the direct convoy having been missed, delays occurred at Falmouth and Gibraltar; it was held that no demurrage was due in respect of delays at places other than Portsmouth and Barcelona.

Discharge Short of Destination.—It has already been observed (*n*) that the contract of carriage is, as regards the payment of freight, so far absolute that, to earn his freight, the ship-

(*j*) 34 L. J. C. P. 10; also The Teutonia, L. R. 4 P. C. 171; The Heinrich, L. R. 3 A. & E. 424.

(*k*) Moorsom *v.* Greaves, 2 Camp. 627.

(*l*) 2 Bro. Parl. C. 60; Carver on Carriage, § 635.

(*m*) 1 Esp. 367.

(*n*) P. 415, *supra*.

owner must carry the cargo to the agreed destination. He may, in certain cases, be absolved from completing his contract, but such an absolution only relates to his liability to pay damages for non-performance, and is beside the question of payment of freight.

In *The Isabella Jacobina* (*o*), the vessel, of Swedish ownership, bound with a cargo of pilchards from Radstow to Venice, put into Falmouth in distress, and was there detained under an embargo laid on all Swedish vessels. The cargo, it was said, could not await a removal of the embargo, and it was, therefore, given up to the shippers. The Court adjudged no freight to be due, but ordered that the cargo should pay any expenses which might have been incurred on its behalf by the ship. It is, however, apparently to be presumed that if the captain had declined to deliver up the cargo, unless against payment of freight, he would have been within his rights; but it would seem as though he had voluntarily parted with his cargo before demanding freight.

In *Liddard* v. *Lopes* (*p*), a contract had been made to carry coals from Shields to Lisbon, freight to be paid on right delivery. Portugal was occupied by the French, and the master being informed of this put into Portsmouth, and there the cargo was, by consent, sold without prejudice. Against the shipowner's claim for *pro-ratâ* freight and for demurrage whilst his ship was under detention at Portsmouth, Lord Ellenborough decided as follows:—

"The parties have entered into a special contract, by which freight is made payable in one event only, that of a right delivery of the cargo according to the terms of the contract, and that event has not taken place; there has been no such delivery, and consequently the plaintiff is not entitled to recover; he should have provided in his contract for the emergency which has arisen."

In *Hunter* v. *Prinsep* (*q*) a vessel captured by the enemy was recaptured, and was subsequently wrecked at St. Kitts, where the cargo was sold. The shipowner claimed the proceeds in respect

(*o*) 4 Rob. 77.

(*p*) 10 East, 526. *Vide* also Curling *v.* Long, 1 Bos. & Pul. 634.

(*q*) 10 East, 378. *Vide* also Cook *v.* Jennings, 7 T. R. 381.

of *pro-ratâ* freight, but Lord Ellenborough decided against this claim, observing that there had been no right and true delivery, and that if the shipowner had neither earned his freight nor was going to earn it, the freighter was entitled to possession of the goods.

In *Smith* v. *Wilson* (r) a vessel under charter from the United Kingdom to Monte Video and back again, was captured on the way out and brought to England. The ship was restored, but in consequence of the delay the charterer refused to proceed with the contract. It was decided by the Court that, inasmuch as no cargo had been delivered in terms of the contract, no freight was due, delivery in the United Kingdom being a condition precedent to payment. The fact that the master was ready and willing to proceed did not get over this condition precedent: if the vessel *had* proceeded freight might still not have been earned. In this case the claim seems to have been solely for freight, *eo nomine*, not, as might have been expected, for damages for breach of contract.

If the cargo be unlivered short of the destination by order of the Court, full freight is due, and the contract is at an end. So, at least, it was laid down by Sir W. Scott; and until a later decision to the contrary (*The Newport*, to be mentioned presently), no doubt seems to have existed as to this principle. Thus, in *The Hoffnung* (s), the vessel, on account of her cargo, had been brought in by captors and was unlivered by authority of the Court. The cargo was ultimately restored, but the master claimed to receive his freight, refusing at the same time to proceed on his voyage. Sir W. Scott decided that "the act of unlivery is binding on the parties, and must be taken to be decisive in producing a complete dissolution of the contract." Full freight, therefore, was held to be due. "At the moment of separation," said the learned judge, "the vessel acquires a right to proceed" (t). In *The Newport* (u), the vessel, whilst under charter to Ambriz out and home, was seized and condemned by the vice-admiralty court at St. Helena for being engaged in the

(r) 8 East, 437.

(s) 6 Rob. 231; The Martha, 3 Rob. 106.

(t) Cf. The Racehorse, p. 426, *infra*.

(u) Swab. 341.

slave trade, the cargo having been unladen and warehoused by order of the Court. An appeal was lodged against this condemnation, and the decree of the local court was, more than three years afterwards, reversed with costs and damages. The latter were claimed under various heads, one of which was that owing to his having been prevented from fulfilling his contract, the shipowner was liable to repay charterers the sum of 400*l.* advanced by them. The question of damages having been referred to the Registrar (H. C. Rothery), he found in favour of this item as follows:—"I am inclined to hold that the circumstances of the capture, detention, and even sale of *The Newport* amount to a mere temporary detention; that they do not fall within the exceptions specified in the charter-party, and that the shipowner was bound, on his property being restored to him, to fulfil his contract by furnishing a suitable ship to carry on the cargo to Ambriz, if so required by the charterers, and on his failing to do so, that the charterers have a right of action against him." Whether this opinion of the learned Registrar will ultimately be found to prevail over the judgments of Sir W. Scott may perhaps be doubted.

Default of Charterer at Port Short of Destination.—If the vessel, either on account of capture, recapture, or other cause, be at a port short of her destination, and for any reason unconnected with the ship the cargo be not ready to proceed when the master is ready and willing to carry it on, the contract is deemed to be dissolved owing to the fault of the cargo, and full freight becomes due. Thus, in *The Racehorse* (*v*), the vessel, bound from Lisbon to an Irish port with fruit and wine, having been captured, was recaptured and brought into Falmouth. The master having been taken off by the first captors, and the owner being dead, no claim for the cargo was put forward till 17th July, the vessel having been restored by consent on 2nd July. In face of these facts it would, the Court considered, have been unreasonable to require the ship to stay and await the result of the proceedings after her own release; for the cargo might be condemned,

(*v*) 3 Rob. 101. *Vide* also Cargo ex Galam, 33 L. J. Ad. 97; Blasco *v.* Fletcher, 32 L. J. C. P. 284; The Soblomsten, L. R. 1 A. & E. 293.

or there might be no cargo left to carry on. Full freight was awarded on the ground that the cargo was not ready to proceed. (The cargo was restored on 17th November.) In coming to this conclusion, Sir W. Scott observed that he did not say that a master was to depart in haste so soon as his ship was restored: a reasonable time was to be allowed, and if it was not allowed a proportion of the freight might be deducted. The circumstances in which the cargo was discharged are not fully reported, but it is to be assumed that no unlivery was ordered by the Court: for, as already indicated, in such case the ship would have been *ipso facto* entitled to full freight,—at least, as the law then stood.

In another case (*x*), where a Danish ship bound to Lisbon had been brought in on account of the cargo, and the cargo was ultimately restored, but the ship, on account of hostilities which had meantime occurred with Denmark, was condemned, freight was ordered to be paid to the Crown on the ground that the circumstances, at the time the ship was brought in, were such as to entitle the master to receive his freight, and that the Crown, as captors, had entered upon his rights. "In this Court," said Sir W. Scott, "it is held that where neutral and innocent masters of vessels are brought into the ports of this country on account of their cargoes, and obliged to unliver them, they shall have their freight, upon the principle that a non-execution of the contract, arising from the incapacity of the cargo to proceed, ought not to operate to the disadvantage of the ship."

It has been said above that unlivery by order of the Court concludes the contract and entitles the master to his freight (*y*). If, however, the unlivery be caused by the fault of the ship, the cargo may be discharged from the lien of freight. Thus, in *The Theresa Bonita* (*z*), a Danish vessel arrived in London during an embargo on Danish property, and the cargo, being perishable, was ordered by the Court to be unladen. By a general Order in Council, the payment of freight to Danish masters had been prohibited. Consequently the captain lost his lien on the cargo, and had to resort to such personal rights as he might have

---

(*x*) The Prosper, 1 Edw. 72.

(*y*) But cf. The Newport, *supra*.

(*z*) 4 Rob. 236.

under the contract of affreightment. And in *The Weldsborgaren* (*a*), a Swedish vessel, bound from Philadelphia to Lisbon, had been brought in under an embargo on Swedish property, and the cargo had to be unlivered. On removal of the embargo, the master applied for freight. The Court, observing that the detention had been occasioned by the fault of the ship only, and that the cargo had been finally compelled to find another vehicle to carry it to its destination, declined to support the master's demand. In *The Fortuna* (*b*), the ship, a Dane, on a voyage to Portugal, had been brought in on account of the cargo. The cargo was restored, but the ship, owing to hostilities which had meantime broken out with Denmark, was confiscated. Freight was claimed by the Crown, standing in the right of captor. The Court, however, decided that the cargo could be charged with no freight at all, inasmuch as the voyage was to end at Portugal, and the contract (through the fault of the ship) had not been performed.

And, generally, if the failure to fulfil the contract be due to the default of the ship, no freight will be due, and the shipowner may in some cases be liable in damages (*c*).

Pro-ratâ Freight.—In the absence of special provision otherwise in the contract of affreightment, a capture or recapture of the vessel does not *ipso facto* operate as a dissolution of the contract, and if the voyage be thus broken up short of the destination the circumstance gives no special right to freight (*d*). There have been, it is true, other decisions, but more recent judgments involving the contract of affreightment seem to place the above principle beyond doubt. In *Luke* v. *Lyde* (1759) (*e*), a ship bound from Newfoundland to Lisbon with fish, after being

(*a*) 4 Rob. 17.

(*b*) 1 Edw. 56.

(*c*) Osgood *v.* Groning, p. 417, *supra;* Atkinson *v.* Ritchie, *ibid.*

(*d*) Moorsom *v.* Greaves, 2 Camp. 627; The Racehorse, *supra*, p. 426; Boystrom *v.* Mills, 3 Esp. 36; cf. Curling *v.* Long, 1 B. & P. 634. And *vide* Carver's Carriage by Sea, p. 243, note. *Vide* also p. 253, *supra.*

(*e*) 2 Burr. 883. *Vide* also Lutwidge *v.* Grey, Carver's Carriage by Sea, p. 556; Mitchell *v.* Darthez, 2 Bing. N. C. 555. For other cases unconnected with war or hostilities, *vide* Carver, §§ 556—561.

captured, was recaptured and brought into Bideford. The fish was transhipped to Bilboa, where there was a good market, and a claim was made for freight. Lord Mansfield ordered *pro-ratâ* freight to be paid to Bideford. There could be no doubt, he said, that some freight was due. But whether this conclusion was based on a recognition of the principle of *pro-ratâ* freight; or whether, as it would rather seem, it was founded on the circumstance that the charterer had voluntarily accepted his goods from the recaptors at Bideford, the report does not clearly establish. In *The Copenhagen* (*f*), however (1799), there can be no doubt that the principle of *pro-ratâ* freight was clearly admitted by the Court. The vessel, on a voyage from Smyrna to London, had put into Milford Haven in distress, and had to discharge cargo for the purpose of her repairs. The ship and cargo were both seized as prize, but the cargo was restored and forwarded, and ultimately the ship was also released. The points for the decision of the Court were several, but it was admitted that some freight was due (though on what grounds does not appear), and Sir W. Scott awarded freight *pro ratâ itineris* to be fixed by the registrar and merchants in the usual way. But more recent decisions seem to indicate that if *pro-ratâ* freight is allowed at all, it will be allowed only in cases where the non-fulfilment of the voyage can be attributed to *force majeure* of some extraordinary kind; or where, possibly, the non-fulfilment may be in some measure attributable to the cargo or cargo-owners. It is, however, impossible to speak with any precision on this point. That it must be regarded as open is certainly to be understood from the concluding words of the judgment in *The Teutonia* (*g*).

Substituted Performance.—If the vessel be incapacitated at a port short of the destination, and the charterers so act as to support the inference that they voluntarily agree to waive full performance of the contract, such action may be deemed to raise an implied promise that they will pay freight (*h*). But "no

(*f*) 1 Rob. 289.

(*g*) *Vide* p. 431, *infra*.

(*h*) The Soblomsten, L. R. 1 A. & E. 293; Castel *v.* Trechman, 1 Cab. & Ell. 276.

such inference can be drawn unless the goods, or their proceeds, have been accepted voluntarily, and in such a way as to show that the further carriage by the shipowner was intentionally dispensed with. If the merchant must either have accepted the goods where they lay, or abandoned them, no promise to pay freight can be presumed from the fact of their being given up to him. The presumption of a promise cannot, therefore, arise unless the shipowner was able and willing to carry on the goods to their destination, or might have become so within a reasonable time" (*i*).

In *Christy* v. *Row* (*k*), a vessel was under contract to proceed with coals to Hamburg, but was warned off by a British naval commander, as the French forces were approaching the port. The consignees thereupon requested the master to proceed to Gluckstadt, where they would send him lighters. He had so discharged part of his cargo when the vessel was again ordered off, and she eventually returned to Shields without completing the discharge. The Court awarded full freight on the coal delivered at Gluckstadt, but on the remainder it was decided that no freight was recoverable.

But, as already set forth (*l*), if the master be both willing and able to carry the cargo to its destination, and from so doing he be prevented by the fault of the cargo, or by the act or default of the cargo-owner, full freight will be due.

The case of *The Teutonia* (*m*) stands alone. This was a Prussian vessel bound from Pisagua with nitrate of soda to Cork, Cowes, or Falmouth, for orders to discharge at any safe port in Great Britain or on the Continent between Havre and Hamburg,—the act of God, the Queen's enemies, and perils of navigation excepted. She received orders to discharge at Dunkirk, and whilst on the way to that port the master learnt that war was on the eve of declaration between France and Germany. Thereupon he proceeded to Dover, where he was informed that war was declared. On this he declined to proceed to Dunkirk, and tendered delivery at Dover against full freight.

(*i*) *Vide* Carver's Carriage by Sea, § 560.

(*k*) 1 Taunt. 298.

(*l*) P. 426, *supra*, and *vide* Carver's Carriage by Sea, § 554.

(*m*) L. R. 3 A. & E. 394; L. R. 4 P. C. 171.

The Court, in adjudicating on a claim for damages put forward by the charterers, held that the master was justified in not exposing his vessel to the risk of confiscation at Dunkirk, and that, moreover, he could not have gone to a French port without exposing himself to penalties for trading with his country's enemies. Mellish, L. J., in delivering judgment for the shipowner, expressed himself thus:—

"Although it is true that the Court ought not to make a contract for the parties which they have not made themselves, yet a mercantile contract, which is usually expressed shortly, and leaves much to be understood, ought to be construed fairly and liberally for the purpose of carrying out the object of the parties; and it would seem very unjust to hold, because the consignee has named a port at which, without any fault on the part of the shipowner, it is impossible for the cargo to be delivered, that, therefore, the consignee is entitled to the possession of the cargo at the nearest neighbouring port, which, in a charter-party framed like this, must necessarily be one of the ports named in the charter-party, without paying for the cargo any freight whatever. The ship, without any breach of contract on the part of the shipowner, has arrived at Dover, the consignee has required the master to deliver him the cargo there, and he has not required the master to proceed to any other port except Dunkirk, where it was impossible for him to go. The charter-party provides what freight is to be paid if the cargo is delivered at Dover, and how it is to be paid; and, therefore, it appears to their Lordships that they ought to hold that the contract was not dissolved by the impossibility of delivering the cargo at Dunkirk, and that the shipowner had not lost his chartered freight, nor his lien for it, at the time when the cargo was demanded at Dover (*i.e.*, freight-free).

"Their lordships having come to the conclusion that the shipowner had still a lien for the full freight, it becomes unnecessary to consider whether, if Dunkirk had been the only port of discharge, the shipowner would have been entitled to freight *pro ratâ itineris*, or to a sum by way of compensation for the carriage of the goods from Pisagua to Dover, and they wish to be understood as giving no opinion on these questions, which, no doubt, are questions of great difficulty and importance."

The judgments recorded above emphasise the expediency both of a more extended provision for war emergencies in charterparties and for more precise language in expressing the same. Having regard also to the fact that such contracts are often signed some months before the anticipated inception of performance, it is obvious that shipowners and merchants would alike do well to see that charterparties make suitable provision for warlike contingencies which may at any time arise to interfere with the due performance of contracts.

If the goods of an enemy be seized on board a neutral vessel, the captor must ordinarily pay full freight to the neutral carrier (*o*).

If the ship of an enemy be seized with neutral cargo on board, the captors are entitled to carry the goods to their destination and to receive the freight thereon (*p*).

If contraband of war be seized on board a neutral vessel, the prohibited goods are subject to confiscation and the carrier will receive no freight (*q*).

(*o*) *Vide* p. 339, *supra*.
(*p*) *Vide* p. 343, *supra*.
(*q*) *Vide* p. 188, *supra*.

XIV.

PIRACY.

It is not within the objects of this work to enter into discussion under the above head; but as it has sometimes occurred that a doubt has arisen whether a certain capture should be deemed to have been effected by lawful belligerents or by pirates, a brief reference to the subject may not be out of place.

"Piracy," says Chancellor Kent, quoting the case of *The United States* v. *Smith* (*a*), "is robbery, or a forcible depredation on the high seas, without lawful authority, and done *animo furandi*, and in the spirit and intention of universal hostility. It is the same offence at sea with robbery on land; and all the writers on the law of nations, and on the maritime law of Europe, agree in this definition." In the case cited, the mutinous crew of a private armed vessel, commissioned by the Buenos Ayres Government, then at war with Spain, had seized a similar vessel commissioned by the Government of Artigas, also at war with Spain. Having appointed officers to the vessel thus seized, the defendant Smith, without any commission, proceeded on a cruise in her, in the course of which a Spanish vessel was encountered and plundered. For this offence he was brought to trial in the United States, the Court finally deciding that the offence "amounted to the crime of piracy as defined by the law of nations." The point to be decided was whether the act was or was not piracy, and the notes to the case are especially valuable as a summary of the definitions of this crime, as collected from the various writers on the law of nations.

It does not in the above case appear that the prisoners had

(*a*) 5 *Wheat.* 153.

been animated, in the strict sense of the words quoted, by a spirit of universal hostility; but this seems not to be an essential condition of the offence. For Dr. Lushington, in *The Magellan Pirates* (*b*), declared that "in the administration of our criminal law, generally speaking, all persons are held to be pirates who are found guilty of piratical acts; and piratical acts are robbery and murder on the high seas. . . . It was never deemed necessary to inquire whether the parties so connected had intended to rob or to murder on the high seas indiscriminately." As the learned judge in this case made reference to our criminal law, it should be noted that while an act may be piratical within the provisions of a country's municipal law, this circumstance will not of itself make the act piracy under the law of nations; for neither municipal laws nor international treaties can make that an offence under the law of nations which is in fact no such offence. Thus, Sir W. Scott, in giving judgment in the case of *The Le Louis* (*c*), declared that slave trade was not piracy in legal consideration, nor was it a crime by the universal law of nations. The slave trade has, however, been, both by international treaty and by municipal law, declared illegal and piratical so far as carried on by subjects of the states thus prescribing it.

"An offence committed on the high seas is not piracy *jure gentium* so long as the ship on which it is committed remains subject to the authority of the state to which it belongs. A chief ingredient of piracy is throwing off this authority" (*d*).

"When an insurrection or rebellion has broken out in any state, the rebel cruisers may be treated as pirates by the established government, if the rebel government has not been recognized as a belligerent by the parent state, or by foreign nations (*e*); but this right ceases to exist on the recognition of the rebels as belligerents. . . . When rebels cannot produce a regular commission from their government, the question of

---

(*b*) Shipg. and Merc. Gaz., 27 July, 1853.

(*c*) 2 Dods. 210.

(*d*) Wheat. Int. Law, 2 Eng. ed. p. 167, ed. note.

(*e*) For a very recent case in connexion with the question of recognition of a *de facto* government, *vide* The Republic of Peru *v.* Dreyfus Bros. & Co., 4 Times L. R. 333 (an. 1888).

whether they are pirates becomes to a great extent one of intention. If their acts are not done with a piratical intent, but with an honest intention to assist in the war, they cannot be treated as pirates. But it is not because they assume the character of belligerents that they can thereby protect themselves from the consequences of acts really piratical. If their acts are at first unauthorized, but are subsequently avowed by the insurgent government, this may or may not take them out of the category of pirates. A recognition of belligerency does not imply that other acts than those of war will be recognized, and the avowal of any past proceedings is not an act of war" (*f*).

In *Att.-Gen. for Hong-Kong* v. *Kwok-a-Sing* (*g*), the following definition was accepted by the Court:—"Piracy is only a sea term for robbery, piracy being a robbery within the jurisdiction of the Admiralty." But it is not every forcible and unlawful depredation on board ship which will constitute the crime of piracy (*h*).

In *The United States* v. *Pirates* (*i*), the Court decided that a vessel at anchor in an open roadstead might well be found by a jury to be on the high seas. Also, that it was no objection that the vessel was within the jurisdictional limits of a foreign state, for those limits, though neutral to war, are not neutral to crime.

Some of the elements of piracy were present in the cases of *The Cagliari*, *The Virginius*, and *The Huascar*. *The Cagliari* (*k*) was a Sardinian merchant steamer which, in the Neapolitan insurrection of 1857, was taken possession of by persons who had shipped as passengers, and who then landed at a Neapolitan island, and released persons imprisoned in a fortress there. The vessel was subsequently seized by Neapolitan warships, and two of her engineers, Englishmen, were imprisoned. They were, however, in no way in complicity with the persons who had seized the ship, and the Neapolitan Government was ultimately prevailed upon to pay the sum of 3,000*l.* as an indemnity for

(*f*) Wheat. Int. Law, 2 Eng. ed. p. 169.
(*g*) L. R. 5 P. C. 179.
(*h*) *Vide* Nesbitt *v.* Lushington, 4 T. R. 783.
(*i*) 5 *Wheat.* 200.
(*k*) Parl. Papers, Vol. 59, 1857-8.

their imprisonment. The circumstances in this case, though interesting, are, however, not of great value in considering the subject of piracy generally.

The case of *The Virginius* occurred in 1873. This vessel was originally registered in the United States, but subsequently, as it would seem, she lost or abandoned the right to carry the American flag. In October, 1873, she sailed from Kingston, Jamaica—where certain arms and ammunition which were on board had been confiscated under the Customs laws—ostensibly for a Costa Rican port, but really for Cuba, where an insurrection was then raging. Whilst thus proceeding under the American flag, she was seized by a Spanish warship, and carried into Santiago de Cuba. Most of the passengers and crew were Cubans, and it appeared that their intention was to assist in the insurrection. The Spanish authorities, having tried the prisoners by court-martial, shot thirty-seven of them, including sixteen British subjects, who, it appeared, had shipped under the belief that the vessel was really going to Costa Rica. Prompt action having been taken by the United States and British Governments, Spain ultimately agreed to restore *The Virginius* and the survivors of the crew to the United States Government, and to compensate the families of the British subjects illegally condemned and shot. *The Virginius* was not a pirate. She was, no doubt, on her way to assist in an insurrection, but at the time she was captured she was on the high seas, and had not as yet committed any overt acts implicating her in the revolt. Spain was entitled, perhaps, to treat her own subjects as she pleased, but the execution of foreigners found on board a foreign ship, upon the mere supposition that they were going to assist rebels, was wholly unjustifiable (*l*).

The third case, *The Huascar*, occurred in 1877 in connexion with a revolutionary outbreak in Peru. *The Huascar*, a Peruvian turret vessel, was seized at Callao by some of her officers and crew, acting in the interests of the insurgents. The vessel then cruised about the coast and stopped several British vessels, demanding despatches destined for the Peruvian Government, and in one case appropriating, without paying for it, a quantity of coal. The British admiral, De Horsey, on the Pacific station

(*l*) Wheat. Int. Law, 2 Eng. ed. p. 171, ed. note.

having been informed of these proceedings, called upon *The Huascar* to surrender, and offered to land the crew on convenient neutral territory. The demand for the surrender of the vessel having been refused, the admiral thereupon opened fire upon her from *The Shah* and *The Amethyst*, two wooden war-ships. Shortly afterwards the vessel surrendered to the Peruvian national squadron. The Peruvian Government, which had previously disclaimed all responsibility for the acts of *The Huascar*, subsequently demanded reparation from the British Government. This, however, was refused, the law officers advising that Admiral de Horsey's proceedings were justifiable. The ship, it was stated by the Attorney-General, had committed acts which made her an enemy of Great Britain, and she was in the hands of insurgents not in a position to claim belligerent rights.

The subject of Piracy is discussed at some length both in Wheaton's International Law (2 Eng. ed. 166—173), and Kent's International Law (2nd ed. 399—414). Pitt Cobbett's "Leading Cases," pp. 82—93, may also be usefully referred to in this connexion. See also p. 91, *supra, sub* Privateering.

Insurance.

The ordinary marine policy specifically undertakes the risk of "pirates, rovers . . . and all other perils," *i. e.* all other perils of the like kind. Therefore, although a loss may fail to come strictly within what may be considered to be the technical definition of piracy, yet, if the loss be *ejusdem generis* with piracy, the underwriters will, under the above general words, be liable.

In *Palmer* v. *Naylor* (*m*), where some coolie passengers rose and murdered the captain and seized the ship for the purpose of getting ashore, Lord Coleridge said that it was admitted that the seizure was "either a direct act of piracy, or an act so entirely *ejusdem generis*, that if not deduced from the general words of the policy, they are included in the general words at the foot of the peril clause."

(*m*) 24 L. T. 83.

In *Nesbitt* v. *Lushington* (*n*), during a famine in Ireland, a corn-laden vessel was forcibly taken possession of by the mob and run upon the rocks. The mob "requisitioned" the cargo, paying for it on their own terms. For the loss thus arising a claim was brought against the underwriters. The first count of plaintiffs' claim was a loss under the words in the policy—"arrests, restraints, and detainments of all . . . people." The second, a loss by "pirates." As regards the first, the Court decided in favour of the underwriters, on the ground that the "people" contemplated under the words relied upon must be taken to mean the ruling power of the country. But on the second count defendants were held liable, the Court deciding that the loss fell within a capture by pirates.

In cases where the insurance excludes the risk of capture generally, an exception—perhaps in consequence of the judgment in *Johnston* v. *Hogg* (*o*)—is sometimes made in favour of capture by pirates. The Lloyd's F. C. & S. clause runs as follows:—

> "Warranted free of capture, seizure and detention, and the consequences thereof, or of any attempt thereat, *piracy excepted*, and also from all consequences of hostilities or warlike operations, whether before or after declaration of war" (*p*).

(*n*) 4 T. R. 783. For further minor references to the subject of Piracy generally, *vide* Arnould's Insurance, 5th ed. p. 756.

(*o*) Page 79, *supra*.

(*p*) Owen's Marine Insurance Notes and Clauses, 2nd ed. p. 19.

APPENDIX.

NAVAL PRIZE ACT, 1864.

(27 & 28 Vict. c. 25.)

An Act for regulating Naval Prize of War.

[23rd June, 1864.]

Whereas it is expedient to enact permanently, with amendments, such provisions concerning naval prize, and matters connected therewith, as have heretofore been usually passed at the beginning of a war:

Be it therefore enacted by the Queen's most Excellent Majesty, by and with the advice and consent of the Lords Spiritual and Temporal, and Commons, in this present Parliament assembled, and by the authority of the same, as follows:

Preliminary.

1. This Act may be cited as the Naval Prize Act, 1864. **Short title.**

2. In this Act— **Interpretation of terms.**

The term "the Lords of the Admiralty" means the Lord High Admiral of the United Kingdom, or the commissioners for executing the office of Lord High Admiral:

The term "the High Court of Admiralty" means the High Court of Admiralty of England:

The term "any of her Majesty's ships of war" includes any of her Majesty's vessels of war, and any hired armed ship or vessel in her Majesty's service:

The term "officers and crew" includes flag officers, commanders, and other officers, engineers, seamen, marines, soldiers, and others on board any of her Majesty's ships of war:

The term "ship" includes vessel and boat, with the tackle, furniture, and apparel of the ship, vessel, or boat:

The term "ship papers" includes all books, passes, sea briefs, charter parties, bills of lading, cockets, letters, and other documents and writings delivered up or found on board a captured ship:

The term "goods" includes all such things as are by the course of Admiralty and law of nations the subject of adjudication as prize (other than ships).

I.—PRIZE COURTS.

High Court of Admiralty and other Courts to be Prize Courts for purposes of Act.

3. The High Court of Admiralty, and every Court of Admiralty or of Vice-Admiralty, or other Court exercising Admiralty jurisdiction in her Majesty's dominions, for the time being authorized to take cognizance of and judicially proceed in matters of prize, shall be a Prize Court within the meaning of this Act.

Every such Court, other than the High Court of Admiralty, is comprised in the term "Vice-Admiralty Prize Court," when hereafter used in this Act.

High Court of Admiralty.

Jurisdiction of High Court of Admiralty.

4. The High Court of Admiralty shall have jurisdiction throughout her Majesty's dominions as a Prize Court.

The High Court of Admiralty as a Prize Court shall have power to enforce any order or decree of a Vice-Admiralty Prize Court, and any order or decree of the Judicial Committee of the Privy Council in a prize appeal.

Appeal; Judicial Committee.

Appeal to Queen in Council, in what cases.

5. An appeal shall lie to her Majesty in Council from any order or decree of a Prize Court, as of right in case of a final decree, and in other cases with the leave of the Court making the order or decree.

Every appeal shall be made in such manner and form and subject to such regulations (including regulations as to fees, costs, charges, and expenses) as may for the time being be directed by Order in Council, and in the absence of any such order, or so far as any such order does not extend, then in such manner and form and subject to such regulations as are for the time being prescribed or in force respecting maritime causes of appeal.

Jurisdiction of Judicial

6. The Judicial Committee of the Privy Council shall have jurisdiction to hear and report on any such appeal, and may

therein exercise all such powers as for the time being appertain to them in respect of appeals from any Court of Admiralty jurisdiction, and all such powers as are under this Act vested in the High Court of Admiralty, and all such powers as were wont to be exercised by the Commissioners of Appeal in prize causes. Committee in prize appeals.

7. All processes and documents required for the purposes of any such appeal shall be transmitted to and shall remain in the custody of the Registrar of Her Majesty in Prize Appeals. Custody of processes, papers, &c.

8 In every such appeal the usual inhibition shall be extracted from the Registry of Her Majesty in Prize Appeals within three months after the date of the order or decree appealed from if the appeal be from the High Court of Admiralty, and within six months after that date if it be from a Vice-Admiralty Prize Court. Limit of time for appeal.

The Judicial Committee may, nevertheless, on sufficient cause shown, allow the inhibition to be extracted and the appeal to be prosecuted after the expiration of the respective periods aforesaid.

Vice-Admiralty Prize Courts.

9. Every Vice-Admiralty Prize Court shall enforce within its jurisdiction all orders and decrees of the Judicial Committee in prize appeals and of the High Court of Admiralty in prize causes. Enforcement of orders of High Court, &c.

10. Her Majesty in Council may grant to the judge of any Vice-Admiralty Prize Court a salary not exceeding five hundred pounds a year, payable out of money provided by Parliament, subject to such regulations as seem meet. Salaries of judges of Vice-Admiralty Prize Courts.

A judge to whom a salary is so granted shall not be entitled to any further emolument, arising from fees or otherwise, in respect of prize business transacted in his Court.

An account of all such fees shall be kept by the registrar of the Court, and the amount thereof shall be carried to and form part of the consolidated fund of the United Kingdom.

11. In accordance, as far as circumstances admit, with the principles and regulations laid down in the Superannuation Act, 1859, her Majesty in Council may grant to the judge of any Vice-Admiralty Prize Court an annual or other allowance, to take effect on the termination of his service, and to be payable out of money provided by Parliament. Retiring pensions of judges, as in 22 & 23 Vict. c. 26.

Returns from Vice-Admiralty Prize Courts.

12. The registrar of every Vice-Admiralty Prize Court shall, on the first day of January and first day of July in every year, make out a return (in such form as the Lords of the Admiralty from time to time direct) of all cases adjudged in the Court since the last half-yearly return, and shall with all convenient speed send the same to the registrar of the High Court of Admiralty, who shall keep the same in the registry of that Court, and who shall, as soon as conveniently may be, send a copy of the returns of each half year to the Lords of the Admiralty, who shall lay the same before both Houses of Parliament.

General.

General orders for Prize Courts.

13. The Judicial Committee of the Privy Council, with the judge of the High Court of Admiralty, may from time to time frame general orders for regulating (subject to the provisions of this Act) the procedure and practice of Prize Courts, and the duties and conduct of the officers thereof and of the practitioners therein, and for regulating the fees to be taken by the officers of the Courts, and the costs, charges, and expenses to be allowed to the practitioners therein.

Any such general orders shall have full effect, if and when approved by her Majesty in Council, but not sooner or otherwise.

Every Order in Council made under this section shall be laid before both Houses of Parliament.

Every such Order in Council shall be kept exhibited in a conspicuous place in each Court to which it relates.

Prohibition of officer of Prize Court acting as proctor, &c.

14. It shall not be lawful for any registrar, marshal, or other officer of any Prize Court, or for the Registrar of Her Majesty in Prize Appeals, directly or indirectly to act or be in any manner concerned as advocate, proctor, solicitor, or agent, or otherwise, in any prize cause or appeal, on pain of dismissal or suspension from office, by order of the Court or of the Judicial Committee (as the case may require).

Prohibition of proctors being concerned for adverse parties in a cause.

15. It shall not be lawful for any proctor or solicitor, or person practising as a proctor or solicitor, being employed by a party in a prize cause or appeal, to be employed or concerned, by himself or his partner, or by any other person, directly or indirectly, by or on behalf of any adverse party in that cause or appeal, on pain of exclusion or suspension from practice in prize matters, by order of the Court or of the Judicial Committee (as the case may require).

II.—PROCEDURE IN PRIZE CAUSES.

Proceedings by Captors.

16. Every ship taken as prize, and brought into port within the jurisdiction of a Prize Court, shall forthwith, and without bulk broken, be delivered up to the marshal of the Court. Custody of prize ship.

If there is no such marshal, then the ship shall be in like manner delivered up to the principal officer of customs at the port.

The ship shall remain in the custody of the marshal, or of such officer, subject to the orders of the Court.

17. The captors shall, with all practicable speed after the ship is brought into port, bring the ship papers into the registry of the Court. Bringing in of ship papers.

The officer in command, or one of the chief officers of the capturing ship, or some other person who was present at the capture, and saw the ship papers delivered up or found on board, shall make oath that they are brought in as they were taken, without fraud, addition, subduction, or alteration, or else shall account on oath to the satisfaction of the Court for the absence or altered condition of the ship papers or any of them.

Where no ship papers are delivered up or found on board the captured ship, the officer in command, or one of the chief officers of the capturing ship, or some other person who was present at the capture, shall make oath to that effect.

18. As soon as the affidavit as to ship papers is filed, a monition shall issue, returnable within twenty days from the service thereof, citing all persons in general to show cause why the captured ship should not be condemned. Issue of monition.

19. The captors shall, with all practicable speed after the captured ship is brought into port, bring three or four of the principal persons belonging to the captured ship before the judge of the Court or some person authorized in this behalf, by whom they shall be examined on oath on the standing interrogatories. Examinations on standing interrogatories.

The preparatory examinations on the standing interrogatories shall, if possible, be concluded within five days from the commencement thereof.

20. After the return of the monition, the Court shall, on production of the preparatory examinations and ship papers, proceed with all convenient speed either to condemn or to release the captured ship. Adjudication by Court.

Further proof.

21. Where, on production of the preparatory examinations and ship papers, it appears to the Court doubtful whether the captured ship is good prize or not, the Court may direct further proof to be adduced, either by affidavit or by examination of witnesses, with or without pleadings, or by production of further documents; and on such further proof being adduced the Court shall with all convenient speed proceed to adjudication.

Custody, &c. of ships of war.

22. The foregoing provisions, as far as they relate to the custody of the ship, and to examination on the standing interrogatories, shall not apply to ships of war taken as prize.

Claim.

Entry of claim.

23. At any time before final decree made in the cause, any person claiming an interest in the ship may enter in the registry of the Court a claim, verified on oath.

Security for costs.

Within five days after entering the claim, the claimant shall give security for costs in the sum of sixty pounds; but the Court shall have power to enlarge the time for giving security, or to direct security to be given in a larger sum, if the circumstances appear to require it.

Appraisement.

Power to Court to direct appraisement.

24. The Court may, if it thinks fit, at any time direct that the captured ship be appraised.

Every appraisement shall be made by competent persons sworn to make the same according to the best of their skill and knowledge.

Delivery on Bail.

Power to Court to direct delivery to claimant on bail.

25. After appraisement, the Court may, if it thinks fit, direct that the captured ship be delivered up to the claimant, on his giving security to the satisfaction of the Court to pay to the captors the appraised value thereof in case of condemnation.

Sale.

Power to Court to order sale.

26. The Court may at any time, if it thinks fit, on account of the condition of the captured ship, or on the application of a claimant, order that the captured ship be appraised as aforesaid (if not already appraised), and be sold.

Sale on condemnation.

27. On or after condemnation the Court may, if it thinks fit, order that the ship be appraised as aforesaid (if not already appraised), and be sold.

28. Every sale shall be made by or under the superintendence of the marshal of the Court or of the officer having the custody of the captured ship.

How sales to be made.

29. The proceeds of any sale, made either before or after condemnation, and after condemnation the appraised value of the captured ship, in case she has been delivered up to a claimant on bail, shall be paid under an order of the Court either into the Bank of England to the credit of her Majesty's Paymaster-General, or into the hands of an official accountant (belonging to the Commissariat or some other department) appointed for this purpose by the Commissioners of her Majesty's Treasury or by the Lords of the Admiralty, subject in either case to such regulations as may from time to time be made, by Order in Council, as to the custody and disposal of money so paid.

Payment of proceeds to Paymaster-General or Official Accountant.

Small armed Ships.

30. The captors may include in one adjudication any number, not exceeding six, of armed ships not exceeding one hundred tons each, taken within three months next before institution of proceedings.

One adjudication as to several small ships.

Goods.

31. The foregoing provisions relating to ships shall extend and apply, *mutatis mutandis*, to goods taken as prize on board ship; and the Court may direct such goods to be unladen, inventoried and warehoused.

Application of foregoing provisions to prize goods.

Monition to Captors to proceed.

32. If the captors fail to institute or to prosecute with effect proceedings for adjudication, a monition shall, on the application of a claimant, issue against the captors, returnable within six days from the service thereof, citing them to appear and proceed to adjudication; and on the return thereof the Court shall either forthwith proceed to adjudication or direct further proof to be adduced as aforesaid, and then proceed to adjudication.

Power to Court to call on captors to proceed to adjudication.

Claim on Appeal.

33. Where any person, not an original party in the cause, intervenes on appeal, he shall enter a claim, verified on oath, and shall give security for costs.

Person intervening on appeal to enter claim.

III.—SPECIAL CASES OF CAPTURE.

Land Expeditions.

Jurisdiction of Prize Court in case of capture in land expedition.

34. Where, in an expedition of any of her Majesty's naval or naval and military forces against a fortress or possession on land, goods belonging to the state of the enemy or to a public trading company of the enemy exercising powers of government are taken in the fortress or possession, or a ship is taken in waters defended by or belonging to the fortress or possession, a Prize Court shall have jurisdiction as to the goods or ship so taken, and any goods taken on board the ship, as in case of prize.

Conjunct Capture with Ally.

Jurisdiction of Prize Court in case of expedition with ally.

35. Where any ship or goods is or are taken by any of her Majesty's naval or naval and military forces while acting in conjunction with any forces of any of her Majesty's allies, a Prize Court shall have jurisdiction as to the same as in case of prize, and shall have power, after condemnation, to apportion the due share of the proceeds to her Majesty's ally, the proportionate amount and the disposition of which share shall be such as may from time to time be agreed between her Majesty and her Majesty's ally.

Joint Capture.

Restriction on petitions by asserted joint captors.

36. Before condemnation, a petition on behalf of asserted joint captors shall not (except by special leave of the Court) be admitted, unless and until they give security to the satisfaction of the Court to contribute to the actual captors a just proportion of any costs, charges, or expenses or damages that may be incurred by or awarded against the actual captors on account of the capture and detention of the prize.

After condemnation, such a petition shall not (except by special leave of the Court) be admitted unless and until the asserted joint captors pay to the actual captors a just proportion of the costs, charges, and expenses incurred by the actual captors in the case, and give such security as aforesaid, and show sufficient cause to the Court why their petition was not presented before condemnation.

Provided, that nothing in the present section shall extend to the asserted interest of a flag officer claiming to share by virtue of his flag.

Offences against Law of Prize.

In case of offence by

37. A Prize Court, on proof of any offence against the law of nations, or against this Act, or any Act relating to naval

discipline, or against any Order in Council or royal proclamation, or of any breach of her Majesty's instructions relating to prize, or of any act of disobedience to the orders of the Lords of the Admiralty, or to the command of a superior officer, committed by the captors in relation to any ship or goods taken as prize, or in relation to any person on board any such ship, may, on condemnation, reserve the prize to her Majesty's disposal, notwithstanding any grant that may have been made by her Majesty in favour of captors.

captors, prize to be reserved for Crown.

Pre-emption.

Purchase by Admiralty for public service of stores on board foreign ships.

38. Where a ship of a foreign nation passing the seas laden with naval or victualling stores intended to be carried to a port of any enemy of Her Majesty is taken and brought into a port of the United Kingdom, and the purchase for the service of her Majesty of the stores on board the ship appears to the Lords of the Admiralty expedient without the condemnation thereof in a Prize Court, in that case the Lords of the Admiralty may purchase, on the account or for the service of her Majesty, all or any of the stores on board the ship; and the Commissioners of Customs may permit the stores purchased to be entered and landed within any port.

Capture by Ship other than a Ship of War.

Prizes taken by ships other than ships of war to be droits of Admiralty.

39. Any ship or goods taken as prize by any of the officers and crew of a ship other than a ship of war of her Majesty shall, on condemnation, belong to her Majesty in her office of Admiralty.

IV.—PRIZE SALVAGE.

Salvage to re-captors of British ship or goods from enemy.

40. Where any ship or goods belonging to any of her Majesty's subjects, after being taken as prize by the enemy, is or are retaken from the enemy by any of her Majesty's ships of war, the same shall be restored by decree of a Prize Court to the owner, on his paying as prize salvage one eighth part of the value of the prize to be decreed and ascertained by the Court, or such sum not exceeding one eighth part of the estimated value of the prize as may be agreed on between the owner and the re-captors, and approved by order of the Court; provided, that where the re-capture is made under circumstances of special difficulty or danger, the Prize Court may, if it thinks fit, award to the re-captors as prize salvage a larger part than one eighth part, but not exceeding in any case one fourth part, of the value of the prize.

Provided also, that where a ship after being so taken is set forth or used by any of her Majesty's enemies as a ship of war, this provision for restitution shall not apply, and the ship shall be adjudicated on as in other cases of prize.

Permission to re-captured ship to proceed on voyage.

41. Where a ship belonging to any of her Majesty's subjects, after being taken as prize by the enemy, is retaken from the enemy by any of her Majesty's ships of war, she may, with the consent of the re-captors, prosecute her voyage, and it shall not be necessary for the re-captors to proceed to adjudication till her return to a port of the United Kingdom.

The master or owner, or his agent, may, with the consent of the re-captors, unload and dispose of the goods on board the ship before adjudication.

In case the ship does not, within six months, return to a port of the United Kingdom, the re-captors may nevertheless institute proceedings against the ship or goods in the High Court of Admiralty, and the Court may thereupon award prize salvage as aforesaid to the re-captors, and may enforce payment thereof, either by warrant of arrest against the ship or goods, or by monition and attachment against the owner.

V.—Prize Bounty.

Prize bounty to officers and crew present at engagement with an enemy.

42. If, in relation to any war, her Majesty is pleased to declare, by proclamation or Order in Council, her intention to grant prize bounty to the officers and crews of her ships of war, then such of the officers and crew of any of her Majesty's ships of war as are actually present at the taking or destroying of any armed ship of any of her Majesty's enemies shall be entitled to have distributed among them as prize bounty a sum calculated at the rate of five pounds for each person on board the enemy's ship at the beginning of the engagement.

Ascertainment of amount of prize bounty by decree of Prize Court.

43. The number of the persons so on board the enemy's ship shall be proved in a Prize Court, either by the examinations on oath of the survivors of them, or of any three or more of the survivors, or if there is no survivor by the papers of the enemy's ship, or by the examinations on oath of three or more of the officers and crew of her Majesty's ship, or by such other evidence as may seem to the Court sufficient in the circumstances.

The Court shall make a decree declaring the title of the

officers and crew of her Majesty's ship to the prize bounty, and stating the amount thereof.

The decree shall be subject to appeal as other decrees of the Court.

Payment of prize bounty awarded.

44. On production of an official copy of the decree, the Commissioners of her Majesty's Treasury shall, out of money provided by Parliament, pay the amount of prize bounty decreed, in such manner as any Order in Council may from time to time direct.

VI.—MISCELLANEOUS PROVISIONS.

Ransom.

Power for regulating ransom by Order in Council.

45. Her Majesty in Council may from time to time, in relation to any war, make such orders as may seem expedient, according to circumstances, for prohibiting or allowing, wholly or in certain cases, or subject to any conditions or regulations or otherwise, as may from time to time seem meet, the ransoming or the entering into any contract or agreement for the ransoming of any ship or goods belonging to any of her Majesty's subjects, and taken as prize by any of her Majesty's enemies.

Any contract or agreement entered into, and any bill, bond, or other security given for ransom of any ship or goods, shall be under the exclusive jurisdiction of the High Court of Admiralty as a Prize Court (subject to appeal to the Judicial Committee of the Privy Council), and if entered into or given in contravention of any such Order in Council shall be deemed to have been entered into or given for an illegal consideration.

If any person ransoms or enters into any contract or agreement for ransoming any ship or goods, in contravention of any such Order in Council, he shall for every such offence be liable to be proceeded against in the High Court of Admiralty at the suit of her Majesty in her Office of Admiralty, and on conviction to be fined, in the discretion of the Court, any sum not exceeding five hundred pounds.

Convoy.

Punishment of masters of merchant vessels under convoy dis-

46. If the master or other person having the command of any ship of any of her Majesty's subjects, under the convoy of any of her Majesty's ships of war, wilfully disobeys any lawful signal, instruction, or command of the commander of obeying orders or deserting convoy.

the convoy, or without leave deserts the convoy, he shall be liable to be proceeded against in the High Court of Admiralty at the suit of her Majesty in her Office of Admiralty, and upon conviction to be fined, in the discretion of the Court, any sum not exceeding five hundred pounds, and to suffer imprisonment for such time, not exceeding one year, as the Court may adjudge.

Customs Duties and Regulations.

Prize ships and goods liable to duties and forfeiture.

47. All ships and goods taken as prize and brought into a port of the United Kingdom shall be liable to and be charged with the same rates and charges and duties of customs as under any Act relating to the customs may be chargeable on other ships and goods of the like description; and

All goods brought in as prize which would on the voluntary importation thereof be liable to forfeiture or subject to any restriction under the laws relating to the customs, shall be deemed to be so liable and subject, unless the Commissioners of Customs see fit to authorize the sale or delivery thereof for home use or exportation, unconditionally or subject to such conditions and regulations as they may direct.

Regulations of customs to be observed as to prize ships and goods.

48. Where any ship or goods taken as prize is or are brought into a port of the United Kingdom, the master or other person in charge or command of the ship which has been taken or in which the goods are brought shall, on arrival at such port, bring to at the proper place of discharge, and shall, when required by any officer of customs, deliver an account in writing under his hand concerning such ship and goods, giving such particulars relating thereto as may be in his power, and shall truly answer all questions concerning such ship or goods asked by any such officer, and in default shall forfeit a sum not exceeding one hundred pounds, such forfeiture to be enforced as forfeitures for offences against the laws relating to the customs are enforced, and every such ship shall be liable to such searches as other ships are liable to, and the officers of the customs may freely go on board such ship and bring to the Queen's warehouse any goods on board the same, subject, nevertheless, to such regulations in respect of ships of war belonging to her Majesty as shall from time to time be issued by the Commissioners of her Majesty's Treasury.

Power for Treasury to remit customs duties in certain cases.

49. Goods taken as prize may be sold either for home consumption or for exportation; and if in the former case the proceeds thereof, after payment of duties of customs, are insufficient to satisfy the just and reasonable claims thereon, the Commissioners of her Majesty's Treasury may remit the whole or such part of the said duties as they see fit.

Perjury.

50. If any person wilfully and corruptly swears, declares, or affirms falsely in any prize cause or appeal, or in any proceeding under this Act, or in respect of any matter required by this Act to be verified on oath, or suborns any other person to do so, he shall be deemed guilty of perjury, or of subornation of perjury (as the case may be), and shall be liable to be punished accordingly.

Punishment of persons guilty of perjury.

Limitation of Actions, &c.

51. Any action or proceeding shall not lie in any part of her Majesty's dominions against any person acting under the authority or in the execution or intended execution or in pursuance of this Act for any alleged irregularity or trespass, or other act or thing done or omitted by him under this Act, unless notice in writing (specifying the cause of the action or proceeding) is given by the intending plaintiff or prosecutor to the intended defendant one month at least before the commencement of the action or proceeding, nor unless the action or proceeding is commenced within six months next after the act or thing complained of is done or omitted, or, in case of a continuation of damage, within six months next after the doing of such damage has ceased.

Actions against persons executing Act not to be brought without notice, &c.

In any such action the defendant may plead generally that the act or thing complained of was done or omitted by him when acting under the authority or in the execution or intended execution or in pursuance of this Act, and may give all special matter in evidence; and the plaintiff shall not succeed if tender of sufficient amends is made by the defendant before the commencement of the action; and in case no tender has been made, the defendant may, by leave of the Court in which the action is brought, at any time pay into Court such sum of money as he thinks fit, whereupon such proceeding and order shall be had and made in and by the Court as may be had and made on the payment of money into Court in an ordinary action; and if the plaintiff does not succeed in the action, the defendant shall receive such full and reasonable indemnity as to all costs, charges, and expenses incurred in and about the action as may be taxed and allowed by the proper officer, subject to review; and though a verdict is given for the plaintiff in the action he shall not have costs against the defendant, unless the judge before whom the trial is had certifies his approval of the action.

Any such action or proceeding against any person in her Majesty's naval service, or in the employment of the Lords of the Admiralty, shall not be brought or instituted elsewhere than in the United Kingdom.

Petitions of Right.

Jurisdiction of High Court of Admiralty on petitions of right in certain cases, as in 23 & 24 Vict. c. 34.

52. A petition of right, under the Petitions of Right Act, 1860, may, if the suppliant thinks fit, be intituled in the High Court of Admiralty, in case the subject-matter of the petition or any material part thereof arises out of the exercise of any belligerent right on behalf of the Crown, or would be cognizable in a Prize Court within her Majesty's dominions if the same were a matter in dispute between private persons.

Any petition of right under the last-mentioned Act, whether intituled in the High Court of Admiralty or not, may be prosecuted in that Court, if the Lord Chancellor thinks fit so to direct.

The provisions of this Act relative to appeal, and to the framing and approval of general orders for regulating the procedure and practice of the High Court of Admiralty, shall extend to the case of any such petition of right intituled or directed to be prosecuted in that Court; and, subject thereto, all the provisions of the Petitions of Right Act, 1860, shall apply, *mutatis mutandis*, in the case of any such petition of right; and for the purposes of the present section the terms "Court" and "judge" in that Act shall respectively be understood to include and to mean the High Court of Admiralty and the judge thereof, and other terms shall have the respective meanings given to them in that Act.

Orders in Council.

Power to make Orders in Council.

53. Her Majesty in Council may from time to time make such Orders in Council as seem meet for the better execution of this Act.

Order in Council to be gazetted, &c.

54. Every Order in Council under this Act shall be published in the *London Gazette*, and shall be laid before both Houses of Parliament within thirty days after the making thereof, if Parliament is then sitting, and, if not, then within thirty days after the next meeting of Parliament.

Savings.

Not to affect rights of Crown; effect of treaties, &c.

55. Nothing in this Act shall—

(1.) give to the officers and crew of any of her Majesty's ships of war any right or claim in or to any ship or goods taken as prize or the proceeds thereof, it being the intent of this Act that such officers and crews shall continue to take only such interest (if any) in the proceeds of prizes as may be from time to time granted to them by the Crown; or

(2.) affect the operation of any existing treaty or convention with any foreign power; or

(3.) take away or abridge the power of the Crown to enter into any treaty or convention with any foreign power containing any stipulation that may seem meet concerning any matter to which this Act relates; or

(4.) take away, abridge, or control, further or otherwise than as expressly provided by this Act, any right, power, or prerogative of her Majesty the Queen in right of her Crown, or in right of her office of Admiralty, or any right or power of the Lord High Admiral of the United Kingdom, or of the Commissioners for executing the Office of Lord High Admiral; or

(5.) take away, abridge, or control, further or otherwise than as expressly provided by this Act, the jurisdiction or authority of a Prize Court to take cognizance of and judicially proceed upon any capture, seizure, prize, or reprisal of any ship or goods, and to hear and determine the same, and, according to the course of Admiralty and the law of nations, to adjudge and condemn any ship or goods, or any other jurisdiction or authority of or exerciseable by a Prize Court.

Commencement.

56. This Act shall commence on the commencement of the Naval Agency and Distribution Act, 1864. Commencement of Act.

GENERAL INDEX.

FINIS.

PRINTED BY C. F. ROWORTH, GREAT NEW STREET, FETTER LANE, E.C.

May, 1894

CATALOGUE

OF

LAW WORKS

PUBLISHED BY

STEVENS AND SONS,

LIMITED,

119 & 120, CHANCERY LANE, LONDON,

(*And at* 14, *Bell Yard, Lincoln's Inn*).

Telegraphic Address—"RHODRONS, London."

A Catalogue of Modern Law Works, *together with a complete Chronological List of all the English, Irish, and Scotch Reports, an Alphabetical Table of Abbreviations used in reference to Law Reports and Text Books, and an Index of Subjects. Corrected to end of* 1893. *Demy* 8*vo.* (100 *pages*), *limp binding. Post free*, 6*d*.

Acts of Parliament.—*Public and Local Acts from an early date may be had of the Publishers of this Catalogue, who have also on sale the largest collection of Private Acts, relating to Estates, Enclosures, Railways, Roads, &c., &c.*

*** For ANNOTATED ACTS, *vide* "Statutes."

ACTION AT LAW.—Foulkes' Elementary View of the Proceedings in an Action in the Supreme Court.—By W. D. I. FOULKES, Esq., Barrister-at-Law. Third Edition. Demy 12mo. 1884. 7*s*. 6*d*.

ADMIRALTY.—Roscoe's Admiralty Practice.—Third Edition. By E. S. ROSCOE, Assistant Registrar, Admiralty Court, and T. LAMBERT MEARS, Esqrs., Barrister-at-Law. [*In preparation.*

ADVOCACY.—Harris' Hints on Advocacy.—Conduct of Cases Civil and Criminal. Classes of Witnesses and Suggestions for Cross-examining them, &c., &c. By RICHARD HARRIS, one of her Majesty's Counsel. Tenth Edition, with an Index. Royal 12mo. 1893. 7*s*. 6*d*.

"Full of good sense and just observation. A very complete Manual of the Advocate's art in Trial by Jury."—*Solicitors' Journal.*

"Deserves to be carefully read by the young barrister whose career is yet before him."—*Law Magazine.*

AGRICULTURAL LAW.—Forster's Manual of the Law relating to Small Agricultural Holdings, with the Small Holdings Act, 1892. By CHARLES D. FORSTER, Solicitor. Demy 12mo. 1892. *Net* 2*s*. 6*d*.

Spencer's Small Holdings Act, 1892.—With Notes. By AUBREY J. SPENCER, Esq., Barrister-at-Law, Editor of "Dixon's Law of the Farm." Demy 8vo. 1892. *Net* 2*s*. 6*d*.

*** *All standard Law Works are kept in Stock, in law calf and other bindings.*

A

ALLOTMENTS.—Hall's Allotments Acts, 1887, with the Regulations issued by the Local Government Board, and Introductory Chapters, Notes, and Forms. By T. HALL HALL, Barrister-at-Law. Author of "The Law of Allotments." Royal 12mo. 1888. 7*s.* 6*d.*

ANGLO-INDIAN CODES.—Stokes's Anglo-Indian Codes.—By WHITLEY STOKES, LL.D. 2 Vols. Demy 8vo. 1887–88. 3*l.* 5*s.*
Supplements to the above. 1889. *Net* 2*s.* 6*d.* 1891. 4*s.* 6*d.*

ANNUAL DIGEST.—Mews'.—*Vide* "Digest."

ANNUAL LIBRARY (LAWYER'S).—(1) The Annual Practice.—SNOW, BURNEY, and STRINGER. (2) The Annual Digest.—MEWS. (3) The Annual Statutes.—LELY. (4) The Annual County Court Practice.—HEYWOOD.

The Complete Series, as above, delivered on the day of publication, *net*, 2*l.* Nos. 1, 2, and 3 only, *net*, 1*l.* 10*s.* Nos. 2, 3, and 4 only, *net*, 1*l.* 10*s.* (*Carriage extra*, 2*s.*)

☞ *Subscriptions, payable on or before August 31st in each year. Full prospectus forwarded on application.*

ANNUAL PRACTICE (THE).—The Annual Practice. Edited by THOMAS SNOW, Barrister-at-Law; CHARLES BURNEY, a Chief Clerk of the Hon. Mr. Justice Chitty, Editor of "Daniell's Chancery Forms"; and F. A. STRINGER, of the Central Office. 2 vols. Demy 8vo. 25*s.*

The Edition for 1894 is now out of print.

*** Supplement to the Annual Practice for 1894, containing the New Rules of the Supreme Court, 1893. Printed on one side of the paper, with Notes by the Editors, and Instructions for their insertion in the present Edition. *Net* 2*s.* 6*d.*

"A book which every practising English lawyer must have."—*Law Quarterly Review.*
"Part of the equipment of every practising lawyer."—*Law Journal.*
"It is only by the help of this established book of practice that a practitioner can carry on his business."—*Law Times.*
"Every member of the bar, in practice, and every London solicitor, at all events, finds the last edition of the Annual Practice a necessity."—*Solicitors' Journal.*

ANNUAL STATUTES.—Lely.—*Vide* "Statutes."

ARBITRATION.—Russell's Treatise on the Power and Duty of an Arbitrator, and the Law of Submissions and Awards; with an Appendix of Forms, and of the Statutes relating to Arbitration. By FRANCIS RUSSELL. Seventh Edition. By the Author and HERBERT RUSSELL, Esq., Barrister-at-Law. Royal 8vo. 1891. 30*s.*

ARCHITECTS.—Macassey and Strahan.—*Vide* "Civil Engineers."

ASSETS, ADMINISTRATION OF.—Eddis' Principles of the Administration of Assets in Payment of Debts.—By ARTHUR SHELLY EDDIS, one of Her Majesty's Counsel. Demy 8vo. 1880. 6*s.*

AVERAGE.—Hopkins' Hand-Book of Average.—Fourth Edition. By MANLEY HOPKINS, Esq. Demy 8vo. 1884. 1*l.* 1*s.*

Lowndes' Law of General Average.—English and Foreign. Fourth Edition. By RICHARD LOWNDES, Average Adjuster. Author of "The Law of Marine Insurance," &c. Royal 8vo. 1888. 1*l.* 10*s.*

"The most complete store of materials relating to the subject in every particular, as well as an excellent exposition of its principles."—*Law Quarterly Review.*

BALLOT.—Fitzgerald's Ballot Act.—With an Introduction. Forming a Guide to the Procedure at Parliamentary and Municipal Elections. Second Edition. By GERALD A. R. FITZGERALD, Esq., Barrister-at-Law Fcap. 8vo. 1876. 5*s.* 6*d.*

BANKING.—Walker's Treatise on Banking Law.—Second Edition. By J. D. WALKER, Esq., Q.C. Demy 8vo. 1885. 15*s.*

*** *All standard Law Works are kept in Stock, in law calf and other bindings.*

BANKRUPTCY.—Lawrance's Precedents of Deeds of Arrangement between Debtors and their Creditors; including Forms of Resolutions for Compositions and Schemes of Arrangement under the Bankruptcy Acts, 1883 and 1890, with Introductory Chapters, also the Deeds of Arrangement Acts, 1887 and 1890, with Notes. Fourth Ed. By H. ARTHUR SMITH, Esq., Barrister-at-Law. 8vo. 1892. *7s. 6d.*

"Concise, practical, and reliable."—*Law Times.*

Williams' Law and Practice in Bankruptcy.—Comprising the Bankruptcy Acts, 1883 to 1890, the Bankruptcy Rules and Forms, 1886, 1890, the Debtors Acts, 1869, 1878, the Bankruptcy (Discharge and Closure) Act, 1887, the Deeds of Arrangement Act, 1887, and the Rules thereunder. By the Hon. Sir ROLAND L. VAUGHAN WILLIAMS, one of the Justices of Her Majesty's High Court of Justice. Sixth Edition. By EDWARD WM. HANSELL, M.A., Esq., Barrister-at-Law Roy. 8vo. 1894. 25*s.*

"This book will now, if possible, since the appointment of its distinguished author as Bankruptcy Judge, take higher rank as an authority than before."—*Law Journal.*

BILLS OF EXCHANGE.—Chalmers' Digest of the Law of Bills of Exchange, Promissory Notes, Cheques and Negotiable Securities. Fourth Edition. By His Honour Judge CHALMERS, Draughtsman of the Bills of Exchange Act. Demy 8vo. 1891. 18*s.*

"This excellent work is unique. As a statement and explanation of the law, it will be found singularly useful."—*Solicitors' Journal.*

BILLS OF LADING.—Leggett's Treatise on the Law of Bills of Lading.—Second Edition. By Eugene Leggett, Solicitor and Notary Public. Demy 8vo. 1893. 30*s.*

"A very complete and useful exposition of the law relating to this most important branch of mercantile law."

BILLS OF SALE.—Stevens' Treatise on the Bills of Sale Acts. By T. M. STEVENS, Esq., Barrister-at-Law. (*In the press.*)

BOOK-KEEPING.—Matthew Hale's System of Book-keeping for Solicitors, containing a List of all Books necessary, with a comprehensive description of their objects and uses for the purpose of Drawing Bills of Costs and the rendering of Cash Accounts to clients; also showing how to ascertain Profits derived from the business; with an Appendix. Demy 8vo. 1884. 5*s.* 6*d.*

"We think this is by far the most sensible, useful, practical little work on solicitors' book-keeping that we have seen."—*Law Students' Journal.*

BRACTON.—Bracton's Note Book. A Collection of Cases decided in the King's Courts during the reign of Henry the Third, annotated by a Lawyer of that time, seemingly by Henry of Bratton. Edited by F. W. MAITLAND, Bar.-at-Law. 3 vols. Demy 8vo. 1887. *Net 3l. 3s.*

BUILDING SOCIETIES.—Wurtzburg on Building Societies.—The Law relating to Building Societies, with Appendices containing the Statutes, Treasury Regulations, Act of Sederunt, and Precedents of Rules and Assurances. Second Edition. By E. A. WURTZBURG, Esq., Barrister-at-Law. Demy 8vo. 1892. 14*s.*

"The work presents in brief, clear, and convenient form the whole law relating to Building Societies."

"Will be of use not only to lawyers but also to secretaries and directors of building societies. It is a carefully arranged and carefully written book."—*Law Times.*

CANADA.—Munro's Constitution of Canada.—By J. E. C. MUNRO. Demy 8vo. 1889. 10*s.*

CANALS.—Webster's Law Relating to Canals.—By ROBERT G. WEBSTER, M.P., Barrister-at-Law. Demy 8vo. 1885. 1*l.* 1*s.*

Street.—*Vide* "Company Law."

*** ***All standard Law Works are kept in Stock, in law calf and other bindings.***

CARRIERS.—Carver's Treatise on the Law relating to the Carriage of Goods by Sea.—Second Edition. By THOMAS GILBERT CARVER, Esq., Barrister-at-Law. Royal 8vo. 1891. 1*l.* 12*s.*

"A recognized authority."—*Solicitors' Journal.*

"A careful and accurate treatise."—*Law Quarterly Review.*

Macnamara's Digest of the Law of Carriers of Goods and Passengers by Land and Internal Navigation.—By WALTER HENRY MACNAMARA, Barrister-at-Law, Registrar to the Railway Commission. Royal 8vo. 1888. 1*l.* 8*s.*

"A complete *epitome* of the law relating to carriers of every class."—*Railway Press.*

CHAMBER PRACTICE.—Archibald's Practice at Judges' Chambers and in the District Registries in the Queen's Bench Division, High Court of Justice; with Forms of Summonses and Orders. Second Edition. By W. F. A. ARCHIBALD, Esq., Barrister-at-Law, and P. E. VIZARD, of the Summons and Order Department, Royal Courts of Justice. Royal 12mo. 1886. 15*s.*

CHANCERY, *and Vide* "Equity."

Daniell's Chancery Practice.—The Practice of the Chancery Division of the High Court of Justice and on appeal therefrom. Sixth Edit. By L. FIELD, E. C. DUNN, and T. RIBTON, assisted by W. H. UPJOHN, Barristers-at-Law. 2 vols. in 3 parts. Demy 8vo. 1882-84. 6*l.* 6*s.*

Daniell's Forms and Precedents of Proceedings in the Chancery Division of the High Court of Justice and on Appeal therefrom. Fourth Edition. With Summaries of the Rules of the Supreme Court, Practical Notes and References to the Sixth Edition of "Daniell's Chancery Practice." By CHARLES BURNEY, B.A. Oxon., a Chief Clerk of the Hon. Mr. Justice Chitty. Royal 8vo. 1885. 2*l.* 10*s.*

Morgan's Chancery Acts and Orders.—With Copious Notes. Sixth Edition. By the Right Hon. GEORGE OSBORNE MORGAN, Q.C. and E. A. WURTZBURG, Barrister-at-Law. Royal 8vo. 1885. 1*l.* 10*s.*

CHARITABLE TRUSTS.—Mitcheson's Charitable Trusts.—The Jurisdiction of the Charity Commission. By RICHARD EDMUND MITCHESON, Esq., Barrister-at-Law. Demy 8vo. 1887. 18*s.*

CHARTER PARTIES.—Carver.—*Vide* "Carriers." Wood.—*Vide* "Mercantile Law."

CHURCH LAW.—Whitehead's Church Law.—Being a Concise Dictionary of Statutes, Canons, Regulations, and Decided Cases affecting the Clergy and Laity. By BENJAMIN WHITEHEAD, B.A., Esq., Barrister-at-Law. Demy 8vo. 1892. 10*s.* 6*d.*

"A perfect mine of learning on all topics ecclesiastical."—*Daily Telegraph.*

CIVIL ENGINEERS.—Macassey and Strahan's Law relating to Civil Engineers, Architects and Contractors.—Primarily intended for their own use. By L. LIVINGSTON MACASSEY and J. A. STRAHAN, Esqrs., Barristers-at-Law. Demy 8vo. 1890. 10*s.* 6*d.*

COAL MINES.—Chisholm's Manual of the Coal Mines Regulation Act, 1887.—With Introduction, Explanatory and Practical Notes. By JOHN C. CHISHOLM. Demy 8vo. 1888. 7*s.* 6*d.*

COLLISIONS.—Marsden's Treatise on the Law of Collisions at Sea.—With an Appendix containing Extracts from the Merchant Shipping Acts, and the International Regulations. By REGINALD G. MARSDEN, Esq., Barrister-at-Law. Third Edition. By the Author and the Hon. J. W. MANSFIELD, Barrister-at-Law. Demy 8vo. 1891. 1*l.* 5*s.*

"One of the standard books on its subject. It is clear in statement and careful in summarizing the results of decisions."—*Solicitors' Journal.*

*** ***All standard Law Works are kept in Stock, in law calf and other bindings.***

COMMERCIAL LAW.—The French Code of Commerce and most usual Commercial Laws.—By L. GOIRAND, Licencié en droit. Demy 8vo. 1880. 2*l.* 2*s.*

COMMON LAW.—Ball's Short Digest of the Common Law; being the Principles of Torts and Contracts. Chiefly founded upon the Works of Addison, with Illustrative Cases, for the use of Students. By W. EDMUND BALL, LL.B., Barrister-at-Law. Demy 8vo. 1880. 16*s.*

Chitty's Archbold's Practice of the Queen's Bench Division of the High Court of Justice and on Appeal therefrom to the Court of Appeal and House of Lords in Civil Proceedings. Fourteenth Edition. By THOMAS WILLES CHITTY, assisted by J. ST. L. LESLIE, Barristers-at-Law. 2 vols. Demy 8vo. 1885. (Published at 3*l.* 13*s.* 6*d.*) Reduced to *net* 30*s.*

Chitty's Forms.—*Vide* "Forms."

Fisher's Digest of Reported Decisions in all the Courts, with a Selection from the Irish; and references to the Statutes, Rules and Orders of Courts from 1756 to 1883. Compiled and arranged by JOHN MEWS, assisted by C. M. CHAPMAN, HARRY H. W. SPARHAM and A. H. TODD, Barristers-at-Law. In 7 vols. Royal 8vo. 1884. (Published at 12*l.* 12*s.*) Reduced to *net* 5*l.* 5*s.*

Mews' Consolidated Digest of all the Reports in all the Courts, for the years 1884–88, inclusive. By JOHN MEWS, Barrister-at-Law. Royal 8vo. 1889. (Pub. at 1*l.* 11*s.* 6*d.*) Reduced to *net* 15*s.*

The Annual Digest for 1889, 1890, 1891, 1892 and 1893. By JOHN MEWS, Barrister-at-Law. Royal 8vo. *Each*, 15*s.*

☞ The above bring Fisher's Common Law and Chitty's Equity Digests down to end of 1893.

Pollock and Wright's Possession in the Common Law.—Parts I. and II. by F. POLLOCK, Barrister-at-Law. Part III. by R. S. WRIGHT, Barrister-at-Law. Demy 8vo. 1888. 8*s.* 6*d.*

Shirley.—*Vide* "Leading Cases."

Smith's Manual of Common Law.—For Practitioners and Students. Comprising the Fundamental Principles, with useful Practical Rules and Decisions. By JOSIAH W. SMITH, B.C.L., Q.C. Tenth Edition. By J. TRUSTRAM, LL.M., Esq., Barrister-at-Law. 12mo. 1887. 14*s.*

COMMONS.—Scrutton's Commons and Common Fields, or the History and Policy of the Laws relating to Commons and Enclosures in England. By T. E. SCRUTTON, M.A. 1887. 10*s.* 6*d.*

COMPANY LAW.—Hamilton's Manual of Company Law: For Directors and Promoters. By WILLIAM FREDERICK HAMILTON, LL.D. (Lond.), assisted by KENNARD GOLBORNE METCALFE, M.A., Esqrs., Barristers-at-Law. Demy 8vo. 1891. 12*s.* 6*d.*

"The work is executed throughout with great care and accuracy . . . . may be safely recommended as a most useful manual of the law with which it deals."—*Law Gazette.*

Mackenzie, Geare, and Hamilton's Company Law.—An Abridgment of the Law contained in the Statutes and Decisions, Alphabetically Arranged. By M. MUIR MACKENZIE, E. A. GEARE, and G. B. HAMILTON, Esqrs., Barristers-at-Law. Roy. 8vo. 1893. 21*s.*

"Ease of reference is one of the most prominent characteristics of this book, and we have never seen it carried to greater perfection."—*Law Times.*

Palmer's Private Companies and Syndicates, their Formation and Advantages; being a Concise Popular Statement of the Mode of Converting a Business into a Private Company, and of establishing and working Private Companies and Syndicates. Eleventh Edition. By F. B. PALMER, Esq., Barrister-at-Law. 12mo. 1894. 1*s.*

Palmer.—*Vide* "Conveyancing" and "Winding-up."

*** *All standard Law Works are kept in Stock, in law calf and other bindings.*

COMPANY LAW—*continued.*

Palmer's Shareholders, Directors, and Voluntary Liquidators' Legal Companion.—A Manual of Every-day Law and Practice for Promoters, Shareholders, Directors, Secretaries, Creditors, Solicitors, and Voluntary Liquidators of Companies under the Companies Acts, with Appendix of useful Forms. Fourteenth edit. By F. B. PALMER, Esq., Barrister-at-Law. 12mo. 1894. *Net*, 2*s*. 6*d*.

Street's Law relating to Public Statutory Undertakings: comprising Railway Companies, Water, Gas, and Canal Companies, Harbours, Docks, &c., with special reference to Modern Decisions. By J. BAMFIELD STREET, Esq., Barrister-at-Law. Demy 8vo. 1890. 10*s*. 6*d*.

COMPENSATION.—Cripps' Treatise on the Principles of the Law of Compensation. Third Edition. By C. A. CRIPPS, Esq., Q.C. Demy 8vo. 1892. 20*s*.

"An accurate exposition of the law on the subject of compensation."—*Law Journal.*

COMPOSITION DEEDS.—Lawrance.—*Vide* "Bankruptcy."

CONSIDERATION.—Jenks' History of the Doctrine of Consideration.—By EDWARD JENKS, Barrister-at-Law. Post 8vo. 1892. 3*s*. 6*d*.

CONSTITUTION.—Anson's Law and Custom of the Constitution. By Sir WILLIAM R. ANSON, Bart., Barrister-at-Law. Demy 8vo.

Part I. Parliament. Second Edition. 1892. 12*s*. 6*d*.

Part II. The Crown. 1892. 14*s*.

CONTRACT OF SALE.—Moyle's Contract of Sale in the Civil Law. With References to the Laws of England, Scotland, and France. By J. B. MOYLE, Barrister-at-Law. 8vo. 1892. 10*s*. 6*d*.

CONTRACTS.—Addison on Contracts.—A Treatise on the Law of Contracts. 9th Edit. By HORACE SMITH, Esq., Bencher of the Inner Temple, Metropolitan Magistrate, assisted by A. P. PERCEVAL KEEP, Esq., Barrister-at-Law. Royal 8vo. 1892. 2*l*. 10*s*.

"A compendium of the law of contracts which is at once minutely accurate, thoroughly reliable, and exhaustive. . . . No law library is complete without Addison up to date."—*Freeman's Journal.*

"This and the companion treatise on the law of torts are the most complete works on these subjects, and form an almost indispensable part of every lawyer's library."—*Law Journal.*

Anson's Principles of the English Law of Contract.—By Sir WILLIAM R. ANSON, Bart., Barrister-at-Law. Seventh Edit. Demy 8vo. 1893. 10*s*. 6*d*.

Finch's Selection of Cases on the English Law of Contract.—By G. B. FINCH, M.A., Barrister-at-Law. Royal 8vo. 1886. 28*s*.

Fry.—*Vide* "Specific Performance."

Leake's Law of Contracts.—A Digest of Principles of the Law of Contracts. Third Edition. By STEPHEN MARTIN LEAKE, Barrister-at-Law. Demy 8vo. 1892. 32*s*.

"The work is complete, accurate, and easy of reference."—*Solicitors' Journal.*

"Clear, concise, accurate, and exhaustive."—*Law Times.*

Pollock's Principles of Contract.—Being a Treatise on the General Principles relating to the Validity of Agreements in the Law of England. Fifth Edition, with a new Chapter. By Sir FREDERICK POLLOCK, Bart., Barrister-at-Law. Demy 8vo. 1889. 1*l*. 8*s*.

"The reputation of the book stands so high that it is only necessary to announce the publication of the fifth edition, adding that the work has been thoroughly revised."—*aw Journal.*

Smith's Law of Contracts.—Eighth Edition. By V. T. THOMPSON, Esq., Barrister-at-Law. Demy 8vo. 1885. 1*l*. 1*s*.

*** *All standard Law Works are kept in Stock, in law calf and other bindings.*

CONVEYANCING.—Dart.—*Vide* "Vendors and Purchasers."

Greenwood's Manual of Conveyancing.—A Manual of the Practice of Conveyancing, showing the present Practice relating to the daily routine of Conveyancing in Solicitors' Offices. To which are added Concise Common Forms and Precedents in Conveyancing. Eighth Edition. Edited by HARRY GREENWOOD, M.A., LL.D., Esq., Barrister-at-Law. Demy 8vo. 1891. 16*s*.

"A complete guide to Conveyancing. . . . . Where and how the author obtained his information is a perfect puzzle to us, and no conceivable state of affairs seems to have been left unprovided for."—*Law Gazette.*

"We should like to see it placed by his principal in the hands of every articled clerk. One of the most useful practical works we have ever seen."—*Law Students' Journal.*

Morris's Patents Conveyancing.—Being a Collection of Precedents in Conveyancing in relation to Letters Patent for Inventions. Arranged as follows:—Common Forms, Agreements, Assignments, Mortgages, Special Clauses, Licences, Miscellaneous, &c. With Dissertations and Copious Notes on the Law and Practice. By ROBERT MORRIS, M.A., Barrister-at-Law. Royal 8vo. 1887. 1*l*. 5*s*.

"Well selected, well arranged, and thoroughly practical."—*Law Times.*

Palmer's Company Precedents.—For use in relation to Companies subject to the Companies Acts, 1862 to 1890. Arranged as follows:—Promoters, Prospectus, Agreements, Memoranda and Articles of Association, Resolutions, Notices, Certificates, Private Companies, Power of Attorney, Debentures and Debenture Stock, Petitions, Writs, Pleadings, Judgments and Orders, Reconstruction, Amalgamation, Arrangements, Special Acts, Provisional Orders, Winding-up. With Copious Notes and an Appendix containing the Acts and Rules. Fifth Edition. By FRANCIS BEAUFORT PALMER, assisted by CHARLES MACNAGHTEN, Esqrs., Barristers-at-Law. Royal 8vo. 1891. 1*l*. 16*s*.

"No company lawyer can afford to be without it."—*Law Journal.*

"As regards company drafting it is unrivalled."—*Law Times.*

Prideaux's Precedents in Conveyancing—With Dissertations on its Law and Practice. Fifteenth Edition. By JOHN WHITCOMBE, Esq., Barrister-at-Law. 2 vols. Royal 8vo. 1893. 3*l*. 10*s*.

"We have always considered that 'Prideaux' is the best work out on Conveyancing, and after a perusal of the latest edition, we certainly see no reason for altering our opinion."—*Law Journal*, Feb. 4, 1893.

"This work is accurate, concise, clear, and comprehensive in scope, and we know of no treatise upon Conveyancing which is so generally useful to the practitioner."—*Law Times.*

Turner's Duties of Solicitor to Client as to Partnership Agreements, Leases, Settlements, and Wills.—By EDWARD F. TURNER, Solicitor, Lecturer on Real Property and Conveyancing, Author of "The Duties of Solicitor to Client as to Sales, Purchases, and Mortgages of Land." Demy 8vo. 1884. 10*s*. 6*d*.

"The work has our full approval, and will, we think, be found a valuable addition to the student's library."—*Law Students' Journal.*

CONVICTIONS.—Paley.—*Vide* "Summary Convictions."

COPYRIGHT.—Slater's Law relating to Copyright and Trade Marks, treated more particularly with Reference to Infringement. By J. H. SLATER, Esq., Barrister-at-Law. 8vo. 1884. 18*s*.

CORONERS.—Jervis on the Office and Duties of Coroners.—With Forms and Precedents. By R. E. MELSHEIMER, Esq., Barrister-at-Law. Fifth Edition. Post 8vo. 1888. 10*s*. 6*d*.

"The present edition will hold the place of that occupied by its predecessors, and will continue to be the standard work on the subject."—*Law Times.*

*** *All standard Law Works are kept in Stock, in law calf and other bindings.*

CRIMINAL LAW—*continued.*

Roscoe's Digest of the Law of Evidence in Criminal Cases.—Eleventh Edition. By HORACE SMITH and GILBERT GEORGE KENNEDY, Esqrs., Metropolitan Magistrates. Demy 8vo. 1890. 1*l.* 11*s.* 6*d.*

"To the criminal lawyer it is his guide, philosopher and friend. What Roscoe says most judges will accept without question. . . . Every addition has been made necessary to make the digest efficient, accurate, and complete."—*Law Times.*

Russell's Treatise on Crimes and Misdemeanors.—Sixth Edition. By HORACE SMITH, Esq., Metropolitan Police Magistrate. 3 vols. Royal 8vo. (*In the press.*)

Shirley's Sketch of the Criminal Law.—By W. S. SHIRLEY, Esq., Barrister-at-Law. Second Edition. By CHARLES STEPHEN HUNTER, Esq., Barrister-at-Law. Demy 8vo. 1889. 7*s.* 6*d.*

"As a primary introduction to Criminal Law, it will be found very acceptable to students."—*Law Students' Journal.*

Warburton.—*Vide* "Leading Cases." Thring.—*Vide* "Navy."

DECISIONS OF SIR GEORGE JESSEL.—Peter's Analysis and Digest of the Decisions of Sir George Jessel; with Notes, &c. By APSLEY PETRE PETER, Solicitor. Demy 8vo. 1883. 16*s.*

DIARY.—Lawyers' Companion (The) and Diary, and London and Provincial Law and Chartered Accountants' Directory for 1894.—For the use of the Legal Profession, Chartered Accountants, Public Companies, Justices, Merchants, Estate Agents, Auctioneers, &c., &c. Edited by EDWIN LAYMAN, B.A., of the Middle Temple, Esq., Barrister-at-Law; and contains Tables of Costs in the High Court of Judicature and County Court, &c.; Monthly Diary of County, Local Government, and Parish Business; Oaths in Supreme Court; Summary of Statutes of 1893; Alphabetical Index to the Practical Statutes since 1820; the New Schedule of Stamp Duties; Legal Time, Interest, Discount, Income, Wages and other Tables; Probate, Legacy and Succession Duties; and a variety of matters of practical utility: together with a complete List of the English Bar, and London and Country Solicitors, with date of admission and appointments. PUBLISHED ANNUALLY. Forty-eighth Issue. (*Now ready.*)

Issued in the following forms, octavo size, strongly bound in cloth:—

1.	Two days on a page, plain	5*s.*	0*d.*
2.	The above, INTERLEAVED for ATTENDANCES	7	0
3.	Two days on a page, ruled, with or without money columns	5	6
4.	The above, with money columns, INTERLEAVED for ATTENDANCES	8	0
5.	Whole page for each day, plain	7	6
6.	The above, INTERLEAVED for ATTENDANCES	9	6
7.	Whole page for each day, ruled, with or without money columns	8	6
8.	The above, INTERLEAVED for ATTENDANCES	10	6
9.	Three days on a page, ruled blue lines, without money columns	5	0

The Diary contains memoranda of Legal Business throughout the Year.

"Combines everything required for reference in the lawyer's office."—*Law Times.*

"The amount of information packed within the covers of this well-known book of reference is almost incredible. In addition to the Diary, it contains nearly 800 pages of closely printed matter, none of which could be omitted without, perhaps, detracting from the usefulness of the book. The publishers seem to have made it their aim to include in the Companion every item of information which the most exacting lawyer could reasonably expect to find in its pages, and it may safely be said that no practising solicitor, who has experienced the luxury of having it at his elbow, will ever be likely to try to do without it."—*Law Journal.*

*** *All standard Law Works are kept in Stock, in law calf and other bindings.*

DICTIONARY.—The Pocket Law Lexicon.—Explaining Technical Words, Phrases and Maxims of the English, Scotch and Roman Law, to which is added a complete List of Law Reports, with their Abbreviations. Third Edit. By HENRY G. RAWSON and JAMES F. REMNANT, Esqrs., Barristers-at-Law. Fcap. 8vo. 1893. 6s. 6d.

"A wonderful little legal Dictionary."—*Indermaur's Law Students' Journal.*
"A very handy, complete, and useful little work."—*Saturday Review.*

Wharton's Law Lexicon.—Forming an Epitome of the Law of England, and containing full Explanations of the Technical Terms and Phrases thereof, both Ancient and Modern; including the various Legal Terms used in Commercial Business. Together with a Translation of the Latin Law Maxims and selected Titles from the Civil, Scotch and Indian Law. Ninth Edition. By J. M. LELY, Esq., Barrister-at-Law. Super-royal 8vo. 1892. 1*l.* 18*s.*

"On almost every point both student and practitioner can gather information from this invaluable book, which ought to be in every lawyer's office."—*Gibson's Law Notes.*

"One of the first books which every articled clerk and bar student should procure." —*Law Students' Journal.*

DIGESTS.—Campbell's Ruling Cases.—Arranged, Annotated, and Edited by ROBERT CAMPBELL, M.A., of Lincoln's Inn, Barrister-at-Law, Advocate of the Scotch Bar, and Late Fellow of Trinity Hall, Cambridge. Author of "Sale and Agency," &c. Assisted by Colleagues of the Bar. With American Notes by IRVING BROWNE, formerly Editor of the American Reports and the Albany Law Journal. Vol. I. ABANDONMENT—ACTION. Royal 8vo. 1894. (*Nearly ready.*) *Half vellum, net,* 25*s.*

It is intended in this Work to collect and arrange in alphabetical order of subjects the useful authorities of English Case Law on points of general application.

The matter under each alphabetical heading is arranged in sections, in an order indicated at the commencement of the heading. The more important and Ruling Cases are set forth at length, subject only to abridgment where the original report is unnecessarily diffuse. The effect of the less important or subordinate cases is stated briefly in the Notes.

The aim of the Work is to furnish the practitioner with English Case Law in such a form that he will readily find the information he requires for ordinary purposes. The Ruling Case will inform him, or refresh his memory, as to the principles; and the Notes will show in detail how the principles have been applied or modified in other cases.

The American Notes, by Mr. IRVING BROWNE, are intended primarily for American use; but it is also considered that, particularly on some points which have been much discussed in American cases, they may be of considerable value to practitioners here and in the Colonies.

Each volume of the Work will contain an Alphabetical Table of Cases reported or referred to; and when the Work is complete there will be a General Index of Subjects as well as a Table of Cases for the whole.

It is estimated that the Work will be carried out in about 25 Volumes, of the size of an average volume of the "*Law Reports*" (about 800 pages), and issued at the rate of 5 volumes per annum.

☞ **Subscribers for Five Volumes in advance will be entitled to them at £1 per Volume.**

*** *All standard Law Works are kept in Stock, in law calf and other bindings.*

DIGESTS—*continued.*

Chitty's Index to all the Reported Cases decided in the several Courts of Equity in England, the Privy Council, and the House of Lords, with a selection of Irish Cases, on or relating to the Principles, Pleading, and Practice of Equity and Bankruptcy from the earliest period. Fourth Edition. Wholly Revised, Re-classified, and brought down to the End of 1883. By HENRY EDWARD HIRST, Barrister-at-Law. Complete in 9 vols. Roy. 8vo. 1883-89. (Published at 12*l.* 12*s.*) *Reduced to net*, 5*l.* 5*s.*

*** The volumes sold separately. *Each net*, 15*s.*

"A work indispensable to every bookcase in Lincoln's Inn."—*Law Quarterly Review.*

"The practitioner can hardly afford to do without such a weapon as Mr. Hirst supplies, because if he does not use it probably his opponent will."—*Law Journal.*

Dale and Lehmann's Digest of Cases, Overruled, Not Followed, Disapproved, Approved, Distinguished, Commented on and specially considered in the English Courts from the Year 1756 to 1886 inclusive, arranged according to alphabetical order of their subjects; together with Extracts from the Judgments delivered thereon, and a complete Index of the Cases, in which are included all Cases reversed from the year 1856. By CHAS. WM. MITCALFE DALE, and RUDOLF CHAMBERS LEHMANN, assisted by CHAS. H. L. NEISH, and HERBERT H. CHILD, Barristers-at-Law. Royal 8vo. 1887. (Published at 2*l.* 10*s.*) *Reduced to net*, 25*s.*

"One of the best works of reference to be found in any library."—*Law Times.*

"The book is divided into two parts, the first consisting of an alphabetical index of the cases contained in the Digest presented in a tabular form, showing at a glance how, where, and by what judges they have been considered. The second portion of the book comprises the Digest itself, and bears marks of the great labour and research bestowed upon it by the compilers."—*Law Journal.*

Fisher's Digest of the Reported Decisions of the Courts of Common Law, Bankruptcy, Probate, Admiralty, and Divorce, together with a Selection from those of the Court of Chancery and Irish Courts from 1756 to 1883 inclusive. Founded on Fisher's Digest. By J. MEWS, assisted by C. M. CHAPMAN, H. H. W. SPARHAM, and A. H. TODD, Barristers-at-Law. 7 vols. Roy. 8vo. 1884. (Published at 12*l.* 12*s.*) *Reduced to net*, 5*l.* 5*s.*

"To the common lawyer it is the most useful work he can possess."—*Law Times.*

Mews' Consolidated Digest of all the Reports in all the Courts, for the Years 1884–88 inclusive.—By JOHN MEWS, Barrister-at-Law. Royal 8vo. 1889. (Published at 1*l.* 11*s.* 6*d.*) *Reduced to net*, 15*s.*

"This work is an indispensable companion to the new edition of Chitty's Digest, which ends with 1883, and also Fisher's Digest ending with the same year. . . . . The work appears to us to be exceedingly well done."—*Solicitors' Journal.*

Or the whole of these Digests, together 18 Volumes, net £10.

The Annual Digest for 1889, 1890, 1891, 1892, and 1893. By JOHN MEWS, Barrister-at-Law. Royal 8vo. *Each*, 15*s.*

*** The above bring Fisher's Common Law and Chitty's Equity Digests down to end of 1893.

Talbot and Fort's Index of Cases Judicially noticed (1865—1890); being a List of all Cases cited in Judgments reported in the "Law Reports," "Law Journal," "Law Times," and "Weekly Reporter," from Michaelmas Term, 1865 to the end of 1890, with the places where they are so cited.—By GEORGE JOHN TALBOT and HUGH FORT, Barristers-at-Law. Royal 8vo. 1891. 25*s.*

"This is an invaluable tool for the worker among cases. . . . The way in which the tool is to be used is this, you find a case that appears to decide the question you have in hand, but you want to know whether it has been subsequently judicially questioned or confirmed. You turn to the name of the case, given in large type in this work, and you find following it in smaller type the names, references to reports, and dates of every reported case since 1865 in the judgments of which it has been in any way noticed."—*Solicitors' Journal.*

*** ***All standard Law Works are kept in Stock, in law calf and other bindings.***

DISCOVERY.—Sichel and Chance's Discovery.—The Law relating to Interrogatories, Production, Inspection of Documents, and Discovery, as well in the Superior as in the Inferior Courts, together with an Appendix of the Acts, Forms and Orders. By WALTER S. SICHEL, and WILLIAM CHANCE, Esqrs., Barristers-at-Law. Demy 8vo. 1883. 12*s.*

DISTRESS.—Oldham and Foster on the Law of Distress.—A Treatise on the Law of Distress, with an Appendix of Forms, Table of Statutes, &c. Second Edition. By ARTHUR OLDHAM and A. LA TROBE FOSTER, Esqrs., Barristers-at-Law. Demy 8vo. 1889. 18*s.*

"This is a useful book, because it embraces the whole range of the remedy by distress, not merely distress for rent, but also for *damage feasant*, tithes, poor and highway rates and taxes, and many other matters."—*Solicitors' Journal.*

DIVORCE.—Browne and Powles' Law and Practice in Divorce and Matrimonial Causes. Fifth Edition. By L. D. POWLES, Esq., Barrister-at-Law. Demy 8vo. 1889. 1*l.* 6*s.*

"The practitioner's standard work on divorce practice."—*Law Quarterly Review.*

DOGS.—Lupton's Law relating to Dogs.—By FREDERICK LUPTON, Solicitor. Royal 12mo. 1888. 5*s.*

"Within the pages of this work the reader will find every subject connected with the law relating to dogs touched upon."—*Law Times.*

EASEMENTS.—Goddard's Treatise on the Law of Easements.—By JOHN LEYBOURN GODDARD, Esq., Barrister-at-Law. Fourth Edition. Demy 8vo. 1891. 1*l.* 1*s.*

"Nowhere has the subject been treated so exhaustively, and, we may add, so scientifically, as by Mr. Goddard. We recommend it to the most careful study of the law student, as well as to the library of the practitioner."—*Law Times.*

Innes' Digest of the Law of Easements. Fourth Edition. By L. C. INNES, lately one of the Judges of Her Majesty's High Court of Judicature, Madras. Royal 12mo. 1893. 7*s.* 6*d.*

"Constructed with considerable care and pains."—*Law Journal.*

EASTERN QUESTION.—Holland's European Concert in the Eastern Question.—A Collection of Treaties and other Public Acts. Edited, with Introductions and Notes, by T. E. HOLLAND, D.C.L. 8vo. 1885. 12*s.* 6*d.*

ECCLESIASTICAL LAW.—Phillimore's Ecclesiastical Law of the Church of England. With Supplement. By the Right. Hon. Sir ROBERT PHILLIMORE, D.C.L. 2 vols. 8vo. 1873-76. (Published at 3*l.* 7*s.* 6*d.*) *Reduced to net,* 1*l.* 10*s.*

Whitehead.—*Vide* "Church Law."

ELECTION IN EQUITY.—Serrell's Equitable Doctrine of Election. By GEORGE SERRELL, M.A., LL.D., Esq., Barrister-at-Law. Royal 12mo. 1891. 7*s.* 6*d.*

"The work is well executed, and will be of service to all who desire to master the doctrine of election."—*Law Journal.*

ELECTIONS.—Day's Election Cases in 1892 and 1893.—Being a Collection of the Points of Law and Practice arising out of the Parliamentary Election Petitions in those Years, together with Reports of the Judgments. By S. H. DAY, Esq., Barrister-at-Law, Editor of "Rogers on Elections," Part II. 16th Edit. Royal 12mo. 1893. 7*s.* 6*d.*

Hedderwick's Parliamentary Election Manual: A Practical Handbook on the Law and Conduct of Parliamentary Elections in Great Britain and Ireland, designed for the Instruction and Guidance of Candidates, Election Agents, Sub-Agents, Polling and Counting Agents, Canvassers, Volunteer Assistants, and Members of Political Clubs and Associations. By T. C. H. HEDDERWICK, Esq., Barrister-at-Law. Demy 12mo. 1892. 7*s.* 6*d.*

"Clear and well arranged."—*Law Quarterly Review.*

*** *All standard Law Works are kept in Stock, in law calf and other bindings.*

ELECTIONS—*continued.*

Rogers on Elections.—In two parts.

Part I. REGISTRATION, including the Practice in Registration Appeals; Parliamentary, Municipal, and Local Government; with Appendices of Statutes, Orders in Council, and Forms. Fifteenth Edition. By MAURICE POWELL, Esq., Barrister-at-Law. Royal 12mo. 1890. 1*l.* 1*s.*

"The practitioner will find within these covers everything which he can be expected to know, well arranged and carefully stated."—*Law Times.*

Part II. ELECTIONS AND PETITIONS. Parliamentary, Municipal, and Local Government, with Appendix of Statutes and Forms. Sixteenth Edition. By SAMUEL H. DAY, Esq., Barrister-at-Law. Royal 12mo. 1892. 1*l.* 1*s.*

"The leading book on the difficult subjects of elections and election petitions."—*Law Times*, April 9, 1892.

"A very satisfactory treatise on election law . . . . well arranged, and tersely expressed."—*Solicitors' Journal.*

ELECTRIC LIGHTING.—Bazalgette and Humphreys.—*Vide* "Local and Municipal Government."

Cunynghame's Treatise on the Law of Electric Lighting, with the Acts, Rules and Orders, a Model Provisional Order, and Forms. By HENRY CUNYNGHAME, Barrister-at-Law. Royal 8vo. 1883. 12*s.* 6*d.*

ELEMENTS OF LAW.—Markby's Elements of Law.—Fourth Edition. Demy 8vo. 1889. 12*s.* 6*d.*

EQUITY, *and Vide* CHANCERY.

Chitty's Index.—*Vide* "Digests."

Kerly's Historical Sketch of the Equitable Jurisdiction of the Court of Chancery.—Being the Yorke Prize Essay for 1889. By D. M. KERLY, M.A., St. John's College. Demy 8vo. 1890. 12*s.* 6*d.*

Mews' Digest.—*Vide* "Digests."

Serrell.—*Vide* "Election in Equity."

Seton's Forms of Judgments and Orders in the High Court of Justice and in the Court of Appeal, having especial reference to the Chancery Division, with Practical Notes. Fifth Edition. By CECIL C. M. DALE, Esq., Barrister-at-Law, and W. CLOWES, Esq., a Registrar of the Supreme Court of Judicature. In 3 vols. Royal 8vo. 1891—3. 6*l.*

*** The Volumes sold separately, 2*l.* each.

"A monument of learned and laborious accuracy."—*Law Quarterly Review.*

"We have no fault to find with the treatment of either editor. Seton in its new guise is well up to the character which it has for so many years sustained of being the best book of forms of judgment which is known on the north side of the Strand."—*Law Times.*

Smith's Manual of Equity Jurisprudence.—A Manual of Equity Jurisprudence for Practitioners and Students, founded on the Works of Story, Spence, and other writers, comprising the Fundamental Principles and the points of Equity usually occurring in General Practice. By JOSIAH W. SMITH, Q.C. Fourteenth Edition. By J. TRUSTRAM, LL.M., Esq., Barrister-at-Law. 12mo. 1889. 12*s.* 6*d.*

"Still holds its own as the most popular first book of equity jurisprudence, and one which every student must of necessity read."—*Law Journal.*

Smith's Practical Exposition of the Principles of Equity, illustrated by the Leading Decisions thereon. For the use of Students and Practitioners. Second Edition. By H. ARTHUR SMITH, M.A., LL.B., Esq., Barrister-at-Law. Demy 8vo. 1888. 21*s.*

"This excellent practical exposition of the principles of equity is a work one can well recommend to students either for the bar or the examinations of the Incorporated Law Society. It will also be found equally valuable to the busy practitioner. It contains a mass of information well arranged, and is illustrated by all the leading decisions."—*Law Times.*

*** *All standard Law Works are kept in Stock, in law calf and other bindings.*

ESTOPPEL.—Everest and Strode's Law of Estoppel. By LANCELOT FIELDING EVEREST, and EDMUND STRODE, Esqrs., Barristers-at-Law. Demy 8vo. 1884. 18*s.*

"A useful repository of the case law on the subject."—*Law Journal.*

EXAMINATION GUIDES.—Bedford's Digest of the Preliminary Examination Questions in Latin Grammar, Arithmetic, French Grammar, History and Geography, with the Answers. Second Edition. Demy 8vo. 1882. 18*s.*

Haynes and Nelham's Honours Examination Digest, comprising all the Questions in Conveyancing, Equity, Common Law, Bankruptcy, Probate, Divorce, Admiralty, and Ecclesiastical Law and Practice asked at the Solicitors' Honours Examinations, with Answers thereto. By JOHN F. HAYNES, LL.D., and THOMAS A. NELHAM, Solicitor (Honours). Demy 8vo. 1883. 15*s.*

"Students going in for honours will find this one to their advantage."—*Law Times.*

Napier & Stephenson's Digest of the Subjects of Probate, Divorce, Bankruptcy, Admiralty, Ecclesiastical and Criminal Law necessary to be known for the Final Examination, done into Questions and Answers. With a Preliminary Chapter on a Course of Study for the above Subjects. By T. BATEMAN NAPIER and RICHARD M. STEPHENSON, Esqrs., Barristers-at-Law. Demy 8vo. 1888. 12*s.*

Napier & Stephenson's Digest of the Leading Points in the Subject of Criminal Law necessary to be known for Bar and University Law Examinations. Done into Questions and Answers. By T. BATEMAN NAPIER and RICHARD M. STEPHENSON, Esqrs., Barristers-at-Law. Demy 8vo. 1888. 5*s.*

Shearwood's Guide for Candidates for the Professions of Barrister and Solicitor.—Second Edition. By JOSEPH A. SHEARWOOD, Esq., Barrister-at-Law. Demy 8vo. 1887. 6*s.*

"A practical little book for students."—*Law Quarterly Review.*

Uttley's How to Become a Solicitor; or, Hints for Articled Clerks.—Showing the necessary steps for getting Articled, passing the Examinations, obtaining Admission, taking out Certificate to Practise; Hints on Reading, Tables of Cases, Statutes and Books; Articled Clerks in the Law Courts: Notes of recent Cases affecting them; with Appendix, comprising many useful Forms and all the Questions set at all the Examinations of 1893. By T. F. UTTLEY, Solicitor. Royal 12mo. 1894. 5*s.*

EXECUTIONS.—Edwards' Law of Execution upon Judgments and Orders of the Chancery and Queen's Bench Divisions of the High Court of Justice.—By C. JOHNSTON EDWARDS, Esq., Barrister-at-Law. Demy 8vo. 1888. 16*s.*

"Very useful, especially to solicitors. . . . In addition to the other good points in this book, it contains a copious collection of forms and a good index."—*Solicitors' Journal.*

EXECUTORS.—Macaskie's Treatise on the Law of Executors and Administrators, and of the Administration of the Estates of Deceased Persons. With an Appendix of Statutes and Forms. By S. C. MACASKIE, Esq., Barrister-at-Law. 8vo. 1881. 10*s.* 6*d.*

Williams' Law of Executors and Administrators.—Ninth Edition. By the Hon. Sir ROLAND VAUGHAN WILLIAMS, a Justice of the High Court. 2 vols. Roy. 8vo. 1893. 3*l.* 16*s.*

"We can conscientiously say that the present edition will not only sustain, but enhance the high reputation which the book has always enjoyed. The want of a new edition has been distinctly felt for some time, and in this work, and in this work only, will the practitioner now find the entire law relating to executors and administrators treated in an exhaustive and authoritative fashion, and thoroughly brought down to the present date."—*Law Journal*, Dec. 9, 1893.

*** *All standard Law Works are kept in Stock, in law calf and other bindings.*

EXTRADITION.—Kirchner's L'Extradition.—Recueil Renfermant in Extenso tous les Traités conclus jusqu'au ler Janvier, 1883, entre les Nations civilisées, et donnant la solution précise des difficultés qui peuvent surgir dans leur application. Avec une Préface de Me GEORGES LACHAUD, Avocat à la Cour d'Appel de Paris. Publié sous les auspices de M. C. E. HOWARD VINCENT, Directeur des Affaires Criminelles de la Police Métropolitaine de Londres. Par F. J. KIRCHNER, Attaché à la Direction des Affaires Criminelles. In 1 vol. (1150 pp.). Royal 8vo. 1883. 2*l.* 2*s.*

FARM, LAW OF.—Dixon's Law of the Farm: including the Cases and Statutes relating to the subject; and the Agricultural Customs of England and Wales; together with the Small Holdings Act, 1892. Fifth Edition. By AUBREY J. SPENCER, Esq., Barrister-at-Law. Demy 8vo. 1892. 26*s.*

"The book is well and carefully edited."—*Law Journal.*
"A complete modern compendium on agricultural matters."—*Law Times.*

FIXTURES.—Amos and Ferard on the Law of Fixtures and other Property partaking both of a Real and Personal Nature. Third Edition. By C. A. FERARD and W. HOWLAND ROBERTS, Esqrs., Barristers-at-Law. Demy 8vo. 1883. 18*s.*

"An accurate and well written work."—*Saturday Review.*

FORMS.—Archibald.—*Vide* "Chamber Practice."

Bullen and Leake.—*Vide* "Pleading."

Chitty's Forms of Practical Proceedings in the Queen's Bench Division of the High Court of Justice. Twelfth Edition. By T. W. CHITTY, Esq., Barrister-at-Law. Demy 8vo. 1883. (Published at 1*l.* 18*s.*) Reduced to *net* 20*s.*

"Brief and clear, and the notes accurate and to the point."—*Law Journal.*

Daniell's Forms and Precedents of Proceedings in the Chancery Division of the High Court of Justice and on Appeal therefrom.—Fourth Edition, with Summaries of the Rules of the Supreme Court, Practical Notes and References to the Sixth Edition of "Daniell's Chancery Practice." By CHARLES BURNEY, B.A. (Oxon.), a Chief Clerk of the Hon. Mr. Justice Chitty. Royal 8vo. 1885. 2*l.* 10*s.*

"The standard work on Chancery Procedure."—*Law Quarterly Review.*

FRAUD AND MISREPRESENTATION.—Moncreiff's Treatise on the Law relating to Fraud and Misrepresentation.—By the Hon. F. MONCREIFF, Barrister-at-Law. 8vo. 1891. 21*s.*

"The task which Mr. Moncreiff has undertaken has been handled carefully and with considerable ability, and the work will well repay perusal."—*Solicitors' Journal.*

GOODWILL.—Allan's Law relating to Goodwill.—By CHARLES E. ALLAN, M.A., LL.B., Esq., Barrister-at-Law. Demy 8vo. 1889. 7*s.* 6*d.*

"A work of much value."—*Solicitors' Journal.*

HIGHWAYS.—Bazalgette and Humphreys.—*Vide* "Local and Municipal Government."

Chambers' Law relating to Highways and Bridges, being the Statutes in full and brief Notes of 700 Leading Cases. By GEORGE F. CHAMBERS, Esq., Barrister-at-Law. 1878. 7*s.* 6*d.*

HOUSE OF LORDS SCOTCH APPEALS.—Paterson's Reports of Scotch Appeals in the House of Lords, A.D. 1851 to 1873.—By J. PATERSON, Barrister-at-Law. 2 vols. Roy. 8vo. 1879. 5*l.* 5*s.*

HOUSE TAX.—Ellis' Guide to the House Tax Acts, for the use of the Payer of Inhabited House Duty in England.—By ARTHUR M. ELLIS, LL.B. (Lond.), Solicitor, Author of "A Guide to the Income Tax Acts." Royal 12mo. 1885. 6*s.*

"We have found the information accurate, complete and very clearly expressed."—*Solicitors' Journal.*

*** *All standard Law Works are kept in Stock, in law calf and other bindings.*

HUSBAND AND WIFE.—Lush's Law of Husband and Wife; within the Jurisdiction of the Queen's Bench and Chancery Divisions. By C. MONTAGUE LUSH, Esq., Barrister-at-Law. 8vo. 1884. 20*s.*
"Mr. Lush has one thing to recommend him most strongly, and that is his accuracy." —*Law Magazine.*

INCOME TAX.—Ellis' Guide to the Income Tax Acts.—For the use of the English Income Tax Payer. Third Edition. By ARTHUR M. ELLIS, LL.B. (Lond.), Solicitor. Royal 12mo. 1893. 7*s.* 6*d.*
"Contains in a convenient form the law bearing upon the Income Tax."—*Law Times.*

INDIAN LAW.—Wilson's Tables showing the Differences between English and Indian Law.—By Sir ROLAND KNYVET WILSON, Bart., M.A., LL.M. Demy 4to. 1890. *net,* 1*s.*

INLAND REVENUE CASES.—Highmore's Summary Proceedings in Inland Revenue Cases in England and Wales.—Second Edition. By N. J. HIGHMORE, Esq., Barrister-at-Law, and of the Solicitors' Department, Inland Revenue. Roy. 12mo. 1887. 7*s.* 6*d.*
"Is very complete. Every possible information is given."—*Law Times.*

INSURANCE.—Arnould on the Law of Marine Insurance.—Sixth Edition. By DAVID MACLACHLAN, Esq., Barrister-at-Law. 2 vols. Royal 8vo. 1887. 3*l.*
"As a text book, 'Arnould' is now all the practitioner can want."—*Law Times.*

Lowndes' Practical Treatise on the Law of Marine Insurance.—By RICHARD LOWNDES. Author of "The Law of General Average," &c. Third Edition. Demy 8vo. (*In preparation.*)

McArthur on the Contract of Marine Insurance.—Second Edition. By CHARLES MCARTHUR, Average Adjuster. Demy 8vo. 1890. 16*s.*
"The work is carefully executed and brought down to date."—*Law Journal.*

INTERNATIONAL LAW.—Hall's International Law.—Third Edit. Demy 8vo. 1890. 1*l.* 2*s.* 6*d.*

Kent's International Law.—Kent's Commentary on International Law. Edited by J. T. ABDY, LL.D., Judge of County Courts. Second Edition. Crown 8vo. 1878. 10*s.* 6*d.*

Nelson's Private International Law.—Selected Cases, Statutes, and Orders illustrative of the Principles of Private International Law as Administered in England, with Commentary. By HORACE NELSON, M.A., B.C.L., Barrister-at-Law. Roy. 8vo. 1889. 21*s.*
"The notes are full of matter, and avoid the vice of discursiveness, cases being cited for practically every proposition."—*Law Times.*

Twiss's Law of Nations considered as Independent Political Communities.—By Sir TRAVERS TWISS, D.C.L. Part I.: On the Rights and Duties of Nations in Time of Peace. New Edition. Revised and Enlarged. 8vo. 1884. 15*s.*

Walker's Science of International Law.—By T. A. WALKER, M.A., LL.M., of the Middle Temple. Demy 8vo. 1893. 18*s.*

Westlake's International Law.—An Introductory Lecture, delivered 17th October, 1888, in the University of Cambridge, by J. WESTLAKE, Q.C., LL.D., Whewell Professor. Demy 8vo. 1888. *net,* 1*s.*

Wheaton's Elements of International Law; Third English Edition. Edited with Notes and Appendix of Statutes and Treaties. By A. C. BOYD, Esq., Barrister-at-Law. Royal 8vo. 1889. 1*l.* 10*s.*
"Wheaton stands too high for criticism, whilst Mr. Boyd's merits as an editor are almost as well established."—*Law Times.*

*** *All standard Law Works are kept in Stock, in law calf and other bindings.*

JOINT STOCKS.—Palmer.—*Vide* "Company Law," "Conveyancing," and "Winding-up."

Thring's Joint Stock Companies' Law.—The Law and Practice of Joint Stock and other Companies, including the Companies Acts, 1862 to 1886, with Notes, Orders, and Rules in Chancery, a Collection of Precedents of Memoranda and Articles of Association, and other Forms required in Making and Administering a Company. By LORD THRING, K.C.B., formerly the Parliamentary Counsel. Fifth Edition. By J. M. RENDEL, Esq., Barrister-at-Law. Royal 8vo. 1889. 1*l*. 10*s*.

JUDGES' CHAMBERS.—Archibald.—*Vide* "Chamber Practice."

JUDICATURE ACTS.—Wilson's Practice of the Supreme Court of Judicature: containing the Acts, Orders, Rules, and Regulations relating to the Supreme Court. With Practical Notes. Seventh Edition. By CHARLES BURNEY, a Chief Clerk of the Hon. Mr. Justice Chitty, Editor of "Daniell's Chancery Forms;" M. MUIR MACKENZIE, and C. A. WHITE, Esqrs., Barristers-at-Law. Roy. 8vo. 1888. 1*l*.

JURISPRUDENCE.—Clark's Practical Jurisprudence. A Comment on AUSTIN. By E. C. CLARK, LL.D. Crown 8vo. 1883. 9*s*.

Holland's Elements of Jurisprudence.—Sixth Edition. By T. E. HOLLAND, D.C.L. Demy 8vo. 1893. 10*s*. 6*d*.

JUSTICE OF THE PEACE.—Stone's Practice for Justices of the Peace, Justices' Clerks and Solicitors at Petty and Special Sessions, in Summary matters, and Indictable Offences, with a list of Summary Convictions, and matters not Criminal. With Forms. Ninth Edit. By W. H. MACNAMARA, Esq., Barrister-at-Law. Demy 8vo. 1882. 1*l*. 5*s*.

Wigram's Justice's Note Book.—Containing the Jurisdiction and Duties of Justices, and an Epitome of Criminal Law. By the late W. KNOX WIGRAM, Esq., Barrister-at-Law, J. P. Middlesex and Westminster. Sixth Edition. By ARCHIBALD HENRY BODKIN, Esq., Barrister-at-Law. Royal 12mo. 1892. 12*s*. 6*d*.

"The style is clear, and the expression always forcible, and sometimes humorous. The book will repay perusal by many besides those who, as justices, will find it an indispensable companion."—*Law Quarterly Review.*

"We can thoroughly recommend the volume to magistrates."—*Law Times.*

Magistrates' Cases, 1893.—Cases relating to the Poor Law, the Criminal Law, Licensing, and other subjects chiefly connected with the duties and office of Magistrates, decided in the House of Lords, the Court of Appeal, the Queen's Bench Division, and in the Court for Crown Cases Reserved, from Michaelmas, 1892, to Michaelmas, 1893. 1 vol. 4to. 1894. 1*l*.

These Reports, which have hitherto been published as part of the Law Journal Reports Series only, will in future be published Quarterly, in response to a large demand by Magistrates and others for an authoritative Series of Reports. *Net* 5*s*.

Subscription per annum, payable in advance, 15*s*. *post free.*

LAND TAX.—Bourdin's Land Tax.—An Exposition of the Land Tax. Including the Latest Judicial Decisions, and the Changes in the Law effected by the Taxes Management Act, and by the Act Converting the Three per Cent. into Two and Three-quarter per Cent. Stock, with other Additional Matter. Fourth Edition. Revised and corrected, to which has been added a New and Exhaustive Index, by the late FREDERICK HUMPHREYS, Deputy Registrar of Land Tax; and Digests of Cases decided in the Courts by CHARLES C. ATCHISON, Deputy Registrar of Land Tax. Royal 12mo. 1894. 7*s*. 6*d*.

**** All standard Law Works are kept in Stock, in law calf and other bindings.*

LAND TENURE.—Baden-Powell's Land-Systems of British India. —By B. H. BADEN-POWELL. 3 vols. 8vo. 1892. With Maps. 3*l*. 3*s*.

Montgomery's History of Land Tenure in Ireland.—By W. E. MONTGOMERY, M.A., LL.M. Demy 8vo. 1889. 10*s*. 6*d*.

LANDLORD AND TENANT.—Woodfall's Law of Landlord and Tenant.—With a full Collection of Precedents and Forms of Procedure; containing also a collection of Leading Propositions. Fifteenth Ed. By J. M. LELY, Esq., Barrister-at-Law. Roy. 8vo. 1893. 1*l*. 18*s*.

"The editor has expended elaborate industry and systematic ability in making the work as perfect as possible."—*Solicitors' Journal.*

Lely and Peck.—*Vide* "Leases."

LANDS CLAUSES ACTS.—Jepson's Lands Clauses Consolidation Acts; with Decisions, Forms, and Table of Costs. By ARTHUR JEPSON, Esq., Barrister-at-Law. Demy 8vo. 1880. 18*s*.

LAW LIST.—Law List (The).—Comprising the Judges and Officers of the different Courts of Justice, Counsel, Special Pleaders, Conveyancers, Solicitors, Proctors, Notaries, &c., in England and Wales; the Circuits, Judges, Treasurers, Registrars, and High Bailiffs of the County Courts; Metropolitan and Stipendiary Magistrates, Official Receivers under the Bankruptcy Act, Law and Public Officers in England and the Colonies, Foreign Lawyers with their English Agents, Clerks of the Peace, Town Clerks, Coroners, Chartered Accountants in England and Wales, &c., &c., and Commissioners for taking Oaths, Conveyancers Practising in England under Certificates obtained in Scotland. Compiled, so far as relates to Special Pleaders, Conveyancers, Solicitors, Proctors and Notaries, by JOHN SAMUEL PURCELL, C.B., Controller of Stamps, and Registrar of Joint Stock Companies, Somerset House, and Published by the Authority of the Commissioners of Inland Revenue. 1893. (*Net cash*, 9*s*.) 10*s*. 6*d*.

LAW QUARTERLY REVIEW—Edited by Sir FREDERICK POLLOCK, Bart., M.A., LL.D., Corpus Professor of Jurisprudence in the University of Oxford. Vols. I.—IX. Royal 8vo. 1885-93. *Each*, 12*s*.

☞ *Subscription for* 1894 *post free* 12*s*. 6*d*. *Single numbers, each* 5*s*.

The Review includes:—The discussion of current decisions of importance in the Courts of this country, and (so far as practicable) of the Colonies, the United States, British India, and other British Possessions where the Common Law is administered; the consideration of topics of proposed legislation before Parliament; the treatment of questions of immediate political and social interest in their legal aspect. Endeavour is also made to take account of the legal science and legislation of Continental States in so far as they bear on general jurisprudence, or may throw light by comparison upon problems of English or American legislation. The current legal literature of our own country receives careful attention.

"The greatest of legal quarterly reviews . . . the series of 'Notes' always so entertaining and illustrative, not merely of the learning of the accomplished jurist (the Editor) but of the grace of language with which such learning can be unfolded."—*Law Journal.*

LAWYER'S ANNUAL LIBRARY.—(1) The Annual Practice.—SNOW, BURNEY, and STRINGER. (2) The Annual Digest.—MEWS. (3) The Annual Statutes.—LELY. (4) The Annual County Court Practice.—HEYWOOD.

Annual prepaid Subscription for the Complete Series, as above, delivered on the day of publication, *net*, 2*l*., or carriage free, 2*l*. 2*s*.

Nos. 1, 2, and 3 only, *net*, 1*l*. 10*s*., or carriage free, 1*l*. 12*s*.

Nos. 2, 3, and 4 only, *net*, 1*l*. 10*s*., or carriage free, 1*l*. 12*s*.

☞ *Subscriptions payable on or before August* 31*st in each year.*

LAWYER'S COMPANION.—*Vide* "Diary."

*** *All standard Law Works are kept in Stock, in law calf and other bindings.*

LEADING CASES.—Ball's Leading Cases. *Vide* "Torts."

Haynes' Student's Leading Cases.—In Constitutional Law, Common Law, Conveyancing and Equity, Probate, Divorce, and Criminal Law. With Notes. Second Edition. By JOHN F. HAYNES, LL.D. Demy 8vo. 1884. 16*s.*

Shirley's Selection of Leading Cases in the Common Law. With Notes. By W. S. SHIRLEY, Esq., Barrister-at-Law. Fourth Edition. By RICHARD WATSON, Esq., Barrister-at-Law. Demy 8vo. 1891. 16*s.*

"A sound knowledge of common law can be gleaned from Shirley."—*Law Notes.*

"The present editor has done his work with great care, and large additions have been made to the cases."—*Law Journal.*

Warburton's Selection of Leading Cases in the Criminal Law. With Notes. By HENRY WARBURTON, Esq., Barrister-at-Law. [Founded on "Shirley's Leading Cases."] Demy 8vo. 1892. 9*s.*

"The cases have been well selected, and arranged. . . . We consider that it will amply repay the student or the practitioner to read both the cases and the notes."—*Justice of the Peace*, Feb. 6, 1892.

LEASES.—Lely and Peck's Precedents of Leases for Years, and other Contracts of Tenancy, and Contracts relating thereto; mainly selected or adapted from existing Collections, including many additional Forms, with a short Introduction and Notes. By J. M. LELY and W. A. PECK, Barristers-at-Law. Royal 8vo. 1889. 10*s.* 6*d.*

"Varied, well considered, and thoroughly practical."—*Law Times.*

LEXICON.—*Vide* "Dictionary."

LIBEL AND SLANDER.—Odgers on Libel and Slander.—A Digest of the Law of Libel and Slander: the Evidence, Procedure and Practice, both in Civil and Criminal Cases, and Precedents of Pleadings. Second Edition, with a SUPPLEMENT, bringing the Law down to June, 1890. By W. BLAKE ODGERS, LL.D., one of Her Majesty's Counsel. Royal 8vo. 1890. 1*l.* 12*s.*

"The best modern book on the law of libel."—*Daily News.*

LIBRARIES AND MUSEUMS.—Chambers' Digest of the Law relating to Public Libraries and Museums, and Literary and Scientific Institutions: with much Practical Information. 3rd Edit. By GEO. F. CHAMBERS, Esq., Barrister-at-Law. Roy. 8vo. 1889. 8*s.* 6*d.*

LICENSING.—Lely and Foulkes' Licensing Acts, 1828, 1869, and 1872—1874; with Notes to the Acts, a Summary of the Law, and an Appendix of Forms. Third Edition. By J. M. LELY and W. D. I. FOULKES, Esqrs., Barristers-at-Law. Roy. 12mo. 1887. 10*s.* 6*d.*

LOCAL AND MUNICIPAL GOVERNMENT.—Bazalgette and Humphreys' Law relating to County Councils.—Third Edition. By GEORGE HUMPHREYS, Esq. Royal 8vo. 1889. 7*s.* 6*d.*

"The most stately as regards size, and the best in point of type of all the works. There is a good introduction . . . the notes are careful and helpful."—*Solicitors' Journal.*

Bazalgette and Humphreys' Law relating to Local and Municipal Government. Comprising the Statutes relating to Public Health, Municipal Corporations, Highways, Burial, Gas and Water, Public Loans, Compulsory Taking of Lands, Tramways, Electric Lighting, &c., with a Table of upwards of 2,500 Cases, and full Index. With Addenda containing the Judicial Decisions and Legislation relating to Local and Municipal Government since 1885. By C. NORMAN BAZALGETTE and GEORGE HUMPHREYS, Esqrs., Barristers-at-Law. Sup. royal 8vo. 1888. 3*l.* 3*s.*

"Thoroughly comprehensive of the law on all points."—*Law Journal.*

"The work is one that no local officer should be without; for nothing short of a whole library of statutes, reports, and handbooks could take its place."—*Municipal Review.*

*** *All standard Law Works are kept in Stock, in law calf and other bindings.*

LOCAL AND MUNICIPAL GOVERNMENT—*continued.*

Chambers' Popular Summary of the Law relating to Local Government, forming a complete Guide to the new Act of 1888. Second Edition. By G. F. Chambers, Barrister-at-Law. Imp. 8vo. 1888. (*Or bound in Cloth with copy of Act*, 5s. 6*d*.) *Net*, 2s. 6*d*.

Humphreys.—*Vide* "Parish Law."

LUNACY.—Elmer's Practice in Lunacy.—Seventh Edition. By Joseph Elmer, Esq., late of the Office of the Masters in Lunacy. Demy 8vo. 1892. 21*s*.

"It is natural for those accustomed to 'Elmer' to find it as carefully compiled and lucidly arranged as ever."—*Law Quarterly Review.*

MAGISTERIAL LAW.—Shirley's Elementary Treatise on Magisterial Law, and on the Practice of Magistrates' Courts.—By W. S. Shirley, Esq., Barrister-at-Law. Roy. 12mo. 1881. 6*s*. 6*d*.

Wigram.—*Vide* "Justice of the Peace."

MALICIOUS PROSECUTIONS.—Stephen's Law relating to Actions for Malicious Prosecutions.—By Herbert Stephen, LL.M., Barrister-at-Law. Royal 12mo. 1888. 6*s*.

MARINE INSURANCE.—*Vide* "Insurance."

MARITIME DECISIONS.—Douglas' Maritime Law Decisions.—Compiled by Robt. R. Douglas. Demy 8vo. 1888. 7*s*. 6*d*.

MARRIED WOMEN'S PROPERTY.—Lush's Married Women's Rights and Liabilities in relation to Contracts, Torts, and Trusts. By Montague Lush, Esq., Barrister-at-Law, Author of "The Law of Husband and Wife." Royal 12mo. 1887. 5*s*.

"Well arranged, clearly written, and has a good index."—*Law Times.*

Smith's Married Women's Property Acts, 1882 and 1884, with an Introduction and Critical and Explanatory Notes, together with the Married Women's Property Acts, 1870 and 1874, &c. 2nd Edit. Revised. By H. A. Smith, Esq., Barrister-at-Law. Roy. 12mo. 1884. 6*s*.

MASTER AND SERVANT.—Macdonell's Law of Master and Servant. Second Edition. By John Macdonell, LL.D., M.A., Esq., a Master of the Supreme Court. (*In preparation.*)

"A work which will be of real value to the practitioner."—*Law Times.*

MERCANTILE LAW.—Smith's Compendium of Mercantile Law.—Tenth Edition. By John Macdonell, Esq., a Master of the Supreme Court of Judicature, assisted by Geo. Humphreys, Esq., Barrister-at-Law. 2 vols. Royal 8vo. 1890. 2*l*. 2*s*.

"Of the greatest value to the mercantile lawyer."—*Law Times.*

"We have no hesitation in recommending the work before us to the profession and the public as a reliable guide to the subjects included in it, and as constituting one of the most scientific treatises extant on mercantile law."—*Solicitors' Journal.*

Tudor's Selection of Leading Cases on Mercantile and Maritime Law.—With Notes. By O. D. Tudor, Esq., Barrister-at-Law. Third Edition. Royal 8vo. 1884. 2*l*. 2*s*.

Wilson's Mercantile Handbook of the Liabilities of Merchant, Shipowner, and Underwriter on Shipments by General Vessels.—By A. Wilson, Solicitor and Notary. Royal 12mo. 1883. 6*s*.

Wood's Mercantile Agreements.—The Interpretation of Mercantile Agreements. By John Dennistoun Wood, Esq., Barrister-at-Law. Royal 8vo. 1886. 18*s*.

"A book of great use in the interpretation of written mercantile agreements."—*Law Journal.*

MERCHANDISE MARKS ACT.—Payn's Merchandise Marks Act, 1887.—By H. Payn, Barrister-at-Law. Royal 12mo. 1888. 3*s*. 6*d*.

"A safe guide to all who are interested in the Act."—*Law Times.*

**** ***All standard Law Works are kept in Stock, in law calf and other bindings.***

METROPOLIS BUILDING ACTS.—Woolrych's Metropolitan Building Acts, together with such clauses of the Metropolis Management Acts as more particularly relate to the Building Acts, with Notes and Forms. Third Edition. By W. H. MACNAMARA, Esq., Barrister-at-Law. 12mo. 1882. 10*s.*

MINES.—Rogers' Law relating to Mines, Minerals and Quarries in Great Britain and Ireland, with a Summary of the Laws of Foreign States, &c. Second Edition Enlarged. By His Honor Judge ROGERS. 8vo. 1876. 1*l.* 11*s.* 6*d.*

MORALS AND LEGISLATION.—Bentham's Introduction to the Principles of Morals and Legislation.—By JEREMY BENTHAM, M.A., Bencher of Lincoln's Inn. Crown 8vo. 1879. 6*s.* 6*d.*

MORTGAGE.—Beddoes' Concise Treatise on the Law of Mortgage.—By W. F. BEDDOES, Barrister-at-Law. Demy 8vo. 1893. 10*s.*

"Compiled carefully and with discretion."—*Law Times*, June 10, 1893.

Coote's Treatise on the Law of Mortgage.—Fifth Edition. Thoroughly revised. By WILLIAM WYLLYS MACKESON, Esq., one of Her Majesty's Counsel, and H. ARTHUR SMITH, Esq., Barrister-at-Law. 2 vols. Royal 8vo. 1884. 3*l.*

Robbins' Treatise on the Law of Mortgage.—By L. G. GORDON ROBBINS, Esq., Barrister-at-Law. Founded on "Coote's Law of Mortgage." (*In preparation.*)

MUNICIPAL CORPORATIONS.—Bazalgette and Humphreys.—*Vide* "Local and Municipal Government."

Lely's Law of Municipal Corporations.—By J. M. LELY, Esq., Barrister-at-Law. Demy 8vo. 1882. 15*s.*

NAVY.—Thring's Criminal Law of the Navy, with an Introductory Chapter on the Early State and Discipline of the Navy, the Rules of Evidence, and an Appendix comprising the Naval Discipline Act and Practical Forms. 2nd Edit. By THEODORE THRING, Esq., and C. E. GIFFORD, Assistant-Paymaster, Royal Navy. 12mo. 1877. 12*s.* 6*d.*

NEGLIGENCE.—Smith's Treatise on the Law of Negligence. Second Edition. By HORACE SMITH, Esq., Barrister-at-Law, Editor of "Addison on Contracts, and Torts," &c. 8vo. 1884. 12*s.* 6*d.*

"Of great value both to the practitioner and student of law."—*Solicitors' Journal.*

NISI PRIUS.—Roscoe's Digest of the Law of Evidence on the Trial of Actions at Nisi Prius.—Sixteenth Edition. By MAURICE POWELL, Esq., Barrister-at-Law. 2 vols. Demy 8vo. 1891. 2*l.* 10*s.*

"Continues to be a vast and closely packed storehouse of information on practice at Nisi Prius."—*Law Journal.*

NONCONFORMISTS.—Winslow's Law Relating to Protestant Nonconformists and their Places of Worship; being a Legal Handbook for Nonconformists. By REGINALD WINSLOW, Esq., Barrister-at-Law. Post 8vo. 1886. 6*s.*

NOTARY.—Brooke's Treatise on the Office and Practice of a Notary of England.—With a full collection of Precedents. Fifth Ed. By G. F. CHAMBERS, Esq., Barrister-at-Law. Demy 8vo. 1890. 1*l.* 1*s.*

OATHS.—Stringer's Oaths and Affirmations in Great Britain and Ireland; being a Collection of Statutes, Cases, and Forms, with Notes and Practical Directions for the use of Commissioners for Oaths, and of all Courts of Civil Procedure and Offices attached thereto. By FRANCIS A. STRINGER, of the Central Office, Royal Courts of Justice, one of the Editors of the "Annual Practice." Second Edition. Crown 8vo. 1893. 4*s.*

"Indispensable to all commissioners."—*Solicitors' Journal.*

*** *All standard Law Works are kept in Stock, in law calf and other bindings.*

PUBLIC MEETINGS.—Chambers' Handbook for Public Meetings, including Hints as to the Summoning and Management of them. Second Edition. By GEORGE F. CHAMBERS, Esq., Barrister-at-Law. Demy 8vo. 1886. *Net*, 2*s*. 6*d*.

QUARTER SESSIONS.—Archbold.—*Vide* "Criminal Law."

RAILWAY RATES.—Darlington's Railway Rates and the Carriage of Merchandise by Railway; including the Provisional Orders of the Board of Trade as sanctioned by Parliament, containing the Classification of Traffic and Schedule of Maximum Rates and Charges applicable to the Railways of Great Britain and Ireland. By H. R. DARLINGTON, Esq., Barrister-at-Law. Demy 8vo. 1893. 1*l*. 5*s*.

RAILWAYS.—Browne and Theobald's Law of Railway Companies.—Being a Collection of the Acts and Orders relating to Railway Companies in England and Ireland, with Notes of all the Cases decided thereon, and Appendix of Bye-Laws and Standing Orders of the House of Commons. Second Edition. By J. H. BALFOUR BROWNE, Esq., one of Her Majesty's Counsel, and H. S. THEOBALD, Esq., Barrister-at-Law. Royal 8vo. 1888. 1*l*. 15*s*.

"Contains in a very concise form the whole law of railways."—*The Times.*

RATES AND RATING.—Castle's Practical Treatise on the Law of Rating.—Second Edition. By EDWARD JAMES CASTLE, Esq., one of Her Majesty's Counsel. Demy 8vo. 1886. 25*s*.

"A correct, exhaustive, clear and concise view of the law."—*Law Times.*

Chambers' Law relating to Local Rates; with especial reference to the Powers and Duties of Rate-levying Local Authorities, and their Officers; comprising the Statutes in full and a Digest of 718 Cases. Second Edition. By G. F. CHAMBERS, Esq., Barrister-at-Law. Royal 8vo. 1889. 10*s*. 6*d*.

"A complete repertory of the statutes and case law of the subject."—*Law Journal.*

REAL PROPERTY.—Digby's History of the Law of Real Property.—Fourth Edition. Demy 8vo. 1892. 12*s*. 6*d*.

Greenwood's Real Property Statutes, 1874—1884. With copious notes. Second Edition. By HARRY GREENWOOD, assisted by LEES KNOWLES, Esqrs., Barristers-at-Law. Demy 8vo. 1884. 1*l*. 5*s*.

Leake's Elementary Digest of the Law of Property in Land.—Containing: Introduction. Part I. The Sources of the Law.—Part II. Estates in Land. By STEPHEN MARTIN LEAKE, Barrister-at-Law. Demy 8vo. 8vo. 1874. *Net*, 15*s*.

Leake's Digest of the Law of Property in Land.—Part III. The Law of Uses and Profits of Land. By STEPHEN MARTIN LEAKE, Barrister-at-Law. Demy 8vo. 1888. *Net*, 15*s*.

Or the above-named 2 vols. together. *Net*, 1*l*. 5*s*.

Shearwood's Real Property.—A Concise Abridgment of the Law of Real Property and an Introduction to Conveyancing. Designed to facilitate the subject for Students preparing for examination. By JOSEPH A. SHEARWOOD, Esq., Barrister-at-Law. Third Edition. Demy 8vo. 1885. 8*s*. 6*d*.

"One of the most obvious merits of the book is its good arrangement. The author evidently understands 'the art of putting things.' All important points are so printed as to readily catch the eye."—*Law Times.*

Shelford's Real Property Statutes.—Comprising the principal Statutes relating to Real Property passed in the reigns of King William IV. and Queen Victoria, with Notes of Decided Cases. Ninth Edition. By THOMAS H. CARSON, Esq., Barrister-at-Law, assisted by HAROLD B. BOMPAS, Esq., Barrister-at-Law. Royal 8vo. 1893. 30*s*.

"Absolutely indispensable to conveyancing and equity lawyers."

*** ***All standard Law Works are kept in Stock, in law calf and other bindings.***

REAL PROPERTY—*continued.*

Smith's Real and Personal Property.—A Compendium of the Law of Real and Personal Property, primarily connected with Conveyancing. Designed as a second book for Students, and as a digest of the most useful learning for practitioners. By JOSIAH W. SMITH, B.C.L., Q.C. Sixth Edition. By the AUTHOR and J. TRUSTRAM, LL.M., Barrister-at-Law. 2 vols. Demy 8vo. 1884. 2*l.* 2*s.*

"A book which he (the student) may read over and over again with profit and pleasure."—*Law Times.*

"Will be found of very great service to the practitioner."—*Solicitors' Journal.*

"The book will be found very handy for reference purposes to practitioners, and very useful to the industrious student as covering a great deal of ground."—*Law Notes.*

"A really useful and valuable work on our system of Conveyancing."—*Law Student's Journal.*

REGISTRATION.—Rogers.—*Vide* "Elections."

Coltman's Registration Cases.—Vol. I. (1879—1885). Royal 8vo. Calf. *Net,* 2*l.* 8*s.*

Fox's Registration Cases.—Vol. I., Part I. (1886), *net,* 4*s.* Part II. (1887), *net,* 6*s.* 6*d.* Part III. (1888), *net,* 4*s.* Part IV. (1889), *net,* 4*s.* Part V. (1890), *net,* 5*s.* 6*d.* (In continuation of Coltman.)

Smith's (C. Lacey) Registration Cases. (In continuation of Fox.) Vol. I., Part VI. (1891), *net,* 4*s.* 6*d.* Part VII. (1892-3), *net,* 4*s.* Part VIII. (1893-4), *net,* 5*s.*

ROMAN LAW.—Abdy and Walker's Institutes of Justinian, Translated, with Notes, by J. T. ABDY, LL.D., and the late BRYAN WALKER, M.A., LL.D. Crown 8vo. 1876. 16*s.*

Abdy and Walker's Commentaries of Gaius and Rules of Ulpian. With a Translation and Notes, by J. T. ABDY, LL.D., late Regius Professor of Laws in the University of Cambridge, and the late BRYAN WALKER, M.A., LL.D. New Edition by BRYAN WALKER. Crown 8vo. 1885. 16*s.*

Goodwin's XII. Tables.—By FREDERICK GOODWIN, LL.D. London. Royal 12mo. 1886. 3*s.* 6*d.*

Greene's Outlines of Roman Law.—Consisting chiefly of an Analysis and Summary of the Institutes. For the use of Students. By T. WHITCOMBE GREENE, Barrister-at-law. Fourth Edition. Foolscap 8vo. 1884. 7*s.* 6*d.*

Grueber's Lex Aquilia.—The Roman Law of Damage to Property: being a Commentary on the Title of the Digest "Ad Legem Aquiliam" (ix. 2). With an Introduction to the Study of the Corpus Iuris Civilis. By ERWIN GRUEBER, Dr. Jur., M.A. 8vo. 1886. 10*s.* 6*d.*

Holland's Institutes of Justinian.—Second Edition. Extra fcap. 8vo. 1881. 5*s.*

Holland and Shadwell's Select Titles from the Digest of Justinian.—Demy 8vo. 1881. 14*s.*

Holland's Gentilis, Alberici, I.C.D., I.C.P.R., de Iure Belli Libri Tres.—Edidit T. E. HOLLAND, I.C.D. Small 4to., half-morocco. 21*s.*

Monro's Digest XIX. 2, Locati Conducti. Translated, with Notes, by C. H. MONRO, M.A., Fellow of Gonville and Caius College. Crown 8vo. 1891. 5*s.*

Monro's Digest XLVII. 2, De Furtis. Translated, with Notes, by C. H. MONRO, M.A., Fellow and Lecturer of Gonville and Caius College. Crown 8vo. 1893. 5*s.*

ROMAN LAW—*continued.*

Moyle's Imperatoris Justiniani Institutiones.—Second Edition. 2 vols. Demy 8vo. 1889—1890. 1*l.* 2*s.*

Poste's Elements of Roman Law.—By Gaius. With a Translation and Commentary. Third Edition. By EDWARD POSTE, Esq., Barrister-at-Law. Demy 8vo. 1890. 18*s.*

Roby's Introduction to the Study of Justinian's Digest, containing an account of its composition and of the Jurists used or referred to therein. By H. J. ROBY, M.A. Demy 8vo. 1886. 9*s.*

Roby's Justinian's Digest.—Lib. VII., Tit. I. De Usufructu, with a Legal and Philological Commentary. By H. J. ROBY, M.A. Demy 8vo. 1886. 9*s.*

Or the Two Parts complete in One Volume. Demy 8vo. 18*s.*

Ruegg's Student's "Auxilium" to the Institutes of Justinian.—Being a complete synopsis thereof in the form of Question and Answer. By A. H. RUEGG, Esq., Barrister-at-Law. Post 8vo. 1879. 5*s.*

Sohm's Institutes of Roman Law.—By RUDOLPH SOHM, Professor in the University of Leipzig. Translated (from the Fourth Edition of the German) by J. C. LEDLIE, B.C.L., M.A. With an Introductory Essay by ERWIN GRUEBER, Dr. Jur., M.A. 8vo. 1892. 18*s.*

Walker's Selected Titles from Justinian's Digest.—Annotated by the late BRYAN WALKER, M.A., LL.D.

Part I. Mandati vel Contra. Digest XVII. I. Crown 8vo. 1879. 5*s.*

Part II. De Adquirendo rerum dominio, and De Adquirenda vel amittenda possessione. Digest XLI. 1, 2. Crown 8vo. 1880. 6*s.*

Part III. De Condictionibus. Digest XII. 1 and 4—7, and Digest XIII. 1—3. Crown 8vo. 1881. 6*s.*

Walker's Fragments of the Perpetual Edict of Salvius Julianus. Collected, arranged, and annotated by BRYAN WALKER, M.A., LL.D., late Fellow of Corpus Christi College, Cambridge. Cr. 8vo. 1877. 6*s.*

Whewell's Grotius de Jure Belli et Pacis, with the Notes of Barbeyrac and others; accompanied by an abridged Translation of the Text, by W. WHEWELL, D.D. 3 vols. Demy 8vo. 1853. 12*s.*

The Translation separate. 6*s.*

RULING CASES.—Campbell.—*Vide* "Digest."

SALE OF GOODS.—Lely and Craies' Sale of Goods Act, 1893. —With Introduction, Notes, and Index. By J. M. LELY and W. F. CRAIES, Esqrs., Barristers-at-Law. Royal 8vo. 1894. *Net* 1*s.*

*** *The above forms No. II. of the "Annotated Acts." Annual Subscription, post free,* 10*s.*

SALES.—Blackburn on Sales. A Treatise on the Effect of the Contract of Sale on the Legal Rights of Property and Possession in Goods, Wares, and Merchandise. By Lord BLACKBURN. 2nd Edit. By J. C. GRAHAM, Esq., Barrister-at-Law. Royal 8vo. 1885. 1*l.* 1*s.*

"We have no hesitation in saying that the work has been edited with remarkable ability and success."—*Law Quarterly Review.*

SALES OF LAND.—Clerke and Humphry's Concise Treatise on the Law relating to Sales of Land. By AUBREY ST. JOHN CLERKE, and HUGH M. HUMPHRY, Esqrs., Barristers-at-Law. Royal 8vo. 1885. 1*l.* 5*s.*

Webster's Particulars and Conditions of Sale.—The Law relating to Particulars and Conditions of Sale on a Sale of Land. By WM. FREDK. WEBSTER, Esq., Barrister-at-Law. Royal 8vo. 1889. 1*l.* 1*s.*

"Characterized by clearness of arrangement and careful and concise statement; and we think it will be found of much service to the practitioner."—*Solicitors' Journal.*

*** *All standard Law Works are kept in Stock, in law calf and other bindings.*

SALVAGE.—Kennedy's Treatise on the Law of Civil Salvage.—By the Hon. Sir WILLIAM R. KENNEDY, a Justice of the High Court. Royal 8vo. 1891. 12s.

"A learned and scholarly exposition of an important branch of maritime law."—*Solicitors' Journal.*

"The best work on the law of salvage that has yet appeared. It is a complete exposition of the subject, and as such is accurate and exhaustive."—*Law Times.*

SHERIFF LAW.—Churchill's Law of the Office and Duties of the Sheriff, with the Writs and Forms relating to the Office. 2nd Edit. By CAMERON CHURCHILL, Esq. Demy 8vo. 1882. 1*l.* 4*s.*

"A very complete treatise."—*Solicitors' Journal.*

Mather's Compendium of the Law relating to the Offices and Duties of the Sheriff.—By PHILIP E. MATHER, Solicitor and Notary Public, formerly Under Sheriff of Newcastle-on-Tyne. (*In the press.*)

SHIPOWNERS.—Holman's Handybook for Shipowners and Masters. Third Edition. By H. HOLMAN, Esq., Barrister-at-Law. Royal 8vo. 1892. 5*s.*

"The work is well arranged and well written."—*Law Journal.*

SHIPPING.—Boyd's Merchant Shipping Laws; being a Consolidation of all the Merchant Shipping and Passenger Acts from 1854 to 1876, inclusive; with Notes of all the leading English and American Cases, and an Appendix. By A. C. BOYD, LL.B., Esq., Barrister-at-Law. 8vo. 1876. 1*l.* 5*s.*

SLANDER.—Odgers.—*Vide* "Libel and Slander."

SOLICITORS.—Cordery's Law relating to Solicitors of the Supreme Court of Judicature. With an Appendix of Statutes and Rules, and Notes on Appointments open to Solicitors, and the Right to Admission to the Colonies. Second Edition. By A. CORDERY, Esq., Barrister-at-Law. Demy 8vo. 1888. 16*s.*

"The book is very clear, accurate, and practical, and will be found of much value. Without being bulky, it contains in a concise and intelligible form all the matters usually occurring in a solicitor's practice."—*Solicitors' Journal.*

Turner.—*Vide* "Conveyancing" and "Vendors and Purchasers."

SPECIFIC PERFORMANCE.—Fry's Treatise on the Specific Performance of Contracts. By the Right Hon. Sir EDWARD FRY. Third Edition. By the Author and E. PORTSMOUTH FRY, Esq., Barrister-at-Law. Royal 8vo. 1892. 1*l.* 16*s.*

"The standard work on Specific Performance."—*Law Gazette.*

STAMP ACTS.—Highmore's Stamp Act, 1891, and the Stamp Duties Management Act, 1891. With an Introduction and Notes, and a copious Index. By NATHANIEL JOSEPH HIGHMORE, Esq., Barrister-at-Law, Assistant-Solicitor of the Inland Revenue. Demy 8vo. 1891. 5*s.*

"A useful guide to those who desire to understand the present state of the stamp laws."—*Law Journal.*

"This edition supplies practising lawyers with all the help that acuteness, sagacity and experience can give to them."—*Justice of the Peace.*

STATE TRIALS.—Willis-Bund's Selection of State Trials.—By J. W. WILLIS-BUND, M.A., LL.B., Barrister-at-Law, Professor of Constitutional Law and History, University College, London. Cr. 8vo. Vols. I. and II. In 3 Parts. Vol. I., 1879. Vol. II., 1882. (Originally published at 46*s.*) 30*s.*

STATUTE LAW.—Wilberforce on Statute Law. The Principles which govern the Construction and Operation of Statutes. By E. WILBERFORCE, Esq., Barrister-at-Law. 1881. 18*s.*

*** *All standard Law Works are kept in Stock, in law calf and other bindings.*

STATUTES, and *vide* "Acts of Parliament."

Chitty's Collection of Statutes from Magna Charta to 1880.—A Collection of Statutes of Practical Utility, arranged in Alphabetical and Chronological order, with Notes thereon. The Fourth Edition. By J. M. LELY, Esq., Barrister-at-Law. In 6 vols. Royal 8vo. 1880. Published at 12*l.* 12*s.*, reduced to *Net* 6*l.* 6*s.*

The following may still be had separately—44 & 45 Vict. (1881), 8*s.* 46 & 47 Vict. (1883), 14*s.* 47 & 48 Vict. (1884), 10*s.* 6*d.* 48 & 49 Vict. (1885), 12*s.* 6*d.* 50 & 51 Vict. (1887), 10*s.* 6*d.* 51 & 52 Vict. (1888), 12*s.* 6*d.* 51 & 52 Vict. (1888, Second Session), *Net* 2*s.* 6*d.* 54 & 55 Vict. (1891), 12*s.* 55 & 56 Vict. (1892), 12*s.* 56 & 57 Vict. (1893), 10*s.* 6*d.*

"It is needless to enlarge on the value of 'Chitty's Statutes' to both the Bar and to Solicitors, for it is attested by the experience of many years."—*The Times.*

The "ANNOTATED ACTS."—An Edition of the Leading Statutes of the Year. With Explanatory Introduction, Notes, and full Index.

The Publishers have arranged to supply the Profession with every Act of importance as promptly as possible after its becoming law, in the form of a Complete Edition, with Notes and Index. Thus for a small Annual Subscription (10/-) the Subscriber will be kept up to date in the legislation of the year.

☞ *Prepaid Subscription for the Twelve Months* (*Jan. to Dec.*), 10*s.*

Already Published:—

The Local Government Act, 1894 (Parish and District Councils), 56 & 57 Vict. c. 73, with Introduction, Notes, and Index. By J. M. LELY and W. F. CRAIES, Barristers-at-Law. *Net* 1*s.* 6*d.*

The Sale of Goods Act, 1893 (56 & 57 Vict. c. 71), with Introduction, Notes, and Index.—By J. M. LELY and W. F. CRAIES. *Net* 1*s.*

SUMMARY CONVICTIONS.—Paley's Law and Practice of Summary Convictions under the Summary Jurisdiction Acts, 1848—1884; including Proceedings Preliminary and Subsequent to Convictions, and the Responsibility of Convicting Magistrates and their Officers, with the Summary Jurisdiction Rules, 1886, and Forms.—Seventh Edition. By W. H. MACNAMARA, Esq., Barrister-at-Law. Demy 8vo. 1892. 24*s.*

Wigram.—*Vide* "Justice of the Peace."

SUMMONSES & ORDERS.—Archibald.—*Vide* "Chamber Practice."

TAXES ON SUCCESSION.—Trevor's Taxes on Succession.—A Digest of the Statutes and Cases, with Practical Observations and Official Forms. Fourth Edit. By EVELYN FREETH and R. J. WALLACE, of the Legacy and Succession Duty Office. Royal 12mo. 1881. 12*s.* 6*d.*

TAXPAYERS' GUIDES.—*Vide* "House," "Income," & "Land Tax."

THEATRES AND MUSIC HALLS.—Geary's Law of Theatres and Music Halls, including Contracts and Precedents of Contracts.—By W. N. M. GEARY, J.P. With Historical Introduction. By JAMES WILLIAMS, Esqrs., Barristers-at-Law. 8vo. 1885. 5*s.*

TITHES.—Easterby's History of the Law of Tithes in England.—By W. EASTERBY, of the Middle Temple. Demy 8vo. 1888. 7*s.* 6*d.*

Studd's Law of Tithes and Tithe Rent-Charge.—Being a Treatise on the Law of Tithe Rent-Charge, with a sketch of the History and Law of Tithes prior to the Commutation Acts, and including the Tithe Act of 1891, with the Rules thereunder. Second Edition. By EDWARD FAIRFAX STUDD, Esq., Barrister-at-Law. Royal 12mo. 1891. 6*s.*

"This work is thoroughly reliable."—*Solicitors' Journal.*

⁂ *All standard Law Works are kept in Stock, in law calf and other bindings.*

TORTS.—Addison on Torts.—A Treatise on the Law of Torts; or Wrongs and their Remedies. Seventh Edition. By HORACE SMITH, Esq., Bencher of the Inner Temple, Metropolitan Magistrate, Editor of "Addison on Contracts," &c., and A. P. PERCEVAL KEEP, Esq., Barrister-at-Law. Royal 8vo. 1893. 1*l*. 18*s*.

"As an exhaustive digest of all the cases which are likely to be cited in practice it stands without a rival."—*Law Journal*, May 13, 1893.

"As now presented, this valuable treatise must prove highly acceptable to judges and the profession."—*Law Times*.

"An indispensable addition to every lawyer's library."—*Law Magazine*.

Ball's Leading Cases on the Law of Torts, with Notes. Edited by W. E. BALL, LL.D., Esq., Barrister-at-Law, Author of "Principles of Torts and Contracts." Royal 8vo. 1884. 1*l*. 1*s*.

Bigelow's Elements of the Law of Torts.—A Text-Book for Students. By MELVILLE M. BIGELOW, Ph.D., Lecturer in the Law School of the University of Boston, U.S.A. Crown 8vo. 1889. 10*s*. 6*d*.

Innes' Principles of the Law of Torts.—By L. C. INNES, lately one of the Judges of the High Court, Madras, Author of "A Digest of the English Law of Easements." Demy 8vo. 1891. 10*s*. 6*d*.

"We have found the work accurate and clear, and believe that it will be a useful addition to any law library."—*Law Quarterly Review*.

"Throughout the work the author is clear in his definitions, and there is no lack of illustrative examples. . . . A welcome addition to the library of the student and the practitioner."—*Law Times*.

Pollock's Law of Torts: a Treatise on the Principles of Obligations arising from Civil Wrongs in the Common Law. Third Edition, to which is added the draft of a Code of Civil Wrongs prepared for the Government of India. By Sir FREDERICK POLLOCK, Bart., Barrister-at-Law. Author of "Principles of Contract," "A Digest of the Law of Partnership," &c. Demy 8vo. 1892. 21*s*.

"Concise, logically arranged, and accurate."—*Law Times*.

"A book which is well worthy to stand beside the companion volume on 'Contracts.' Unlike so many law-books, especially on this subject, it is no mere digest of cases, but bears the impress of the mind of the writer from beginning to end."—*Law Journal*.

Shearwood's Sketch of the Law of Tort for the Bar and Solicitors Final Examinations. By JOSEPH A. SHEARWOOD, Esq., Barrister-at-Law. Royal 12mo. 1886. 3*s*.

TRADE MARKS.—Aston.—*Vide* "Patents."

Graham's Designs and Trade Marks.—By JOHN CAMERON GRAHAM, of the Middle Temple, Barrister-at-Law. Demy 8vo. 1889. 6*s*.

Sebastian on the Law of Trade Marks and their Registration, and matters connected therewith, including a chapter on Goodwill; together with the Patents, Designs and Trade Marks Acts, 1883-8, and the Trade Marks Rules and Instructions thereunder; Forms and Precedents; the Merchandize Marks Act, 1887, and other Statutory Enactments; the United States Statutes, 1870-81, and the Rules and Forms thereunder; and the Treaty with the United States, 1877. Third Edition. By LEWIS BOYD SEBASTIAN, Esq., Barrister-at-Law. Demy 8vo. 1890. 1*l*. 5*s*.

"The work stands alone as an authority upon the law of trade-marks and their registration."—*Law Journal*.

"It is hardly necessary to tell anyone who has consulted the last edition of this book that it is characterized by mastery of the subject, exemplary industry, and completeness and accuracy of statement It is rarely we come across a law book which embodies the results of years of careful investigation and practical experience in a branch of law, or that can be unhesitatingly appealed to as a standard authority. This is what can be said of Mr. Sebastian's book."—*Solicitors' Journal*.

*** *All standard Law Works are kept in Stock, in law calf and other bindings.*

TRADE MARKS—*continued.*

Sebastian's Digest of Cases of Trade Mark, Trade Name, Trade Secret, Goodwill, &c., decided in the Courts of the United Kingdom, India, the Colonies, and the United States of America. By LEWIS BOYD SEBASTIAN, Esq., Barrister-at-Law. 8vo. 1879. 1*l.* 1*s.*

"A digest which will be of very great value to all practitioners who have to advise on matters connected with trade marks."—*Solicitors' Journal.*

TRAMWAYS.—Sutton's Tramway Acts of the United Kingdom; with Notes on the Law and Practice, an Introduction, including the Proceedings before the Committees, Decisions of the Referees with respect to Locus Standi, and a Summary of the Principles of Tramway Rating, and an Appendix containing the Standing Orders of Parliament. Rules of the Board of Trade relating to Tramways, &c. Second Edition. By HENRY SUTTON, assisted by ROBERT A. BENNETT, Barristers-at-Law. Demy 8vo. 1883. 15*s.*

TRUST FUNDS.—Geare's Investment of Trust Funds.—Incorporating the Trustee Act, 1888. By EDWARD ARUNDEL GEARE, Esq., Barrister-at-Law. Second Edition. Including the Trusts Investment Act, 1889. Royal 12mo. 1889. 7*s.* 6*d.*

"The work is written in an easy style, it can very well be read by all trustees, whether they are lawyers or not; and if they will take our advice, and invest their money here before they invest other people's elsewhere, they may be spared much trouble in the future."—*The Jurist.*

TRUSTS AND TRUSTEES.—Ellis' Trustee Act, 1893, including a Guide for Trustees to Investments. By ARTHUR LEE ELLIS, M.A., B.C.L., Barrister-at-Law. Fifth Edit. Roy. 12mo. 1894. 6*s.*

Godefroi's Law Relating to Trusts and Trustees.—Second Edit. By HENRY GODEFROI, of Lincoln's Inn, Esq., Barrister-at-Law. Royal 8vo. 1891. 1*l.* 12*s.*

"The second edition of this work which lies before us is a model of what a legal text-book ought to be. It is clear in style and clear in arrangement."—*Law Times.*

Hamilton's Trustee Acts.—Containing the Trustee Act, 1850; the Trustee Extension Act, 1852; and the Trustee Act, 1888; with Supplement of the Lunacy Act, 1890 (53 Vict. c. 5), so far as relates to Vesting Orders. By G. BALDWIN HAMILTON, Esq., Barrister-at-Law, Author of "A Concise Treatise on the Law of Covenants." Demy 8vo. 1890. 6*s.*

"This is a very useful little book. We have perused it with much care, and we have come to the conclusion that it may be safely trusted to as a guide to the complicated law to which it relates."—*Law Quarterly Review.*

VENDORS AND PURCHASERS.—Dart's Vendors and Purchasers.—A Treatise on the Law and Practice relating to Vendors and Purchasers of Real Estate. By the late J. HENRY DART, Esq., one of the Six Conveyancing Counsel of the High Court of Justice, Chancery Division. Sixth Edition. By WILLIAM BARBER, Esq., one of Her Majesty's Counsel, RICHARD BURDON HALDANE, and WILLIAM ROBERT SHELDON, both of Lincoln's Inn, Esqrs., Barristers-at-Law. 2 vols. Royal 8vo. 1888. 3*l.* 15*s.*

"The new edition of Dart is far ahead of all competitors in the breadth of its range, the clearness of its exposition, and the soundness of its law."—*Law Times.*

Turner's Duties of Solicitor to Client as to Sales, Purchases, and Mortgages of Land.—Second Edition. By W. L. HACON, Barrister-at-Law. Demy 8vo. 1893. 10*s.* 6*d.*

"The most skilled in practical conveyancing would gain many useful hints from a perusal of the book, and we recommend it in all confidence."—*Law Notes.*

See also Conveyancing.—"Turner."

**** All standard Law Works are kept in Stock, in law calf and other bindings.***

WAR, DECLARATION OF.—Owen's Declaration of War.—A Survey of the Position of Belligerents and Neutrals, with relative considerations of Shipping and Marine Insurance during War. By DOUGLAS OWEN, Barrister-at-Law. Demy 8vo. 1889. 21s.

WILLS.—Theobald's Concise Treatise on the Law of Wills.—Third Edition. By H. S. THEOBALD, Esq., Barrister-at-Law. Royal 8vo. 1885. 1l. 10s.

"A book of great ability and value. It bears on every page traces of care and sound judgment. It is certain to prove of great practical usefulness."—*Solicitors' Journal.*

Weaver's Precedents of Wills.—A Collection of Concise Precedents of Wills, with Introduction, Notes, and an Appendix of Statutes. By CHARLES WEAVER, B.A. Post 8vo. 1882. 5s.

WINDING UP.—Palmer's Winding-up Forms and Practice.—A Collection of Forms and Precedents. With Notes on the Law and Practice under the Companies Acts, 1862—1890. Second Edition. By FRANCIS BEAUFORT PALMER, Author of "Company Precedents," &c., assisted by FRANK EVANS, Esqrs., Barristers-at-Law. Royal 8vo. 1893. 1l. 10s.

"It is simply invaluable, not only to company lawyers, but to everybody connected with companies."—*Financial News.*

Pitt-Lewis' Winding-up Practice.—A Manual of the Practice as to Winding-up in the High Court and in the County Court; forming a SUPPLEMENT to "A Complete Practice of the County Courts." By G. PITT-LEWIS, Q.C., Recorder of Poole. Demy 8vo. 1891. 7s. 6d.

"This is a book that we can cordially recommend, and forms a fitting supplement to the aptly-named larger work of the same author."—*Law Gazette.*

WRECK INQUIRIES.—Murton's Law and Practice relating to Formal Investigations in the United Kingdom, British Possessions and before Naval Courts into Shipping Casualties and the Incompetency and Misconduct of Ships' Officers. With an Introduction. By WALTER MURTON, Solicitor to the Board of Trade. Demy 8vo. 1884. 1l. 4s.

WRONGS.—Addison, Ball, Pollock, Shearwood.—*Vide* "Torts."

REPORTS.—The largest Stock in London. Prices on application.

BINDING.—Executed in the best manner at moderate prices and with dispatch.

The Law Reports, Law Journal, and all other Reports, bound to Office Patterns, at Office Prices.

PRIVATE ACTS.—*The Publishers of this Catalogue possess the largest known collection of Private Acts of Parliament (including Public and Local), and can supply single copies commencing from a very early period.*

LICENSED VALUERS for Probate, Partnership, &c.

LIBRARIES PURCHASED OR EXCHANGED.